RUSSIA'S MILITARY STRATEGY AND DOCTRINE

Glen E. Howard and
Matthew Czekaj, *Editors*

Foreword by
Former NATO SACEUR
General Philip M. Breedlove

The JAMESTOWN
FOUNDATION

Washington, DC
February 2019

THE JAMESTOWN FOUNDATION

Published in the United States by
The Jamestown Foundation
1310 L Street NW
Suite 810
Washington, DC 20005
http://www.jamestown.org

For more information on this book of The Jamestown Foundation, email pubs@jamestown.org.

ISBN: 978-0-9986660-1-3

Cover art provided by Peggy Archambault of Peggy Archambault Design.

Jamestown's Mission

The Jamestown Foundation's mission is to inform and educate policy makers and the broader community about events and trends in those societies which are strategically or tactically important to the United States and which frequently restrict access to such information. Utilizing indigenous and primary sources, Jamestown's material is delivered without political bias, filter or agenda. It is often the only source of information which should be, but is not always, available through official or intelligence channels, especially in regard to Eurasia and terrorism.

Origins

Founded in 1984 by William Geimer, The Jamestown Foundation made a direct contribution to the downfall of Communism through its dissemination of information about the closed totalitarian societies of Eastern Europe and the Soviet Union.

William Geimer worked with Arkady Shevchenko, the highest-ranking Soviet official ever to defect when he left his position as undersecretary general of the United Nations. Shevchenko's memoir *Breaking With Moscow* revealed the details of Soviet superpower diplomacy, arms control strategy and tactics in the Third World, at the height of the Cold War. Through its work with Shevchenko, Jamestown rapidly became the leading source of information about the inner workings of the captive nations of the former Communist Bloc. In addition to Shevchenko, Jamestown assisted the former top Romanian intelligence officer Ion Pacepa in writing his memoirs. Jamestown ensured that both men published their insights and experience in what became bestselling books. Even today, several decades later, some credit Pacepa's revelations about Ceausescu's regime in his bestselling book *Red Horizons* with the fall of that government and the freeing of Romania.

The Jamestown Foundation has emerged as a leading provider of information about Eurasia. Our research and analysis on conflict and instability in Eurasia enabled Jamestown to become one of the most reliable sources of information on the post-Soviet space, the Caucasus and Central Asia as well as China. Furthermore, since 9/11, Jamestown has utilized its network of indigenous experts in more than 50 different countries to conduct research and analysis on terrorism and the growth of al-Qaeda and al-Qaeda offshoots throughout the globe.

By drawing on our ever-growing global network of experts, Jamestown has become a vital source of unfiltered, open-source information about major conflict zones around the world—from the Black Sea to Siberia, from the Persian Gulf to Latin America and the Pacific. Our core of intellectual talent includes former high-ranking government officials and military officers, political scientists, journalists, scholars and economists. Their insight contributes significantly to policymakers engaged in addressing today's newly emerging global threats in the post 9/11 world.

Table of Contents

Cont. next page...

...Contents, cont. from last page

Acknowledgements

As one of the premier research and analysis organizations in Washington, DC, not funded by any branch of the US government, The Jamestown Foundation occupies a unique niche in providing timely, opinion-free and data-driven analysis to the policymaking community. And since its founding in 1984, the key to Jamestown's success has always been our rich and unmatched network of international experts and researchers. Within the core group of our regular writers, however, is another sub-strata of Jamestown analysts, who represent our own elite of sorts—the best of the best within the analytical community of Russia and Eurasia experts. It is these elite analysts that we immediately turned to in order to make this book possible. The majority of the contributors who have written chapters for *Russia's Military Strategy and Doctrine* are not freshly graduated from universities; they are specialists who have been writing about this region and closely examining Russian actions and behavior for decades. Each of this book's chapters, therefore, is informed by the author's extensive professional experience and, in many cases, invaluable retrospective analysis combined with modernity. That analytical approach provides an unmatched collective assessment of Russian goals and regional strategies emerging from Syria to the Arctic that blend together the lessons of the Soviet past with the present to help us understand the course of Russia's future military strategy and behavior.

Such a volume has been long overdue. The field of Russian military studies, as a whole, has noticeably declined in the United States. And this has been the case despite three Eurasian wars since 2008: the Russian invasion of Georgia in August 2008, the invasion and annexation of Crimea in February–March 2014, and the subsequent Russian invasion of eastern Ukraine in mid-2014 (four if one includes Russia's brutal suppression of the militant insurgency in Chechnya).

As such, one would have thought the US think tank and policy community would had supported such a reference work on the Russian military long before 2019. But living up to Jamestown's mission statement, our faithful Board of Directors stepped forward last year to make this book possible, providing constructive encouragement and opening their pocketbooks.

The list of backers of this project is quite long, but a debt of gratitude is owed first and foremost to our Board Chairman, Willem de Vogel, who provided the leadership and support for this project as part of his ceaseless quest to assist Jamestown and make it truly what it is today. A very special note of thanks is also due to Board Member Robert Spring, who played a distinctive role in coming up with the idea to create this edited volume of articles on Russian military strategy and then stepped forward to provide the effort with his generous backing. We would also like to recognize the two co-founders of Jamestown, James G. Gidwitz and Clint Smullyan, for their contributions to this project and for never saying no when asked. We would additionally like to express our thanks to Board Member Michael Kavoukjian, who is always there to support this organization.

Moreover, we wish to thank the former Supreme Allied Commander of Europe, retired General Philip Breedlove, for taking the time to write the Foreword to this book as well as offering his insights along the way as the project was being finalized.

And last but not least, we thank the readers of our publications for their continued interest in our work, helping sustain Jamestown year and after and continually allowing us to reach new generations of policymakers and experts.

Foreword

The Russian invasion of Crimea in February 2014 was a turning point in Washington's relations with Moscow. Learning from that experience remains important. As the former Supreme Allied Commander for Europe, I witnessed these events first hand. The crisis both transformed our relationship with Russia and reinvigorated our ties with allies in the North Atlantic Treaty Organization (NATO).

This book comes at a critical time in US-Russian relations. Based upon the experience of Crimea and Donbas, the United States and its NATO allies need to be more prepared in how we think about our strategy for the future. Certainly, the West does not want to end up in a shooting war with Russia and we need to continue to engage the Russians—but we must do so from a position of readiness and strength. Anything less will be apparent to them, likely undermining our bargaining position vis-à-vis Moscow.

The present rancorous political climate in Washington, however, prevents us from effectively engaging with Russia. We, therefore, must move beyond our political quagmire (where taking any position is seen as partisan to one or the other side) in order to somehow reach a constructive internal agreement on how to deal with Russia.

Importantly, Russia represents a multi-domain challenge: Moscow applies an all-of-government approach, including diplomatic, military, economic, and informational tools against us or anybody else they perceive as a threat. Washington's approach, however, has so far been largely limited to fighting the Russians economically. A fuller and more effective response—one that can also offset Russian pressure on other vulnerable allies and partners—will require us to compete while making use of the full spectrum of US government tools at our disposal.

From a policymaker's perspective, we have dropped our focus on great power rivalry with Russia for many (and often good) reasons. Our soldiers, airmen and sailors had been focused for almost two decades on Afghanistan and Iraq. What we need to do now is regain our "Operational" and "Tactical" views about Russia.

First of all, we need to understand that Vladimir Putin's Russia does not want to be our partner. For the last two decades, our efforts to turn Moscow into one have repeatedly failed. Instead, of seeking to integrate itself into the Western rule-based system, Russia has used force to change internationally recognized borders on several different occasions: Georgia in 2008 and then Ukraine in 2014. This should serve as an important lesson to us as we assess the paths ahead for how to contend with a revanchist Russia.

The United States has a substantially different posture today than during the Cold War. And while the Cold War era was reasonably contained and well understood, today the threat coming from Moscow is much broader in terms of its geographic scope, stretching from the Levant to the North Pole. *Russia's Military Strategy and Doctrine* should serve as a valuable reference guide for policymakers and all those seeking to comprehend the multifaceted challenges posed by Moscow—particularly when it comes to understanding the various theaters in which Russia operates as well as regarding issue-based threats, such as this country's nuclear or cyber strategies. Jamestown has made an important contribution to helping us achieve this goal. I commend their efforts to bring together such a diverse array of authors and perspectives about Russian strategy and trust you will benefit from the resulting study as well.

General Philip M. Breedlove, former NATO SACEUR
November 1, 2018

Introduction

In the early morning of November 25, 2018, four Ukrainian naval vessels rounded the Russian-occupied Crimean Peninsula, on their way to the Kerch Strait. The ships, two Gyurza-M-class artillery boats, accompanied by a tug and a transport ship, had left Odesa several days earlier and were headed toward the Ukrainian port of Berdyansk, on the Azov Sea. At 3:58 a.m., local time, the Ukrainian detachment radioed its request to enter the strait to Russia's Kerch/Kavkaz port control—*de facto* in charge of monitoring all maritime traffic there since Moscow's forcible annexation of Crimea in 2014. The Russians never responded, nor even acknowledged the Ukrainian radio message. About one and a half hours later, leaving the transport vessel behind, the two Gyurza-Ms and the naval tugboat began heading north toward the mouth of the strait, crossing inside the 12-mile zone around Crimea at 6:08 a.m.[1]

Within 15 minutes, the Ukrainian ships found themselves surrounded by Russian coast guard and Black Sea Fleet naval forces. Two Federal Security Service (FSB) Coast Guard corvettes and three patrol boats carried out dangerous maneuvers around the Ukrainian vessels, repeatedly attempting to ram the Ukrainian tug and eventually damaging its engine.

For the next several hours, as the Ukrainian detachment slowly moved northward to enter the Kerch Strait, Russian naval surface and air assets continued to harass them. Starting at 11:00 a.m., and lasting for the next six hours, the Gyurzas and their accompanying tug repeatedly lost communications as a result of Russian jamming, while their crews were targeted by various psychological pressure tactics. As Russian Ka-52 attack helicopters circled overhead, two Su-25SM attack jets overflew the Ukrainian ships at an altitude of 50 meters, with their fire-control systems activated.

At 1:42 p.m., Russia dramatically escalated the situation by hauling a container ship underneath the main archway of the Kerch Strait Bridge, thus blocking all maritime traffic through the strait until the following day. Images of the large ship standing under the Kerch Bridge flashed across media outlets around the world, thus driving home the narrative that Moscow can and is willing to close off the Azov Sea whenever it chooses.

Having received stern warnings from Russian authorities that passage through the strait would be prohibited, the Ukrainian vessels, under orders from Navy Headquarters, turned around and began heading back to Odesa, around half past five in the evening. Yet, less than 30 minutes later, even as the Ukrainian ships were proceeding southward, an FSB corvette suddenly attempted to physically impede their passage. An hour after that, the Ukrainian crews found their radio link with HQ jammed.

Night fell. And at 7:48 p.m., after the two Gyurza-Ms and the tug moved beyond the 12-mile zone around Crimea, the Russian vessels opened fire, hitting the superstructure of one of the Ukrainian artillery boats and injuring three of its sailors. The damaged ship's captain radioed "Mayday," around 8:00 p.m. But just minutes later, Russian FSB special forces troops forcibly began boarding the Ukrainian vessels, as Su-30, Su-25 and attack helicopters fired on the ships from above. The Russian forces seized and hauled away the three Ukrainian naval ships overnight and took the 24 Ukrainian crew members into custody. As of early February 2019, they remain in Russia, awaiting trial.

Some analysts have focused on the *ad hoc* nature of Russia's reaction during the November 25 incident in the Black Sea and Kerch Strait, noting the confused, profanity-laden and frantic-sounding orders as well as the accidental collision between two of the Russian vessels during their aggressive maneuvers.[2] Nonetheless, the actual Russian attack and seizure of Ukrainian vessels in international waters that day represented a culmination of related, regional activities Moscow had been undertaking for months.

Since the spring of 2018, Russia had deployed well over 40 warships to the Azov Sea as well as strengthened its aerial and coastal assets in Crimea. It had been using its greatly enhanced naval presence to obstruct international shipping to and from Ukraine's ports on the Azov Sea. The long-term goal of this approach is clearly to reinforce the perception of Moscow's total control over maritime navigation in the Azov Sea as well as to strangle the economy of Ukraine's industry-heavy southeastern coast. Thus, the dramatic November 25 naval skirmish served to further buttress that narrative, with almost certain lasting implications for commercial actors' willingness to do business with the Ukrainian ports of Mariupol and Berdyansk.[3]

Russia's reaction to the approach of the three Ukrainian vessels to the Kerch Strait that late-autumn morning also did not appear entirely improvised. Nor did it conclude with the seizure of the Ukrainian ships and their crew. Most notably, some advanced planning must have been required to tow a large Russian cargo ship into place to close off all maritime traffic through the Kerch Strait. And in the week prior to the November 25 naval clash, Russia's Ministry of Foreign Affairs and Foreign Minister Sergei Lavrov pointedly declared that Moscow was not bound by international law in the Kerch Strait, allowing it to unilaterally close this passage at will. Moreover, several days after the incident, as Ukraine was debating the passage of Martial Law, Russian Electronic Warfare (EW) units sent out spoof mobile phone text messages to residents of Ukrainian border areas, which called for mobilization or presented other fake news stories.[4] To date, Russia continues to hold the captured Ukrainian ships and their crews, which will likely be used as a means to pressure Kyiv and President Petro Poroshenko during the run-up to the Ukrainian presidential elections in March 2019.

*   *   *

Russia's November 25, 2018, assault in the Black Sea on three small Ukrainian naval boats traveling through international waters toward the port of Berdyansk provides a valuable case study for how Russia engages in conflicts while operating below the threshold of war. Indeed, an even more extreme manifestation of this *modus operandi* was the annexation of Crimea in February–March 2014, followed weeks later by the use of surrogate forces to invade eastern Ukraine. These events ushered in the era of "Hybrid War" as the West struggled to define Russian President Vladimir Putin's use of non-linear warfare—just as Western journalists adopted the term "Blitzkrieg" to describe the use of German tactics used in their 1939 invasion of Poland. To the degree that Poland was a testing ground for new weapons and tactics used by the Wehrmacht, Ukraine is also becoming a modern laboratory for 21st century warfare. For this reason it is important to understand how Russia is adjusting, calibrating, and even redefining our description of non-linear means used for achieving objectives short of open conflict. In other words: limited war.

The concept of limited war often defined inter-state conflict in Early Modern Europe, starting from the Peace of Westphalia in 1648 to the French Revolutionary Wars, and then from the Congress of Vienna in 1815 until the outbreak of World War One, when "total war" again became ascendant.[5] Many Western experts have thus argued that the style of warfare used by Russia in Crimea and Donbas was nothing new—simply a revival of old Soviet concepts used to fit the strategic objective. Putin's wars today, in other words, represent a return to limited war as Russia seeks to Finlandize its periphery by pursuing strategic goals such as gaining unfettered access to the Russian Black Sea naval base at Sevastopol or the domination of the steel industry in eastern Ukraine. The case of Ukraine certainly exemplifies this approach, although the stakes are much larger: were Russia to consume Ukraine, this would radically change the regional balance of power. The late Dr. Zbigniew Brzezinski, a former US National Security Adviser to President Jimmy Carter and former member of the board of Jamestown, famously noted that, "without Ukraine, Russia ceases to be an empire, but with Ukraine suborned and then subordinated, Russia automatically becomes an empire."[6] Indeed, by regaining Ukraine, Russia would once again become a Balkan power and further consolidate its control over the Black Sea basin.

To alter the balance of power throughout Europe's East, Putin's Russia is returning to the notion of limited war by exercising a multi-pronged approach. First, it is changing state borders along the country's non-NATO periphery in order to carry out the Kremlin's neo-imperialistic aims. Short of outright conflict with the North Atlantic Alliance, Putin is focused for the time being on NATO's new borderland, or the "gray areas" between Russia and the West. Influenced by both Soviet and Tsarist nostalgia, Putin is in fact a hybrid post-Soviet man, a product of two systems—the old Soviet Union and the new post-Soviet Russia minus the Warsaw Pact and former republics. Armed with an aging, predominantly legacy Soviet-era arsenal of weaponry, while suffering from decaying infrastructure and steep demographic decline, Putin's Russia does not have the immense military and economic resources of the Soviet Union. Nevertheless, compared to the former captive nations along Russia's western and southern periphery, there is still an enormous strategic mismatch. Within the post-Soviet space, Putin's Russia is a powerful force in its own right and can adequately confront any of its non-NATO and even NATO neighbors, such as the Baltic States, Romania and Bulgaria, if these somehow find themselves alone and without outside support.

With each irredentist move in the post-Soviet space, Putin has redefined the threshold of war by following a common model: achieving a short-term military gain, pausing hostilities, then seeking diplomatic negotiations and international assent or at least passive acceptance of the *status quo*, followed, ideally at the time of Moscow's choosing, by a further grab for territory, thus starting the cycle all over again. Essentially this *modus operandi* created most of the so-called "frozen conflicts' of the former Soviet space—the forgotten battlefields of Crimea, Donbas, Abkhazia, South Ossetia and Transnistria—which Moscow maintains in an indefinite state of unresolved tension, with the hope that the West will ultimately lose interest. The idea of frozen conflicts is nothing particularly new to Russian/Soviet behavior. It was certainly a part of the Tsarist toolkit in its occupation of 19th century Poland, and Putin—as well as his predecessor, Boris Yeltsin—revived the concept with a post-Soviet touch.

Relatedly, limited war was a hallmark of Soviet behavior. During the Cold War, Moscow became involved in several conflicts on its Eurasian periphery that were confined to one geographic theater and never became global or reached the scale of total war. Indeed, conflicts in Korea, Greece, and Vietnam were referred to as "brushfire wars" along the Eastern Bloc's European and Asian periphery. These short-lived conflicts were started but never finished satisfactorily for the aggrieved side, becoming strategic stalemates until one side eventually lost, either through imperial overstretch or was simply overrun by conventional forces. The "frozen conflict" on the Korean Peninsula ended with a paranoid, hostile and aggressively nationalistic, Soviet-supported Communist regime north of the 38th parallel; but the US-backed government in Seoul eventually oversaw the development of a regional political-economic success story in South Korea that is today much more capable of defending itself. In Greece, the planning and on-the-ground efforts of American military advisers inserted at the battalion level through President Harry Truman's newly created Military Assistance Advisory Groups (MAAG) successfully defeated the Stalin-backed insurgency. As for Vietnam, the United States proved unable to win a limited war against the northern Communist forces and hastily abandoned its southern ally. Alone, South Vietnam could not stop a conventional conquering attack across the 17th parallel spearheaded by seventeen North Vietnamese divisions backed by Moscow.[7] Each of the above-mentioned limited wars were fought with limited aims but, collectively, ended with mixed results for the Soviet Union.

Vladimir Putin, on the other hand, has proven to be a master at limited war. In the footsteps of his Tsarist and Soviet predecessors, the Russian leader has pursued a series of limited wars in the post-Soviet space, using his proclaimed aim of halting the expansion of NATO up to Russia's borders as the strategic pretext to Finlandize the non-NATO European periphery. Whether it be Ukraine, Moldova, Georgia or Azerbaijan, Russian goals remain the same: weaken their national identities through prolonged territorial division, using force when necessary.

Putin's long-term goal in this approach is to show that NATO is unable to respond militarily to situations in its neighborhood below the threshold of war—to build up the perception that Russian aggression will always end in an unchallenged *fait accompli*. And in so doing, he is further laying the groundwork for the questioning of NATO's Article V itself, if and when Russia attempts to employ limited war against an exposed Alliance member. When that day comes, it will be at Putin's choosing. For him, Eurasia represents a vast playing field, and he is the Kremlin quarterback, running a spread offense against an overextended NATO defense accustomed to the old rules of the game, completely unaware that offensive innovations are being developed in the plan of attack. And as the rules of the of the game have changed, NATO's old-school defense has shed the ground forces and the military command structure required to prevent Putin from running team Russia up and down the Eurasian playing field, outmaneuvering the West at every turn, whether it be Crimea, Donbas, or Syria.

Not since Otto von Bismarck, has a European leader more skillfully redrawn the borders of his country's periphery than Putin. During the latter half of the 19th century, Bismarck sought to unify Germany through a series of short-lived campaigns, first by defeating Denmark in the Second Schleswig War in 1864, then, two years later, beating the Austrians at Königgrätz in 1866, followed four years after that by summarily defeating France in 1870/1871 in the Franco-Prussian war, which led to the French loss of Alsace-Lorraine. In each case, these conflicts were short wars, fought with limited aims, designed to help Prussia consolidate itself into a modern German state while isolating France. And in a manner reminiscent of the 19th century Prussian statesman, Putin has repeatedly changed existing state borders by force in the pursuit of Russia's rebirth. The Kremlin leader is determined to chart a path of imperial conquest for a greater Russia focusing on achieving short, limited objectives, with each step aimed at incremental changes to the regional balance of power.

Within the post-Soviet space, Putin is applying a boa constrictor strategy, seeking to regain lost territory without resorting to total war as he suffocates his neighbors. However, the boa constrictor understands its limits, as it can only digest one prey at a time. Likewise, Putin keenly understands Russia's own military limitations and its ability to project power—today's Russia cannot match the full strength of NATO once the latter's forces have been mobilized. At the same time, however, he is cognizant of the North Atlantic Alliance's own limitations in East-Central Europe as well as Paris or Berlin's reluctance to directly confront Moscow. Based upon these strategic goals and realities, one can easily understand why notions of non-linear war or "hybrid war" fit into the toolkit of Russian military strategy.

*   *   *

Against this setting, a major objective of this book is to outline and identify the trends in contemporary Russian strategy, military affairs and the lessons learned from Putin's spread offense. While the analysis found therein is highly comprehensive and carefully contextualized, we leave it up to the reader to draw his or her own policy conclusions as to how the US should respond to a revanchist Russia. That said, in identifying a possible strategy for dealing with Moscow, it would be worthwhile to briefly retrace the US's military involvement in Europe since World War I. Doing so may shed some light on why Russia has been so successful recently in resorting to non-linear warfare methods as part of its warfighting toolkit.

First of all, Russian strategists understand that the American experience in European warfare is relatively new compared to Russia's. The battlefields of East-Central Europe, the Balkans, Ukraine and the Black Sea basin are quite familiar to Russia. Its greatest *polkovodets,* or military commanders, ranging from Viktor Suvorov to Georgy Zhukov, fought wars in these regions with great success, alternating between carrying on regional wars on a limited scale or total war, such as against Napoleonic France or Nazi Germany.

Compared to Russia, the US experience in Europe and Eurasia, is only about a century long and limited to waging war on the western side of the European continent. US involvement in Europe since 1917 has been dominated by either total war—as seen through its involvement in the First and Second World Wars—or by the Cold War stalemate that resulted in dividing lines between East and West. Strategically, the situation of two vast opposing military camps facing off at the Fulda Gap was easier to deal with for US policymakers and grand strategists than, say, developing the operational concepts necessary for fighting limited wars.

As the Cold War ramped up, the US posture in Europe went from President Dwight D. Eisenhower's New Look defense strategy, which relied on technology and air power, to soon be overtaken by John F. Kennedy's conventional buildup, rooted in the doctrine of Flexible Response and strategic mobility. However, little room was left to adapt to social instability or upheaval on the Soviet periphery. And this visibly restricted Washington's ability to react to unrest in the Soviet empire, such as the 1956 Hungarian uprising or the Soviet/Warsaw Pact invasion of Czechoslovakia in 1968. Even in retirement, Eisenhower deliberated at great length over his own perceived failure to respond adequately to the Hungarian rebellion and bloody Soviet repression that occurred afterward. As he noted,

"Hungary was in the circumstances as inaccessible to us as Tibet… and… was the last provocation that my temper could stand.[8] Indeed, the geographic complexities of Eastern Europe always seem to have intimidated and even eluded US policymakers. It was not until they were faced with a real crisis—like the Berlin Crises of 1947 and 1961— that they were forced to change their thinking. To their credit, in each such case, US policymakers came up with creative solutions to these strategic problems. That said, for the first three decades, the American response always avoided full-scale confrontation. It was not until the Soviet invasion of Afghanistan in 1979 and the effort to contest Soviet power head on by President Ronald Reagan that the Soviet colossus was stopped in its tracks. Reagan did so by arming the Afghan rebels through National Security Decision Directive (NSDD) 166, eventually pushing the Soviets to withdraw from Afghanistan.[9]

American officials tended to be more comfortable with the ideas of *détente* and peaceful coexistence than confrontation until the Cold War struggle shifted to areas outside of Europe, such as Afghanistan, the Middle East or Africa. And with the bipolar struggle metastasizing to the Third World in the 1960s via regional proxies and client states, the concept of limited war finally began to make its way into American strategic thinking. Noted strategists like B. H. Liddell Hart stimulated this debate on how best to confront limited war. Indeed, Hart's 1960 book *Deterrent or Defense* ended up influencing the thinking of then-Senator John F. Kennedy.[10]

Today, we are again seeing a return to limited war. As was the case with the US experience of Korea (38th parallel) and later Vietnam (17th parallel), demarcation lines are again influencing US policymakers in their strategic decision-making as policy responses are being shaped by dividing lines between old and new Europe and between what constitutes an actual violation of NATO's sacred Article V. For all practical purposes, NATO response lines seem to end at the Alliance's edge. But serious uncertainties lie in the new demarcation lines of the non-NATO periphery. This is the current challenge for policymakers as they seek to chart a course for strategy and response—similar to the challenge faced, in the late 1950s and early 1960s, by strategists from Bernard Brodie to Liddell Hart, who understood the necessity to replace Eisenhower's New Look based on a reliance on airpower and nuclear missiles.

It is important to keep in mind that the military strategies formed in response to the Cold War's various regional conflicts in the Third World were imposed by civilian political leaders and not by the American military. General (ret.) H. R. McMaster's book *Dereliction of Duty* goes to great lengths to describe how these dividing lines often influenced strategy as the Joint Chiefs of Staff were sidelined by civilian policymakers during the critical phases of the Vietnam War. Notably, it was George Kennan's long cable that conceived the concept of containment, which defined US strategy during the Cold War—and from this overarching approach, Washington developed a suitable military strategy. However, over time, the Soviet Union learned to "leap frog" containment by shifting its activities to the Third World, forcing the US to develop new strategic concepts to counter these efforts.

The United States now appears to be at a similar juncture in formulating its grand strategy. Conflict at the margins of NATO has restricted the ability of US strategists to consider ways to deal with limited wars—particularly in the zones just beyond the reach of Article V. The Russian Federation of today is not the Soviet Union of old; it is not likely to engage in full-on proxy wars against the United States in the Developing World. Rather, Moscow will continue to ignite new instances of limited warfare on the margins of Europe, especially in vulnerable areas of particular strategic value to Russia, like the Baltic and the Black Sea. The contours of this new battlefield make up what geopolitical theoretician Nicholas J. Spykman referred to as the "Eurasian Rimland," the giant buffer zone between sea power and land power. As Spykman famously noted in his 1944 book *The Geography of the Peace*, "he who controls the Rimland rules Eurasia, [and he] who rules Eurasia controls the destinies of the world."[11] Indeed, in many ways, today's struggles are returning to the Rimland, as the balance of power of world politics lies in Eurasia. Moreover, it was Spykman who asserted that it would be up to the United States to be the chief balancer in the competition to control the balance of power in Eurasia.[12]

Frozen conflicts are at the heart of the struggle being fought in the Rimland. The post-Soviet space is emerging as a contest where Russian-backed rebellions threaten state sovereignty and political stability in Georgia, Ukraine, Moldova and now Ukraine. Understandably as the United States charts a new strategy of deterrence, open conflict is no longer to be found only at the geopolitical margins or in the Developing World, as was the case in the 1960s. Instead, conflict threatening Western security and transatlantic solidarity has now shifted to the borderlands of the post-Soviet space, where a revanchist Russia endangers NATO's youngest and most exposed members. In order to safeguard the North Atlantic Alliance's eastern flanks, the United States should formulate a new model of deterrence to not only safeguard those NATO member states that border Russia but also their transatlantic-leaning neighbors, such as Georgia and Ukraine.

Today, the entire center of gravity of NATO is shifting to the east, with the critical allies of Poland, the Baltic States and Romania making up the Alliance's vulnerable flanks. It took the United States decades to adjust to the geopolitical realities of the Cold War before becoming comfortable with its presence in Western Europe and in its ability to deter the Soviet Union. But that strategy was significantly more geographically limited: over 360,000 US ground forces manned the Fulda Gap, and its immediate flanks were guarded by NATO member Italy in the South and Norway in the North. Now, NATO must adjust to a new center of gravity east of the Oder River, an expansive region where the US lacks geographic familiarity and operational certainty. The Baltic and Black Seas, for example, were once areas that NATO feared to tread, as the maritime chokepoints of Skagerrak and the Bosporus formed the geographic dividing lines for power projection. Former NATO SACEUR Admiral James Stavridis echoed this view by noting that the US Navy largely viewed the Black Sea as a potential death trap for US warships.[13] And despite the lessons of Ukraine in 2014, this mentality still seems to dominate in Washington and across European capitals. Euro-Atlantic policymakers habitually retreat into the cocoon of thinking that "if it is not a violation of Article V, then everything is fine along NATO's flanks"—even as the balance of power in Eurasia changes. NATO's reluctance to think about ways to operate along those flanks must change as well, and for good reason. An often-overlooked mechanism the Alliance possesses is Article IV, which allows any member that feels threatened to invoke this clause and bring it to the North Atlantic Council for discussion—something of particular value for the exposed NATO members along the eastern flanks.[14]

*   *   *

Since Russia's invasion of Ukraine in 2014 and start of its operations in Syria in 2015, Western analysts, policymakers and military leaders have grappled with what lessons to draw from the Russian involvement in those military campaigns as well as how to confront the growing threat to the international order from an increasingly belligerent Moscow. Russia's pullout from the Conventional Forces in Europe (CFE) treaty in 2007 as well as its aggression against Georgia in August 2008 were two clear shots across the bow of the transatlantic community. But it was not until Russia forcibly changed borders on the European continent by annexing Crimea that the West realized Russia has become more threat than partner. Indeed, in July 2015, then-nominee for Chairman of the Joint Chiefs, General Joseph Dunford, testified before Congress that Russia posed the greatest "existential" threat to the United States. As such, the US and the NATO alliance have been upgrading their deterrence posture along Europe's eastern flank. Meanwhile, Russia's bold reassertion of political and military influence across the wider Middle East has hampered and complicated the US-led international coalition's anti-terrorism operations against the Islamic State in Syria and beyond.

To effectively confront Russia, Western policymakers and military commanders will need a more thorough understanding of the strategic calculus behind Russia's behavior in each global region it is involved in—the Arctic, the Far East, the Greater Middle East and Europe's eastern flank. In addition, there is a need to better comprehend the Russian Armed Forces' strategic and doctrinal approaches to all the various domains in which they operate. *Russia's Military Strategy and Doctrine* is designed to educate Russia watchers, policymakers, military leaders, and the broader foreign policy community about the Russian Armed Forces and security apparatus across the full spectrum of geographic, doctrinal and domain areas.

This book is divided into three main sections. Part I focuses on the four main geographic vectors of Russia's strategy, delving into the most important regions and front lines against which Moscow arrays its forces and political-military efforts. Part II features chapters that explore key functional aspects of Russia's warfighting and defense posture. Whereas, Part III includes analysis of the lessons Moscow has learned from its two ongoing foreign wars, in Syria and Donbas, as well as how its national security and defense strategies have impacted changes to mobilization and military reforms domestically.

One of the key takeaways of this collective study is that Moscow continues to view its southwest vector, including the Black Sea, Middle East and Eastern Mediterranean—or what Russian military planners call the *Iugo-Zapadnoe Napravlenie* (Southwestern Direction)—as most consequential to the security of the state. As such, the book begins with twin pieces on Russia's strategy in this direction. The first chapter, "The Russian Strategic Offensive in the Middle East," is written by long-time Moscow-based defense analyst Pavel Felgenhauer. His contribution delves heavily into Russia's prosecution of its military intervention in Syria as well as the political-informational strategy surrounding building regional coalitions and attracting international support for Moscow's broader policies there. Additionally, Felgenhauer examines Russia's wider Middle East posture from a political, economic and security standpoint. Importantly, he argues that Russia's intervention and ongoing military presence in Syria and the wider region needs to be understood as first and foremost helping to assert Russian control over its access to the Black Sea and Mediterranean via the Turkish Straits. In other words, Russia's newly acquired and expanded bases in Syria offer strategic depth to the *Iugo-Zapadnoye Napravleniye*.

Former chief of Ukrainian naval operations Ihor Kabanenko echoes many of these points in his contribution to this book, "Strategy in the Black Sea and Mediterranean." As he notes in his chapter, Russia's Black Sea strategy naturally extends into the Mediterranean since the country's only year-round ice-free ports with access to the world ocean are all located there. Examining Russia's regional strategy though a naval and maritime security lens, Kabanenko outlines the steps Moscow has been taking to reinforce its military posture in the Black Sea. Specifically, and exploiting its occupation of the geostrategically located Crimean peninsula, Russia has been creating progressively stronger anti-access and area-denial (A2/AD) bubbles over the Black Sea region. Moreover, Russian actions in the Black Sea have been characterized by the continual creation of new high-probability offensive threats and then periodically raising their perceived likelihood for political-military reasons.

The third chapter, "Russia's Arctic and Far East Strategies," by Pavel K. Baev, pointedly links these two regions in light of Moscow's focus on developing the Northern Sea Route, which will connect the European and East Asian markets via a maritime passage along the country's Arctic coastline. As the Arctic continues to open up, the strategically important Northern Sea Route as well as economic opportunities associated with extracting natural resources from the

High North have been translating into growing focus on this region by Moscow. However, as Baev points out, the inflated and entirely unrealistic threat assessments pushed by the Russian military have resulted in an unreasonable resource allocation to the Arctic, resulting in more attention paid to building a string of new military bases and A2/AD bubbles than actual economic development or commercial investment there. The Far East, on the other hand, suffers from the exact opposite situation, he notes. Despite quite real security challenges to Russian Siberia and the Asia-Pacific region stemming from an increasingly confident China and a nuclear North Korea, for example, Moscow has been naively trying to link itself politically to Beijing's rise while misallocating billions on dubious economic and infrastructure projects that have no hope of ever turning a profit.

The final chapter of the geography-driven section is Swedish defense ministry advisor Jörgen Elfving's "Baltic Sea Strategy." Specifically, his contribution details the steps Russia has been taking to counteract NATO's growing presence and activities in the Baltic region that, themselves, were spurred by Russian aggression in Ukraine. Additionally, he looks at Moscow's attempts to ensure that Sweden and Finland remain outside of the North Atlantic Alliance. As he contends, particularly when it comes to armament acquisition and creating new military units, Russian military planners are currently giving the most attention to the country's western strategic direction—i.e., the Baltic Sea Region—because of NATO's increased activities there as well as the area's history as an east-west invasion corridor.

The second section of this book pulls back and focuses on the non-conventional elements of Russian strategy and doctrine that are common to most if not all areas of conflict or political-security competition with other powers that Moscow engages in around the world. Chapter 5, "Not 'Hybrid' but New Generation Warfare," by Latvian defense analyst Jānis Bērziņš, seeks to dispel some of the pervasive myths in the West about what role asymmetric, non-conventional, informational and below-the-threshold-of-conflict elements play in Russian military thought. His chapter not only defines the overlapping terms and concepts found in Russian military theory but also importantly provides a framework for how these elements fit together in practice under the overarching concept of New Generation Warfare. Of particular value is Bērziņš's outline of the eight phases of New Generation Warfare, which the Russian military is likely to follow—though, as he cautions, not necessarily in a purely linear fashion—as hostilities in a conflict escalate.

Nuclear weapons clearly form a key element of such a non-conventional war-fighting or military-political intimidation strategy for Russia. Thus, the following pair of chapters tackles this topic head on. Well-known Finnish defense researcher, Stefan Forss, provides a detailed background and history of the role nuclear arms play in Russian strategy and doctrine. In particular, he offers an overview of the various missiles and nuclear warheads in Russia's inventory as well as analyzes the major US-Russian arms control treaties that have limited Moscow's deployments. At the same time, he notes that since the end of the Cold War, and particularly after having recovered from the politically and economically turbulent 1990s, Russia has been undertaking a massive rearmament and modernization program of its nuclear stockpiles—an effort that has picked up significantly in recent years as ties to the West have deteriorated.

Long-time expert on the Russian Armed Forces, Stephen Blank, drills down further on this topic while also expanding the discussion in his contribution, "Putin's 'Asymmetric Strategy': Nuclear and New-Type Weapons in Russian Defense Policy." In particular, he explores Moscow's use of nuclear saber-rattling and intimidation to try to control every phase of a conflict. And through a close reading of the writings produced by Russian military theorists, Blank provides an important corrective to the popular but misleading idea in the West of an ostensible Russian "escalate to deescalate" doctrine of nuclear weapons use. Additionally, Blank's chapter looks at the increasing focus by Russian military planners on boosting deterrence via ultra-modern "new-type" weapons, such as lasers, robotics, energy beam systems, hypersonics or even genetically modified biological agents.

The final chapter in this section, "Russia's Offensive and Defensive Use of Information Security," by Russian researcher Sergey Sukhankin, examines the role that cyberspace and the broader information domain play in Russian war making. Of particular note, Sukhankin writes that Moscow's attitude toward the information domain strongly retains many of its Soviet legacies, including its use as both an offensive weapon against outside enemies as well as a means to internally control the domestic population. As he points out, modern Russian theorists frequently ascribe the collapse of the Soviet Union to the authorities' forfeiture of control over information flows in and out of the country. At the same time, he writes that, when it comes to defense, Russia's view of information security differs dramatically from the Western approach, with practice regularly outrunning theory, thus making Russian actions more difficult to predict.

Part III of this book begins with two chapters analyzing the lessons Russia has learned from its ongoing wars abroad and how those lessons are being incorporated into its military reforms, rearmament processes as well as doctrine and strategy. Chapter 9, "Deciphering the Lessons Learned by the Russian Armed Forces in Ukraine, 2014–2017," by Russian military expert Roger N. McDermott, concludes that the "covert" campaign in Donbas, first and foremost, revitalized the General Staff's support for large, heavy armor maneuvers. It also pushed a reorganization of Russia's military structure back to reintroducing some divisional units. In turn, analyst Dima Adamsky contributed a chapter on Russia's "open" foreign war: "Russian Lessons Learned From the Operation in Syria: A Preliminary Assessment." One of the key points he makes is that the Russian intervention in Syria has provided invaluable combat experience for the country's military commanders, who have been rotated in and out of the campaign continually for the past several years. Moreover, his chapter looks at the ways in which the Syrian campaign has been influencing how Russia utilizes intelligence, surveillance and reconnaissance (ISR) assets in combat, as well as the war's impact on Russian disinformation operations.

The final chapter in this collective study is written by the well-known Russian military analyst and defense journalist Aleksandr Golts. In "The Concept of Mass Mobilization Returns," Golts turns to the ongoing reforms to Russia's domestic mobilization system. Specifically, he outlines how and why the leadership of the Russian Armed Forces is progressively turning away from previous plans to create a fully voluntary army. Moreover, he analyzes what a reliance on a Soviet-style conscript-based force will mean for the capabilities of the Russian military to deal with the types of conflicts it can actually expect to face, versus the kind the Kremlin appears to be preparing for under the guidance of the General Staff.

The key questions emphasized by this book are "how Russia fights wars" and "how its experiences with modern conflicts are shaping the evolution of Russia's military strategy, capabilities and doctrine." The book's value comes not only from a piecemeal look at granular Russian strategies in each of the theaters and domains where its Armed Forces may act, but also from the collective work's unifying description of Russia's military strategy as a declining but still formidable global power. It is our sincere hope that *Russia's Military Strategy and Doctrine* will be an essential reference for US national security thinkers, NATO defense planners and policymakers the world over who deal with the potential military and security challenges posed by a revanchist Russia.

Glen E. Howard
President, The Jamestown Foundation

Matthew Czekaj
Editor-in-Chief, Eurasia Daily Monitor *and*
Senior Program Associate for Europe and Eurasia, The Jamestown Foundation

February 5, 2019
Washington, DC

Notes

[1] The presented timeline of events can be found in "Russian Attack Against Ukrainian Navy Ships," Presentation, Ukrainian Navy, December 14, 2018; "How Russia occupied Sea of Azov: full chronology," *Empr.media*, https://empr.media/opinion/analytics/how-russia-occupied-sea-of-azov-full-chronology/, accessed January 4, 2019.

[2] Michael Kofman, "The Kerch Strait Naval Skirmish," *Russia Military Analysis*, November 28, 2018, https://russianmilitaryanalysis.wordpress.com/2018/11/28/the-kerch-strait-naval-skirmish/.

[3] Maryna Vorotnyuk, "In Serious Escalation, Russia Openly Attacks Ukrainian Vessels in Azov Sea," *Eurasia Daily Monitor*, Volume 15, Issue 165, November 26, 2018, The Jamestown Foundation, https://jamestown.org/program/in-serious-escalation-russia-openly-attacks-ukrainian-vessels-in-azov-sea/; Ihor Kabanenko, "Strategic Implications of Russia and Ukraine's Naval Clash on November 25," *Eurasia Daily Monitor*, Volume 15, Issue 167, November 28, 2018, The Jamestown Foundation, https://jamestown.org/program/strategic-implications-of-russia-and-ukraines-naval-clash-on-november-25/.

[4] Yuri Lapaiev, "Martial Law in Ukraine: A Rehearsal for War," *Eurasia Daily Monitor*, Volume 15, Issue 175, December 12, 2018, The Jamestown Foundation, https://jamestown.org/program/martial-law-in-ukraine-a-rehearsal-for-war/.

[5] See for example: Robert Endicott Osgood, *Limited War: The Challenge to American Strategy* University of Chicago Press, 1957, p. 62. Osgood's book, written in 1957, is considered the classic work on the term limited war that heavily influenced American strategic thinkers in the 1960s. Many experts consider this time period to be the golden age of academic thinking on strategy.

[6] Zbigniew Brzezinski, *Strategic Vision: America and the Crisis of Global Power*, New York: Basic Books, 2012, p. 95.

[7] Harry G. Summers, Jr. *On Strategy: The Vietnam War in Context*, Strategic Studies Institute, US Army War College, Carlisle Barracks, Pennsylvania (Fifth Printing), January 1989, p. 70.

[8] Ralph Gordon Hoxie, *Command Decision and the Presidency: A Study of National Security Policy and Organization*, New York: Readers Digest Press, 1977, p. 208.

[9] "National Security Decision Directive 166," The White House, Washington, DC, March 27, 1985, https://fas.org/irp/offdocs/nsdd/nsdd-166.pdf.

[10] Basil H. Liddell Hart, *Deterrent or Defense: A Fresh Look at the West's Military Position*, New York: Frederick A. Praeger Publishers, 1960.

[11] Nicholas J. Spykman, *The Geography of the Peace*. New York: Harcourt Brace and Company, 1944, p. 43.

[12] Geoffrey R. Sloan, *Geopolitics in United States Strategic Policy, 1890–1987*, Brighton, United Kingdom: Wheatsheaf Books Ltd, 1988, p. 16.

[13] James Stavridis, *Seapower: The History and Geopolitics of the World's Oceans*, New York: Penguin Press, 2017, p. 133.

[14] Stavridis, op. cit., p. 161

Part I

The Geographic Vectors of Russia's Strategy

1. The Russian Strategic Offensive in the Middle East

Pavel Felgenhauer

Introduction

As Russian military forces began to massively deploy to Syria in September 2015, questions proliferated about Moscow's true objective. It seemed difficult to understand why Russia was undertaking a new massive overseas combat mission while already engaged in other conflicts and a serious standoff with the West over Crimea and Donbas. Moreover, the Russian budget suffered from sizeable deficits, household incomes were steadily decreasing, and sanctions were harming the flow of Russia's capital and technologies. Some, in Moscow and abroad, posited that the Syrian encounter may have been designed to deflect public opinion away from the doldrums of a seemingly unending Ukrainian crisis. Others suggested that Moscow may have been trying to somehow "exchange" Syria for Ukraine—by joining the West in fighting the Islamic State (IS) and other jihadists, Russia could obtain sanctions reprieve or maybe *de facto* parole for its other presumed transgressions. Subsequent developments soon suggested, ostensibly at least, that this latter group of observers seemed closer to the mark.

3

In September 2015, speaking in Dushanbe, Tajikistan, at a summit of the Collective Security Treaty Organization (CSTO—the Russian-dominated regional defense alliance), President Vladimir Putin called for a joint effort by the international community to resist the IS threat. Furthermore, he promoted the formation of a "broad coalition" to support the Iraqi and Syrian government forces "that are already fighting ISIS [Islamic State of Iraq and Syria—the former name for IS]." Putin also called on other countries to join in providing military assistance to Syrian President Bashar al-Assad.[1] Later that same month, speaking at the United Nations General Assembly, in New York, Putin repeated his call for forming a grand anti-terrorist coalition along the outlines of the Second World War anti-fascist alliance. In addition, however, Putin condemned "the export of democracy" by the West as one of the main reason for the destabilization of the Middle East and the original rise of the Islamic State.[2]

Moscow's pitch to the West—joining forces in a grand anti-terrorist coalition with al-Assad, Hezbollah and the Iranian Revolutionary Guard (IRGC) Quds Force militias—did not work. Indeed, the main targets of Russia's military campaign in Syria turned out to be Syrian opposition groups that Moscow labeled "terrorist." The Syria operation, thus, did not help build up confidence between Moscow and the West, and in some cases it actually created additional lines of tension. In October 2015, Putin offered to send to Washington a high-level delegation headed by Prime Minister Dmitry Medvedev to discuss Syria and "to work together and find solutions"; but the United States, according to Foreign Minister Sergei Lavrov, "refused to send a top delegation to Moscow to discuss Syria and declined to receive a delegation led by Medvedev." According to Lavrov, the US agrees to discuss only purely military measures to avoid mid-air clashes between US and Russian aircraft.[3] In an interview published in Moscow in December 2017, first deputy defense minister and the chief of General Staff, Army General Valery Gerasimov, confirmed that the bilateral memorandum on air safety or "de-confliction" in

Syria, signed in 2015 with the US military, had been working fine for more than two years, with both sides fully complying. But according to Gerasimov, all further Russian proposals for joint operations "did not interest the Americans."[4]

The Syrian overseas campaign was not particularly popular with the Russian public. The Russian military effort in Syria seemed at times like an outdated, imperialistic foray into the Middle East and the Mediterranean—a theater in which the Russian tsars and Communist leaders traditionally wrestled against Western opponents for influence. Putin's Russia seemed to be acting out of its depth, taking on too heavy a strategic role it did not have the resources or manpower to complete, for reasons that did not seem clear-cut or imperative.

But the real reason for entering the Syrian civil war was complex, involving different internal and foreign policy considerations. On the one hand, preventing the fall of the al-Assad regime and reversing the course of the Syrian civil war was seen as another manifestation of Russian national state revival, of its military demonstrating the ability to take on a logistically and organizationally challenging overseas mission. The world and the Middle East were supposed to see that Russia is once again on par with the mighty United States, like the Soviet Union during the Cold War. And on the other hand, the Kremlin believed, thanks to the Russian intervention, the balance of power in a strategically sensitive region of the world could be significantly altered—with global ramifications.

The Southern Dimension of Russia's Global Anti-Western Standoff

In February 2007, at the Munich Security Conference, in Germany, Putin declared a watershed change in Russia's national security, defense and foreign policies. As such, he negated any future possibility of comprehensive strategic cooperation with the West and the US, while retaining the option of limited collaboration on some issues, like fighting terrorism.[5] The Cold War–tested strict rules of global zero-sum gaming had once again become the true international rules of the game for Moscow.

A year and a half later, in August 2008, Russia invaded Georgia—Moscow's first direct use of military power to roll back assumed Western encroachment into what the Kremlin considered Russia's security backyard. In the immediate aftermath of the short Russian-Georgian war, the United States and the North Atlantic Treaty Organization (NATO) deployed naval forces to the Black Sea, setting off alarm bells in Moscow. Its dilapidated Black Sea Fleet (BSF) was clearly no match for North Atlantic Alliance vessels; and both Moscow and the *de facto* second Russian capital, Sochi, where Putin stays about half of the year, suddenly seemed under threat from a potential stealthy and massive precision cruise missile attack.

As a countermeasure, Russian authorities planned a massive rearmament of the Black Sea Fleet, including the establishment of a cruise missile–armed attack submarine force and the introduction of new Bastion long-range land-based anti-ship missiles. But the revamping of the BSF was considered insufficient for building an impenetrable southwestern Russian defense perimeter. Thus, in February 2013, soon after the government adopted the country's main top-secret strategic defense document—the "Plan of Defense of the Russian Federation" ("*Plan Oborony Rossyskoy Federatsiy*"—PORF)—a decision was announced to reinstitute a permanent Mediterranean naval operational task force (*Operativnoye Soedineniye VMF RF na Sredizemnom More*—OSVMFRFSM) "to defend Russian national interests." And a reinvigorated BSF would form this reconstituted naval group's backbone.[6] Officials declared that the OSVMFRFSM would be modeled on the Cold War–era 5th Mediterranean Soviet Naval Squadron, which numbered 30–50 ships and was deployed until 1992 to counter the US 6th Fleet as well as to support Moscow's client Arab states in the region.[7] Acting in concert with the Black Sea Fleet and under BSF operational command, the

OSVMFRFSM could help prevent a massive breakthrough of NATO naval forces into the Black Sea, as occurred in August 2008.

The PORF is a top-secret document incorporating threat assessment, rearmament, mobilization and integrated defense plans. As reported by the Kremlin Press Service, on January 29, 2013, Defense Minister Sergei Shoigu and Gerasimov presented Putin with the draft text of the PORF. According to Shoigu, "the PORF is very detailed and has been worked out with the input of 49 ministries and [government] departments." The PORF, continued Shoigu, will define Russian defenses for decades and serves as a "live document" that integrates all defense plans and efforts and will be regularly corrected to take into account the changing threat environment and "other events."[8] The PORF seems to be a new type of integrated strategic blueprint that does not have a direct equivalent in old Soviet planning practice. In January 2013, Shoigu told Putin that the PORF was ready to be signed into law—which apparently did take place.

Concrete military plans to defend Russia and its allies against all possible threats are kept under wraps, as are most of the tactical/technical capabilities of deployed and newly developed weapons systems. And yet, the underlining threat assessment seems to be less of a secret. Just two weeks after the PORF was approved by the Kremlin, Gerasimov delivered public remarks at a conference in Moscow, where he presented a gloomy forecast of impending danger, apparently based on the PORF threat assessment analysis: "In the period until 2030, the level of existing and potential military threats may grow substantially." Leading world powers will be fighting to control natural energy resources, markets and "Lebensraum [Nazi German term meaning 'living space'; a call for eastward territorial expansion]," actively using military means to achieve national goals.[9] Since the adaption of the PORF, the concept of Russia under siege and the growing threat of enemy attack has dominated strategic military planning, rearmament, as well as the country's foreign and domestic policies. Moscow has been reinforcing its defenses in all strategic directions: North, West, East and South. But the southwestern direction (*Iugo-Zapadnoye Napravleniye*)—the Black Sea, the Mediterranean and the Turkish Straits connecting the two—is seen from the Kremlin as one of the most important and potentially vulnerable.

In September 2016, the battle-readiness of the *Iugo-Zapadnoye Napravleniye* was tested in the massive Kavkaz ("Caucasus") 2016 strategic military exercises in southwestern Russia and occupied Crimea. The General Staff mobilized over 220,000 soldiers and civilian defense ministry contractors. Gerasimov told journalists the reinforced BSF (possibly with the help of OSVMFRFSM vessels) had the capacity to destroy "potential enemy [NATO]" ships "before they leave home ports [apparently in the Mediterranean] or in the Bosporus—we have long-range targeting reconnaissance capabilities and land-based Bastion anti-ship missiles with a range of 350 km, in addition to submarines with [long-range] Kalibr cruise missiles, naval attack jets, strategic bombers with cruise missiles and more." According to Gerasimov, "The enemy will never come close to Crimea, no matter from where they come."[10]

The takeover of Crimea in March 2014 tremendously reinforced Russia's control of the Black Sea, but this did not negate the need to continue to maintain the OSVMFRFSM. To keep the OSVMFRFSM operational, Russian command needed a permanent naval base in the Mediterranean and a large military airbase to provide the flotilla task force with air cover and support. The small mothballed Cold War–era naval supply base in Tartus, Syria, was increasingly dysfunctional because of the Syrian civil war, while the seemingly imminent collapse of al-Assad's regime threatened to result in its permanent shutdown. Moreover, there was no airbase in Tartus. In 2015, in coordination with Damascus and Tehran, the Russian military began preparations to establish a major airbase at Hmeymim, in Syria's Latakia province. At the end of September 2015, the Russian military, in coordination with Damascus and Iranian-led Shia militias, began a major military operation in Syria that has since turned the course of the civil war. At the same time, however, Moscow's Syria intervention has secured a possibly much more fundamental strategic goal: reinforcing the *Iugo-Zapadnoye Napravleniye* and providing it with strategic depth. Only a couple of weeks into the operation, in October 2015, the Russian General Staff announced that Hmeymim, together with the Tartus naval facility, would become "permanent" naval, army and air force bases on the Syrian Mediterranean coast.[11] The al-Assad regime, dependent on Russian military support for its survival, immediately consented that the Russians could have any bases they wish.[12]

In December 2017, the Russian parliament ratified an agreement with the al-Assad regime in Damascus, establishing Tartus as a permanent naval base for 49 years with the option of an automatic prolongation of the lease for another 25 years. According to Deputy Defense Minister Nikolai Pankov, Russian personnel, equipment and facilities in Tartus will be covered by full legal immunity, effectively granting them exterritorial status. The territory of the previously small Russian naval facility in Tartus will be expanded to some 24 hectares (about 60 acres). The base has been reinforced by anti-aircraft batteries and anti-ship Bastion guided missiles. New piers, warehouses and living facilities are being constructed. Tartus may eventually have the capacity to house up to 11 warships, including nuclear-powered ones. Air and sea defenses of Tartus are the responsibility of the Russian Armed Forces, with the local Syrian forces providing outer perimeter defenses on land. Tartus is apparently planned to be the main home-port of the OSVMFRFSM and "will enable the expansion of Russia's naval presence and influence in the Mediterranean," according to Pankov.[13] Dmitry Sablin, a Duma deputy from the ruling United Russia party, noted, "NATO was doing its best to expel Russia from the Mediterranean," but these plans have been thwarted. The transformation of the small Tartus supply facility into a major naval base implies Russia has a long-term strategy of military presence in the Mediterranean, according to Sablin. [14]

The Russian military intervention in Syria was always primarily about countering the United States in the Middle East and the Mediterranean. Fighting the Islamic State and other jihadist groups, together with al-Assad forces, the IRGC Quds Force and Iranian-backed militias, is an important, but secondary task. In May 2017, speaking at a session of the upper house of parliament—the Federation Council—Shoigu announced the main strategic accomplishment of the Russian Syrian campaign was the establishment of a strong military force (*Gruperovka*) "on the south flank of NATO, which dramatically changed the strategic balance of power in the region." In the same speech, the defense minister called on the Russian people "not to be blind" to the growing menace "of NATO activities on the borders of Russia."[15] Building an impenetrable southwestern defense perimeter in the Black Sea region and the Caucasus against the US and its allies apparently continues to be the main strategic objective. Occupying a position of overall influence in the Middle East is considered equally important, especially if this undermines US positions in the region in zero-sum game terms.

Tank Generals in Command of the Syrian Air Campaign

The desire to hold on to the Tartus naval base may have been one of the main strategic reasons behind why the Russian military began its prolonged and costly foray in Syria to secure the survival of Bashar al-Assad. Indeed, the embattled Syrian president, in turn, could guarantee continued Russian military permanent presence in the Eastern Mediterranean. But during the Russian campaign in Syria from 2015 through 2017, the Tartus naval facility, though an important logistics hub on the Syrian coast, did not see much military action *per se*. Importantly, it is situated in a region inhabited by friendly pro-al-Assad Alawites, with practically no insurgent activities by armed opposition or jihadist groups. The most notable exception was a series of brazen drone attacks on the Tartus and Hmeymim bases in early January 2018. Although these terrorist strikes ultimately caused little damage and were repelled by Russian forces.[16]

The headquarters and the main operational base of the Russian forces in Syria were instead located in Hmeymim. High-ranking Russian generals regularly rotated through this military airfield. In an interview published in December 2017, Gerasimov mentioned five colonel generals—Aleksandr Dvornikov (56), Andrei Kartapolov (54), Sergey Surovikin (51), Vladimir Zarudnitsky (59) and Alexander Zhuravlyov (52)—who rotated as commanders of the Armed Forces *Gruperovka* in Syria. According to the General Staff chief, each of these generals arrived in Hmeymim with his own operational staff, intelligence and reconnaissance chiefs, artillery and rocket commanders, and so on from one or another of Russia's military districts. The constant rotation of top military commanders and staffs through Syria (a typical tour lasts three months) have allowed, according to Gerasimov, to provide all the military districts and army staffs, together with 90 percent of divisional command staffs, with firsthand combat experience. In all, over 48,000 servicemen did tours in Syria in 2015–2018, and a quarter of them were decorated. Zhuravlyov commanded the Syria *Gruperovka* in 2016 and took over for a second tour in December 2017.[17]

The Kremlin has been portraying its Syrian campaign as a non-contact, low-casualty Western-style war, mostly being carried out via bombing by the Russian Aerospace Forces (*Vozdushno-Kosmicheskiye Sily*—VKS). The ground fighting was the responsibility of al-Assad's Syrian Arab Army (SAA) as well as various local and Iranian-backed militias, including Hezbollah. Gerasimov complained of serious problems during the beginning of the campaign in organizing effective cooperation between the VKS and different local allied military units and militias. Other challenges for Russia related to organizing the logistics of supplying and training these foreign ground forces. In 2015, the SAA controlled only 10 percent of the territory, according to Gerasimov; but with the help of the VKS and Russian advisors, the SAA, supplied with new weapons, dramatically improved. Russian military advisors are present in SAA units up to the battalion level: "They gather intel, [as well as] plan and command operations under orders coming from the *Gruperovka* headquarters in Hmeymim."[18]

Though the VKS and its bombers were the decisive military arm of the *Gruperovka*, its commanders were all tank and mechanized infantry (motor-rifle) generals. All of them have since been decorated and promoted. Dvornikov, Surovikin and Zhuravlyov received the Order of Heroes of Russia medal. Only Zarudnitsky, who is approaching retirement age from active service, was appointed to the honorary position of commandant of Russia's top military school—the Academy of the General Staff—following his Syria tour. The Syrian campaign was hailed by state propaganda as a spectacular VKS operation, but not a single flyer general was in overall command of the *Gruperovka*. Apparently, Gerasimov, himself a tank general (*tankyst*), used the Syrian campaign as an opportunity to promote fellow tank and army generals who traditionally dominate the Russian military and the General Staff and do their best to keep the admirals, the flyers and the rocket generals at bay. In November 2017, in an unprecedented move, Surovikin was appointed the commander of the VKS. Surovikin, a "tank" general, replaced Army General (ret.) Viktor Bondarev, a former pilot, who was recently appointed chairman of the Federation Council defense and security committee.[19]

Surovikin, a veteran of the Soviet war in Afghanistan in the late 1980s and both Chechen wars in the 1990s and 2000s, reportedly several times wounded in action, has a notorious reputation. After the unsuccessful August 1991 coup that eventually terminated the Soviet Union, Surovikin spent some six months in prison after solders under his command killed three anti-Communist protesters in the streets of Moscow. But he was eventually released without trial. In 1995, Surovikin received a suspended sentence for illegal arms trade. This felony conviction was later overturned. In the army, Surovikin has a reputation for total ruthlessness. In 2005, while commander of the 42nd mechanized (motor-rifle) division in Chechnya, Surovikin reportedly announced he would kill three Chechens for every one of his soldiers killed.[20] In 2004, Surovikin, as commander of the 34th motor-rifle division, was accused of physically assaulting subordinate officers. Colonel Andrei Shatkal reportedly fatally shot himself in the head using his service sidearm in Surovikin's office after a dress-down by the general.[21]

Surovikin made a stellar career in the top echelons of the General Staff and defense ministry after 2008, during the radical military reform that required ruthlessness in dismissing unneeded veterans and building a more battle-ready and leaner force. Surovikin's readiness to vigorously execute any orders trounced any potential questions about his checkered curriculum vitae.[22]

The Navy's Shortcomings in Syria Campaign

Today, Russia has four main military districts (West, South, Central and East). Russia's most powerful Northern Fleet was expanded in December 2014 into a separate Joint Strategic Command "North," in charge of the entire Arctic, reinforced by an Army corps and VKS units.[23] Joint Strategic Command North is seemingly on par with the other four military districts, but its commander, Admiral Nikolai Yevmenov, has never command the *Gruperovka* in Syria—nor has any other Russian admiral. Russia's navy, the Military-Maritime Fleet (*Voyenno-Morskoy Flot*—VMF), played a vital part in the Russian expansion in the Middle East. It could be said the entire operation in Syria was in large part undertaken to establish a solid home base for the OSVMFRFSM in the Eastern Mediterranean. But the VMF apparently did not gain much in terms of top echelon influence and was often criticized for its deficiencies.

Navy frigates, corvettes and submarines repeatedly fired long-range Kalibr cruise missiles at targets in Syria. In the first spectacular attack on October 7, 2015 (Putin's 63rd birthday), four corvettes of the Caspian Flotilla launched 26 Kalibr-NK 3M14 missiles, which flew more than 1,500 km over Iran and Iraq from the Caspian Sea to reach targets in Latakia and Idlib provinces. Russian state TV propaganda aggressively played up this first launch of Kalibr-NKs at Syria—a demonstration of Russian military might and a snub to the Americans. Moreover, the Kremlin press service released footage of Shoigu personally briefing Putin, who was spending his birthday at his Black Sea residence in Sochi.[24]

Over the next three years, the VMF continued to launch Kalibr-NK missiles, but none of the individual volleys were as massive as the October 7, 2015, strike. Since that first attack and through the end of 2017, over 25 volleys of, together, more than 140 Kalibr-NK missiles were reportedly fired by Russian Black Sea Fleet frigates operating in the Eastern Mediterranean, over a hundred miles off the Syrian coast. Each Kalibr-NK volley consisted of four to eight missiles. Newly built Project 636.3 (Kilo) diesel-electric BSF submarines fired Kalibr-PL (the submarine version of the Kalibr) cruise missiles at targets in Syria, some of them as the subs were transiting from the Baltic Sea, where they were built. In all, some 40 Kalibr-PLs were reportedly fired at targets in Syria, in volleys of 2 to 4, through the end of 2017. By this time, the BSF had received six 636.3 (Kilo) submarines. The Kalibr missiles launched by the navy from the Mediterranean hit targets 400–900 km away in Syria. The Kalibr missiles appeared to be a reliable weapon, but the navy apparently had insufficient stockpiles of these cruise missiles to organize more massive attacks. Moreover, the VMF could not properly test the ability of the Kalibr-NK to pierce enemy defenses, because the Syrian opposition and jihadists groups lacked any anti-aircraft capabilities or early-warning radars.[25]

The need to assess the ability of new Russian ships, including frigates, small corvettes and diesel-electric submarines, to launch long-range missiles was clearly one of the main reasons to use a relatively large number of different ships. The Kalibr missiles are extremely expensive, reportedly some $3 million–$6.5 million apiece, and there was no clear tactical reason to use these stealthy weapons against targets that lack air defenses and were already being bombed with impunity by Russian jets.[26]

It seems, Russian admirals wanted to impress the Kremlin with the navy's ability to effectively intervene in overseas conventional regional conflicts in order to be able to lobby for financing of expensive shipbuilding projects. Despite the obvious propaganda success of spectacular sea and underwater Kalibr launches, the strategic result was rather mixed: The VMF apparently did not demonstrate the ability to perform massive conventional cruise missile attacks. Having small corvettes and nonnuclear submarines as carriers of long-range missiles that may potentially be nuclear-tipped is strategically important in a possible standoff with a strong enemy like the US. An attack by just several missiles can be effective if they are nuclear and at least one reaches its target with a 200-kiloton warhead. But the ability of the Russian navy to perform effectively in conventional local overseas battle zones is clearly still limited.

In another apparent attempt to demonstrate to the world and the Kremlin its battle capabilities, the VMF sent the aircraft carrier *Admiral Kuznetsov* with a battle group to the Mediterranean. On October 15, 2016, the *Kuznetsov*, nuclear battle cruiser *Pyotr Velikiy*, along with two guided-missile frigates and several support vessels departed Severomorsk—the main naval base of the Northern Fleet, on the Barents Sea. This naval grouping returned to port on February 9, 2017. During its voyage around Europe, via the Channel and through the Strait of Gibraltar, the *Kuznetsov* was belching dark smoke reminiscent of a coal-driven World War I battleship and moving at an incredibly slow pace for an aircraft carrier—less than ten nautical miles per hour, on average—from Severomorsk to Gibraltar.[27] This, together with the thick smoke, indicated serious engine trouble.

After returning to its home port in February 2017, the *Kuznetsov*—Russia's only aircraft carrier—has remained moored, awaiting serious renovation. The defense ministry and the government evidently disagree on how much money the Russian budget can allocate to remodel the *Kuznetsov* and how substantial the renovations should be. The vessel's main engine must be replaced, but the extent of other overhauls are still under discussion. A "minimal sum" of 50 billion rubles ($850 million) was reportedly allocated for the renovation; but later news reports suggested only one half of that amount may ultimately be spent.[28] As of August 2018, the *Kuznetsov* remained in limbo, moored, not battle-ready and awaiting repairs and modernizations that "may last some years."[29]

The *Kuznetsov* has the capacity to carry up to 50 jets and helicopters, but it sailed to the Mediterranean in October 2016, with only 14 jet fighters (10 Su-33s and 4 new MiG-29K/KUBs) and several helicopters. The *Kuznetsov* air wing was reportedly incomplete because of lack of jets and trained carrier pilots. The vessel lacks a catapult, and its jet fighters take off using a jump ramp and thrust; the forward motion of the carrier in the water helps provide additional take-off speed to the jets. Because of its faulty main engine, however, the *Kuznetsov*'s maximum speed seems to be less than 20 nautical miles per hour, thus further impeding its capability to launch fixed-wing aircraft into the air while carrying heavy bomb payloads. According to official reports, the *Kuznetsov*'s jets flew 420 combat sorties in Syria, but more than two thirds of them were from the Hmeymim airbase: The jets took on attack payloads and fuel at the land base, instead of flying into action directly from the carrier's deck. The *Kuznetsov* also lost two jet fighters (an Su-33 and a MiG-29K), which sank in the sea because of either technical failure related to the landing gear or pilot errors caused by insufficient training, or both.[30]

The *Pyotr Velikiy*'s voyage to the Mediterranean was uneventful: It traveled with the *Kuznetsov* but did not take part in any action. Plans exist to eventually refit the *Pyotr Velikiy* with 3S14 universal launch tubes, so it may fire Kalibr-HK or other land-attack and anti-ship missiles. The *Pyotr Velikiy* may be docked for renovation in 2019—

repairs and refits that may take several years. At present, the nuclear cruiser is not designed to attack land targets.

The frustrated Russian navy will have to make do without any aircraft carriers for some years to come, and the fleet's land-attack capabilities are limited. Still, the VMF played a decisive role in the logistics of the Syrian campaign by organizing the so called "Syrian express" route to deliver weapons, munitions and other essential supplies to Russian troops and their local allies from Black Sea ports (mostly Novorossiysk) to Syria (Tartus). According to the chief of staff of the Russian naval base in Tartus, Alexei Tarasov, the port handles 100,000 tons of traffic a month "and most of that traffic is to supply the *Gruperovka* in Syria"[31] The overall supply traffic from 2015 to 2017 through the "Syrian express" could be over two million tons. To handle this massive traffic, the VMF mobilized its landing ships, first of all Project 775 Ropucha-class vessels built in Poland in the 1970s and 1980s, which have the capacity to carry a marine battalion, 12 tanks and supplies. The landing ships moved troops and supplies and were supplemented by a number of old general-transport and container-cargo vessels purchased in Turkey, Greece and Ukraine. These ships, though unarmed and operated by civilian crews, were repainted and carried the naval Russian flag as Black Sea Fleet support vessels so that they could not be stopped and searched by the Turks as they passed through the Straits. Il-76 and heavy An-124 military transport jets flying directly to Hmeymim have been supplementing the "Syrian express" maritime route. Military and civilian personnel has been moved to and from Hmeymim by transport planes and defense ministry passenger jets.[32]

Gerasimov has commended the logistics part of the overseas operation in Syria and compared it with the secretive deployment of a massive Russian nuclear-armed military *Gruperovka* in Cuba in 1962, during the Cuban Missile Crisis—"operation Anadyr." Strategic mobility is seen today as a key component of Russian military strategy, since the Russian Armed Forces are much smaller than during the

Cold War. Effective strategic mobility is being tested by the Russian military in multiple massive snap exercises and has been successfully implemented, according to Gerasimov, during the Syrian operation.[33] In March and again in December 2016, Putin publicly announced the military mission in Syria "mostly accomplished," saying that the *Gruperovka* shall be withdrawn home. Some withdrawals did happen, but they were soon secretly reversed while the war continued. This flexibility and mobility is seen in Moscow as an important achievement. In any crisis in the Middle East, the Russian military believes it can swiftly reinforce and possibly play a decisive future role.[34]

The Israeli Connection Revolutionizes Russian War-Making

Putin, Shoigu, the Russian state TV propaganda machine and the expert community have been heaping praise on the VKS for an exemplary air campaign in Syria. The Syrian opposition, jihadists and Islamic State fighters are portrayed as a formidable foe, a well-organized "terrorist army" that was gallantly defeated by the VKS with minimal casualties. Of course, this foe had no radars and only a small number of old Soviet-made shoulder-launched anti-aircraft missiles or short-range man-portable air-defense systems (MANPADS). To avoid risk, VKS attack jets tended to bomb from heights of over 5 km, where the opposition's MANPADS could not reach. As a result, only four jets were reportedly lost in Syria before the end of 2017, of them only one directly in action—an Su-24M bomber shot down in November 2015 by a Turkish F-16, after briefly flying into Turkish airspace. Two jets were lost by the *Kuznetsov* due to some technical mishaps. Russian helicopters, attack and transport, did fly much lower than the bomber jets: They frequently operated in harms' way and at least six were lost in action.[35] On October 10, 2017, an Su-24M bomber ran off the runway at Hmeimim during takeoff, crashed and exploded, killing its crew of two. [36]

The Russian military insists all of its bombing missions were super accurate, hitting only jihadist and opposition fighters designated as terrorists. During the Syrian campaign, the Russian military has employed some precision-attack weapons: hundreds of long-range naval (Kalibr) and air-launched (KH-555 and Kh-101) cruise missiles, guided bombs, as well as Iskander and Tochka-U tactical ballistic missiles. According to Shoigu, the VKS "in two years, flew some 34,000 combat [bombing] sorties" and killed over 60,000 enemy combatants or "terrorists." Yet, most of the bombing missions were carried out using "dumb" OFAB bombs of various caliber. It is claimed the new Su-34 bombers have modern targeting equipment, while older Su-24M and Tu-22M3 swing-wing bombers have been modernized and equipped with the SVP-24 targeting devices that allowed them to use simple OFAB bombs as precision weapons, "never hitting schools or mosques"[37]

Targeting intelligence was collected by satellites and, for the first time in any Russian air campaign, by drones. According to Gerasimov, there are some 50–70 drones in action over Syria one any given day. The targeting intelligence and footage is provided simultaneously to the command staff in Hmeymim and the General Staff in Moscow. According to Gerasimov, the Russian military "made great strides" in drone usage in the last five years. "Today, it is impossible to fight without drones, and everybody uses them—special forces, the pilots and artillery units," concluded Gerasimov.[38]

The Russian defense ministry's narrative about the super-accurate targeting of its mostly "dumb" OFAB bombs is highly exaggerated at best. But it also reflects a genuine effort to enact a new, probably revolutionary by Russian standards, strategy of effective surgical-precision air campaigns, surely mimicking the US aerial warfare practices over the former Iugoslavia and Iraq, replacing the traditional Russian model of massive use of brute firepower exercised in Afghanistan in the 1980s and in the two Chechen wars. Investment in the use of drones to provide live targeting information and the development and mass production of various precision-guided weapon systems is seen as a new and highly important part of Russia's strategic outlook and how the General Staff believes it will fight wars in the future.[39]

Gerasimov is correct: Only five years ago, the Russian military did not have any modern usable unmanned aerial vehicles (UAV), and the acute need to acquire them was not universally recognized. Aerial reconnaissance and attack missions were carried out by manned aircraft, either taking photos or the crew simply observing visually. This situation began to change when, in 2012, the Yekaterinburg (Urals)–based Uralskiy Zavod Grazhdanskoy Aviatsii (UZGA) began producing the Forpost UAV, using Israeli-provided components. The Forpost is a Russian-assembled licensed replica of the Israeli Aerospace Industries' Searcher II reconnaissance UAV. This Russian drone is produced together with Israeli-designed command, control and communications (C3) equipment. The Forpost has been the backbone of successful Russian military UAV operations in Syria and Donbas. According to defense ministry sources the Israeli-designed Forpost is still the most potent operational Russian UAV, with the biggest payload (up to 70 kilograms) and the longest flight endurance (some 18 hours). The Russian-designed Orlan-10 UAV, also used by Russian forces in Syria, can carry only a 5 kg payload.[40]

The Russian military has built up special drone units and successfully integrated the Forpost and other drones to provide targeting information to artillery, multiple rocket-launch systems (MRLS) and attack aircraft. Footage provided by UAVs in Syria has been regularly displayed by the Russian military for PR purposes. But while images and videos of jets, helicopters and other attack systems are frequently distributed by official government sources, the UAVs operating in Syria are never pictured. In particular, the Forpost is not even mentioned at all. It would appear that the Russian authorities are embarrassed and hesitant to display Israeli-designed Russian UAVs deployed on Arab soil and used against Muslim (jihadist) rebels.

In Syria and in Donbas, Russian UAVs have been used exclusively on reconnaissance missions, which has revolutionized Russian war-making. Russia inherited heavy-load land- and air-based attack systems from the Soviet Union that it has been modernizing; but until recently, the Russian Armed Forces lacked effective reconnaissance and targeting capabilities. So by integrating Israeli-designed UAV assets with preexisting attack systems, including precision-guided ones, the Russian military leapfrogged into the future, acquiring abilities it did not have even as recently as during the two Chechen wars and the August 2008 short war with Georgia. Still, Russia does not possess attack UAVs and cannot perform the types of stealthy surgical assaults from unmanned aerial platforms that have become a trademark of US military operations. Numerous reports have alleged that various Russian companies are developing "heavy" attack UAVs; but as of the end of 2017, nothing usable or deployable has been revealed. This is seen as a serious deficiency, especially in running low-intensity anti-guerrilla or anti-terrorist operations.

When Russia imported Israeli UAV technology some five years ago, it did not manage to buy any drones more advanced or bigger than the Searcher II. On the condition of anonymity, some Russian officials say Washington forbid the Israelis from selling bigger or more modern attack-capable UAVs. In an apparent sign of desperation, the Russian defense ministry allocated budgetary funds to modernize the Forpost, providing it with attack capabilities. It has been announced that, in 2019, the Yekaterinburg-based military contractor UZGA will begin producing a modernized Forpost-M, "using Russian-made components and with attack capabilities."[41] Russian defense industry sources boast the Forpost-M will be "the best UAV in Russia and possibly in the world."[42] Of course, a modernized Searcher II is too light and small to be an effective attack UAV on par with the US MQ-1 Predator, MQ-9 Reaper, Israeli Elbit Hermes 450 or IAI Heron. But at present, it seems to be the only reliable and usable UAV Russia might be able to convert to perform attack missions.

The Russian Deployment Stays Focused on the Coast

In addition to bombers, attack jets and helicopters, the VKS deployed in Hmeymim Su-35S, Su-30SM and Su-27SM3 fighter jets to fend off possible NATO or US-led aerial attacks on Russian troops, aircraft or bases. The fighters escorted Russian bombers as they flew attack sorties close to the zones of deployment of US and coalition air forces. Moreover, the Russian aerial platforms were reinforced with an elaborate anti-aircraft system, including S-400, S-300B4 and short-range Pantsir-S1 systems. The Russian fighters in Syria apparently did not fire a single shot in anger at least until 2018. Nor did the anti-aircraft missile batteries, with the exception of the Pantsir-S1 that, according to Shoigu, was used to intercept opposition drones and rockets (apparently 122-millimeter Grad-type munitions) fired at Russian troops and bases.[43]

By 2018, Russian command reorganized the VKS anti-aircraft defenses in Syria. A mobile anti-aircraft missile battery ("division" in Russian military terminology) of S-300B4s—apparently the foundation of anti-aircraft defenses of the Tartus naval base—was withdrawn back to Russia. The battery had been deployed in Syria since October 2016 but did not fire a shot. Nonetheless, its long-range targeting radars locked on "US tactical jets and recon aircraft at distances of 200–300 kilometers," according to Lieutenant General Aleksandr Leonov, the commander of the Army Anti-Aircraft Forces (*Voyskavaya PVO Booruzhonykh Syl RF*). "The US tactical pilots were rattled by the radar lock on," added Leonov.[44]

The S-300B4 has been replaced by a second battery or "division" of S-400s, which has been reportedly deployed close to the city of Masyaf—once the stronghold-capital of the historical Assassins (*Hashashin*) in the Levant—on the border of Hama and Latakia provinces. One S-400 battery is deployed together with several Pantsir-S1 launchers directly in the vicinity of Hmeymim to defend the base. But the eastward radar outlook from Hmeymim is hampered by the Syrian Coastal Mountain

Range. A second S-400 battery (together with Pantsir-S1) has apparently been based on top of the Coastal Mountain Range close to Masyaf, overlooking Hmeymim and Tartus, providing both bases with an air-defense umbrella and good radar coverage in all directions.[45]

During the fall of 2017, the main campaign effort shifted to the northeast corner of Syria, close to the Iraqi border. There, Russian bombers, special forces and privateers or mercenaries from the notorious private military company (*Chastnye Voennie Companiy*— ChVK) "Wagner" were helping pro-al-Assad forces to take over the oil and natural gas–rich province of Deir el-Zour. Russian sappers were rushed into Syria using heavy-load An-124 transport jets. Equipped with the newest PP-2005 pontoon bridge complex equipment, the sappers built a 210-meter floating bridge over the Euphrates River at Deir el-Zour for the pro-al-Assad forces to cross.[46] On September 23, 2017, a number of top Russian commanders were killed and wounded in Deir el-Zour, including the commander of the 5th Army in the Eastern Military District, Lieutenant General Valery Asapov, as well as the commander of the 61st Marines Brigade of the Northern Fleet, Colonel Velery Fedyanin. Other Russian casualties included fighters from the Private Military Company (ChVK) Wagner Group.[47]

The Deir el-Zour operation was seen as the climax of the Syrian campaign to vanquish the Islamic State and reinstall President al-Assad's rule. By December 2017, the joint efforts of Russian, pro-al-Assad and pro-Iranian forces, along with the Syrian Democratic Forces (SDF—a militia alliance composed of Arab and Kurdish fighters, backed by the US coalition and US Special Forces) effectively crushed the Islamic State as an organized semi-state. On December 11, 2017, Putin landed on the tarmac of Hmeymim for a surprise visit. At the airbase, Putin met with his Syrian counterpart, whose regime had been salvaged by the Russian and Iranian war effort. Putin announced victory over the Islamic State—"the vanguard of terror"—

thanked Russian pilots and soldiers, and announced the withdrawal of "a large part" of the Russian forces. The bases in Hmeymim and Tartus and their garrisons were to stay, of course.[48]

When the fighting in Deir el-Zour was at its height, the Hmeymim base turned out to be somewhat too far from the action: Su-25 attack jets were simply out of range, and Su-24M bombers were operating at the limit of their effective combat radius. The VKS does not have any air-refueling capabilities over Syria. To step up the bombing, a force of heavy Tu-22M3s from different bomber units across Russia was gathered at the Mozdok airbase, in the steppes of the North Caucasus, to fly missions from there to Deir el-Zour province—a return sortie of some 5,000 km.[49] Significantly, the Russian military did not try to establish another airbase somewhere in central Syria in addition to Hmeymim to better cover all the battlefields. Before the war broke out, Hmeymim was a civilian airfield; the Russian VKS had transformed it into a military facility. Russia's helicopter fleet has established some refueling and operational stations outside of Hmeymim, but the VKS jets stubbornly stayed, even though al-Assad would surely have given the Russians any additional base they might have asked for.

For now, Moscow appears to be focusing on the core mission of securing the Tartus and Hmeymim bases and does not seem particularly interested in spreading its thin, limited resources all over Syria. The Russian force in Syria has dug in where it always wanted to be: a strategic naval and airbase area on the coast, with a long-range, multilayer anti-air and anti-ship defensive perimeter. From there, the Russian military is capable of projecting naval and aerial forces deep into the Mediterranean and focusing on the always all-important Turkish Straits.

The Intricate Network of Russian Middle Eastern Alliances

By the end of 2017, the Islamic State had been almost entirely defeated in both Iraq and Syria. The course of the Syrian civil war had reversed, and the al-Assad regime now seems more secure than at any point since the war started, back in 2011. The revived government in Damascus signed agreements with Moscow, securing for Russia permanent sea and airbases in Tartus and Hmeymim, on the Mediterranean coast. Russian Army ("tank") generals have extended and fortified their dominance in the main center of gravity of military (strategic) power in Moscow—the General Staff—at the expense of the VMF and the VKS commanders. Putin, his generals and the state propaganda machine are trumpeting a victory in Syria; and Russia has surely dramatically extended its presence and influence in the Middle East—in some aspects probably outdoing the mighty Soviet Union's outreach in the region at the height of the Cold War, in the 1970s and 1980s.

Moscow cannot match Washington's military, financial or technological capabilities in the Middle East or the Mediterranean, but it seem to be in a unique position to have workable relations with almost all the different warring parties in the region: Iran, Israel, Turkey, Iraq (Baghdad government), Damascus (al-Assad), Egypt, Saudi Arabia, Jordan, the Kurds, different Lebanese and Libyan fractions, Algeria, Qatar, and other Gulf states. Moscow looks to be trying to position itself as an indispensable force and middleman everywhere across the Middle East. Putin's grand all-inclusive anti-terrorist coalition proposal made in 2015, thus, looks to be materializing at least on a regional level. The ultimate strategic goal of this initiative is to weaken Washington's key Middle Eastern alliances, diminishing overall US influence and presence in the region.

Moscow has managed to build up a significant military/security/political relationship with Israel—something Moscow previously enjoyed only in the 1940s, during the Israeli War of Independence, and never since. Putin regularly meets and talks with Israeli Prime Minister Benjamin Netanyahu. And Russian top military/intelligence chiefs meet, talk and coordinate activities in Syria with their Israeli counterparts. In December 2017, Avi Dichter, the chairman of the Knesset Foreign Affairs and Defense Committee, from the ruling Likud party, visited Moscow leading a parliamentary delegation. Dichter—a Sayeret Matkal soldier under commander Ehud Barak, career Shin Bet (internal security service) officer and later Shin Bet director, as well as former minister of internal security and home front defense—told *Interfax*, "Russia is not an enemy, and we [Israel] have no problem with permanent Russian military presence in Syria." Dichter described Russia as a "superpower and ally" that wants a strategic presence in the Mediterranean, "and we say: 'Welcome!'" According to Dichter, there are some 10,000 Hezbollah fighters in Syria and some 20,000 other, mostly Iraqi, pro-Iranian Shia militia combatants. Israel will not allow these forces to establish positions anywhere close to the Golan Heights and has been regularly bombing Iranian and Hezbollah positions in Syria "to send a message" as well as to prevent offensive arms transfers to Hezbollah, he noted. Israel has no problem with continued al-Assad rule in Syria as long as the Iranian influence is kept in check; the government hopes Moscow will help ensure that happens.[50]

Russia and Israel have been closely cooperating. Moscow tacitly accepts intermittent aerial strikes by the Israel Defense Forces (IDF) inside Syria, though they have been hitting Russia's battlefield allies. Based on unconfirmed reports coming from Iran, the Russian military allegedly may have provided the IDF with aircraft transponder "friend or foe" (IFF) identification codes that would automatically prevent the intentional or accidental launches of SAA or VKS anti-aircraft missiles from land, air or sea against IDF jets.[51] Such an arrangement would allow the IDF to carry out attack sorties over Syria with impunity, as a *de facto* Russian ally; but the IFF codes change often, and the IDF would lose this privilege (if it indeed obtained it) as soon as the Russian military command decides Israel should no longer be counted as an ally. By the end of 2017, both Israel and Russia were doing their best to keep the tacit alliance alive. It was reported that Moscow had protested the IDF allegedly helping Syrian rebels. The Israeli military explained that it was only providing humanitarian aid to villages in a zone close to the Golan Heights.[52] Apparently, both sides are doing their best to keep their cooperation agreement on an even keel.

Moscow seems not to mind too much when the IDF selectively attacks Hezbollah and Iran in Syria. In contrast, when Washington condemned the clampdown by the Iranian authorities and the IRGC on street protests inside Iran, Moscow decisively sided with Tehran. The Russian representative at the UN, Vasily Nabehzya, accused the US of infringing on Iranian internal affairs and of seeking an excuse to undermine the 2015 Iran nuclear deal.[53]

Fighting Sunni jihadists in the Middle East and propping up the al-Assad regime together with Iran and Hezbollah is seen in Moscow an important task, but clearly secondary in the overall zero-sum standoff with the US. The Russian military command accuses the US military of being in league with the Islamic State and former al-Nusra jihadists in Syria. It is unclear how much of that is propaganda and what Russia's top brass truly accepts (in a zero-sum mindset) as covert interactions that any reasonable military leader would presumably do. In any case, this level of institutionalized mutual mistrust greatly prohibits any meaningful US-Russian anti-terrorist cooperation.

After dark, on December 31, 2017, when the Russians at Hmeymim and apparently the local Alawite-dominated Syrian security forces were busy celebrating the New Year, the base was shelled by mortar fire. The Russian defense ministry acknowledged two fatalities of service members and an unspecified number of wounded. Several aircraft were reportedly hit, though the authorities refused to confirm this. The severity of the damage to the base and aircraft is unclear as is whether there are plans to restore or eventually scrap any or all of the hit aircraft. Unconfirmed reports say the two servicemen killed in the attack were helicopter pilots. Apparently, a small group of repels (sources in the Russian Defense Ministry say they were from the former al-Nusra Front) infiltrated the outer perimeter of Hmeymim, sprayed the tarmac with mortar shells from several kilometers away and escaped undetected. The outer perimeter defenses were reportedly the responsibility of the Syrian (Alawite) forces that are now accused of failing their mission. Hmeymim—a former civilian airstrip—did not have reinforced concrete hangers for the aircraft, known in Russia as "*caponiers*," or bunkers for the personnel. While occupying Hmeymim since 2015, the Russian military did not bother to build permanent fortifications, and the VKS's highly expensive aircraft, armed and fueled, stood out in the open.[54]

The Russian military is now responding by reinforcing the Hmeymim airbase's defenses. *Caponiers* and bunkers will most likely be built. The Russian military will dig in and mine the entire perimeter with anti-personnel mines.[55] The spectacular New Year's attack on Hmeymim, however, raises more serious concerns for Moscow. Its strategic airbase—where Russia has deployed a bomber and fighter force, long-range anti-aircraft assets, as well as theater Iskander and Bastion missiles that potentially may be nuclear tipped—was apparently vulnerable to a sudden artillery strike and might even be targeted by a suicide bomb attack in the future. Of course, Russian propaganda swiftly accused the US and its Special Forces of being behind the attack on Hmeymim. And angry threats materialized about organizing attacks on US bases in the Middle East in a similar fashion.[56]

Conclusion

Russia returned to Syria and the Middle East primarily to secure an operational base to deter NATO and the United States in the Mediterranean. But will its Middle Eastern bases ever truly be secure? Can those bases be an effective strategic asset? And what will be the cost of keeping them, surrounded by a hostile, unstable and unruly security environment in Syria? If Hmeymim could be hit by motivated rebels, so might Tatrus—particularly since both bases were already targeted by a swarm aerial drone attack in January 2018.

Moscow has a clear strategy in the Middle East, and so far it appears to be working fairly well. Deadly glitches occur regularly, but they seem to be manageable and are seen as mostly the result of sloppiness by the "unreliable" locals the Russian military has always disdained. The most important fundamental detractor to Russian efforts to return to the Middle East, looks to be a lack of overall resources to match Moscow's overly ambitious objectives. In contrast, Washington possesses abundant resources, military and otherwise, but no obvious coherent strategy in the region: US strategy was reactive under President Barack Obama and apparently has not improved much since. It is a fascinating contest.

Notes

1 "Sammit ODKB," *Kremlin.ru*, September 15, 2015, http://www.kremlin.ru/events/president/news/50291.

2 "S tribuny k miru," *Interfax*, September 29, 2015, http://www.interfax-russia.ru/print.asp?id=656523&type=view.

3 "SSHA otkazalis' prinyat' delegatsiyu vo glave s Medvedevym dlya obsuzhdeniya Sirii," *Interfax*, October 14, 2015, http://www.interfax.ru/world/473318.

4 "Nachal'nik Genshtaba Vooruzhennykh sil Rossii general armii Valeriy Gerasimov: 'My perelomili khrebet udarnym silam terrorizma,' " *Komsomolskaya Pravda*, December 27, 2017, https://www.kazan.kp.ru/daily/26775/3808693/.

5 "Vystupleniye i diskussiya na Myunkhenskoy konferentsii po voprosam politiki bezopasnosti," *Kremlin.ru*, February 10, 2007, http://www.kremlin.ru/events/president/transcripts/24034.

6 "Operativnoye soyedineniye VMF zashchitit interesy RF v Sredizemnom more RIA Novosti," *RIA Novosti*, February 27, 2013, https://ria.ru/defense_safety/20130227/924884303.html.

7 *RIA Novosti*, "Operativnoye soyedineniye VMF zashchitit interesy RF v Sredizemnom more RIA Novosti."

[8] "Prezidentu predstavlen Plan oborony Rossiyskoy Federatsii," *Kremlin.ru*, January 29, 2013, http://www.kremlin.ru/events/president/news/17385.

[9] "Uroven' voyennykh ugroz dlya RF k 2030 godu mozhet sushchestvenno povysit'sya," *RIA Novosti*, February 14, 2013, https://ria.ru/defense_safety/20130214/922846600.html.

[10] "VS RF na ucheniyakh 'Kavkaz-2016' otrabotali bor'bu s krylatymi raketami," *Interfax*, September 14, 2016, http://www.interfax.ru/russia/528124.

[11] "General-polkovnik Andrey Kartapolov: U Rossii mozhet poyavit'sya baza v Sirii. Ona budet i morskoy, i vozdushnoy, i sukhoputnoy," *Komsomolskaya Pravda*, October 16, 2015, https://www.kp.ru/daily/26446/3316981/#close.

[12] "Mesto raspolozheniya voyennoy bazy RF v Sirii poka ne opredeleno," *Interfax*, October 16, 2015, http://www.interfax-russia.ru/print.asp?id=663181&type=view.

[13] "Soglasheniye s Siriyey o rasshirenii voyenno-morskoy bazy v Tartuse usilit pozitsii Rossii v Sredizemnom more - Minoborony RF," *Interfax-AVN*, December 21, 2017, http://www.militarynews.ru/story.asp?rid=1&nid=469716.

[14] "U Rossii yest' dolgosrochnaya strategiya voyennogo prisutstviya v Sredizemnom more-Sablin," *Interfax-AVN*, December 21, 2017, http://www.militarynews.ru/story.asp?rid=1&nid=469750.

[15] "Ministr oborony vystupil na zasedanii Soveta Federatsii v ramkakh 'pravitel'stvennogo chasa," *Interfax-AVN*, May 24, 2017, https://function.mil.ru/news_page/country/more.htm?id=12125102@egNews&.

[16] Pavel Felgenhauer, "Despite Putin's Declaration of Victory, Fighting Escalates in Syria," *Eurasia Daily Monitor*, Volume 15, Issue 4, The Jamestown Foundation, January 11, 2018, https://jamestown.org/program/despite-putins-declaration-victory-fighting-escalates-syria/.

[17] *Komsomolskaya Pravda*, "Nachal'nik Genshtaba Vooruzhennykh sil Rossii general armii Valeriy Gerasimov: 'My perelomili khrebet udarnym silam terrorizma.' "

[18] *Ibid.*

[19] "Glavkomom VKS RF naznachen general Surovikin," *Interfax-AVN*, November 29, 2017, http://www.militarynews.ru/story.asp?rid=1&nid=467806.

[20] *Interfax*, October 31, 2008.

[21] "Ofitser pokonchil zhizn' samoubiystvom," *Kommersant*, April 23, 2004, https://www.kommersant.ru/doc/469455.

[22] "Voyennuyu prokuraturu ne ustroil politseyskiy kandidat," *Kommersant*, December 14, 2011, https://www.kommersant.ru/doc/1837567.

[23] "Na vooruzhenii Sevflota nakhodyatsya samyye sovremennyye podvodnyye lodki, korabli i samolety – komanduyushchiy," *Interfax-AVN*, December 15, 2017, http://www.militarynews.ru/story.asp?rid=1&nid=469233.

[24] "Demonstratsiya vozmozhnostey: chem i iz chego Rossiya udarila po IGIL s Kaspiyskogo morya," *Vesti*, October 7, 2015, http://www.vesti.ru/doc.html?id=2672786&cid=3962.

[25] " 'Kalibr' na chas," *Voenno-Promyshlennyi Kurier*, December 26, 2017, https://vpk-news.ru/articles/40592.

[26] "Zachem kaspiytsy obnazhili 'Tomagavki,' " *Fontanka*, October 7, 2015, https://www.fontanka.ru/2015/10/07/159/.

[27] "SSHA nadeyutsya ostavit' 'Kuznetsova' bez topliva," *Vzglyad*, October 26, 2016, https://vz.ru/politics/2016/10/26/674906.html.

[28] "Byudzhet remonta i modernizatsii avianostsa, 'Admiral Kuznetsov' mozhet byt' sokrashchen pochti vdvoye," *Interfax-AVN*, October 7, 2017, http://www.militarynews.ru/story.asp?rid=1&nid=463650.

[29] "Tochnyye sroki nachala remonta 'Admirala Kuznetsova' poka ne opredeleny," *Interfax-AVN*, December 14, 2017, http://www.militarynews.ru/story.asp?rid=0&nid=469168.

[30] *Interfax-AVN*, "Na vooruzhenii Sevflota nakhodyatsya samyye sovremennyye podvodnyye lodki, korabli i samolety – komanduyushchiy."

[31] "Punkt material'no-tekhnicheskogo obespecheniya VMF Rossii v Tartuse. Dos'ye," *TASS*, December 13, 2017, http://tass.ru/info/4808523.

[32] " 'Siriyskiy ekspress' zabuksoval," *Free Press*, September 20, 2017, http://svpressa.ru/war21/article/181633/.

[33] *Komsomolskaya Pravda*, "Nachal'nik Genshtaba Vooruzhennykh sil Rossii general armii Valeriy Gerasimov: 'My perelomili khrebet udarnym silam terrorizma.' "

[34] "Pokoreniye voyny," *Izvestia*, December 27, 2017, https://iz.ru/688413/konstantin-bogdanov/pokorenie-voiny.

[35] "Ni razu ne promazali," *Voenno-Promyshlennyi Kurier*, December 20, 2017, https://vpk-news.ru/articles/40474.

[36] "Bombardirovshchik okazalsya ne v tom polozhenii," *Kommersant*, October 11, 2017, https://www.kommersant.ru/doc/3435128.

[37] *Voenno-Promyshlennyi Kurier*, "Ni razu ne promazali"; "Rasshirennoye zasedaniye kollegii Ministerstva oborony," *The Kremlin*, December 22, 2017, http://www.kremlin.ru/events/president/news/56472.

[38] *Komsomolskaya Pravda*, "Nachal'nik Genshtaba Vooruzhennykh sil Rossii general armii Valeriy Gerasimov: 'My perelomili khrebet udarnym silam terrorizma.' "

[39] "Tochnaya Stavka," *Voenno-Promyshlennyi Kurier*, December 26, 2017, https://vpk-news.ru/articles/40587.

[40] "Samyy tsennyy bespilotnik Rossiyskoy armii rusifitsiruyut za 2 mlrd rubley," *Vedomosti*, June 7, 2016, https://www.vedomosti.ru/politics/articles/2016/06/07/643859-mlrd-rublei-beskonechnii-forpost.

[41] "Razvedyvatel'nyye drony 'Forpost' prevratyat v udarnyye bespilotniki," *Rossyskaya Gazeta*, May 5, 2017, https://rg.ru/2017/05/05/razvedyvatelnye-drony-forpost-prevratiat-v-udarnye-bespilotniki.html.

[42] "Izrail'skiy BPLA 'Forpost' moderniziruyut v Rossii," *Defense.ru*, March 17, 2017, https://defence.ru/article/izrailskii-bpla-forpost-moderniziruyut-v-rossii/.

[43] *Kremlin.ru*, "Rasshirennoye zasedaniye kollegii Ministerstva oborony."

[44] "Divizion sistemy PVO S-300V4 vozvrashchen iz Sirii v punkt postoyannoy dislokatsii – Minoborony," *Interfax-AVN*, December 28, 2017, http://www.militarynews.ru/story.asp?rid=1&nid=470316.

[45] *Voenno-Promyshlennyi Kurier*, "Ni razu ne promazali."

[46] "Rossiyskiye voyennyye privezli mashiny dlya forsirovaniya Yevfrata siriyskoy armiyey-SMI," *Interfax-AVN*, September 24, 2017, http://www.militarynews.ru/story.asp?rid=1&nid=462598; "Most cherez Yevfrat dlya perebroski voyennoy tekhniki i lichnogo sostava na vostochnyy bereg vozveli v Sirii rossiyskiye avtodorozhniki," *Interfax-AVN*, September 26, 2017, http://www.militarynews.ru/story.asp?rid=1&nid=462689.

[47] "Ikh prosto net. Rassledovaniye," *Novaya Gazeta*, October 9, 2017, https://www.novayagazeta.ru/articles/2017/10/09/74125-ih-prosto-net.

[48] "Putin prikazal nachat' vyvod voysk iz Sirii," *Interfax-AVN*, December 11, 2017, http://www.militarynews.ru/story.asp?rid=0&nid=468860.

[49] "V Murmanskuyu oblast' vernulis' samolety Tu-22M3, uchastvovavshiye v nanesenii aviaudarov po terroristam v Sirii," *Interfax-AVN*, December 12, 2017, http://www.militarynews.ru/story.asp?rid=1&nid=468988.

[50] "Avi Dikhter: yesli kto-to iz terroristov poschitayet Siriyu spasitel'noy gavan'yu, my prevratim yego zhizn' v ad," *Interfax*, December 5, 2017, http://www.interfax.ru/interview/590501.

[51] "Report: Iran accuses Russia of giving Israel codes for Syrian air defenses," *Jerusalem Post*, March 21, 2017, http://www.jpost.com/Arab-Israeli-Conflict/Report-Iran-accuses-Russia-of-giving-Israel-codes-for-Syrian-air-defenses-484777.

[52] "Rossiya zayavila protest v svyazi s okazaniyem Izrailem pomoshchi siriyskim povstantsam," December 14, 2017, http://www.newsru.co.il/mideast/14dec2017/ru_il_103.html.

[53] "Postpred Rossii pri OON prizval SSHA ne vmeshivat'sya vo vnutrenniye dela Irana," *Interfax*, January 6, 2018, http://www.interfax.ru/world/594491.

[54] "Khmeymim pod udarom: pochemu rossiyskaya aviabaza v Sirii popala pod obstrel," *RBK*, January 4, 2018, https://www.rbc.ru/politics/04/01/2018/5a4def379a7947a9e3f00a5b.

[55] "Ekspert rasskazala, kak zashchitit' samolety na aviabaze Khmeymim," *RIA Novosti*, January 5, 2018, https://ria.ru/syria/20180105/1512157084.html.

[56] "Obstrel Khmeymima vyyavil probely vo 'vtorom kol'tse' oborony," *Vzglyad*, January 5, 2018, https://vz.ru/politics/2018/1/5/902400.html.

2. Strategy in the Black Sea and Mediterranean

Ihor Kabanenko

Introduction

The current Maritime Doctrine of the Russian Federation Until 2030 defines six important regional directions for the country's maritime policy: Atlantic, Pacific, Indian Ocean, Arctic, Antarctic and Caspian. And of those, the Atlantic direction—which includes the Baltic, Black Sea and Sea of Azov, the Mediterranean Sea, as well as the Atlantic Ocean—is ranked first. The Black Sea region (BSR)—composed of the Black Sea and the Sea of Azov, and which is closely connected with the Eastern Mediterranean—is a particularly notable geopolitical space for Moscow. This region plays an important role in Russia's military policy and features its own specifics determined by historical, geopolitical and other aspects that significantly affect Russia's broader southwestern military strategy.

One year prior to Moscow's illegal annexation of Crimea, Russian Defense Minister Sergei Shoigu stressed that,

> The Black Sea Fleet of Russia (BSF) is protecting Russia's interests in the southwestern direction, where the most essential threats to our national interests are concentrated. The fleet is able to carry

out tasks in any areas of the World Ocean important for our national interests, including, currently, the Mediterranean Sea.[1]

Additionally, Shoigu has called Ukraine, Syria and the Korean peninsula strategically important [regions] for Russia.[2] And Ukraine, whose sovereignty has repeatedly been violated as a result of these "important interests," is not the only country under threat as a result.

This chapter will analyze Russia's BSR strategy across the full spectrum of historical, geopolitical, doctrinal and other domains as related to the Russian military. Of particular focus will be Russia's regional naval and maritime doctrines, the roles electromagnetic warfare and nuclear weapons play in its strategy, Moscow's posture in the Black Sea, as well as the lessons its Armed Forces have learned from their ongoing operations in Syria and eastern Ukraine.

Historical and Geopolitical Context

For millennia, the Black Sea region, with its complex ethnic diversity, difficult geography and variable climactic conditions, played the role of a natural barrier between various civilizations that would otherwise have clashed. This began to dramatically change with the rise (1299–1453) and expansion (1453–1566) of the Ottoman Empire, which eventually became the dominant naval power in the Black Sea, in control of much of the wider region's transport routes, including the sea lanes.

The expansion of Islamic frontiers to the north of the Black Sea bumped into growing resistance from the Russian Empire.[3] Beginning in the 17th century, the rivalry between the Russian and Ottoman empires transformed into a hard confrontation, with Russia's goal becoming the destruction of its rival. The littoral Black Sea territories of Crimea, Bessarabia, the Caucasus and the adjacent Balkans thus became centers of gravity in Russia's imperial efforts to secure unimpeded passage for its ships and vessels passing through the

Bosporus and Dardanelles straits. Since that time, Russia's southwestern geopolitical ambitions became intimately tied to the geostrategic goal of dominating the Black Sea.

Throughout this period, slogans of "Slavic (Orthodox) unity" served as a useful tool or justification for securing control over the wider region's strategic territories. Similarly, political-diplomatic rhetoric about "protecting Orthodox populations outside Russia from oppression under the Ottoman Empire" as well as "supporting Orthodox Slavic national liberation movements" served as useful pretexts for the Russian Empire to annex additional territories around the Black Sea. Though once under control, the Kremlin's cruel treatment of populations living on the annexed lands led to mass forced migrations of various indigenous peoples, as the historical record shows. Indeed, it is worth pointing out that Moscow's modern interpretation of this centuries-old approach, today characterized as "protecting Russian-speaking population outside Russia," served as an ideological basis for the Russian invasions of Georgia (2008) and Ukraine (2014).

The conviction of Russian and Ottoman leaders in the historical correctness of their ambitions for Black Sea dominance turned the region into a theater of nearly continuous bloody wars, with varying levels of success for the two warring sides. In the Russo-Turkish War (1768–1774), Russia won a number of Crimean territories and, in line with its rights negotiated under the Treaty of Küçük Kaynarca, took the opportunity to conduct sea trade and create new naval forces on the peninsula. Indeed, since its creation in 1783, the Russian Black Sea Fleet has been an important hard power instrument of Russian policy in the region. Its offensive nature, strongly shaped by autocratic Russia's 18th-century desire to "restore Orthodox Byzantium," was further developed in the years of World War I, World War II and the Cold War; and these capabilities were explicitly demonstrated during the annexation of Crimea in 2014.[4]

Also in 1783, the Russian Empire forcefully annexed the Crimean Khanate and, later, Ukrainian lands between the Southern Bug and the Dniester rivers. Then, in 1791, the Sea of Azov became an internal Russian waterway. Subsequently, the Russian Empire concentrated its efforts on strengthening its position along the northwestern part of the Black Sea. Whereas, during succeeding wars with the Porte, Tsarist Russia moved into Bessarabia, the Caucasus and the Balkans.

Russia's defeat in the Crimean (Eastern) War of 1853–1856 suspended and limited Moscow's expansion in the region for 15 years. Under the terms of the Paris Peace Treaty of 1856, Russia lost its fleet on the Black Sea. Moreover, Russia was forced to give up the rights it had been accorded as a result of the earlier Treaty of Küçük Kaynarca (1774) it signed with the Ottomans: its protectorate over Moldavia and Wallachia as well as the exclusive right to protect the Christian of the Ottoman Empire. However, after the Russo-Turkish War of 1877–1878, Russian soldiers returned to the southern part of Bessarabia, the Karsk region inhabited by Armenians and Georgians, as well as the strategically important eastern Black Sea port of Batumi. And a series of victories over the Turkish army in January 1878 allowed Russian troops to reach Istanbul's outskirts. Only English ships deployment to the Sea of Marmara as well as political-diplomatic efforts by Great Britain and Austria-Hungary forced the Russian tsar's government to abandon further offensive actions.[5]

The Black Sea region played a key role in Russia's southwestern policy for centuries. But for most of this long historical era, Russian Black Sea maritime strategy was oriented along the vertical, "North-South" axis. The collapse of the Ottoman Empire after WWI and subsequent friendly relations between the newly born Republic of Turkey and Bolshevik Russia turned the latter's regional maritime policy 90 degrees, to proceed along the horizontal "East-West" axis. Following the end of WWII, the Soviet Union's Black Sea horizontal vector became dominated by hard power. The Kremlin took control over most of the Black Sea the Balkan countries, and advanced to North

Africa and the Middle East. When Turkey joined the North Atlantic Treaty Organization (NATO) in 1952, this was seen in Moscow as vindication of the Soviet naval strategy, which from the 1970s was built according to the formula "keep Turkey below the 43rd parallel and the US beyond the 23rd meridian."

After the end of the Soviet period, Russia lost much of its influence in the Black Sea territories occupied or annexed during the bloody wars of the 18th–20th centuries because Moscow's former Soviet republics and satellites, including Ukraine, became independent states. Russian naval bases, in particular Sevastopol, survived in Crimea, but their status was not clear. In 1997, the Partition Treaty on the Status and Conditions of the Black Sea Fleet gave Russian naval forces the opportunity to stay in Crimea up to 2017. In 2010, this agreement was prolonged to 2042 by the so-called Kharkiv Pact, signed by then-president Viktor Yanukovych.

Russia's Naval Strategy at the Turn of the 20th Century

Historically, Russian (both imperial- and Soviet-era) maritime policy was militarily and politically motivated, rather than geared toward maximizing the benefits of maritime commercial activity. Modern Russia is no exception—the aging and withdrawal of the main Russian naval assets in the 1990s triggered new thinking on the development of strategic views and doctrinal provisions of Russian maritime policy, with no major effort put into addressing the dismal state of the country's merchant fleet. The Russian naval leadership's vision as to the place and role of Russia in the world/s oceans, built mainly on the basis of theory and practice of the strategic use of the Soviet Navy, has become the determining factor in the further development of Russia's maritime strategy.

The Russian naval lobby initiated the development of Russian naval policy in 2000—in particular, "The Fundamentals of the Russian Federation's Policy in the Sphere of Naval Activities for the Period

Until 2010."[6] One year later, the "The Maritime Doctrine of the Russian Federation for the period until 2020"[7] was signed by the president of Russia and the Maritime Board under the government of the Russian Federation, headed by the prime minister, was formed. His deputy became the commander-in-chief of the Russian navy (*Voyenno-Morskoy Flot*—VMF).[8] The influence of Russian admirals resulted in the adoption of "The Fundamentals of the Russian Federation State Policy in the Field of Naval Activities" in 2012,[9] this document's significant revision in 2017,[10] as well as an updated version of the Maritime Doctrine of Russia in 2015.[11]

Like during the Soviet era, the Kremlin today links Russia's naval activities in the Atlantic direction to opposing NATO and the United States. Notably, "The Maritime Doctrine of the Russian Federation for the period until 2020" states,

> Growing economic, political and military pressure from NATO, its enlargement to the East was clarified as a determining factor of Russia's national policy in the Atlantic direction.[7]

And Russian wording in 2015 became even more stringent: "The Maritime Doctrine of the Russian Federation" declares that Moscow must prevent the advancement of

> the [North Atlantic] Alliance's military infrastructure toward [Russia's] borders and attempts to confer global functions [to NATO].[12]

While in 2017, one of the main threats to Russian national security was clarified as,

> A number of states' desire to dominate in the World Ocean, primarily the United States of America and its allies.[13]

Key provisions of "Russia's Naval Policy Until 2030"[14] should also be recognized:

> The Russian Navy's operational and combat capabilities must be maintained at one of the leading positions in the world, and second place in terms of combat capabilities;

> The Russian Navy must pursue balanced development in order to prevent the exclusive superiority of the US Navy and other leading naval powers over it;

> Strategic (nuclear and non-nuclear) deterrence, including the prevention of a "global strike" by the United States [is vital];

> The Russian Navy is one of the main instruments of the Russian Federation's foreign policy;

> The Black Sea Fleet's operational and combat capabilities [are to be increased] by developing an interspecific grouping of forces (troops) on the territory of the Crimean peninsula;

> The Russian Federation must keep a permanent naval presence in the Mediterranean and other strategically important areas of the world's oceans, including areas of major maritime transport communications;

> Priority must be given to the development of long-range naval high-precision cruise missiles with a qualitatively new task of destroying the enemy's military and economic potential by hitting its vital facilities from the sea;

> Common, interconnected and unified next-generation systems of naval armaments, ships, submarines, naval aviation and coastal complexes must be created.

The adoption of these basic strategic maritime policy documents required a clear long-term concept for the rearmament and development of the Russian navy. Admiral Vladimir Vysotsky, the commander-in-chief of theVMF (2007–2012) proposed this concept in April 2008.[15] The triad of strategic nuclear submarines, heavy combat systems (based on aircraft carrier, cruiser and amphibious forces) and mobile multipurpose offshore platforms (non-nuclear submarines, corvettes, frigates and destroyers) equipped with long-range high-precision cruise missiles and air-defense systems permeates the above-mentioned concept. But in the reality, budgetary and other restrictions during 2012–2017 significantly hampered Russia's naval ambitions.[16] Nonetheless, in December 2017, a new state armament program (covering 2018–2027) was announced. It placed a special emphasis on equipping troops (forces) with high-precision air-, land- and sea-based weapons, unmanned strike complexes, as well as the newest reconnaissance, communications and electronic warfare systems.[17]

Domination of the Black Sea Region: From Hidden Underwater Threats to 'All-Inclusive' Naval Platforms and Beyond

The illegal annexation of Crimea opened the door for the implementation of the Kremlin's aggressive southwestern ambitions. Broadly speaking Moscow has resurrected the former Soviet southwestern policy that envisioned the Black Sea as an "internal Russian lake" from which it could project naval power into the Eastern Mediterranean.

In the 1970s and 1980s, the BSF primarily concentrated on sea power projection to the Mediterranean in order to be able to carry out so-called "sea control and strike" missions in important sea zones. Today, however, at least two strategic developments have modified this primary mission profile: the appearance of General Valery Gerasimov's doctrine of modern warfare as well as the creation of Russian naval long-range cruise missile capabilities.

Modern Russian Black Sea strategy requires maintaining regional dominance, predicated on developing key combat capabilities that allow Moscow to:

1. Block attempts by any regional adversary to obstruct Russian ambitions to dominate the Black Sea or impede its passage through the Turkish Straits;

2. Provide anti-access, area denial (A2/AD) bubbles in the Black Sea and Eastern Mediterranean maritime zones (areas);

3. Create a balanced composition of naval forces able to fight on land, sea, air and the electro-magnetic domains;

4. Provide amphibious power projection into the Black Sea and the Eastern Mediterranean;

5. Keep Crimean infrastructure and naval assets ready for nuclear weapons deployments.

Countering Opponents' Attempts to Obstruct Russian Dominance of the Black Sea and Free Access to the Mediterranean

Since 2014, Russia has significantly increased the number of its Black Sea military assets capable of carrying out hidden and covert missions. Notably, between 2014 and 2016, it has deployed six recently built Improved Kilo–class submarines to Crimea.[18] Thus, at least two Russian Kilos are likely carrying out 24/7 combat duties in the Black Sea and beyond, at any given time.

The Kilo-class submarine's noise-reducing attributes have earned this vessel the nickname "the Black Hole." Moreover, it is armed with land-attack (Kalibr-PL), anti-ship, and anti-submarine weaponry and can carry out long-term hidden underwater missions, ready to hit surface or land targets not only within the vicinity of its region of operation, but far beyond. Throughout the summer of 2017, the *Krasnodar*, an Improved Kilo–class submarine subordinated to the BSF, engaged in a prolonged cat-and-mouse chase with NATO Anti-Submarine Warfare (ASW) forces during its deployment in the Eastern Mediterranean. Subsequently, US Navy Captain Bill Ellis, commander of US ASW planes in Europe, declared, "One small submarine has the ability to threaten a large capital asset like an aircraft carrier."[19]

Russian could also use Improved Kilos as hidden platforms for naval special forces (SEAL) operations, particular against undersea cables connecting the global economy in the Atlantic and the Mediterranean.[20] And it appears Moscow has already attempted such actions. US Navy Rear Admiral Andrew Lennon, the commander of NATO's submarine forces, observed in late 2017,

> We are now seeing Russian underwater activity in the vicinity of undersea cables that I don't believe we have ever seen. Russia is clearly taking an interest in NATO and NATO nations' undersea [possessions].[21]

At the same time, Russia demonstrates a readiness for overt military actions in the Black Sea. Near the Russian-occupied Odeske and Holitsynske oil and natural gas fields, located within Ukraine's exclusive maritime economic zone (EEZ), Russia has created mobile A2/AD bubbles. BSF combat ships and other assets operate there around the clock. The 41st Missile Boats Brigade (12 missile corvettes and boats with 68 cruise and anti-ship missiles on board) is subordinated to the so-called Crimean Naval Base, located in Donuzlav Lake, in the northern part of the peninsula.[22] In 2016, this naval unit approached the northwestern part of the Black Sea and began operating within the vicinity of ten Russian-captured rigs in four gas fields inside Ukraine's EEZ. Based on the ranges of their onboard missiles, these Russian naval assets based out of Donuzlav could threaten the maritime industrial-port facilities of at least two littoral states.

The creation of high-probability offensive threats and periodically raising their perceived likelihood for political-military reasons is, in fact, characteristic of Russian activities in the region. An important element of this practice is the flexing of Russian military muscle whenever NATO members, particular the US, bring warships or patrol aircraft into the Black Sea. Frequently, these types of demonstrations by Moscow have resulted in potentially dangerous military incidents. It should be pointed out that there is not only a political-military, but also a psychological aspect to these incidents, associated with Russia's paranoid desire to "show the Americans."[23] Since the illegal annexation of Crimea, several dangerous military episodes took place in the Black Sea:

Perhaps the most publicized cases have involved provocative overflights of NATO ships by Russian strike aircraft. The first such incident in the Black Sea took place in April 2014, when an Su-24 tactical bomber simulated an attack on the USS *Donald Cook* (DDG-75). Soon thereafter, in September 2014, a group of Russian bombers performed flight maneuvers near the Canadian frigate HMCS *Toronto* (F333); one of the aircraft flew at an altitude of only about 300 meters above the vessel. In June 2016, a Russian aviation group, including four Tu-22M3 strategic missile bombers, four Su-27 fighters and an A-50 aerial early warning (AEW) aircraft, carried out a mock bombing run seemingly targeting a group of NATO ships located in Constanța (Romania).[24] Three incidents in which four Russian aircraft made low passes occurred on February 2017, as the USS *Porter* (DDG-78) was operating in international waters in the Black Sea. One Russian bomber even came within 200 yards of the US ship.[25]

Russian fighters have also periodically performed unsafe interceptions of NATO aircraft. Such incidents took place, notably, on May 9, 2017, and on November 25, 2017, involving US P-8A Poseidon patrol jets.[26]

Additionally, Russian intelligence and combat ships routinely track Alliance joint naval exercises in Black Sea international waters.[27] And indeed, the Russian Ministry of Defense unequivocally warns NATO countries that their ships will be tracked by Russian radars during their maneuvers in the Black Sea and that they will be explicitly targeted by Russian anti-ship missile systems.[28]

These types of incidents increase the possibility of a serious military accident with casualties. Moreover, all the above-cited examples took place in or over international waters, and thus in violation (by Russia) of the principle of freedom on the high seas recognized by the Convention on the High Seas (1958) and the United Nations Convention on the Law of the Sea (UNCLOS, 1982). According to international law, no state has the right to extend its sovereignty to any part of the high seas or to the airspace above it or to prevent other states from exercising their right of freedom of the high seas, including when it comes to shipping and/or overflights. Instead, Moscow uses its naval buildup, provocative military activities, and a wide spectrum of hidden and overt security threats in the region to gain sea and air superiority and thus demonstrate—explicitly through hard power— to its regional neighbors "who owns the Black Sea."

Russian A2/AD Bubbles in Key Maritime Areas

Russia has deployed Bastion and Bal mobile coastal-defense missile systems, its most advanced S-400 Triumph air-defense missile system, and high-tech electronic-warfare equipment to Crimea. The occupied peninsula is also undergoing ongoing refurbishment of Soviet-era bunkers there and the reanimation of early-warning radar stations. Together, these upgrades and deployments have effectively transformed Crimea into the epicenter of a nearly impenetrable land-based anti-access, area denial bubble, barring enemy forces from entering or freely operating in the region during a conflict.[29]

The Crimean peninsula–centered A2/AD bubble is further reinforced via a "a fortress fleet" in the Black Sea composed of minelayers and submarines, land-based air support, and coupled with ground-based anti-ship cruise missiles (ASCM), surface-to-air missiles (SAM) and electronic warfare systems. This kind of force mixture arguably represents the most cost-effective and hardest-to-counter method of controlling littorals and nearby seas. It is characterized by echeloned missile warfare and coastal-defense systems—in a sense, replicating the strengths of a naval fleet without its vulnerabilities and thus playing a prominent role in littoral operations. Indeed, in a tactical engagement in the littorals, numerous land-based ASCM and SAM systems can either reinforce the fleet's firepower in a cost-effective way, batter the adversary navy, or give the littoral state's vessels the opportunity to engage the enemy on more favorable terms.

The installation of a Black Sea A2/AD zone was essentially acknowledged by the chief of the General Staff of the Russian Armed Forces, General Valery Gerasimov, in September 2016. He clearly noted that,

> The balance of forces in the Black Sea has changed in recent years, and the Turkish navy cannot be called the master in the region anymore.[30]

Importantly, Russia's A2/AD zone in the Black Sea encompasses Ukrainian waters near Odesa since at least 2015. Though this maritime territory is part of Ukraine's continental shelf and EEZ, Russia has been illegally extracting natural resources from this area's seabed, including annual extraction of up to 2 billion cubic meters of natural gas.[31] BSF assets (ships, missile boats, air defense and aviation, as well as special forces) have routinely and aggressively (including with the use of weapons) denied Ukrainian naval forces and the State Border Service of Ukraine access to this area.[32]

The Black Sea exclusion and area-denial bubble is complemented by a similar A2/AD zone in the Eastern Mediterranean. Russia began creating the latter already in 2013, with the deployment of a Russian Naval Operational Group to the logistics port of Tartus, in Syria. For now, however, despite the widely advertised deployment of Russian air-defense systems to Syria in order to defend the country's air bases from US cruise missiles,[33] those Russian A2/AD asset deployments have not been sufficient to prevent such Western aerial attacks.[34]

Tensions Between Modern Naval Warfare Requirements and Russian Capabilities

One of the key objectives of modern Russia's "Naval Policy Until 2030"[35] is the creation of a balanced composition to the VMF:

> The Russian Federation in 2030 has to possess powerful balanced fleets in all strategic directions, including designed ships capable of performing tasks in littoral and blue waters as well as ocean areas; naval aviation and coastal troops equipped with high-precision weapons; and an advanced system of naval bases and logistic support.[36]

But in practice, Moscow has been visibly tilting the balance of its fleet more strongly toward underwater capabilities. In the last decade, Russia has dramatically boosted its submarine activity near the maritime borders of various NATO members.[37] At the same time, it has been actively building blue-water nuclear ballistic-missile submarines as a key element of Russia's nuclear triad, as well as multi-purpose nuclear-powered and conventional submarines. Conversely, Moscow has paid relatively less attention to the development of its surface naval forces and maritime aviation. As a result, Russia's blue-water surface fleet experienced a dramatic decline in the 1990s and early 2000s. Only one of its eight Soviet-built Kirov-class battlecruisers, the *Pyotr Velikiy*, can still be put out to sea.[38] Meanwhile, the Russian aircraft-carrying cruiser, *Admiral Kuznetsov*, is undergoing repairs after its late-2016 campaign in Syria, and it is not clear when it will again be fully operational.[39] Russian Krivak-class frigates have limited capabilities, according to modern naval standards. Moreover, the Russian navy urgently needs to replace its Sovremenny-class destroyers and Udaloy-class frigates because their service lives are ending.[40]

The same is true of the Black Sea Fleet. More than 80 percent of its surface ships were built in Soviet times, and their capabilities are now quite limited. The BSF's maritime aviation is old as well, excluding the Su-24M bombers and Su-30 fighters that were deployed in Crimea in 2014–2016. Thus, Moscow's ambition to create a well-balanced fleet is being undermined due to two factors: by the BSF's limited surface forces capabilities as well as insufficient financing and shipbuilding capacities. That inherent tension has forced the Russian leadership to look for alternatives to a balanced naval capabilities development. And under influence from these factors, Moscow has been looking to develop operational means to carry out combat actions against an enemy located within a Russian anti-access, area denial bubble.

The land-based air-defense, anti-surface and early-warning capabilities that are integral components of Russia's A2/AD bubbles, together with long-range offensive and defensive naval means, provide the BSF with impressive capabilities to hit the enemy and, at the same time, maintain the combat resilience of Russia's own naval assets operating inside the A2/AD zone. Russian military leaders have assured that this approach is effective in the Black Sea, where operational dimensions are commensurate with size of the local A2/AD bubble,[41] as well as when engaging in warfare with a weaker enemy in a small-to-medium-intensity conflict. High-intensity war, on the other hand, would require maritime activities beyond the vicinity of land-based A2/AD bubbles. So Russian naval assets could remain vulnerable while in the Mediterranean, outside of the Syrian A2/AD bubble.

In the past, Russian naval capabilities development never fully matched the comprehensive requirements for modern naval warfare; often, Russian political-military authorities have tried to figure out a separate way. Notably, the Kremlin decided to postpone building a previously advertised nuclear destroyer until 2025[42]; whereas, a new Russian aircraft carrier was never constructed,[43] because of financial and technological constrains. Instead, Russia plans to build six multi-purpose Admiral Gorshkov–class blue-water frigates. This decision was facilitated by some key aspects: though the Admiral Gorshkov frigates are smaller and substantially cheaper than destroyers and cruisers, at the same time they have a long-enough range to carry out multipurpose missions in so-called (in Russia) "far maritime zones" that include the Mediterranean as well. Russian authorities believe that multi-purpose frigates will allow the country's surface forces to increase their capabilities by up to 30 percent. Such outcomes are expected to be achieved through modern onboard naval weapons: Kalibr long-range cruise missiles, Onyx anti-ship missiles and Polyment-Redut missile-defense systems.

Nonetheless, not everything appears to be going smoothly with the production of the new Russian frigates. Construction of the original, titular ship of this class, the *Admiral Gorshkov*, took more than decade. Russia was supposed to build ten such frigates by the end of 2020.[44] But in March 2017, Russian Defense Minister Shoigu admitted that only two of these ships will be commissioned in 2020.[45] Their number is planned to be increased by up to six in 2025[46]; however, problems with building the needed gas turbines as well as installing the Polyment-Redut missile-defense system and other equipment on these frigates have still not been solved, as of summer 2018.[47]

Realizing that the mass construction of new Admiral Gorshkov–class frigates will not take place in the near future, Russia commissioned three less capable Krivak V–class frigates and deployed them in Crimea.[48] And three additional frigates are waiting on gas turbines in their shipyard. Originally designed for India, but ultimately purchased by the Russian VMF, the Krivak V–class frigates are equipped with Kalibr-NK cruise missiles and should be counted as part of Russia's blue-water fleet in the Eastern Mediterranean.

Although loudly voiced as a "success" story by Russian officials, the indigenous shipbuilding program has been far less impressive in reality—since 2013, only 16 blue-water-capable multi-purpose naval platforms (frigates, corvettes and conventional submarines) were commissioned. Of those, 12 can carry long-range cruise missiles[49] and seven were deployed to the Black Sea.

Chronic delays in the Russian shipbuilding program have forced the VMF leadership to resuscitate old heavy ships through repair and modernization. But warship repair plans have been postponed several times.[50] The Slava-class missile cruiser *Moskva*, the flagship of the Black Sea Fleet, has been waiting for renovations and modernization since January 2016.[51] Another Russian heavy Kirov-class battlecruiser, *Pyotr Velikiy,* part of the Russian campaign in the Mediterranean in late-2016, needs deep repairs as well. While the battlecruiser *Admiral Nakhimov*, which could potentially also undertake such deployments, is still undergoing long-time repairs that are not scheduled to end until 2021–2022. Earlier, Moscow planned to install 80 universal vertical launchers for cruise, anti-ship and air-defense missiles onboard these warships.[52]

Based on the above-cited capabilities, Russia may be creating operational warship groups for short-term, blue-water missions in limited areas. Therefore, the periodic use of new frigates and submarines, along with modernized old ships, primarily in the Eastern Mediterranean, should be expected in the coming years. Yet, this composition of ships is not enough to deploy balanced naval groups far from the Russian coast on an ongoing basis—which would be important to maintain constant sea control. Nevertheless, two former Supreme Allied Commanders Europe (SACEUR), General (ret.) Philip Breedlove and Admiral (ret.) James Stavridis, believe

Russian naval activities near NATO's borders require an adequate assessment and response from the Alliance.[53]

Russian Amphibious Capabilities in the Black Sea: Naval Assault Power Projection

Following the August 2008 Russian-Georgian war, Moscow discovered a huge gap in its military capabilities—especially when it came to carrying out offensive operations. At this time, Russia became interested in acquiring French Mistral-class helicopter-carrier landing ships. Their capabilities were considered invaluable for to Russian-style rapid amphibious-assault operations, allowing for the seizure of enemy coastal infrastructure via simultaneous attacks from the sea and air. The commander-in-chief of the VMF at the time, Admiral Vladimir Vysotsky, bluntly stated in 2011, "The Mistral would give the Black Sea Fleet the opportunity to carry out its mission in Georgia in 40 minutes instead of the 26 hours that were required to deliver Russian troops to the coast."[54]

Moscow planned to build four such ships—two in France and then two in Russia. Notably, Russian President Vladimir Putin stated, "When we buy [these] ships, we will use them however we please."[55] In other words, the Mistral's appearance in the Black Sea could not be excluded. Thus, on September 3, 2014, then–French President François Hollande decided that the Mistrals would not be delivered to Russia due to Moscow's "recent actions in Ukraine."[56]

After Russia's failure to procure the French Mistrals, a new doctrinal provision appeared in Russian naval policy aimed at "increas[ing] the BSF's operational and combat capabilities by developing an interspecific [sic] grouping of forces (troops) on the territory of the Crimean peninsula."[57]

Within Russian naval doctrine, "interspecific" means simultaneous military forces at sea, on land and in the air to fulfill operational and strategic tasks. Historically, amphibious operations have been the most revealing example of these types of BSF activities. Marine infantry makes up the main component of these kinds of operations today—specifically, the 801st Marine Infantry Brigade, traditionally a well-equipped and well-trained amphibious-assault unit. The capabilities of this unit have increased substantially since 2014.[58] And in line with the above-mentioned doctrinal shift, Russian military authorities made the decision to work out joint amphibious operations. A series of exercises of this type were conducted in Crimea in 2014–2017, with the largest (as of fall 2018) land, air and sea drills taking place on March 2017, at the Opuk combat training area, located near the city of Theodosia. These well-coordinated exercises, involving thousands of troops, notably marked the first time that the Russian military "simultaneously alerted" its three large airborne units—the 7th Mountain Airborne-Assault Division (Novorossiysk), the 11th Airborne-Assault Brigade (Ulan-Ude) and the 56th Airborne-Assault Brigade (Kamyishin). During the exercises, these airborne units worked out joint offensive actions in close interaction with the 801st Marine Infantry Brigade, the 126th Coastal Defense Brigade, aviation and ships, as well as units of the Russian Aerospace Forces. In total, more than 2,500 troops, up to 600 combat and auxiliary vehicles as well as combat ships (including landing vessels), and more than 45 fixed-wing aircraft and helicopters took part in these land-air-sea exercises.[59]

After these exercises, Russia deployed the 171st Separate Airborne Assault Battalion to Crimea.[60] This battalion is subordinated to the 7th Guard Airborne Mountain Assault Division of the Southern Military District. The 171st Airborne Assault Battalion's specialization is reconnaissance-assault operations in mountainous and urban areas along with raid actions. But, the unit's most important mission is to establish a forward airborne bridgehead to provide the 7th Division's deployment in Crimea, if needed.

At the same time, Russian landing ships' capabilities in the Black Sea remain limited. Moscow is attempting to close this gap by building Priboy-class amphibious-assault ships.[61] Two such ships are included in the state armament program for 2018–2025. According to Russian Deputy Defense Minister Yuri Borisov, the first of these new ships will be commissioned in 2022, and the second—five years later.[62] And given Russia's broader southwestern strategy, it cannot be ruled out that these vessels will eventually also make an appearance in the Eastern Mediterranean.

Russian Electronic Warfare Operations in the Black Sea Region

Russia has consistently invested in Electronic Warfare (EW) capabilities for the Armed Forces since 2009. Indeed, modernization of the EW inventory is a key element of the State Armaments Program up to 2025.

Traditionally, Russian EW has been part of so-called "combat support," aimed to provide forces (troops) sustainability/resilience during combat operations. It is clearly tailored to target NATO's command, control, communications, computers, intelligence, surveillance and reconnaissance (C4ISR) and is an integral part—an "electronic bastion"—of Russia's A2/AD bubbles in the Black Sea. Russian military strategists and experts believe that electronic warfare capabilities can increase the combat potential of military forces by up to two times, reduce aircraft losses by up to six times, and combat ship losses—up to three times. Namely, Russian EW involves damaging/destroying command-and-control networks through jamming, disrupting and interfering with radio communications, hampering the work of radar and other sensor systems, and muting GPS signals of Unmanned Aerial Vehicles (UAV) and other assets[63].

Russia is actively developing a "total package" of EW systems to include a broad frequency range; these seem advanced and capable. In addition to systems for surveillance, protection and countermeasures (jamming), it has also introduced measures to protect Russia's own usage of the electromagnetic spectrum (EMS). These systems offer countermeasures against "Western" civilian and military usage of the EMS. Much of this technology in the Russian inventory is highly mobile, including small systems deployable on UAVs, making targeting and neutralizing them more complex and challenging.

More than a dozen different Russian EW systems have been created in recent years. And many are already being introduced in units across all the services stationed in the Southern and Western Military Districts as well as the BSF. The most capable such systems in the Black Sea region are:

- Murmansk-BN[64]—designed for electronic suppression of enemy radio reconnaissance. The complex, which is included in the 475th Electronic Warfare Center of the Black Sea Fleet, can "stun" and "dazzle" reconnaissance sensors of "intelligent" enemy weapons at distances of up to 5,000 kilometers;

- Moskva-1[65]—designed to conduct radio-technical intelligence. It gathers information about sources of electromagnetic radiation within a radius of 400 km, including from aircraft, homing missiles, mobile and stationary air-defense systems, radio transmitters, and other objects emitting radio waves. Data from the Moskva-1 is useful for anti-aircraft missile systems, including the latest S-400 complex, which has the same range of detection as the Moskva-1;

- Krasuha-4[66]—designed to defend against enemy attacks on command posts, force groupings, as well as industrial and administrative facilities. The system suppresses the functioning of electronics-powered stationary and mobile objects with the help of interference effects in what one

Russian source describes as "smart" operations in order to distinguish between enemy and friendly signals inside the Krasuha's area of operations. This system is capable of blinding not only enemy fighters or bombers, but also ground-based radars, airborne early-warning and control (AWACS) aircraft, and even spy satellites. The complex's horizontal and vertical ranges reach 300 km. It also counters enemy drones and unmanned systems. It should be noted that, in 2015, the "Krasuha-4 was deployed at Russia's Khmeimim military airbase in Syria;

- Mi-8MTPR-1[67]—electronic warfare helicopters equipped with Rychag-AV jamming stations. One of the main ways these systems have been employed by Russia has been to deal with counter-air-defense systems and complexes by reducing their effectiveness though muting and jamming their radio signals.

Moscow is stepping up its efforts to renew and modernize the Russian EW inventory; and this effort is complemented by changes to organization, doctrine, command structure, training and tactics, as well as techniques and procedures. The effect of those changes is evident in Russia's aggression against Ukraine, where EW forms an organic part of Russia's kinetic and non-kinetic operations—both in support of proxy forces and conducted independently.

Currently, Russian EW development is shifting from combat support operations to a legitimate electromagnetic warfighting domain—on par with the air, sea or land. Major General Yuriy Lastochkyn, the chief of the Russian EW Troops, in an interview on April 24, 2017, outlined five key Russian EW transformations, including what had been accomplished in 2009–2017 and what should be done by 2020[68]:

1. Modern stage of Russian EW Troops development—extension of the range of their tasks, aimed at the effect of

using advanced EW assets comparable in effectiveness with high-precision weapon strikes;

2. Defining the objectives of innovative EW development in five areas: the deployment of controlled fields of radio suppression in enemy territory on the basis of unified small-size reconnaissance and jamming modules delivered by UAVs; the creation of the means of destruction via powerful electromagnetic radiation on the basis of the application of specialized ammunition and mobile complexes; the development of software impact technologies against highly organized management systems to violate the availability, integrity and confidentiality of information; the introduction of techniques to spoof radio electronic signals and confuse enemy command-and-control systems; increasing the level of information security of EW management bodies (points), improving the algorithms of decision-making support at the expense of a single contour of command and control of forces and assets;

3. Practical commendation of the promising results of "Electron 2016," a special Armed Forces research exercise involving Russia's EW. The troops practiced creating an EW grouping in a strategic direction as well as carried out military-technical experiments prepared by the specialists of the Defense Research Institute. Most importantly, the exercise resulted in new recommendations to military command agencies on organization and operational doctrines;

4. Formation of the EW Situational Center and automation of integrated information in EW units will be complete with the creation of the Unified Information Space of the Russian Armed Forces in the coming years. At that point, the Russian military will be able to use all available data in the operational and radio electronic environment;

5. Forecasts to 2020—the whole complex of measures for the development of EW Troops will significantly increase their contribution to gaining battlefield superiority in the management and use of weapons. The volume of effectively performed EW tasks in various strategic directions will increase by 2–2.5 times and will reach 85 percent by 2020.

Certainly, strong Russian ambitions have not translated to 100 percent implementation. But, the trends are clear. Moscow is looking to secure integrated and synchronized C2 and EW capabilities that will not only contribute to greater force resilience, but will also allow Russia to conduct independent and joint EW operations with other military assets—from the strategic to the tactical level. In this way, the "BAIKAL-1" automated C2 system has been upgraded to the "BAIKAL-1ME" version.[69] Such developments allow Russian forces to, for instance, establish highly integrated air-defense networks and, thus, improve response times, promote situational awareness and enhance coordination between force elements.

One more notable example of Russian advances in EW could be observed in a peculiar case of satellite navigation problems in the Black Sea, on June 22, 2017. The master of a ship off the Russian port of Novorossiysk, not so far from Kerch Strait, discovered that his GPS put him in the wrong spot—more than 32 kilometers inland, at Gelendzhik Airport. After double-checking that the navigation equipment was working properly, the captain contacted other nearby ships. Their AIS traces—signals from the automatic identification system used to track vessels—placed them all at the same airport. At least 20 ships were affected this way. Experts now consider this a documented use of GPS misdirection—a spoofing attack of the type long warned about but that, heretofore, had never been seen in the wild. As such, it is evidence of Russian experiments with new forms of electronic warfare.[70]

All of the above incidents and stated goals illustrate Russia's growing confidence in its ability to operate in the electromagnetic (and cyber) warfighting domain.

The Growing Threat of Naval Mines in the Black Sea

Historically, naval mines played an important role in maritime warfare in the Black Sea. Spurred on by lessons learned during World War I and World War II, the Soviet Black Sea Fleet deployed considerable numbers of offensive and defensive mines in the Black Sea littoral waters, particularly in the northwestern portion of this body of water.[71] Unexploded WWI- and WWII-era naval mines still lay at the bottom of the Black Sea to this day, threatening local shipping.[72]

The modern BSF has accumulated considerable experience in mine warfare in the region. This fleet has traditionally been the navy's leader when it comes to its ability to lay multiple large minefields.[73] The Fleet's minesweepers and landing ships as well as maritime aviation are able to lay more than 1,000 naval mines at once. It fields 500–1,500-kilogram anchor and bottom mines, equipped with combined fuses, which can be used by aircraft, surface ships and submarines. Among the modern types are MDM-1 and MDM-3 mines, which weigh about a ton each.[74] The depth of their setting can reach 120 meters, and the radius of the affected zone—up to 50–70 meters. A significant number of traditional anchor mines (mostly non-contact mines), including deep-sea mines, can be used at depths of up to 1,500 meters. The Russian arsenal also includes a considerable number of RM-1 and PM-2 reactive-emerging mines. The most modern model is the anti-submarine complex PMK-2. Russia increased the production of naval mines after annexing Crimea.

Naval mines, which are characterized by great destructive power and cost-effectiveness, are particularly difficult to detect and neutralize. As such, they have a powerful psychological effect. Minefields to blockade particular sea areas, naval bases or ports can be installed densely (whereby the probability of detonation is 0.6–0.8) or sparsely (with probability of detonation being 0.1–0.3). Even a single naval mine could be used in order to pose a threat to freedom of navigation in an area where merchant shipping is particularly heavy. The northwestern part of the Black Sea is particularly prone to naval mines. And the operational size of this area is such that were a mine to suddenly explode beneath the hull of even just one or two commercial vessels, this would likely entirely hinder further maritime navigation throughout the Black Sea until adequate counter-measures could be taken—negatively affecting the economies of all littoral states. The Crimean annexation underscored that surprise, stealthiness and *maskirovka* are key elements of Russia's military approach. Therefore, it would not be outside the realm of possibility for Russia to carry out concealed offensive mine activities in the northwestern portion of the Black Sea. Whereas, in the event of open hostilities, the probability of more intensive and more overt mine warfare in the Black Sea should be expected.

The BSF intensively trains for minelaying and mine countermeasure operations; landing ships, corvettes, minesweepers and other assets are all involved in these activities.[75] Admiral Alexander Vitko, the commander of the BSF, noted that, in 2017, "Crew training for laying minefields was resumed for the first time after a long break."[76]

Taking this threat of mines into consideration, therefore, NATO and its regional partners will need to develop relevant naval capabilities for systematic and "on-call" mine-countermeasure (MCM) operations in the Black Sea.

Russian Black Sea Nuclear Policy: Crimean Nuclear Intrigue and Pragmatic Reality

During the December 2017 Defense Ministry Collegium, Russian President Vladimir Putin noted that, within the context of the modernization of the Russian Armed Forces, special attention will be accorded to the Strategic Nuclear Forces.[77]

The Black Sea was never excluded from Moscow's nuclear policy. Indeed, a developed system of nuclear ammunition bases, transportation and loading facilities has existed in Crimea since Soviet times. And during the 1970s–1980s, Black Sea Fleet assets carried out their combat duties with nuclear munitions on board. Nuclear-capable ships and submarines would sail out into the Mediterranean Sea, while the 2nd Naval Missile-Carrying Air Division (Tu-22M3 aircrafts) operated out of an airbase near Simferopol.

As the Cold War came to a close, nuclear warheads were moved out of Crimea based on a set of strategic agreements made in 1991 by George H. W. Bush and Mikhail Gorbachev to remove nuclear sea-launched cruise missiles from ships and submarines—a decision subsequently confirmed by Russian President Boris Yeltsin.[78] At the same time, however, the relevant systems for operating or safeguarding onboard nuclear munitions were never dismantled from BSF vessels. These systems have been maintained in good working order to this day.

Intrigue over whether Moscow might be planning to redeploy nuclear weapons to Crimea was rekindled based on a statement by Russian Foreign Minister Sergei Lavrov in December 2014—asked whether the annexed peninsula could host Russian nuclear weapons, he pointedly answered in the affirmative. This pronouncement was further exacerbated by news suggesting that the Crimean nuclear base Feodosia-13, located underneath a mountain, was being renovated.[79] According to the Main Intelligence Directorate of the Ministry of Defense of Ukraine,

> Nuclear weapons delivery systems are now located on the territory of Crimea—at military airfields and at the Sevastopol naval base. The nuclear warheads themselves are located on the

territory of the Southern Military District of the Russian Federation. They can be delivered either to Crimea to equip naval assets there, or these nuclear munitions can be placed onto [Crimean-based] aircraft that land at airfields of the Southern Military District.[80]

Drills to work out the logistical models for supplying nuclear munitions to Crimea should be noted as well.[81]

Undoubtedly, nuclear ammunition facilities located on the territory of the Russian Southern Military District allow for the delivery of nuclear warheads to ships, submarines and aircraft. The Novorossiysk naval base, equipped with piers and loading capabilities, as well as the Southern Military Districts' network of military airfields already exist in part for this very purpose. Therefore, there is no direct expediency to deploy nuclear weapons to Crimea. Moreover, Russia's sensitivity to the political consequences associated with a unilateral repudiation of the above-cited 1991 agreement by, for example, deploying cruise missiles with nuclear warheads to Crimea, should also be taken into account.

At the same time, the Kremlin may be willing to use "nuclear blackmail" within the Crimean context at various levels of intensity— from exacerbating the rumors and intrigue about purported deployments of nuclear arms to Crimea (low threat level) to actual transfers and their deployment to naval vessels in the Black Sea (high threat level). Simultaneously, a wide spectrum of "hybrid"-style contingencies likely exist between these threat levels. Experience shows that nuclear saber rattling and rhetoric has always been of a purely strategic nature for Russia and been employed as part of a broader military-political package—as was particularly notable during the Cold War. Time will tell exactly how modern-day realities shape up.

Conclusion

The Kremlin's ambitions for the military-strategic domination of the Black Sea region have not faded away since the collapse of the Soviet Union. Particularly in the recent decade, Russia activities in the region have trended toward encouraging instability, confrontation and wars. Armed conflict in Georgia, the illegal annexation of Crimea and war in Donbas, as well as the involvement in the Syrian civil war all represent separate links in a single chain connecting the Kremlin's southwestern ambitions with new rounds of regional turbulence.

Russia's military strategy in the Black Sea region is highly centralized, as the leadership of the Russian Armed Forces seeks to strictly follow the Kremlin's strategic and doctrinal provisions and decisions. First of all, the Kremlin is determining the Russian navy's combat capabilities development until 2025 and beyond. According to expert estimates, in 2014–2017, total missile salvo capacities of the Black Sea Fleet increased by 2.4 times and its capabilities to project sea power into the Eastern Mediterranean grew 1.4 times. Strike, assault and fighter aviation units were deployed to airfields across Crimea; the 22nd Russian Army Corps was formed; and the 810th Marine Infantry Brigade was reinforced with modern weapons. Additionally, modern Russian air-defense systems, including the S-400 Triumph, were deployed to the peninsula. Finally, A2/AD zones were created in the Black Sea and the Eastern Mediterranean.

The rise in military incidents in the Black Sea over the last several years have correlated with Russia's growing vision of this body of water as an "internal Russian lake" and mounting ambition in Moscow to "return Russia to its former greatness" in the region via hard power domination. Generally, the degree of Russia's hard-power activity in the Black Sea, the transformation of Crimea into a "peninsula-fortress" and further plans to build up Russian military capabilities in the rest of Black Sea region, including the Sea of Azov as well as the Eastern Mediterranean, should be taken seriously.

Lessons from the Caucasus, Crimea and Donbas seem to underscore that the Kremlin's southwestern policy agenda again includes territorial claims on regional neighbors, which Russia is willing to act on using military force. Meanwhile, the Kremlin continues to seek out weaknesses in its neighbors, directly influencing the most vulnerable areas in order to create advantageous condition for the potential use of military power.

Russian logic to adopt "all-inclusive" naval platforms for simultaneous warfare in the sea, land and air domains is clear. At the same time, budgetary shortfalls, technological problems and import restrictions due to Western sanctions have significantly impacted the implementation of Russia's ambitious southwestern plans. Undoubtedly, at least a portion of the number of doctrinal provisions in Russia's naval strategy has become declarative. The BSF is far from a balanced force: even as most of its naval forces still date back to the Soviet period, shipbuilding, repair and modernization processes have been progressing too slowly, thus preventing Russia from achieving its blue-water ambitions in the medium-term perspective. An estimated ratio of BSF warships presently under operational use is only about 22–25 percent, thus highlighting the fleet's low technical and operational readiness. The military assets newly deployed to Crimea in 2014–2017, including EW complexes, fell short of their planned operational capabilities. Furthermore, the lack of modern amphibious ships limits the BSF's actual offensive capabilities on shore. In recent years, only two multipurpose frigates were commissioned instead of the originally planned six such vessels. However, it would be a mistake to consider Russia's Black Sea strategy purely from the standpoint of traditional military capabilities. In accordance with the Russian style of so-called "Hybrid" or, more accurately, New Generation Warfare, Moscow's regional strategy pointedly includes different interconnected hidden and overt actions. Thus, Russian activities in the Black Sea and beyond over the past decade or so have included propaganda, disinformation and the dissemination of "fake news"; the subversion of spies, agents of influence and "useful idiots"; foreign infiltration, forced disintegration, subversion and defection; as well as assassinations, sabotage, coup d'états and so on. Such politico-diplomatic, informational, and special forces actions, along with other New Generation Warfare tactics have been complemented periodically through the overt use of military force of various scale and intensity.

Russian Black Sea naval assets play an important role in this type of warfare, which has clear similarities with Soviet-style "Political Warfare."[82] The BSF has accumulated a great deal of political warfare experience thanks to the use of the fleet's so-called "cultural-enlightenment institutions" (officers' and sailors' clubs, theater troupes, music bands, military newspapers, etc.) to influence the local Crimean community and even to engage in direct information warfare. Not only Ukraine, but the Balkans and the Caucasus have been identified as bridgeheads for Russian expansion into the region.

In general, Moscow's Black Sea strategy of achieving regional dominance is based upon a multi-pronged approach: 1) naval activities specifically designed to threaten other regional states; 2) the creation of A2/AD bubbles to boost the resilience of Russian naval forces; 3) the intimidation of Black Sea neighbors by pumping Russian military muscles; 4) the identification of the United States and NATO as the main threat to Russia's maritime interests; 5) the development of naval capabilities based on long-range missiles; 6) the establishment of a geopolitical *raison d'être* for Russia's regional military ambitions; 7) the maintenance of the other littoral states under Moscow's influence, with a peculiar policy concerning Turkey aimed at ensuring unimpeded passage through the Turkish Straits for Russian naval assets; and 8) the achievement of superiority in the EW warfighting domain. Overall, the goal of this strategy is to allow the Russian state to be able to push itself out beyond the geopolitical triangle composed of:

- The US and non-Black Sea NATO countries—to allow Russia to operate freely both in the Black Sea and, if possible, the Eastern Mediterranean;

- The Black Sea NATO countries (except Turkey), as well as Ukraine and Georgia—to ensure freedom of action near their coast lines;

- Turkey—for the ability of its naval forces to operate below the 43rd parallel and out in the Mediterranean; at the same time, to convince Ankara that Moscow's political-military game in the region complements their bilateral "common regional interests."

In this situation, NATO's southern flank is becoming a problem for the Alliance. The way to solve these problems is largely determined by two aspects: the Alliance's ability to properly assess the security situation in the region as well as its subsequent response. NATO and, in particular, US maritime activities in the region, with the involvement of Ukraine and Georgia, are thus vital in this regard. The creation of a common regional naval project (a Black Sea NATO Naval Formation that would include Ukraine and Georgia) and its activation could be a particularly useful response to Russia's Black Sea strategy and its activities. Of particular importance to such a NATO Black Sea partnership policy would be a Turkey-Ukraine tandem due to these countries' geostrategic locations (both have the longest Black Sea coastlines and largest exclusive maritime economic zones, with Ukraine's bordering with Russia, while Turkey borders Syria and Iraq) as well as their chosen geopolitical orientations (Turkey is member of NATO, while Ukraine is a distinctive partner of the Alliance). Strengthening the Turkey-Ukraine security and defense partnership could thus help catalyze the efforts of other Black Sea states as well as jumpstart the integration of their approaches into a common, rational whole.

At the same time, however, Russia could try to take advantage of Turkey's steadfast position on the principles of the Montreux Convention, the Black Sea Harmony framework as well as the prerogatives of the region's countries to solve their own problems— i.e., without the involvement of outside powers like the US. The Russian proposal to build a Black Sea security agenda "exclusively [with the involvement of] the two main regional powers" could encourage Turkey to turn eastward geopolitically while exerting additional political pressure on the Alliance. Nevertheless, the budding relationship between Moscow and Ankara could be more fragile that it may outwardly appear: ultimately, Moscow is more than likely to once again show Turkey Russia's real face by unilaterally violating international agreements or playing geopolitical games even as Russian diplomats continue to promise Ankara they can be "partners and friends."[83]

Notes

[1] Andrey Gavrylenko "Na Chernomorskom rubezhe," *Red Star*, February 22, 2013, http://www.redstar.ru/index.php/nekrolog/item/7671-na-chernomorskom-rubezhe.

[2] "Shoygu nazval Ukrainu, Siriyu i Koreyskiy poluostrov strategicheski vazhnymi dlya RF regionami," *TASS*, May 24, 2017, http://tass.ru/armiya-i-opk/4276229.

[3] Olga Kovalevska "Chorne more v heopolitychnykh viziyakh ukrayintsiv," *Tyzhden*, October 22, 2016, http://tyzhden.ua/History/176543.

[4] "Kak Rossiya zakhvatila Krym: Minyust sozdal khronologiyu anneksii," *Segodnya.ua*, June 1, 2017, http://www.segodnya.ua/politics/pnews/kak-rossiya-zahvatyvala-krym-minyust-sozdal-hronologiyu-anneksii-1026294.html.

[5] Ihor Kabanenko "Strategic Overview of the Russian Maritime Threat to Ukraine: Mariupol and Odesa at Stake," *Eurasia Daily Monitor*, The Jamestown Foundation, July 13, 2017 https://jamestown.org/program/strategic-overview-russian-maritime-threat-ukraine-mariupol-odesa-stake/.

[6] "Osnovy politiki Rossiyskoy Federatsii v oblasti voyenno-morskoy deyatel'nosti na period do 2010 goda," *Flot*, March 4, 2000, http://flot.com/nowadays/concept/osn_napr.htm.

[7] "Morskaya doktrina Rossiyskoy Federatsii na period do 2020 goda," Ministry of Foreign Affairs of the Russian Federation, August 18, 2004, http://www.mid.ru/foreign_policy/official_documents/-/asset_publisher/CptICkB6BZ29/content/id/462098.

[8] "Morskaya kollegiya pri pravitel'stve Rossiyskoy Federatsii," http://marine.gov.ru/.

[9] "Osnovy gosudarstvennoy politiki Rossiyskoy Federatsii v oblasti voyenno-morskoy deyatel'nosti na period do 2020 goda," *BlackSeaFleet*, January 20, 2013, http://blackseafleet-21.com/news/20-01-2013_osnovy-gosudarstvennoj-politiki-rossijskoj-federatsii-v-oblasti-voenno-morskoj-dejatelnos.

[10] "Osnovy gosudarstvennoy politiki Rossiyskoy Federatsii v oblasti voyenno-morskoy deyatel'nosti na period do 2030 goda," President of the Russian Federation, decree № 327, July 20, 2017, http://kremlin.ru/acts/bank/42117.

[11] "Osnovopolagayushchiye dokumenty Morskoy kollegii pri pravitel'stve Rossiyskoy Federatsii," http://marine.gov.ru/about/maindocs/.

[12] "Morskaya doktrina of the Russian Federation," July 26, 2015, http://kremlin.ru/events/president/news/50060.

[13] President of the Russian Federation, "Osnovy gosudarstvennoy politiki Rossiyskoy Federatsii v oblasti voyenno-morskoy deyatel"nosti na period do 2030 goda."

[14] Ibid.

[15] "Glavnokomanduyushchiy VMF Rossii admiral Vladimir Vysotskiy vstretilsya s predstavitelyami SMI," Ministry of Defence of Russian Federation, February 17, 2012, http://mil.ru/et/news/more.htm?id=10956737@egNews.

[16] "Avianostsam byt," *Lenta.ru*, July 28, 2008, https://lenta.ru/articles/2008/07/28/carrier/; "Perspektivnyy esminets rossiyskogo VMF budet mnogotselevym, osnashchen udarnym raketnym oruzhiyem i pochti nevidim," *Novosti OPK*, June 23, 2009; "MO RF reshilo zakazat' vosem' atomnykh esmintsev 'Lider,' " *TASS*, September 10, 2016, http://tass.ru/armiya-i-opk/3610760.

[17] Alexey Zakvasyn, "'Rossiya dolzhna byt' sredi gosudarstv-liderov': Putin prizval k stroitel'stvu armii novogo pokoleniya," *RT*, December 22, 2017, https://russian.rt.com/russia/article/463425-putin-armia-minoborony-shoigu.

[18] Anastasiia Ivanova, "'Rasshireniye voyennogo prisutstviya': v Krymu sozdana samodostatochnaya gruppirovka voysk," November 7, 2017, https://russian.rt.com/russia/article/447129-genshtab-krym-gruppirovka.

[19] Christopher Woody, "A cat-and-mouse game between NATO ships and a Russian sub hints at changes happening in naval warfare," October 20, 2017, *Business Insider*, http://www.businessinsider.com/nato-ships-russian-sub-in-mediterranean-hint-at-changing-naval-warfare-2017-10.

[20] Submarine Cable Map, TeleGeography, https://www.submarinecablemap.com/#/.

[21] Christopher Woody, "Russia's undersea naval activity is at record levels, and NATO is worried about a crucial lifeline to the world," *Business Insider*, December 24, 2017, http://www.businessinsider.com/russia-increased-naval-activity-threatening-undersea-cables-2017-12.

[22] Pavel Zavolokyn, "Krymskaya VMB: vozrozhdeniye utrachennogo," *Red Star*, December 5, 2014, http://www.redstar.ru/index.php/newspaper/item/20382-krymskaya-vmb-vozrozhdenie-utrachennogo.

[23] "On this day: Russia in a click," *RT Russiapedia*, July 26, 2017, https://russiapedia.rt.com/on-this-day/july-26/.

[24] Andrey Klymenko, "Voyenno-morskoye prisutstviye NATO v Chernom more i militarizatsiya Kryma," Black Sea News, July 08, 2016, http://www.blackseanews.net/read/116989.

[25] Sam LaGrone, "USS Porter Buzzed by Russian Planes in Black Sea," February 14, 2017, https://news.usni.org/2017/02/14/uss-porter-buzzed-russian-planes-black-sea#sthash.C5DFZ6NG.dpuf.

[26] Sergey Gromenko, "Rossiya i SSHA v nebe nad Krymom: nazrevayet li voyennyy konflikt?" *Krym Realii*, May 25, 2017, https://ru.krymr.com/a/28508483.html; Ryan Browne, "Russian jet makes 'unsafe' intercept of US Navy aircraft," *CNN*, November 27, 2017, http://edition.cnn.com/2017/11/27/politics/russia-us-unsafe-intercept/index.html.

[27] "V rayone provedeniya 'Si Briz-2016' obnaruzheny rossiyskiye korabli-razvedchiki," *112 Channel*, July 27, 2016, https://112.ua/obshchestvo/v-rayone-provedeniya-si-briz-2016-obnaruzheny-rossiyskie-korabli-razvedchiki-327694.html; "Za ucheniyami 'Si Briz – 2016' v Chernom more sledyat korabli-razvedchiki Rossii," *Gordonua*, July 29, 2016, http://gordonua.com/news/politics/za-ucheniyami-si-briz-2016-v-chernom-more-sledyat-korabli-razvedchiki-rossii-142932.html.

[28] "Shoygu rasskazal, chto Rossiya sdelayet s flotom NATO u Kryma," *Pravda.ru*, February 6, 2017, https://www.pravda.ru/news/world/06-02-2017/1324015-nato-0/.

[29] Bleda Kurtdarcan, Barın Kayaoğlu, "Russia, Turkey and the Black Sea A2/AD Arms Race," *The National Interest*, March 5, 2017, http://nationalinterest.org/feature/russia-turkey-the-black-sea-a2-ad-arms-race-19673.

[30] "Genshtab: Chernomorskiy flot Rossii mozhet unichtozhit' desant protivnika yeshche v portakh," *TASS*, September 14, 2016, http://tass.ru/armiya-i-opk/3619937.

[31] "Rossiya nezakonno dobyvayet na shel'fe Chernogo morya 2 milliarda kubometrov gaza v god – 'Chernomorneftegaz,' " *UNIAN*, November 3, 2016, https://economics.unian.net/energetics/1604426-rossiya-nezakonno-dobyivaet-na-shelfe-chernogo-morya-2-milliarda-kubometrov-gaza-v-god-chernomorneftegaz.html.

[32] "Ukrayins'kyy litak obstrilyaly nad morem iz zakhoplenykh RF vyshok," *Ukrainska Pravda*, February 1, 2017, http://www.pravda.com.ua/news/2017/02/1/7134135/.

[33] Andrey Rezchikov, Nikita Golobokov, Mikhail Moshkin, "Rossiyskiye S-300 zakryli nebo Sirii ot amerikanskikh krylatykh raket," *Vzglyad*, October 7, 2016, https://vz.ru/politics/2016/10/7/836801.html.

[34] Tom Balmforth, "After U.S. Strikes Syrian Air Base, Russians Ask: 'Where Were Our Vaunted Air Defense Systems?' " *Radio Free Liberty, Radio Liberty*, April 7, 2017, https://www.rferl.org/a/weher-was-the-s-300-s-400-missile-defense-systems/28417014.html.

[35] President of the Russian Federation, "Osnovy gosudarstvennoy politiki Rossiyskoy Federatsii v oblasti voyenno-morskoy deyatel'nosti na period do 2030 goda."

[36] Ibid.

[37] *112 Channel*, "V rayone provedeniya 'Si Briz-2016' obnaruzheny rossiyskiye korabli-razvedchiki."

[38] "'Petr Velikiy' postavyat na remont posle 2018 goda," *RIA Novosti*, November 16, 2016, https://ria.ru/defense_safety/20161116/1481474295.html.

[39] "Remont 'Admirala Kuznetsova' nachnetsya srazu posle soglasovaniya goskontrakta," Voenno-Promyshlenniy Kuryer, December 25, 2017, https://vpk-news.ru/news/40575.

[40] Andrey Rezchikov, "Rossiya bol'she ne mozhet pozvolit' sebe okeanskiy flot," *Vzglyad*, April 21, 2017, https://vz.ru/politics/2017/4/21/324418.html.

[41] Voenno-Promyshlenniy Kuryer, "Remont 'Admirala Kuznetsova' nachnetsya srazu posle soglasovaniya goskontrakta."

[42] Alexander Chrolenko, "Atomnyy esminets 'Lider': kak Rossiya poluchit prevoskhodstvo v Mirovom okeane," *RIA Novosti*, July 29, 2017, https://ria.ru/analytics/20170729/1499181539.html.

[43] "Avianostsam byt'," *Lenta.ru*, July 28, 2008, https://lenta.ru/articles/2008/07/28/carrier/.

[44] Voenno-Promyshlenniy Kuryer, "Remont "Admirala Kuznetsova" nachnetsya srazu posle soglasovaniya goskontrakta."

[45] "VMF poluchit dva novykh fregata s 'Kalibrami' do 2020 goda," *Red Star*, March 7, 2017, https://tvzvezda.ru/news/opk/content/201703071208-rjte.htm.

[46] "VMF Rossii poluchit noveyshiye fregaty s opozdaniyem," *Lenta.ru*, May 4, 2016, https://lenta.ru/news/2016/05/04/frigates/.

[47] Oleg Winer, "Proklyat'ye rossiyskogo 'importozameshcheniya,'" *Defense Express*, January 13, 2017, https://defence-ua.com/index.php/statti/2222-proklyat-e-rossijskogo-importozameshcheniya.

[48] "VMF poluchil noveyshiy fregat "Admiral Essen," *Red Star*, June 07, 2016, https://tvzvezda.ru/news/forces/content/201606071654-z5gu.htm; "Fregat 'Admiral Makarov' voshel v sostav Voenno-Morskogo flota RF," *Regnum*, December 27, 2017, https://regnum.ru/news/2363058.html.

[49] Alexander Mozgovoy, "Zhdet li nas novaya Tsusima," *Nezavisimoye Voennoe Obozreniye*, December 22, 2017, http://nvo.ng.ru/armament/2017-12-22/1_978_cusima.html.

[50] "Remont korabley dalney morskoy zony," *Oruzhiye Rossyi*, December 24, 2017, http://www.arms-expo.ru/news/novye_razrabotki/su_57_poluchil_dvigatel_vtorogo_etapa/.

[51] "Kreyser 'Moskva' otremontiruyut v Sevastopole," *Rossiyskaya Gazeta*, August 21, 2017, https://rg.ru/2017/08/21/reg-ufo/krejser-moskva-otremontiruiut-v-sevastopole.html.

[52] Kirill Ryabov, "Novosti modernizatsii kreyserov 'Orlan,' " *Voennoye Obozreniye*, April 18, 2017, https://topwar.ru/113686-novosti-modernizacii-kreyserov-orlan.html.

[53] Andrew Chuter, "Report flags NATO's naval shortfalls vis-a-vis Russia," *Defence News*, March 5, 2017, https://www.defensenews.com/naval/2017/03/06/report-flags-nato-s-naval-shortfalls-vis-a-vis-russia/.

[54] Yevgen Tzybulenko, "Hruzyns'ka viyna: pravo i Pravda," *Tyzhden.ua*, August 8, 2011, http://tyzhden.ua/World/28165; "Vertoletonostsy 'Mistral' sushchestvenno povysyat boyevyye vozmozhnosti VMF Rossii," *Interfax*, June 17, 2011, http://www.interfax.ru/business/195096.

[55] " 'Chernaya smert" nastupayet: morskuyu pekhotu zhdet global'naya modernizatsiya," *Red Star*, November 27, 2017, https://tvzvezda.ru/news/forces/content/201411270254-tpal.htm.

[56] "Ukraine crisis: France halts warship delivery to Russia," *BBC News*, September 3, 2014, http://www.bbc.com/news/world-europe-29052599; "France Suspends Mistral Warship Delivery to Russia," *Defense News*, November 25, 2014 https://www.defensenews.com/global/europe/2014/11/25/france-suspends-mistral-warship-delivery-to-russia/.

[57] President of the Russian Federation, "Osnovy gosudarstvennoy politiki Rossiyskoy Federatsii v oblasti voyenno-morskoy deyatel'nosti na period do 2030 goda."

[58] " 'Chernaya smert" nastupayet: morskuyu pekhotu zhdet global'naya modernizatsiya," November 27, 2017.

[59] Ihor Kabanenko, "Large Russian Land-Air-Sea Exercises in Crimea Highlight Vulnerabilities in Ukrainian Navy and Coastal Defense," *Eurasia Daily Monitor*, The Jamestown Foundation, April 12, 2017, https://jamestown.org/program/large-russian-land-air-sea-exercises-crimea-highlight-vulnerabilities-ukrainian-navy-coastal-defense/.

[60] "Krymchane budut osnovoy dislotsiruyemogo v Krymu desantno-shturmovogo batal'ona," *RIA Novosti*, December 2, 2017, https://ria.ru/defense_safety/20171202/1510076738.html.

[61] Alexander Chrolenko, "Bez frantsuzskogo aktsenta: rossiyskiy vertoletonosets prevzoydet 'Mistrali,' " *RIA Novosti*, July, 1, 2017, https://ria.ru/analytics/20170701/1497624360.html.

[62] Victor Baranets, "Avianosets 'Shtorm': proyekt korablya super-klassa oboydetsya v Z50 milliardov," *Komsomolskaya Pravda*, July 6, 2017, https://www.crimea.kp.ru/daily/26701/3725840/.

[63] Roger N. McDermott, Michael Hayden, "Russia's Electronic Warfare Capabilities to 2025" International Centre for Defence and Security, Tallinn, Estonia, September 2017, https://www.icds.ee/fileadmin/media/icds.ee/doc/ICDS_Report_Russias_Electronic_Warfare_to_2025.pdf.

[64] "Voyennyye razvernuli sverkhmoshchnyy kompleks REB 'Murmansk' v Krymu," *Red Star*, March 10, 2017, https://tvzvezda.ru/news/forces/content/201703101746-kdgq.htm.

[65] "Ucheniye "Elektron-2016," Concern Radio-Electronic Technologies, August 20, 2016, http://kret.com/media/news/uchenie-elektron-2016/.

[66] Vladimir Tuchkov, "Amerikanskiy general: "My bessil'ny pered 'Krasukhoy' i 'Moskvoy,' *Svobodnaya Pressa*, August 28, 2017, http://svpressa.ru/war21/article/180142/.

[67] "Perekhoplennya radioefiru helikoptera REB VPS RF (Mi-8MTPR-1) u Krymu," *InformNapalm*, October 4, 2017, https://informnapalm.org/ua/perehoplennya-mi-8mtpr-1-krym/.

[68] Yuri Lastochkin, Oleg Falichev, "Kupol nad Minoborony," Voenno-Promyshlenniy Kuryer, April 24, 2017, https://vpk-news.ru/articles/36422.

[69] "Avtomatizirovannaya sistema upravleniya 'BAYKAL 1-ME,'" *Raketnaya Technika*, September 28, 2012, http://rbase.new-factoria.ru/gallery/avtomatizirovannaya-sistema-upravleniya-baykal-1-me.

[70] "Ships fooled in GPS spoofing attack suggest Russian cyberweapon," *New Scientist*, August 10, 2017, https://www.newscientist.com/article/2143499-ships-fooled-in-gps-spoofing-attack-suggest-russian-cyberweapon/.

[71] "Boyevoye traleniye v pervyye poslevoyennyye gody - surovoye prodolzheniye voyny," Voennoye Obozreniye, September 5, 2016, https://topwar.ru/100116-boevoe-tralenie-v-pervye-poslevoennye-gody-neotemlemaya-chast-velikoy-otechestvennoy-voyny.html.

[72] "Vnimaniye! V Sevastopole iz-za opasnoy 1000-kilogrammovoy miny polnost'yu ostanovyat sudokhodstvo," *Sevastopolskiye Novosti*, June 6, 2017, http://sevastopolnews.info/2017/06/lenta/sobytiya/069271045/.

[73] "Kapkan na vsekh moryakh," Voenno-Promishlennuy Kuryer, September 16, 2015, https://vpk-news.ru/articles/27023.

[74] "V lyubom rayone Mirovogo okeana," *Nezavisimoye Voennoye Obozreniye*, June 23, 2017, http://nvo.ng.ru/armament/2017-06-23/8_953_ocean.html.

[75] "Korabli Chernomorskogo flota otrabatyvayut postanovku minnykh zagrazhdeniy i protivominnyye deystviya," *Red Star*, December 4, 2017, https://tvzvezda.ru/news/forces/content/efd4c5dd4ee05752ba0c5f85b7c43901d0ac35b5e26745ee7616fa6e886f743f; Evgeniya Artemova, Yevgeniya Artemova "Proverka flota," *Interfax-Russia*, March 18, 2015, http://www.interfax-russia.ru/Crimea/view.asp?id=592667.

[76] "Komanduyushchiy CHF: v blizhaysheye vremya flot poluchit shest' korabley s 'Kalibrami,' " *Interfax*, December 1, 2017, http://www.interfax.ru/interview/589923.

[77] "'Rossiya dolzhna byt' sredi gosudarstv-liderov': Putin prizval k stroitel'stvu armii novogo pokoleniya." *RT*, December 22, 2017, https://russian.rt.com/russia/article/463425-putin-armia-minoborony-shoigu.

[78] "Lavrov ne isklyuchil razmeshcheniya yadernogo oruzhiya v Krymu," *Interfax*, December 15, 2014, http://www.interfax.ru/russia/413164; Vladimir Belous, "Opasny, kak i strategicheskiye nastupatel'nyye vooruzheniya," *Nesavisimoye Voennoye Obozreniye*, November 20, 2009, http://nvo.ng.ru/concepts/2009-11-20/1_control.html.

[79] "Muzhenko: Rossiya vosstanavlivayet ob'yekty dlya khraneniya yadernogo oruzhiya v Krymu," *Krym Realii*, July 7, 2017, https://ru.krymr.com/a/news/28601314.html.

[80] "V Krymu mogut primenit' yadernoye oruzhiye – razvedka," *Korrespondent.net*, August 11, 2016, https://korrespondent.net/ukraine/3730077-v-krymu-mohut-prymenyt-yadernoe-oruzhye-razvedka.

[81] "Rossiya otrabatyvayet postavki yadernykh boyepripasov v Krym – GUR," *Segodnya*, July 30, 2016, https://www.segodnya.ua/regions/krym/rossiya-otrabatyvaet-postavki-yadernyh-boepripasov-v-krym-gur-738252.html.

[82] Jeffrey V. Dickey, Thomas B. Everett, Zane M. Galvach, Matthew J. Mesko, Anton V. Soltis, "Russian political warfare: origin, evolution, and application," Monterey, California: Naval Postgraduate School, June 2015, https://calhoun.nps.edu/bitstream/handle/10945/45838/15Jun_Dickey_Everett_Galvach_Mesko_Soltis.pdf.

[83] Dave Majumdar, "Why are Russia and Turkey Holding Joint Naval Exercises in the Black Sea?" *National Interest*, April 5, 2017, http://nationalinterest.org/blog/the-buzz/why-are-russia-turkey-holding-joint-naval-exercises-the-20041.

3. Russia's Arctic and Far East Strategies

Pavel K. Baev

Introduction

Development of the enormous economic resources of the Arctic and the Far East is one of the main challenges for the Russian state, and asserting control over these vast and thinly populated regions is one of Russia's core national interests. The Russian leadership understands these interests and is aware of the scope of the associated challenges; it thus seeks to allocate efforts and resources, including military power, accordingly. At the same time, however, the evolving confrontation with the West, triggered by the annexation of Crimea in spring 2014 and sustained by the ongoing war in Ukraine, has determined deep shifts in Russia's national security strategy. Political attention in Moscow is centered on managing this confrontation, and resource allocation necessarily prioritizes the Western theater.[1]

This distortion has a profound impact on setting political goals, executing economic projects, and engaging in military activities in the Arctic and the Far East. In the most general terms, it is possible to establish that Arctic matters receive plenty of political attention, perhaps even more than they would rationally deserve. Thus, at the long press conference on December 14, 2017, in which he announced his intention to claim yet another presidential term, Vladimir Putin made a particular point on military security in the Arctic. He followed up on this theme in his presentation at the Collegium of the Ministry of Defense, noting the capacity for "rapid reinforcement of the units in the Arctic."[2] At the very end of that long press conference, President Putin also praised the "breakthrough" in the development of Vladivostok, but the only foreign policy issue in the problem-rich Asia-Pacific region that received attention was the cultivation of the "strategic partnership" with China. The crisis in North Korea was mentioned solely in the context of Russia's relations with the United States, as if it were happening far away from Russia's borders.

The sustained political attention to the Arctic remains seriously incoherent because the emphasis on preserving the pattern of international cooperation and bracketing this region out of the new pattern of confrontation is poorly compatible with the commitment to expand Russia's military presence and activities in the High North. The desire to ensure economic development of the Far East is also in conflict with Moscow's expectations that great-power competition is bound to escalate in the Asia-Pacific region; moreover, that development is highly unlikely to be achieved only by expanding the partnership with China.[3] These contradictions are reflected in the strategic assessments of, and military planning for, possible security risks in these regions.

These assessments and guidelines should have been summarized and elaborated in the series of fundamental and recently updated state documents, from the National Security Strategy (approved on December 31, 2015) to the Military Doctrine (approved December 25, 2014). These documents, however, provide long lists of threats and dangers in the most general terms, while giving little in terms of priorities. For instance, among the tasks for the Russian Armed Forces, the Military Doctrine mentions "the contribution to the construction in the Asia-Pacific region of a new security model based on collective non-aligned foundations," and gives as the last one in the long list "guaranteeing the national interests of the Russian Federation in the Arctic."[4]

This traditional vagueness of those key documents raises an important question about the real content of Russian doctrinal and strategic propositions. This chapter attempts to address this question regarding the Arctic and Far Eastern regions, which are compared and juxtaposed to one another. It starts with the examination of Moscow's threat assessments to the perceived security interests in these regions. Then, the nuclear strategic level of assessments and goals is examined, followed by the naval strategic guidelines for the Northern and Pacific fleets, and preparations for countering conventional and "hybrid" threats. The range of possible implications for the US and its allies is outlined before the conclusion.

Security Interests and Threat Assessments

The gradual maturing of Putin's corrupt authoritarian regime has brought about a re-evaluation of Russia's security interests, which are increasingly identified with guaranteeing the survival of this regime against perceived hostile Western attempts at "regime change." Such means as, for instance, strengthening the newly created National Guard, are directed toward this key interest.[5] In this strategic perspective, both the Arctic and the Far Eastern regions are rather peripheral, since few disturbances in these remote areas could resonate in Moscow, which is the natural focal point of Russian security interests. The remoteness and vastness of these regions, as well as their underdeveloped infrastructure, determine the particular character of national interests, with a pronounced emphasis on the issue of sovereignty over harsh and essentially uncontrollable spaces; consequently, the question of Russia's territorial integrity looms large. It is, therefore, quite remarkable that this question has quite different manifestations and answers in the Arctic and in the Far East.

In the Arctic, the Russian leadership sees an urgent need to ascertain sovereignty over uninhabited and uninhabitable islands as well as the continental shelf, despite the absence of any territorial disputes (after the settlement of the maritime border with Norway in 2010).[6] At the aforementioned December 2017 press conference, Putin found it opportune to refer to some foreign tourist guides who allegedly claimed that Russia had only recently took control over the Franz Josef Land—which makes a rather peculiar justification for the construction of a modern military base there.[7] A string of new northern bases spans all the way to the tip of Kamchatka, where the Arctic theater meets the Far Eastern theater. Those bases are meant to assert Russia's control over the Northern Sea Route (*Sevmorput*) and to guarantee its right to enforce the rules for maritime communications in the Arctic.

Moscow's main concerns include the official claim to expand its continental shelf between the Lomonosov and Mendeleev underwater ridges up to the North Pole. After much work on gathering scientific evidence, Russia resubmitted this claim to the United Nations Commission on the Limits of the Continental Shelf (UN CLCS) in August 2015. Putin, who repeatedly extolled the prospect of expanding Russia's Arctic "possessions" after Arthur Chilingarov's famous flag-planting expedition to the North Pole seabed in August 2007, has stopped mentioning it since deliberations over the claim started in February 2016.[8] It is entirely possible that the UN CLCS will ultimately postpone its recommendation on the Russian claim, particularly since it clashes with the claim submitted by Denmark. This procrastination may prompt Moscow to resort to unilateral measures for asserting control over the icy waters to the north of its 200 nautical mile exclusive economic zone (EEZ).

In the Far East, there are several unresolved issues with Russia's maritime and land borders, and a looming threat to its sovereignty over that region. Russia's claim for expanding its continental shelf in the Sea of Okhotsk was approved by the UN CLCS in November 2013, making it possible for Russian energy giants Gazprom and Rosneft to proceed with exploration and drilling.[9] However, the 1990 Maritime Boundary Agreement with the United States (known as the Baker-Shevardnadze line) is yet to be ratified by the Russian parliament.

Perhaps the most controversial territorial dispute in the Far East involves Russia's control over the South Kurile Islands (Iturup, Kunashir, Shikotan, and the Habomai rocks), which are claimed by Japan as the Northern Territories. While bilateral negotiations on the status of those islands continues to drag on, Moscow has been strengthening its military presence there, including the deployment of Bastion-P (SS-C-5 Stooge) and Bal-E (SS-C-6 Sennight) coastal defense missile systems, as well as declaring the resolve to respond to the increasing US military activities in the region.[10]

In contrast, border issues with China have been resolved quietly through a series of compromises and concessions, starting with the border agreement ratified by the newly-empowered Russian parliament in February 1992. Most of the islands on the Amur River, including Damansky (Zhenbao), which saw fierce fighting in 1969, were transferred under China's control, and in October 2004, Putin signed an additional agreement on the Eastern part of this border, which granted China even more territory.[11] In May 2016, China's President Xi Jinping visited the recently gained Heixiazi Island (Bolshoi Ussuriisky), close to Khabarovsk, and extolled the prospects of cross-border ties, but also reminded about the need to increase the readiness and capabilities of border troops.[12] Russia assumes that the issue is closed, but China still harbors reservations about the border problem. For that matter, the installation of granite markers on the newly-demarcated border near the city of Hunchun provoked an explosion of protests on Chinese social networks against accepting this "colonial" border.[13] Beijing's official position asserts the absence of any territorial claims, but the authorities routinely employ discourse on rejecting the historical injustice of "unequal treaties," including the 1858 Aigun Treaty with Russia.[14]

Overall, it is apparent that the threats to Russia's sovereignty in the Arctic are significantly overestimated in Moscow, while the problems in the Far East are downplayed. Great symbolic value is attached to the capacity and determination to "conquer" the Arctic, and military capabilities are presented as the main instrument ensuring Russia's control over the hydrocarbon riches believed to exist there. Meanwhile Eastern Siberia and the Far East are also extraordinarily rich in natural resources, but these vast regions have been steadily losing the scant population they retain from earlier Soviet efforts at channeling internal eastward migration. Military power might be necessary to guarantee Russia's security interests because it is at a deep disadvantage compared to its more dynamic and assertive Asia-Pacific neighbors. Yet, there are few signs of acknowledgment of this imperative in the doctrinal thinking and hardly any indications of prioritization of the Far East in the distribution of military resources.

Strategic Designs and Calculations

In Russia's military security outlook, the Arctic and the Far East are the two frontiers in which strategic matters have the highest priority. The naval component of the country's strategic nuclear deterrent—reduced to just 12 nuclear submarines with ballistic missiles (SSBN)—is divided between the Northern and Pacific fleets. Moreover, the main "corridors" for strategic patrols by long-range aviation—consisting of 66 aging bombers—stretch across the Northern Atlantic and Northern Pacific. Many early-warning radars are located in the High North and the Far East, from Olenegorsk, in the Murmansk region, to Vorkuta, in the Komi republic, and Zeya, in the Amur region. Russia's two space-launch facilities (*cosmodrome*) are the small-capacity Plesetsk, Arkhangelsk region, and the newly-built Vostochny, Amur region. Plans for modernizing these assets and the tasks of ensuring their safety determine the key guidelines for regional development in Russia's Arctic and the Far East, as well as define the international profile of these regions.

Providing that the Russia-US system of arms control is preserved, submarine-launched nuclear warheads will increasingly make up a greater share of Russian strategic capabilities in the near future.[15] The single most expensive item in the 2020 State Armament program was the introduction of the new generation of strategic submarines; three Borei-class (Project 955) SSBNs are currently operational, and five more are in different stages of construction. The need to complete this program ensures that the new 2027 State Armament program, which was finalized only at the end of 2017, after a fierce struggle between various military-industrial lobbies, is also significantly tilted in favor of the naval leg of the strategic nuclear triad.[16] Given the fact that three Delta III–class submarines (the *Podolsk*, *Ryazan* and *Georgy Pobedonosets*), which are assigned to the Pacific Fleet, have to be retired in the next few years, it makes perfect strategic sense to concentrate all SSBNs in the Northern Fleet. Putin, nevertheless. claims personal credit for the decision to modernize the strategic submarine base in Vilyuchinsk, Kamchatka, whatever the costs of such a division of forces.[17] The two basing areas are connected, so that submarines from the Pacific Fleet travel for repairs and overhaul to Severomorsk and Severodvinsk, and most missile tests are fired from the Barents Sea to the Sea of Okhotsk.

The real problem with the sea leg of Russian deterrence is, however, the main weapons system for the Borei-class submarines—the Bulava (SS-N-32) ballistic missile. It has a checkered record of tests, and was fired from the *Yuri Dolgoruki* (the first submarine in the series) only once in 2016 and once in 2017, and the four-missile salvo from the same submarine on May 22, 2018 has not eliminated all issues.[18] Two of the Boreis (the *Aleksandr Nevsky* and the *Vladimir Monomakh*) are presently based in Vilyuchinsk, but they did not partake in the exercises of strategic forces in October 2017, when Putin allegedly launched personally (as technically improbable as that is) three missiles from two submarines.[19] Moscow apparently finds it necessary to maintain strategic naval capabilities in the Pacific theater, but the sustainability of this deployment in the logistically isolated Kamchatka is rather uncertain.

In the course of the on-going confrontation with the West, Russia has found that long-range aviation is in fact its most useful element of deterrence for demonstrating resolve and putting North Atlantic Treaty Organization (NATO) forces on alert, as well as for delivering an occasional strike in Syria.[20] The usual pattern of activity consists of a pair of bombers flying from the Engels base, Saratov region, northward toward the Arctic and then westward into the North Atlantic, and a pair of bombers from the Ukrainka base, Amur region, fly into the North Pacific with an occasional detour to Guam.[21] The fleet of Russia's 55 Tu-95MS (Bear-H) and 11 Tu-160 (Blackjack) strategic bombers is aging fast, however, and the deadly crashes of two Bears at the Ukrainka base in summer 2015 showed that logistics has not quite been able to cope with wear and tear. The plan for resuming serial production of Tu-160s at the Kazan plant is technologically challenged, and the proposition for developing a new generation of strategic bombers (PAK-DA) has not been translated into a clear target in the 2027 State Armament program.[22]

Despite the fact that Russia now cannot build anything resembling the old Soviet "bastion" in the Barents Sea, its strategic assets in the Kola Peninsula are reasonably safe and can perform efficiently. The strategic capabilities in the Far Eastern theater are far less solid and cannot in any meaningful way counter-balance the US naval or air power deployed in the Pacific region. Furthermore, the fast modernization of China's strategic forces constitutes another indirect challenge to Russia, even if there is no official acknowledgement of the task of balancing the capabilities of this senior partner. Russian strategic offensive forces have never had any interactions with their Chinese counterparts; however, in December 2017, the first ever joint Chinese-Russian command missile defense exercise was held in Beijing.[23] Undoubtedly, the escalation of the crisis driven by North Korea's nuclear and missile programs has prompted this advance in cooperation, but Russia's readiness to deal with the potentially grave consequences of this fluid situation is highly uncertain. According to informed Russian experts, the country's early-warning system— designed for quite different tasks—provided rather imprecise data when it came to monitoring North Korean missile launches and nuclear tests. Moscow has nevertheless made no effort at strengthening missile defenses around its very vulnerable Pacific port city of Vladivostok.[24] Beijing is perfectly aware of this weakness; it requested and obtained support from Moscow in opposing the deployment of the US THAAD system in South Korea, but then opted to resolve this issue with Seoul without any involvement from its Russian partner.[25]

Russia's strategic deterrence capabilities in the Far Eastern theater are crucially important for asserting Moscow's control over this remote periphery, but they are clearly insufficient for the traditional task of counter-balancing US capabilities—and entirely unprepared for dealing with a potential real crisis developing in the immediate vicinity of Russia's borders. This unsatisfactory posture is pre-determined by the vague and unrealistic doctrinal guidelines that are focused on maintaining strategic parity with the United States, but which give few considerations to the specific features and vulnerabilities in the Far East.

Naval Ambitions and Deficiencies

The Arctic and the Far Eastern theaters are open to the sea as no other areas of the Russian Federation, and this determines the key role of naval forces in military planning and activities there. While Russia is historically and geopolitically a land power, the navy has secured for itself major functions in guaranteeing national security and plays a prominent symbolic role.[26] This role was performed with great fanfare during the unprecedented naval parade on July 30, 2017, which involved all naval bases from Severomorsk and Vilyuchinsk to Tartus, Syria, and was attended by Putin in St. Petersburg.[27] A week prior to that demonstration of sea power, Putin signed a document entitled, "The Foundations of State Policy in the Area of Naval Activity for the Period up to 2030."[28] The document is essentially doctrinal in scope and presents the usual wide range of threats and dangers, based on the fundamental assumptions of further escalation of competition between global powers and increasing instability in all parts of the world ocean.

The new naval policy sets as a general aim preventing other states from achieving "significant superiority" over the Russian navy, which has to retain "the second place in the world in combat capabilities" (Article 39). It is quite clear from many statements in the document that the US Navy is perceived as the main source of threat, but it is not acknowledged that the fast build-up and modernization of China's navy makes the proposition of securing second place quite unrealistic.[29] Characteristically, the situation in the Asia-Pacific is not mentioned once in the document, while there are several references to the Arctic. Additionally, there is no hint in the official guidelines that the Russian navy is set to suffer particularly painful cuts in funding in the 2027 State Armament program, which has been curtailed due to the sustained contraction of Russia's economic base.[30] The July 2018 naval parade, for that matter, was a more modest affair.

It is possible to figure out, nevertheless, that the Northern Fleet is set to receive the bulk of new funding and is going to be significantly reshaped. Its flagship, Russia's only aircraft carrier, the *Admiral Kuznetsov*, is scheduled to undergo long repairs after its rather unsuccessful combat deployment to the Eastern Mediterranean in 2016–2017. Whereas, the long-cherished desire to build a nuclear-powered ship of this class will almost certainly only materialize in design models.[31] The nuclear battle cruiser *Petr Velikii* is also going into overhaul, so Russia's new flagship will be its sister-ship, the *Admiral Nakhimov*, which is about to come out of protracted modernization.[32] The main strength of the Northern Fleet is going to be its submarine divisions, which are to be strengthened with the arrival of the new generation of nuclear attack submarines armed with cruise missiles (SSGN). Five Yasen-class (Project 885) submarines are in different stages of construction. The design has been highly ranked by naval experts, but the *Severodvinsk*, the first in the series (started back in 1993) has entered the combat order only in mid-2014, while the *Kazan* is still undergoing tests.[33] The reasons for such delays are never entirely explained, but it may presumably have to do with the fact that the Severodvinsk shipyard has to prioritize the Borei program, while also working on the *Admiral Kuznetsov* and proceeding with the planned overhauls of the Delta IV–class SSBNs.

A new and hard task for the Norther Fleet is to ensure control over the *Sevmorput*, and the new naval policy specifically points out among the threats to Russia's interests "military pressure on the Russian Federation aimed at […] weakening its control over the Northern Sea Route—the historically established national transport route of the Russian Federation" (Article 24). Yet, the fact of the matter is that, historically, the Northern Fleet operated primarily in the ice-free Barents Sea and the Northern Atlantic, and even now lacks a single ice-class surface combatant. So its annual (since 2012) summer cruises into the Kara and Laptev seas require the mobilization of several icebreakers.[34] A new Ivan Papanin (Project 23550) series of ice-class patrol ships was started at the St. Petersburg shipyard, but only two ships have been contracted.[35] The Northern Fleet received, in December 2017, its first icebreaker, the *Ilya Muromets* (Project 21180), but no more ships of this class are planned, while the construction of the nuclear icebreaker *Arktika* for the Atomflot corporation has run into delays.[36]

The Pacific Fleet is facing a far more difficult situation and receives far less attention. Its combat order was supposed to be reconfigured around two *Mistral*-class amphibious assault ships, but the cancelation of the deal with France in mid-2014, due to sanctions, has left it with indefinite prospects.[37] Its flagship cruiser, the *Varyag* (Project 1164, launched in 1983), needs an overhaul and modernization. The arrival, in 2017, of the corvette *Sovershenny* (Project 20380) is not going to add significantly to the Pacific Fleet's strength, even if three more ships of this class are in construction.[38] Problems with new designs for diesel submarines prompted the Russian high command to focus on the still useful Kilo-class

(Varshavyanka, Project 636.3) ships, so six submarines were quickly built in St. Petersburg for the Black Sea Fleet, and two are presently under construction for the Pacific Fleet, with four more contracted.[39] The plan for building a new naval base on the Kurile Islands is much advertised, but it is unclear what ships could be possibly based there.[40]

The Pacific Fleet has a key role in achieving the goal vaguely formulated in the new naval policy as "engagement of foreign states in joint actions aimed at ensuring security and strategic stability in the World Ocean" (Article 29), which means primarily expanding cooperation with China. Joint naval exercises in the South China Sea in September 2016 attracted much international speculation about whether they signify an implicit support from Russia to Chinese claims in this region.[41] In September 2017, joint exercises were hold in the Sea of Japan in order to establish that the US Navy grouping concentrated near the Korean peninsula did not have total dominance in the theater.[42] Moscow is aware that Beijing is particularly interested in exercising amphibious operations, but it is exactly this capability that the Pacific Fleet increasingly lacks. The Ropucha-class (Project 775) large landing ships, including the *Admiral Nevelsky* and *Oslyabya* (built in Poland in 1981–1982), based in Vladivostok, are worn out beyond repair, and the new Ivan Gren series (Project 11711) has been reduced to just two ships, which are supposed to join the Northern Fleet—where this capability is even more exhausted.[43]

Ambitious goals in the naval doctrine translate into increased demands that the Northern and Pacific fleets are able to perform a wide range of tasks; and this accumulating stress increases the risk of accidents, particularly as the aging ships receive insufficient maintenance. In the Arctic seas, harsh conditions are the main challenge. But in the Pacific, military tensions are growing, and Russia's naval grouping is unprepared for possible escalations and de-prioritized when it comes to resource allocations.

Conventional Deterrence and Unconventional Challenges

Russian strategic thinking has evolved fast and far in the last few years when it comes to placing new emphasis on conventional (rather than nuclear) deterrence and on defending against a wide variety of unconventional challenges, often conceptualized as "hybrid wars." In the former proposition, the main instrument is long-range high-precision missiles, particularly the 3M-54 Kailbr (SS-N-27 Sizzler) missile deployed on various naval platforms. As for the latter—though Russia is often portrayed in Western analysis as the main perpetrator of "hybrid wars"—in the Russian perspective, it is the US strategic combination of counter-terrorism, information warfare, and "regime change" methods that brings about a new quality of unconventional warfare.[44] Both doctrinal propositions have different manifestations in the Arctic and Far Eastern theaters.

In the High North, Moscow saw a need to unite various elements of its Armed Forces to be able to perform a particular set of tasks, so a new Arctic (or North) Joint Strategic Command was established in December 2014 on the basis of the Northern Fleet command. The newly created Arctic brigade (based rather inconveniently in Alakurtti, near the border with Finland) thus came directly under the command of the Northern Fleet HQ; but the plan to deploy a second Arctic brigade on the Yamal peninsula was quietly abandoned.[45] The main effort was directed instead on strengthening the air defense system in the western part of the Arctic theater, so several units of S-300 and S-400 surface-to-air missiles (modified for the extreme cold conditions) were deployed on the Kola Peninsula and even on Novaya Zemlya.[46] Instead of the old Soviet naval "bastion," these missiles and radars now form an Anti-Access, Area Denial (A2/AD) "bubble" that protects the main base and the patrol area of Russian strategic submarines and extends into NATO's northern flank.[47] This air superiority grants the army and marine brigades of Russia's Arctic Command, which are brought together in a newly-formed army corps, a significant offensive edge in Northern Europe.[48]

In the Far East, it is difficult to turn conventional deterrence into a workable proposition for Russia. One feasible task is to strengthen the defense of the Kurile Islands: a battery of new Bastion (SS-C-5 Stooge) anti-ship missiles was deployed on Iturup, and a battery of older Bal (SS-C-6 Sennight) anti-ship missiles was delivered to Kunashir. The plan to deploy a new army division to the Kuriles has been corrected—instead, these units will be spread over the Sakhalin, Maritime and Amur regions.[49] The large-scale exercise Vostok 2018, held in August–September of that year, tested the plans for moving reinforcements to the Far Eastern theater, including by the Northern Fleet.[50] The shortage of combat-ready forces in this theater is, however, so deep that Russian experts assume operational planning will focus on the use of non-strategic (tactical) nuclear weapons—even if no strategic guidelines have officially been issued regarding the character of the strikes by the thousands of munitions in this arsenal.[51]

In both the Arctic and the Far East, unconventional security challenges have lower intensity than in such Russian frontier regions as, for instance, the Caucasus, not to mention the barely contained war zone in eastern Ukraine. The threat of terrorism, in particular, is barely present. And yet, this has not stopped the Arctic Command from defining many of its military exercises as counter-terrorist.[52] The only justification for that is the Greenpeace action against the Prirazlomnaya oil platform in September 2013, but there is no shortage of quasi-expert claims about Western "hybrid" encroachments.[53] In fact, international cooperation is crucial for dealing with the many unique challenges in the Arctic, from the disposal of empty barrels and other garbage around the old Soviet bases to containing outbreaks of Anthrax.[54] The responsibility for managing many of these problems is given to the Ministry of Defense, while funding for many civilian projects in the areas of environmental protection and health care is cut.[55] In the Far East, the security issue that is both exaggerated and ignored is the illegal cross-border migration from China, while Moscow's policy of stimulating domestic mobility into the depopulated areas, for instance by such megaprojects as the Vostochny Cosmodrome, is entirely ineffectual.[56] The poaching of fish resources is another major problem, but its international dimension is deeply intertwined with domestic corruption, which is notorious even by Russian standards.[57] The military command stays clear of engaging with these challenges, keeping a low profile in all matters that concern relations with China.

Overall, the pronounced trend of militarization of Russia's policy in the Arctic, only slightly camouflaged by the rhetoric of promoting international cooperation, is not present in the Far East, where Russian conventional military capabilities are insufficient for any power projection and increasingly under-prioritized.

Implications and Prospects

Russian doctrinal views are expansionist in the interpretation of threats that need to be proactively countered but too general to capture the significant differences between the Arctic and the Far Eastern theaters. In fact, Russia finds itself in nearly opposite security situations in these two vast frontiers. In the Arctic, it has a position of military superiority, but cannot find a way to capitalize on it politically or to exploit it for tangible benefit. In the Far East, its position is militarily vulnerable, while its political strategy of building a partnership with China cannot compensate for this weakness.[58] China, in fact, is a hidden but major part of Russia's security problem, and definitely not a part of the solution. Moscow can invite Chinese units to partake in the Vostok 2018 exercises but this cannot alleviate its concerns about the accelerated modernization of the Chinese Armed Forces. The Russian navy can monitor the execution of Beijing's aircraft carrier construction program but cannot hope to see a domestic workable design of such a dream ship.[59]

It is the assessment of Chinese intentions in the Arctic that drives Moscow to expand its military infrastructure along the coast of the Eastern Siberia. China is currently following the new Russian regulations for the Northern Sea Route, but Russian experts warn that climate change could make it possible for Chinese vessels, accompanied by Chinese icebreakers, to set a polar course outside Russia's territorial waters.[60] In the US security community, concerns about Russia's superiority in icebreakers are often emphasized, particularly as the Northern Fleet adds icebreakers to its combat order.[61] Such worries are generally misplaced, since this Russian capability presents no threat to US interests and is aimed at strengthening control over the growing maritime traffic in the long sea lines of communications in the Arctic. The transfer of management of the *Sevmorput* to the state corporation Rosatom, which owns the fleet of nuclear icebreakers, follows the same aim.[62]

Implications of the Russian military build-up in the western part of its Arctic frontier are more difficult for NATO in terms of finding adequate answers. It is hard to say whether Putin's repeated statements about US nuclear submarines "concentrated" off the coast of Norway reflect serious worries about missiles reaching Moscow in just 15 minutes.[63] It is certain, however, that Russian SSBNs are indeed concentrated in the Barents Sea, and that the A2/AD "bubble" covering their patrol area has been strengthened to such a degree that the Arctic Command has gained capabilities to launch offensive operations against NATO's northern flank. The units of this Command train for operations in harsh conditions and have gained combat experience in the Donbas war zone as well as in Syria, where Colonel Valery Fedyanin, the commander of the 61st Marine Brigade of the Northern Fleet, was killed in action.[64]

The Nordic states seek to find a balanced response to this threat, increasing their defense budgets and military cooperation, while also preserving the pattern of cooperation with Russia in various political frameworks. The United States could contribute greatly to the effectiveness of this response by demonstrating a commitment to strengthening the defensive capabilities on NATO's northern flank— and to engage in various cooperative enterprises with Russia in the

High North.[65] It is essential to acknowledge, however, that the modernized US early warning radar at Vardø, Norway, may be among the first targets, should Moscow ever attempt a real power projection experiment in the Arctic.[66] The Svalbard archipelago, over which Norway exercises sovereignty according to the Spitsbergen Treaty (1920), is perceived by the Russian high command as an easy target because it is demilitarized and has a Russian settlement.[67] In the annual assessment of maritime national security, the Russian defense ministry singled out Norway's alleged attempts to establish full sovereignty over Spitsbergen as a particular kind of threat.[68] In this fluctuating and tense situation, both sides are closely monitoring every turn in military activities; and each seeks to compensate for its perceived vulnerabilities. Together, this increases the probability of accidents and miscalculations. And on the Russian side, every technical failure (even of a smaller scale than the *Kursk* disaster in August 2000) could be interpreted as a hostile act by NATO.[69]

In the Far East, Russia is in no position to attempt any proactive military move, but it might find itself compelled to respond to events entirely outside its control. The naval strategic deterrent based in Kamchatka is in no immediate danger but is also of little use in a crisis situation. Whereas, Vladivostok—a major population center and the base of the Pacific Fleet—is quite vulnerable to a possible crisis on the Korean Peninsula. Moscow is trying to enhance its security by following Beijing's lead in managing this crisis, even if it has reservations against the steady tightening of the sanctions regime against Pyongyang. The Russian leadership is worried, however, that China has developed a working cooperative relationship with the US to put pressure on North Korea and has even proceeded to discuss options for sorting out a sudden collapse of the over-militarized regime.[70] Putin may resent being taken for granted by Xi Jinping, but unlike in the Western theater, he cannot put into play military instruments of policy. And the Vostok 2018 exercises, in which a small People's Liberation Army contingent actually took part in for the first time, were ultimately unlikely to impress the Chinese high command.

Overall, in the Far East, Russian strategic thinking centers not on a forthcoming conflict with the United States, as the development of the on-going confrontation would demand, but on a macro-conflict between the US and China, in which Russia would presumably have the advantage of flexibility. In the Arctic, the Russian doctrine aims at both eliminating vulnerabilities in the eastern part of the theater and asserting superiority in the western part, where limited opportunities for projecting power give Russia some leverage in the confrontation with NATO.

Conclusion

The reality of Moscow's evolving confrontation with the West has necessitated changes in the Russian military doctrine. But these changes are only partly reflected in the new set of doctrinal documents, which have actually increased the discrepancy between formal and actual guidelines. The expanded demands on the Armed Forces reveal a mix of the old geopolitical thinking about the multi-polar world, in which competition between centers of power is driven by the struggle to control natural resources, and the new perceptions of a real and growing possibility of a large-scale conflict with the West. The necessary preparations for such conflict, however, cannot square the need for a military build-up with the reality of Russia's domestic economic stagnation. This confusion has different manifestations in the strategic perspectives on the threats and opportunities in the Arctic and Far Eastern theaters.

In the Arctic, the security assessments still do not reflect the economic assessments of the negative cost-efficiency of projects for developing off-shore oil and natural gas resources and continue to confirm the need for Russia to assert control over these presumed natural riches by military means.[71] The strategic guideline to expand Russian military infrastructure in the eastern part of this vast theater—in order to assure control over the Northern Sea Route—clashes with the guideline to build up the capabilities to project power in its western part, which is one of the few areas where Russia has an advantage over NATO. The risks related to maintaining and exploiting this position of power are typically underestimated.

In the Far East, Russian strategic thinking struggles with finding adequate responses to the challenges generated by fast-developing crises, first of all on the Korean Peninsula. The military doctrine is traditionally far less optimistic than high-level politics regarding the rapprochement with China and does not discount the possibility of a conflict.[72] It cannot, however, find any way to counter this threat short of multiple use of non-strategic nuclear weapons, including on Russia's own soil. Any option for proactive engagement in the fluid conflict situations in this theater demands a significant reinforcement of the thinly stretched grouping of forces. But this strategic direction is significantly de-prioritized in the distribution of funding and other resources.

The gap between strategic goal-setting and economic resource allocation is widening across all directions and theaters in Russia's security posture. It is possible to establish that it is in the Far East that the shortage of capabilities is particularly acute, while the Arctic receives more attention and provisions in the 2027 State Armament program than it deserves on the basis of realistic threat/counter-measure calculations. This makes the High North a theater where the Russian high command can, in the short term, contemplate a range of opportunities for using military force as an instrument of confrontational policy. This option could disappear in the medium term as priorities in resource allocation shift to more demanding theaters.

Notes

[1] This trend is examined in Pavel K. Baev, "The military dimension of Russia's connection with Europe," *European Security*, vol. 27, no. 1, 2018, pp. 82–97.

[2] Both statements can be found on the Kremlin website; the former at http://kremlin.ru/events/president/transcripts/56378, and the latter at http://kremlin.ru/events/president/news/56472.

[3] On the disappointment in expectations of an inflow of cross-border investments, see Ivan Zuenko, "The ports of the Far East do not see Chinese investments," *Carnegie.ru* (in Russian), June 26, 2017, http://carnegie.ru/commentary/71383.

[4] Both documents are available at the Russian Security Council website; the former at http://www.scrf.gov.ru/security/docs/document133/, and the latter at http://www.scrf.gov.ru/security/military/document129/.

[5] One useful analysis of this priority is Mark Galeotti, "National Guard: The watchdog that could break the leash", *Raamop Rusland*, August 14, 2017, https://raamoprusland.nl/dossiers/militair-beleid/677-national-guard-the-watchdog-that-could-break-the-leash.

[6] Useful examination of this case is Arild Moe, Daniel Fjærtoft & Indre Øverland, "Space and timing: Why was the Barents Sea delimitation dispute resolved in 2010?" *Polar Geography*, vol. 34, no. 3, pp 145–162.

[7] Russian Defense Ministry presented on its website a virtual tour of this base; see http://mil.ru/files/files/arctic/Arctic.html.

[8] For my initial assessments of that claim, see Pavel K. Baev, "Russia's Race for the Arctic and the New Geopolitics of the North Pole," *Occasional Paper*, Washington DC: Jamestown Foundation, October 2007.

[9] "Gazprom Neft has discovered new offshore field in the Okhotsk Sea," *Press release*, 4 October 2017, http://www.gazprom-neft.com/press-center/news/1166743/.

[10] Nikolai Surkov, Aleksei Ramm, "Bastion on the Kurils," *Izvestia* (in Russian), November 29, 2017, https://iz.ru/676106/nikolai-surkov-aleksei-ramm/bastion-na-kurilakh; Seth Robson, "Putin: Russian buildup on disputed islands is response to

US military," *Stars and Stripes*, June 2, 2017, https://www.stripes.com/news/putin-russian-buildup-on-disputed-islands-is-response-to-us-military-1.471616.

[11] Elena Masyuk, "To love the dragon," *Novaya Gazeta* (in Russian), July 4, 2015, https://www.novayagazeta.ru/articles/2015/07/04/64786-lyubit-drakona.

[12] See Peter Wood, "Xi visits China's Northeast, emphasises revitalization, environment, and food security," *China Brief*, The Jamestown Foundation, June 1, 2016, https://jamestown.org/program/xi-visits-chinas-northeast-emphasizes-revitalization-environment-and-food-security/.

[13] Miles Yu, "Storm over Russian border rages," *Washington Times*, November 12, 2015, http://www.washingtontimes.com/news/2015/nov/12/inside-china-storm-over-russia-border-rages/.

[14] One informed Russian opinion is Igor Denisov, "Aigun, Russia, and China's 'century of humiliation,' " *Commentary*, Carnegie Moscow Center, June 10, 2015, http://carnegie.ru/commentary/60357.

[15] Thomas Nilsen, "Larger portion of Russia's nukes will be on subs in Arctic waters," *Barents Observer*, March 3, 2017, https://thebarentsobserver.com/en/security/2017/03/larger-portion-russias-nukes-will-be-subs.

[16] Aleksandra Dzhordzhevich, Ivan Safronov, "Trillions have two allies – the Army and the Navy," *Kommersant* (in Russian), November 18, 2017, https://www.kommersant.ru/doc/3500710?query=2027.

[17] Vladimir Putin, "Being strong: National security guarantees for Russia," *Rossiiskaya Gazeta* (in Russian), February 20, 2012, https://rg.ru/2012/02/20/putin-armiya.html.

[18] Nikolai Litovkin, "What's wrong with Russia's new Bulava missile?" *Russia Beyond the Headlines*, October 23, 2016, https://www.rbth.com/defence/2016/10/03/whats-wrong-with-russias-new-bulava-missile_635311.

[19] "Putin launched four ballistic missiles in the course of nuclear triad exercises," *Interfax*, October 27, 2017, http://www.interfax.ru/russia/584940.

[20] On the "homecoming" of a pair of Tu-22M3 bombers to the Olenegorsk base from the forward base in Mozdok, North Ossetia, see Thomas Nilsen, "Murmansk

governor welcomes home Syria bombers," *Barents Observer*, December 13, 2017, https://thebarentsobserver.com/en/security/2017/12/murmansk-governor-welcomes-home-syria-bombers.

[21] Bill Gertz, "Russian bombers again circle Guam," *Washington Free Beacon*, December 4, 2015, http://freebeacon.com/national-security/russian-bombers-again-circle-guam/.

[22] Matthew Bodner, Aaron Mehta, "Op tempo, sustainment flaws hit Russian Air Force," *Defense News*, July 12, 2015, http://www.defensenews.com/story/defense/air-space/2015/07/12/russian-fleets-crashing-ukraine-nato-fighter-bomber/29962399/.

[23] Franz-Stephen Gady, "China claims 'new breakthrough in anti-missile cooperation with Russia," *The Diplomat*, December 19, 2017, https://thediplomat.com/2017/12/china-claims-new-breakthroughs-in-anti-missile-cooperation-with-russia/.

[24] Vladimir Dvorkin, "The global threat from the North Korean nuclear-missile capabilities," *Nezavisimoe Voennoe Obozrenie* (in Russian), September 8, 2017, http://nvo.ng.ru/realty/2017-09-08/1_964_korea.html.

[25] David Jozef Volodzko, "China wins its war against South Korea's US THAAD missile shield – without firing a shot," *South China Morning Post*, November 18, 2017, http://www.scmp.com/week-asia/geopolitics/article/2120452/china-wins-its-war-against-south-koreas-us-thaad-missile.

[26] Tom Fedyszyn, "Russia: A land power hungry for the sea," *War on the Rocks*, April 19, 2017, https://warontherocks.com/2017/04/russia-a-land-power-hungry-for-the-sea/.

[27] Bruce Jones, "Russia's Navy sets international strategic markers," *Jane's Navy International*, August 1, 2017, http://www.janes.com/article/72763/russia-s-navy-day-sets-international-strategic-markers.

[28] The text (in Russian) is available at the Kremlin website, http://kremlin.ru/acts/news/by-date/20.07.2017.

[29] Aleksandr Golts, "The Russian Navy: To deter US and to compete with China," *Eurasia Daily Monitor*, The Jamestown Foundation, August 1, 2017, https://jamestown.org/program/the-russian-navy-to-deter-the-us-and-to-compete-with-china/.

[30] Alexei Nikolsky, "New State Armament program will have new priorities," *Vedomosti* (in Russian), May 19, 2017, https://www.vedomosti.ru/politics/articles/2017/05/19/690524-novoi-gosprogrammi.

[31] The original estimate of costs for *Admiral Kuznetsov* overhaul was about $US 900 million, but in the updated plan it is reduced by half, so that modernization would be much reduced; see Mikhail Khodarenok, "Kuznetsov is not in the same league with Washington," *Gazeta.ru* (in Russian), October 15, 2017, https://www.gazeta.ru/army/2017/10/15/10944080.shtml.

[32] Matthew Bodner, "Russia's most anachronistic warship is getting an overhaul," *Moscow Times*, August 31, 2015, https://themoscowtimes.com/articles/russias-most-anachronistic-warship-is-getting-an-overhaul-49252.

[33] Dave Majumdar, "Russia's most powerful nuclear attack submarine is almost ready for sea," *The National Interest*, March 15, 2017, http://nationalinterest.org/blog/the-buzz/russias-most-powerful-nuclear-attack-submarine-ever-almost-19775.

[34] Thoman Nilsen, "Warships of Russia's Northern Fleet sail to Arctic waters," *Barents Observer*, August 15, 2017, https://thebarentsobserver.com/en/security/2017/08/warships-russias-northern-fleet-sail-arctic-waters.

[35] Nikolai Novichkov, "Russian Project 23550 Arctic patrol ship laid down," *Jane's Defence Weekly*, April 25, 2017, http://www.janes.com/article/69803/russian-project-23550-arctic-patrol-ship-laid-down.

[36] On the criminal investigation of this delay, see Anastasiya Vedeneeva, Ivan Safronov, et al, "Arktika is adrift," *Kommersant* (in Russian), July 12, 2017, https://www.kommersant.ru/doc/3351960.

[37] John C.K. Daly, "Russia's Pacific Fleet receives new ships, missions," *Eurasia Daily Monitor*, The Jamestown Foundation, March 12, 2014, https://jamestown.org/program/russias-pacific-fleet-receives-new-ships-missions/.

[38] Alexander Zudin, "Russia's first Pacific-built 20380 frigate sets out on sea trials," *Jane's Defence Weekly*, February 3, 2017, http://www.janes.com/article/67441/russia-s-first-pacific-built-20380-frigate-sets-out-on-sea-trials.

[39] Franz-Stefen Gady, "Russia's Pacific Fleet to receive 10 new warships in 2018," *The Diplomat*, November 29, 2017, https://thediplomat.com/2017/11/russias-pacific-fleet-to-receive-10-new-warships-in-2018/.

[40] Ivan Petrov, "A new Russian naval base will appear on the Kurils," *Rossiskaya Gazeta*, October 26, 2017, https://rg.ru/2017/10/26/reg-dfo/na-kurilah-poiavitsia-baza-vmf-rossii.html.

[41] Aleksandr Khrolenko, "What is interesting about Russian-Chinese exercises in the South-China Sea," *RIA Novosti* (in Russian), September 12, 2016, https://ria.ru/analytics/20160912/1476705773.html.

[42] Matthew Little, "Russia and China send message to US, North Korea with military drills," *The Epoch Times*, December 12, 2017, https://www.theepochtimes.com/russia-and-china-send-message-to-us-north-korea-with-military-drills_2385698.html.

[43] "Large landing ship Ivan Gren resumed trials in the Baltic," TASS (in Russian), June 5, 2017, http://tass.ru/armiya-i-opk/4313765.

[44] Mark Galeotti, *Hybrid War or Gibridnaya Voina?* Prague: Mayak Intelligence, 2016.

[45] Steve Micallef, "Russia's evolving Arctic capabilities," Center for International Maritime Security, February 7, 2017, http://cimsec.org/russias-evolving-arctic-capabilities/30712.

[46] Andrei Kots, "Cold arms: How Russia protects its interests in the Arctic," *RIA Novosti* (in Russian), August 17, 2017, https://ria.ru/defense_safety/20170817/1500406740.html.

[47] Alexei Ramm, Evgeny Andreev, "Russia will be protected from the North by an impenetrable screen," *Izvestia* (in Russian), February 20, 2017, https://iz.ru/news/665208.

[48] Alexei Ramm, Evgeny Andreev, "A new army corps is formed in Murmansk," *Izvestia* (in Russian), April 13, 2017, https://iz.ru/news/681638. The broader perspective is given in Andrew Foxall, "Russia's Policy Toward a Changing Arctic: Implications for UK Security," *Research Paper* 12, Russia Studies Centre, June 2017, http://henryjacksonsociety.org/wp-content/uploads/2017/09/Russias-Policies-towards-a-Changing-Arctic-1.pdf.

[49] "The Ministry of Defense emphasised the defensive character of the division to be deployed in the Kurils," *Interfax*, March 20, 2017, http://www.interfax.ru/russia/554387.

[50] "Shoigu told when the Vostok-2018 exercises would be conducted," *RIA Novosti*, December 5, 2017, https://ria.ru/defense_safety/20171205/1510222671.html.

[51] Vasily Kashin "Each party has its own victory," *EastRussia*, December 12, 2017, https://www.eastrussia.ru/material/vasiliy-kashin-u-vsekh-uchastnikov-svoya-pobeda/.

[52] "The Northern Fleet ships conducted counter-terrorist exercises near the Prirazlomnaya platform," *VPK News* (in Russian), September 5, 2016, https://vpk.name/news/162629_korabli_severnogo_flota_proveli_antiterroristiches kie_ucheniya_u_platformyi_prirazlomnaya.html.

[53] Aleksandr Bartosh, "Hybrid threats have appeared in the Arctic," *Nezavisimoe Voennoe Obozrenie* (in Russian), December 2, 2016, http://nvo.ng.ru/gpolit/2016-12-02/1_928_arctic.html.

[54] Boris Nikolaev, "Garbage in the High North," *Nezavisimaya Gazeta* (in Russian), April 11, 2017, http://www.ng.ru/ng_energiya/2017-04-11/11_6971_north.html.

[55] "Russia postpones implementation of some Arctic projects," *Lenta.ru* (in Russian), July 27, 2017, https://lenta.ru/news/2017/07/27/arcticmedvedev/.

[56] Ivan Tselichtchev, "Chinese in the Russia Far East: A geopolitical time bomb?" *South China Morning Post*, July 8, 2017, http://www.scmp.com/week-asia/geopolitics/article/2100228/chinese-russian-far-east-geopolitical-time-bomb. On the failure to stimulate domestic migration, see Dmitry Shcherbakov, "Outflow of population exceeds explanations," *EastRussia* (in Russian), July 18, 2017, https://www.eastrussia.ru/material/ottok-naseleniya-vykhodit-iz-pod-obyasneniya/.

[57] "Salmon season 2017: How to stop poaching in the rivers of the Far East," TASS (in Russian), May 21, 2017, http://tass.ru/v-strane/4268367.

[58] Pavel K. Baev and Stein Tønnesson, "The troubled Russia-China partnership as a challenge to East Asian peace," *Fudan Journal of the Humanities and Social Sciences*, vol. 10, no. 2, 2017, pp. 209–225.

[59] Alekasndr Ermakov, "Flying sharks of the Celestial Empire," Russian Council, April 27, 2017, http://russiancouncil.ru/analytics-and-comments/analytics/letayushchie-akuly-podnebesnoy/.

[60] Anastasia Bashkatova, "China is looking for alternatives to the Northern Sea Route," *Nezavisimaya Gazeta* (in Russian), October 2, 2017, http://www.ng.ru/economics/2017-10-02/1_7085_china.html.

[61] Robert Farley, "How Russia could win a war in the Arctic," *National Interest*, June 13, 2017, http://nationalinterest.org/blog/the-buzz/how-russia-could-win-war-the-arctic-21134.

[62] Anastasia Vedeneeva, Vladimir Dzaguto, Evgenia Krychkova, Ivan Safronon, "Atomic sea route: Vladimir Putin approved the transfer of the Arctic to Rosatom," *Kommersant* (in Russian), November 8, 2017, https://www.kommersant.ru/doc/3460569.

[63] "Putin: Russia will monitor the activity of US Navy in the Arctic," *RIA Novosti* (in Russian), June 15, 2017 https://ria.ru/defense_safety/20170615/1496565509.html.

[64] Natalya Demchenko, Ilya Nemchenko, "The commander of marine brigade died in Moscow from wounds inflicted in Syria," *RBC* (in Russian), October 1, 2017, https://www.rbc.ru/society/01/10/2017/59d0eb1f9a794765768648ca.

[65] Stephanie Pezard, Abbie Tingstad, Kristin Van Abel, Scott Stephenson, *Maintaining Arctic Cooperation with Russia*. Santa Monica: RAND, 2017, https://www.rand.org/pubs/research_reports/RR1731.html.

[66] Ilya Plekhanov, "In the mountain king's cave: What US marines are hiding in Norway," *RIA Novosti* (in Russian), June 20, 2017, https://ria.ru/analytics/20170620/1496856112.html.

[67] Timo Koivurova, Filip Holiencin, "Demilitarisation and neutralisation of Svalbard," *Polar Record*, vol. 53, no. 2, March 2017, pp. 131–142, https://www.cambridge.org/core/journals/polar-record/article/demilitarisation-and-neutralisation-of-svalbard-how-has-the-svalbard-regime-been-able-to-meet-the-changing-security-realities-during-almost-100-years-of-existence/907DA8BACCA9FE39204C7FBBFC6E1024.

[68] Aleksandra Dzhordzhevich, Ivan Safronov, Dmitri Kozlov, "Geopolitics in support of logistics," *Kommersant* (in Russian), October 10, 2017, https://www.kommersant.ru/doc/3428044.

[69] Mathiew Boulege, "The Russia-NATO relations between a rock and a hard place: How 'defensive inferiority syndrome' is increasing the potential for error," *Journal of Slavic Military Studies*, vol. 30, no. 3, 2017, pp. 361–380.

[70] Charles Clover, "US and China broach sensitive topic of N Korea regime collapse," *Financial Times*, December 19, 2017, https://www.ft.com/content/074feca0-e485-11e7-97e2-916d4fbac0da.

[71] Anastasia Bashkatova, "Arctic is a net loss," *Nezavisimaya Gazeta* (in Russian), March 30, 2017, http://www.ng.ru/economics/2017-03-30/1_6961_arktic.html.

[72] Eugene K. Chow, "Are Russia and China preparing for war?" *National Interest*, August 15, 2017, http://nationalinterest.org/blog/the-buzz/are-russia-china-preparing-war-21907.

4. Baltic Sea Strategy

Jörgen Elfving

Introduction

"First and foremost I would like to point out that the military-political situation on our western border remains tense and has a tendency to intensify."
– Sergei Shoigu, Russian minister of defense, October 27, 2017[1]

The above quotation describes in a nutshell how Russia perceives the situation in the Baltic Sea Region (BSR)—an area comprising not only the Baltic Sea but also the littoral territories that drain into the Baltic, inhabited by more than 85 million people.[2] The BSR has been of crucial importance to Russia throughout its history. But does modern-day Russia have what could be accurately considered a comprehensive and coherent Baltic Sea strategy? One possible answer to this question might draw on the declarations in official documents or statements made by Russian officials and politicians. Indeed, the Russian military doctrine, which calls on deterring and preventing military conflicts "through political, diplomatic and other non-military means," strongly hints at one—especially in the context of Moscow opposing the North Atlantic Treaty Organization's (NATO) enhanced presence in the Baltic States or seeking to block Finnish and Swedish NATO membership.[3] But another approach is to analyze actual Russian activities targeting the countries of the BSR to discern whether they show commonalities suggestive of an underlying strategy. The following chapter will seek to pursue both methodologies in order to build up a detailed outline of Russia's goals in the BSR as well as the ways in which it has been trying to accomplish them.

The Operational Environment

The BSR is a multifaceted and complex area. Its dominant central feature, the Baltic Sea itself, is a brackish inland body of water with a surface area of 377,000 square kilometers (146,000 square miles), the size of Montana; its maximum depth is 459 meters (1506 feet), but with an average depth of only 55 meters (180 feet).[4] These hydrological conditions make the Baltic well suited for submarine warfare. A series of artificial waterways connect the Baltic to the White Sea via the White Sea Canal and to the German Bight of the North Sea via the Kiel Canal.[5] The Baltic Sea is composed of several areas that throughout history have been, and still are, of strategic importance: the mouth of the Gulf of Finland, the Åland Islands, the island of Gotland, and the exit to Kattegat and Skagerrak.

Since ancient times, the Baltic Sea has been an important waterway and remains one of the most heavily trafficked seas in the world, with about 15 percent of global cargo transportation. About 2,000 ships navigate the area at any given time; and on a yearly basis, 7,600 tankers, 17,500 passenger ships and 25,000 other vessels travel through the Baltic.[6] Along the coastline, there are about 200 ports. Russia has led in total port handlings since 2011.[7]

The Baltic Sea is also an important transit corridor for Europe-bound energy resources. Of particular note is the offshore dual-string Nord Stream natural gas pipeline (with an annual capacity of 55 billion cubic meters), which stretches along the seafloor from Vyborg, Russia, to Greifswald, Germany. Presently, Russian Gazprom plans to double its capacity by constructing a parallel dual-string pipeline: Nord

Stream Two. This project has generated protests from a number of European Union members—especially Poland and the Baltic States (Lithuania, Latvia, Estonia), in addition to non-member Ukraine—which argue that it will divert trade and transit revenues away from them and increase European dependence on Russian gas.[8]

Within the BSR, Sweden, Denmark, Germany, Poland, the Baltic States and Finland are members of the European Union. All of the above-mentioned countries are also members of NATO, except for Sweden and Finland, which nevertheless maintain close cooperation with the Alliance. Since 2009, Sweden has maintained a solidarity declaration in addition to a number of bilateral agreements with its neighbors, not least with Finland. The solidarity declaration specifically says that "Sweden will not remain passive if another EU Member State or Nordic country suffers a disaster or an attack. We expect these countries to take similar action if Sweden is affected. Sweden should, therefore, be in a position to both give and receive military support."[9] Following its adoption, the declaration was soon forgotten and remained so until 2014, when Russia annexed Crimea.[10] But in the ensuing, more uncertain European security environment, the solidarity declaration has helped Sweden assure its neighbors and other regional actors of its commitment to common action in case of a crisis in the BSR.

A number of multinational projects further promote regional cooperation within the BSR:

- The European Union Strategy for the Baltic Sea Region (EUSBSR), initiated in 2009, is an agreement between the member states of the EU and the European Commission to strengthen cooperation between the countries bordering the Baltic Sea in order to meet common challenges and to benefit from common opportunities facing the region. The countries involved in the project are Denmark, Estonia, Finland, Germany, Latvia, Lithuania, Poland and Sweden.[11]

- The Council of the Baltic Sea States, a political forum for regional inter-governmental cooperation, brings together Denmark, Estonia, Finland, Germany, Iceland, Latvia, Lithuania, Norway, Poland, Russia, Sweden and a representative from the European Union.[12]

- The Baltic Marine Environment Protection Commission–Helsinki Commission—the governing body of the Convention on the Protection of the Marine Environment of the Baltic Sea Area, known as the Helsinki Convention (HELCOM)—involves the European Union, Denmark, Estonia, Finland, Germany, Latvia, Lithuania, Poland, Russia and Sweden.[13]

- Euroregion Baltic, an institutionalized form of sub-state-level cross-border cooperation in the southeastern part of the BSR, involves eight regions/provinces in Denmark, Lithuania, Poland, Russia, and Sweden.[14]

Finally, it is worth pointing out that each of the Western countries in the BSR are also trade partners with Russia. Indeed, in 2016, Germany and Poland were among Russia's top ten export partners.[15]

History

Throughout recorded history, the BSR has been a battleground for the states situated along the Baltic Sea, which frequently entered these wars in ever-shifting constellations of alliances.[16] Since the 16th century, Russia has strived to reach the eastern seaboard of the Baltic Sea, an aspiration driven by the fact that Russia at that time was in a disadvantageous situation from a maritime point of view: The Black Sea was blocked by Tatars and the Ottoman Turks, whereas the White Sea was remote and hard to reach, both by sea and by land from central Russia.

The Russian "*Drang nach Westen*" resulted in a number of wars with the Swedes. And after defeating Sweden in the Great Nordic War (1700–1721), Russia emerged as the dominant power in in the BSR. This position was soon reinforced by the partition of Poland at the end of the 18th century and Russia's annexation of Finland in 1809. As a result of the 1917 revolutions, however, Russia (soon, the Union of Soviet Socialist Republics, or USSR) temporarily lost its foothold in the Baltic when the Baltic States and Finland emerged as sovereign countries. That situation was reversed thanks to the Molotov-Ribbentrop Pact in August 1939. That led to an unsuccessful war with Finland 1939–1940 and basing of troops in the Baltic States in 1939, followed by their occupation in 1940. In 1941, Finland once more went to war with Soviet Russia—the so-called Continuation War. In order not to be seen as the aggressor, Finland did not initiate hostilities on June 22, when Operation Barbarossa began, but four days later, when Soviet air attacks against Finland gave the Finnish government the pretext needed to open hostilities.[17] The Continuation War ended in 1944; but unlike other countries siding with Nazi Germany, Finland was not occupied by the Soviet Union.

The outcome of the Second World War resulted in the Baltic States being reoccupied, but an active armed resistance against Soviet power raged there from 1944 to 1953.[18] Finland remained free. And in 1947, it signed a peace treaty with the Soviet Union, limiting the size of the Finnish armed forces as well as ceding the Petsamo area, on the Arctic coast, and the Karelian Isthmus, in southeastern Finland, to Moscow. Another provision, in force until 1956, was leasing the Porkkala area near Helsinki to the Soviet Union to use as a naval base, which included free access to the area across Finnish territory.[19] In 1948, Finland signed The Treaty of Friendship, Cooperation, and Mutual Assistance with the Soviet Union; this document was the basis of Soviet-Finnish relations until 1992.[20] The key provisions of the treaty included military cooperation between Finland and the Soviet Union if Germany or a country allied with it attempted to invade Finland or the Soviet Union using Finnish territory as well as military consultations prior to actual cooperation.[21] As such, the 1948 friendship treaty was a tool for the Soviet Union to influence Finland's internal affairs during the Cold War.

In addition to other territorial gains as a result of its victory in WWII, Moscow took possession of the northern part of former East Prussia—today, Kaliningrad oblast. All this, in connection with the establishment of Communist regimes throughout Eastern Europe and the creation of the Warsaw Pact, meant that the Baltic Sea essentially became a *Mare Sovieticum*. That situation lasted until 1991, when the demise of the Soviet Union resulted in a regional security environment rather reminiscent of the period between the first and second world wars. However, there was one major exception: Kaliningrad oblast was now an enclave, effectively cut off from Russia proper, like Germany's East Prussia in 1920–1939.

To a certain extent, it can be said that the history in the BSR is repeating itself. The geopolitical situation in the region today is quite similar to both the beginning of the 1920s as well as the period during the Crimean War, when the combined English and French fleet was able to blockade Russian trade in the Gulf of Finland in 1854 and then bombarded Russian naval bases the following year.[22] At present, due in large part to the annexation of Crimea and subsequent events in eastern Ukraine, NATO's naval activity in the Baltic Sea has significantly intensified.

Doctrines and Concepts

Several preexisting doctrines and concepts, found within five key Russian government documents, offer guidelines for a potential Russian Baltic Sea strategy or at least the principles that might form the basis for such a strategy. The official documents of interest are:

- "The National Security Strategy of the Russian Federation"

- "The Foreign Policy Concept of the Russian Federation"
- "The Military Doctrine of the Russian Federation"
- "The Naval Doctrine of the Russian Federation"
- "Fundamentals of Russia's State Naval Policy Through 2030"

Of the above, the "National Security Strategy" and the "Foreign Policy Concept" are fairly modern, with their most recent iterations written since the events of 2014—the annexation of Crimea and subsequent war in eastern Ukraine.

The "National Security Strategy of the Russian Federation," approved by President Vladimir Putin in December 2015, provides the basis for forming and realizing the state's security-related polices.[23] The strategy opens with an observation that, "In the areas bordering Russia, a process of militarization and an arms race are developing." Both phenomena are ascribed to the United States and the North Atlantic Alliance—particularly, due to the deployment of US missile-defense and high-precision weapons systems close to Russia's borders and due to NATO enlargement. In order to protect Russia's national interests, the document advocates an open, rational and pragmatic foreign policy that avoids a costly confrontation with neighbors, including avoiding a new arms race.

The second vital planning document to consider, the "Foreign Policy Concept of the Russian Federation," was approved by President Putin on November 30, 2016. It provides "a systemic vision of the basic principles, priority areas, goals and objectives of the foreign policy of the Russian Federation."[24] The introduction lists the main objectives of Russia's foreign policy. Among them there are several that arguably, could form part, or even a foundation, of a Baltic strategy:

- To consolidate the Russian Federation's position as a center of influence in today's world.

- To pursue neighborly relations with adjacent States, assist them in eliminating existing as well as preventing the emergence of new hotbeds of tension and conflicts on their territory.
- To ensure comprehensive, effective protection of the rights and legitimate interests of Russian citizens and compatriots residing abroad, including within various international frameworks.
- To bolster the standing of Russian mass media and communication tools in the global information space and convey Russia's perspective on international process to a wider international community.

When it comes to the BSR, it is specifically included in part IV of the document—"Regional Foreign Policy Priorities of the Russian Federation." On the one hand, this section of the foreign policy strategy lauds Russia's role in "Northern Europe" as maintaining trust and stability. But on the other hand, it warningly refers to NATO's expansion, which has "accumulated systemic problems in the Euro-Atlantic region."

On December 25, 2014, a new, fourth version of the "Russian Military Doctrine" was approved, replacing its predecessor from 2010.[25] Interestingly, the doctrine was approved prior to the "National Security Strategy" and not the other way around, which would have been more logical. The "Military Doctrine" differentiates between military risks and military threats. A risk is defined as "a situation in inter-state or intra-state relations characterized by the totality of factors, which can lead to a military threat under certain conditions"; whereas, a threat is described in the document as "a situation in inter-state or intra-state relations characterized by a real possibility of an outbreak of a military conflict between opposing sides and by a high degree of readiness of a given state (group of states) or separatist (terrorist) organizations to resort to military force (armed violence)." The BSR is not specifically mentioned in the doctrine. And yet, there are passages applicable to that area, and these echo analogous points in the "Foreign Policy Concept." Notably, the mentioned military risks include NATO deploying military contingents close to Russia's borders and the enlargement of the Alliance. Other described military risks are the establishment and deployment of strategic missile defense systems and implementation of the global strike concept by Russia's competitors or enemies. Military threats consist of, *inter alia*, "the demonstration of military power during exercises carried out on the territory of countries bordering on the territory of the Russian Federation or its allies' territories." The wording is particularly poignant considering the increased tempo, in recent years, of NATO exercises in Central-Eastern Europe, which routinely receive extensive coverage in the Russian media.[26]

In a 2017 study written for the European Parliament's Sub-Committee on Security and Defense, Isabelle Facon, a senior research fellow at the Fondation Pour la Recherche Stratégique, compares and analyzes the "National Security Strategy" and the "Military Doctrine of the Russian Federation."[27] Her study concludes that the present strained relations between Russia and the West long predates 2014 and the Ukrainian crisis.[28] Furthermore, according to Facon's analysis, the Strategy and the Doctrine both focus on the challenges that the Western states supposedly create for Russia's security and, tellingly, the two documents "emphasize the importance of the role of military force in international relations, suggesting that Russia has a legitimate right to develop adequate military power to answer this international trend (which, again, it tends to attribute primarily to the West)." Finally, the study draws attention to Moscow's perception of the West as an obstacle to realizing its ambitions in the post-Soviet space—i.e., in the former, and now independent, Soviet republics.[29]

The 2015 Russian "Naval Doctrine" is, according to its preamble, the primary document determining the country's national naval policy.[30] It comprises of four functional sections—sea transportation, exploitation and preservation of natural resources, maritime science, and maritime military activities. Additionally, the "Naval Doctrine" is divided into six geographic sections—the Atlantic Ocean, the Arctic, the Caspian Sea, the Indian Ocean and the Antarctic. Of these areas, the Atlantic Ocean and the Arctic are accentuated due, according to the doctrine, to NATO activities in those theaters and the Alliance moving closer to Russia's borders. The Baltic Sea might been expected to be highlighted, but that is actually not the case. The section covering the Baltic is relegated to a subsection within the portion on the Atlantic Ocean. Moreover, it is described in rather general terms, mentioning only the need to develop maritime transportation, the shipbuilding industry, tourism and fishing, as well as to create preconditions for stable economic development in cooperation with other BSR countries, to jointly use the Baltic's maritime natural assets in a sensible way, and to generate comprehensive confidence-building measures in all areas of maritime activities. In addition to this, the Naval Doctrine mentions the development of Baltic Fleet basing, but it avoids going into any details on the matter.

On July 20, 2017, the Russian president approved the "Fundamentals of Russia's State Naval Policy Through 2030."[31] This document does not replace, but rather supplements the above-described 2015 "Naval Doctrine" and reflects the Russian Military-Maritime Fleet's (*Voyenno-Morskoy Flot*—VMF) improved capabilities, evolving strategic and operational role, and future ambitions. The document might probably be linked to the finalization of the armament program for the period 2018–2027, with the intention to strengthen the VMF's hand regarding its future development

The conclusion is interesting and says a little about how Russia views the role of its navy: "Trends in the development of the current geopolitical situation in the world convincingly confirm that only the presence of a strong Navy will secure the Russian Federation a leading position in a multipolar world in the 21st century, as well as enable the state to effectively implement and protect its national interests."

Like the "Military Doctrine," the "State Naval Policy" document differentiates between what Moscow views as military risks and military threats. Among these, two (characterized somewhat ambiguously as both risks and threats) are presumably directly applicable to the BSR:

- The pursuit by a number of countries of means to limit the Russian Federation's access to assets in the World Ocean and its access to vital maritime lines of communication.
- The deployment of ship-based strategic, non-nuclear, high-precision weapons, but also ship-based anti-missile systems, in waters and the World Ocean adjacent to the Russian Federation.

The document outlines a series of primary objectives of naval operations in support of Russia's foreign policy. And among those, it lists ensuring "a sufficient naval presence of the Russian Federation in strategically important areas of the World Ocean, as well as showing the flag and demonstrating the military power of the Russian Federation." Another frequent theme is cooperation with foreign countries, for example to ensure security and stability in the World Ocean.

Russia and the Baltic States

As a result of having been part of the Russian Empire between the 18th century until 1918, and then undergoing nearly continuous occupation by the Soviet Union from 1940 to 1991, the Baltic States have a distinct relationship to Russia. Based on that historical heritage, and reinforced by an uncertainty concerning how post-Soviet Russia would develop politically, Lithuania, Latvia and Estonia put membership in NATO and the EU high on their foreign policy agendas soon after recovering their independence in 1991; those twin goals were accomplished in 2004. Yet, Euro-Atlantic integration, combined with diverging views on their shared history with Russia strained the Baltic States' relations with their large eastern neighbor. It is worth noting that in 1991, neighborly relations could easily have developed in a more positive trajectory. At first, the newly independent Baltic States and Russia followed similar paths to transition—i.e. democratization and market economy reforms. Furthermore, the Baltics' strive for independence at the time coincided with then–Russian president Boris Yeltsin's ambitions to dismantle the Soviet Union. However, this congruence of interests did not last, leading to decades of various levels of crises and conflicts that culminated in the aftermath of Russia's annexation of Crimea and the ongoing Moscow-sponsored war in eastern Ukraine.[32] The widely held notion, and hope, of the Baltic States acting as "a bridge" between Europe and Russia has, for the time being, been shelved; but Lithuanian President Dalia Grybauskaitė has hinted that it might one day still be possible.[33]

The Russian view of the Baltic States is perhaps best characterized by a passage published on the news portal *RuBaltic.ru*, whose chief editor, Sergey Rekeda, is a well-known expert on the Baltic States at the Moscow State University:

> The international situation has discarded the last decades' balance of power. The world now oscillates between trying to form a new international security architecture and ossifying into opposing blocs. In this context Lithuania, Latvia and Estonia emerge as some of the most active lobbyists of the realization of the second scenario in European region. This activity of the Baltic republics corresponds with the internal political processes presently developing in Lithuania, Latvia and Estonia—the growth of authoritarian tendencies, deterioration of the economic situation, social degradation, etc.[34]

That view not only influences Moscow's relations with the Baltic States, but also Russian activities directed against them.

One important aspect in the BSR is the presence of a Russian minority still living in the Baltic States. As a percentage of the overall population, Russians made up 25 percent in Estonia (as of 2017), 25.6 percent in Latvia (2016) and 5.8 percent in Lithuania (2011).[35] The levels of integration of these minorities in their respective societies are mixed; and as such, they represent a possible tool of subversion for Russia against these countries. Indeed, the unrest in connection with the removal of a Soviet war memorial in Tallinn (the Bronze Soldier), in 2007, illustrates how Moscow has previously exploited this tool.[36] That said, the present-day level of susceptibility among the younger generation of Baltic Russians to ideas linked to the so-called "Russian World" (*Russkiy Mir*), or whether they can truly be characterized as Russian "compatriots," is open to debate. Indeed, judging by the conclusions reached by Agnia Grigas in her book *Beyond Crimea: The New Russian Empire*, neither may be particularly strong today—a trend that may become even more pronounced as the older generation of Baltic Russians fades away.[37]

Nonetheless, several political parties in the Baltic States continue to attract the local Russian minority and maintain links to Russia:

- The Center Party in Estonia holds 27 seats in the parliament as of mid-2018. Since November 23, 2016, it has headed a coalition government, with Center Party leader, Jüri Ratas, serving as Estonian prime minister.[38] The party has maintained a cooperation agreement with United Russia since 2004.[39] In May 2017, the then–minister of public administration and member of the Center Party, Mihhail Korb, stated at a meeting with army that he was not in favor of Estonia's membership in NATO, which later led to his resignation.[40]
- The Harmony Party in Latvia won 22 seats in the parliament in the October 2018 elections, but it is not represented in the current coalition government. Its leader, Nils Ušakovs, stated in connection with a visit to Russia in September 2014, that

Putin is the best president for Latvia.[41] The party signed a cooperation agreement with United Russia. And though this agreement was recently said to have been canceled, Riga mayor and Saskaṇa (Harmony) Party leader Nils Ušakovs declared that "a pragmatic cooperation with Russia would remain important in the future."[42] Another party with Russian links is the Latvian Russian Union. Presently, this political faction has no seats in the national legislature.

- In Lithuania, the chairman of the Farmers and Greens Union, Ramunas Karbauskis, is thought to maintain close ties to Russia.[43]

Russia also supports non-governmental organizations (NGO) in the Baltic States that are supportive of Russian policies. An investigation in 2015 revealed that more than 40 such NGOs had received financial support from Russia.[44]

This mixture of local Russian minorities, political parties with links to Russia and Moscow-funded NGOs provides Russia with potential leverage to influence the Baltic States. As Igor Korotyenko, the editor of the Russian journal *National Defense* and a conservative military hardliner, noted in a March 2016 interview with *Pravda,*

We [Russia] have enough powerful resources to influence the Baltic countries both using economic tools and via the media. In that aspect we should strengthen our informational and propaganda activities to influence the media market in the Baltic States because "nothing ventured, nothing gained." [...] We should engage in a coherent reformatting of the political area, which today is not friendly to us, and make it either neutral or friendly.[45]

In March 2014, the EU imposed sanctions on Russia in response to the latter's actions against Ukraine's sovereignty and territorial integrity. Later that year, in August, Russia responded to the Western sanctions by adopting a ban on selected agricultural products from the EU, the US, Canada, Australia and Norway.[46] Both the European sanctions and the Russian ban are still in effect, as of early-2019. They have had a deleterious economic impact on the Baltic States, particularly for their food exports. For instance, over 90 percent of the Baltic States' cheese exports went to Russia prior to the ban.[47]

The seaports of the Baltic States are also closely linked to Russian infrastructure, such as important transnational east-west roadways, along which Russian goods are exported to global markets. But in the last 10–15 years, the volume of Russian goods transiting through the Baltic countries has declined.[48] For example, in 2015, nine million tons of Russian oil exports transited via the Baltic States, compared with five million tons in 2016; and this transit of oil products was projected to completely cease in 2018.[49]

Intertwined electricity and gas networks represent another Soviet legacy. The Baltic States operate on a Soviet-era power system, connecting them with Russia and Belarus. But as a result of the changed geopolitical situation, they are now determined to separate their systems to become more independent of the Russian operator.[50] It is important to point out that Russia has never cut the electricity flow to the Baltics or threatened to do so. Nevertheless, by 2025 the Baltic States will, with the support of the EU, decouple their power networks from Russia.[51] Meanwhile, dependence on Russian natural gas had allowed Moscow to charge high prices and made the gas networks vulnerable to Russian influence. This situation is now changing, however, thanks to imports of liquefied natural gas (LNG), increasing connections with the rest of Europe, and Gazprom's decreasing influence as a supplier to Baltic gas markets. All these above-mentioned measures aim explicitly at decreasing the Baltic States' dependence on Russia for gas imports.[52]

In addition, Russia has frequently challenged the Baltic States' sovereignty via military aircraft intruding their airspace. Among the most provocative cases involved the abduction, in 2014, of an Estonian security service operative by Russian agents from an Estonian border post, on Estonian territory. The kidnapped Estonian officer was later taken to Moscow and tried for espionage.[53]

Russia has responded to the presence of multinational NATO forces in the three Baltic States by apparently orchestrating the publishing and propagating of so-called "fake news," reporting on supposed incidents involving Alliance soldiers, with the aim of undermining NATO's regional presence.[54] Such false media accounts often describe NATO soldiers as rapists or drunkards seeking fights with local inhabitants. In one example, Russian-linked media outlets charged German soldiers stationed in Lithuania with fabricated rape claims— bringing to mind the earlier "Lisa case" in Germany. Emails claiming that German soldiers had raped an underage Lithuanian girl were sent to the speaker of the Lithuanian parliament and Lithuanian media. The allegations were investigated by the Lithuanian police, which found no evidence of any wrongdoing or any truth to the sent emails.[55]

Russia and the Other Countries in the BSR

Russia views its western BSR neighbors, Denmark, Finland, Germany, Poland and Sweden, as countries in decay due to their emerging multicultural societies, the influx of immigrants, the legal recognition of same-sex marriage, and so on. In a speech in 2013, President Putin notably claimed,

> We can see how many of the Euro-Atlantic countries are actually rejecting their roots, including the Christian values that constitute the basis of Western civilization. They are denying moral principles and all traditional identities: national, cultural, religious and even sexual. They are implementing policies that equate large families with same-sex partnerships, belief in God with the belief in Satan.[56]

Additionally, the countries in question are, to varying degrees, depicted in Russia as "russophobic."

These states' relations with Russia and the way Moscow behaves against them varies, depending on a number of key factors, including history, membership status in NATO, as well as the actual degree—perceived or real—of their levels of "russophobia."

Denmark

Denmark is a major Arctic power and a small European nation. In the wake of the annexation of Crimea and the ensuing events in Ukraine, its relations with Russia have notably developed in a negative direction.[57] According to the Russian propaganda outlet *Sputnik*, "Over the past [few] years, Denmark's relations with Russia have been marked by tension, which was exacerbated by EU sanctions and the Nordic countries' paranoid fear of Russian 'aggression.' "[58] On the other hand, a 2016 report by the Danish Ministry of Foreign Affairs notes,

> Denmark should support the EU position on a common, robust and principled stance externally, as well as cohesion and resilience internally. This is to be accomplished especially through joint EU sanctions and NATO commitments, including Danish participation in training exercises in the neighboring area. Firmness should not stand alone, but must be backed by dialogue with Russia on the basis of established principles and cooperation in areas of mutual interest.[59]

Moreover, in recent years, Danish media has continued to depict Russia in a negative way. Pointedly, an August 2017 article in the Danish newspaper *Jyllands-Posten* asserts that Russia is a substantial threat.[60]

The deterioration in bilateral Danish-Russian relations stems from more than just Crimea and the Ukraine crisis; it also dates back to the hacking attacks of the Danish defense ministry, in 2015 and 2016, by the group APT 28 (also known as Pawn Storm, Sofacy and Fancy Bear), which is linked directly to the Russian government and security services. The APT 28 hacks managed to gain access to Danish defense ministry employees' emails.[61] Moreover, relations suffered in 2015, when the Russian ambassador to Copenhagen warned Denmark against becoming part of the US missile defense shield, stating that in such a case, Danish warships could become targets for Russian nuclear strikes.[62]

The right-wing populist *Danish People's Party (DPP), which won* 21.1 percent of the vote in the 2015 elections and became Denmark's second-biggest political faction in the parliament, has been accused of pro-Russian leanings.[63] Indeed, in its appearances on Danish media, the party frequently seems to express opinions favorable to Russian positions. Moreover, Russia's propaganda news channel *RT* mentions the DPP twice as much as other Danish parties.[64]

Germany

Germany has enjoyed an on-and-off special relationship with Russia since the time of Chancellor Otto von Bismarck. Subsequently, bilateral relations became notably cordial during the 1920s, with closer military cooperation, culminating perhaps most dramatically for Central-Eastern Europe with the 1939 German-Soviet Non-Aggression Pact signed by foreign ministers Joachim von Ribbentrop and Vyacheslav Molotov. During the Cold War, in the 1960s, the German government's policy of *Ostpolitik* also encouraged closer ties with Moscow. Following the collapse of the Soviet Union, the two countries again grew closer due to expanding trade and cultural ties. This situation reversed abruptly in 2014, however. German President Frank-Walter Steinmeier, in connection with his visit to Moscow in October 2017, characterized the bilateral situation as "...far from [having] normal ties, open wounds are still out there, there are unresolved issues, first and foremost it concerns the takeover of Crimea and the conflict in eastern Ukraine, which are a burden and continue to be a burden for our ties."[65] And a Swiss paper described the present German-Russian relations more bluntly as being in a state of permafrost.[66] Russian analyst Olga Lebedeva ascribes these current tensions to the political agreements Germany has signed with the EU and NATO.[67] Nevertheless, a majority of respondents (58 percent) to a German poll conducted in fall 2017 supported improving relations with Russia—an opinion that has also been increasingly entering German political debate.[68]

Frozen relations have also impacted on Russo-German trade. Russian exports to Germany in 2016 declined by 16.1 percent, and Russia's imports from Germany dropped by 4.8 percent.[69]

Russian media is frequently accused of waging an information war against Germany. As such, Moscow is assumed to be pursuing the following objectives: exaggerate problems for Germany connected to the European migrant crisis, push Berlin to relax its backing for EU sanctions against Russia, as well as weaken voter trust in Chancellor Angela Merkel.[70] A particularly famous example has been the above-mentioned "Lisa case": In January 2016, Russian television reported on a 13-year-old Russian-German girl who had allegedly been raped by migrants. The story turned out to be a fake but was given extensive coverage in Russian domestic and foreign media and resulted in diplomatic tensions between Berlin and Moscow.[71]

Two German political parties exhibit significantly more pro-Russian attitudes than any other domestic party: Alternative for Germany *(AfD) and the* National Democratic Party (NPD). The latter is a right-wing extremist faction with practically no national political influence. The nationalist-populist AfD, however, received 12.6 percent of the vote in the September 2017 parliamentary elections and entered the parliament. It is routinely accused of having been financed by Russia, and some of its members have acted as unofficial election observers in eastern Ukraine and Crimea.[72]

Between 1950 and 2014, 2.4 million Russian-Germans immigrated to Germany from the former Soviet Union. Consequently, this immigrant group has the largest number of eligible voters in Germany,[73] a fact that makes them a tempting target for Russian propaganda and might, to a certain extent, help explain the AfD's electoral success.[74]

Prior to the 2017 German parliamentary elections, speculation was rife that Russia would attempt to influence the vote, as happened with the earlier US and French presidential elections. Ultimately, however, no such attempts were noted, to the disappointment of some observers.[75]

Poland

Poland's traditional distrust of Russia, its usual strong support for common EU policies as well as its complex history with neighboring Ukraine all impact on bilateral relations with Moscow. That relationship became even chillier following then-president Lech Kaczyński's death in a plane crash in 2010 over Smolensk and its aftermath as well as the 2014 annexation of Crimea. Indeed, according to current Polish President Andrzej Duda, speaking in late 2017, "After all, it was not only with Ukraine, but also earlier with Georgia, in 2008; and one should not pretend that it [Russian invasions of both of those former Soviet countries] did not happen. If we pretend that this does not exist, then this will lead to a tragic ending as history has already taught us." Duda added that Russia is constantly acting in a way that cannot in any way be politically accepted.[76] And former Polish foreign minister Witold Waszczykowski asserted around the same time that, in his view, Russia is not interested in maintaining a dialogue with Poland.[77]

A June 2017 report published by the Polish Ministry of Defense explicitly describes Russia as a threat to Poland and other countries in the region, but also for other state actors desiring a stable international order. Furthermore, the report claims that it is not unrealistic that Russia could incite a regional conflict and drag one or several NATO countries into it.[78]

Gazprom estimates that Russian gas deliveries meet 60 percent of Poland's domestic demand.[79] Poland, like the Baltic States, wants to phase out these Russian energy imports in order to address its vulnerability to potential "political actions" by Moscow using the "energy weapon." Warsaw's intention is to become completely independent of Russian gas supplies after 2022, when the present gas purchase agreement expires.[80]

Russian trade with Poland has halved since 2014, as a result of Russia banning the import of Polish fruit and vegetables. In 2013, Poland exported €1.3 billion ($1.5 billion) worth of agricultural products to Russia; and by 2015, that amount dropped to €398 million ($476 million).

While Poland is also subjected to Russian soft power, a recent study by the Budapest-based think tank Political Capital concludes that such leverage has been significantly less successful than in neighboring Hungary, Slovakia or Czechia (the Czech Republic).[81] Moscow's attempted use of soft power in Poland is driven by the fact that Russian political influence over the country is limited; the political establishment and Poles in general have a largely unfavorable attitude toward Russia due to deep social, historical and political preconditions. Moscow's direct political influence extends to only a handful of domestic actors, mainly around the fringe political party Zmiana (Polish for "change"). Founded in 2015, with Mateusz Piskorski as its chairperson, Zmiana espouses a strong anti-American position, openly supports Putin's politics, and sees Russia as a natural ally for both Poland and the European Union.[82] In the spring of 2016,

Piskorski was detained by Poland's Internal Security Agency and charged with "cooperation with Russian intelligence services, meeting intelligence officers, and undertaking operational tasks from them as well as accepting payments."[83] The pro-Russian Zmiana leader also founded the European Center for Geopolitical Analysis in Warsaw, an organization financed at least in part with obfuscated Russian money. Over the past decade, the Center has organized a series of trips for non-official election observers to dubious elections, including in Abkhazia and Transnistria.[84]

Finland

Sweden and Finland are special cases within the BSR: they are not NATO members but carry on extensive cooperation with the Alliance and maintain intense internal debates regarding possible future membership. Finland also differs markedly in its bilateral relations with Russia compared with the other countries in the region. Despite the changed European security situation since 2014, Helsinki has preserved high-level contacts with Moscow, such as the visits to Finland by the Russian foreign minister in May 2017 and the Russian president that following July.[85] According to Finnish Foreign Minister Timo Soini, "We have been here for centuries and we know them [Russia] and they know us. They respect our consistent approach to them. They do not respect crawling on knees."[86] This attitude seems to be largely reflected by the Russian side: its foreign ministry spokesperson, Maria Sacharova, noted in a 2016 interview that Russia and Finland have managed to maintain positive cooperation despite negative relations between the EU and Russia.[87] This attitude on the part of Helsinki can be explained by Finland having a 1,340 km (830-mile) border with *Russia, the experience of relations with Russia since the presidency of* Urho Kekkonen (president in 1956–1982), and high levels of bilateral trade. In 2016, Finnish exports to Russia amounted to €6.145 billion ($7.589 billion) and imports from Russia totaled €2.977 billion ($3.561billion), making Russia Finland's third most important trade partner.[88]

One stumbling block in relations between the two countries is the possibility of Finland one day choosing to join NATO. Today, that outcome still seems quite distant. The majority of Finns are against membership: in a fall 2017 poll, 59 percent of respondents rejected Finland becoming part of the Alliance, and only 22 percent approved of joining.[89] Considering such limited popular support, it is unlikely that Finnish politicians will actively pursue NATO membership any time soon, particularly since any move to join the North Atlantic bloc would require public approval via a referendum.[90] Nevertheless, Russia continues to actively warn Finland against joining NATO. Illustratively, in October 2017, the Russian ambassador to Finland stated, "While each country has the right to define its own national security and defense policy, everyone understands that should the NATO infrastructure advance towards our borders, Russia would be forced to take appropriate countermeasures.[91] A similar warning has also been given to Sweden at several occasions.

In comparison with other BSR countries, Finland appears to be relatively less targeted by Russian subversion. Yet, potential cases can be observed. During the first two months of 2016, about 1,000 asylum seekers entered Finland from Russia compared with 700 in 2015.[92] This breached common border practices without actually breaking any official agreements and might have been a signal from Moscow that good working relations cannot be taken for granted and that the consequences of losing Russia's trust could be significant for Finland. Indeed, during subsequent bilateral negotiations over the asylum seekers, a Russian official appeared to underscore the above sentiment when he told his Finnish counterpart that Russia has 11 million foreigners living on its territory.[93] In another example, a 2016 report from the Finnish security police notes that foreigners, "Russians," have bought property in sensitive areas on Finnish soil in anticipation of a future "crisis situation."[94]

Sweden

In comparison with Finland, relations between Sweden and Russia are more strained and more similar to those of other countries in the BSR. One contributing factor is probably also the fact that Russia is domestically seen as Sweden's archenemy as a result of the wars fought with Russia. A 2017 poll published by the Pew Research Center showed that only 18 percent of Swedes had a positive view of Russia.[95]

Swedish-Russia trade contracted in recent years. In 2016, Swedish exports to Russia amounted to 14 billion Swedish crowns ($1.700 billion) compared with 23 billion ($2.793 billion) in 2012; while, imports from Russia in 2016 amounted to 32 billion crowns ($3.887 billion), almost half of what it had been in 2012.[96]

Like the Finns, a majority of Swedes are opposed to NATO membership: a poll from July 2017 showed 43 percent against and 32 percent in favor of joining the North Atlantic Alliance.[97] At the same time, however, the debate concerning NATO membership seems also to be more intense in Sweden than Finland—although it tends to flare up in connection with activities related to cooperation with the Alliance or sudden appearances of Russian submarines off the Swedish coast or similar provocative incidents. Sweden has also frequently been warned by Russia against joining NATO. In June 2017, Putin declared, "We will consider this [Sweden's joining NATO] as an additional threat to Russia and will search for ways to eliminate it."[98] The same message has also been delivered on separate occasions by the Russian foreign minister, the Russian ambassador to Sweden and the Russian foreign ministry's spokesperson.[99] Due to Swedish and Finnish participation in NATO exercises, the development of their interoperability with NATO, and Sweden's host nation agreement with the Alliance, Russia regards Sweden, and possibly also Finland, as covert NATO members.[100] This accusation particularly comes to the surface when Russian media comments upon Swedish participation in Alliance exercises or other activities related to NATO. Therefore, it is possible to assume that the measures Moscow has threatened to take as a result of a Swedish and Finnish NATO membership have already been implemented as part of Russia's military planning.

Sweden has also been a target of what is assumed to be Russian "active measures," for example:

- Fake letters. One such forged document, which surfaced on online social media, was purportedly signed by the Swedish minister of defense and concerned the sale of artillery pieces to Ukraine.[101]
- Infiltration of local political parties.[102]
- Attempts to influence public opinion in order to prevent the signing of a *Host Nation* Support *Agreement* with NATO.[103]
- A simulated bombing attack on Good Friday 2013.[104]
- A series of articles by the Russian ambassador in Swedish papers. In an October 2017 piece, he pleaded for better relations between Sweden and Russia.[105]

In addition, there are also the recurring reports of suspicious underwater activities in the Swedish archipelago, but so far none of these have been conclusively linked to a specific country.

Besides what is mentioned above, the Russian intelligence and security services—the Foreign Intelligence Service (SVR), Federal Security Service (FSB) and military intelligence (GRU)—are active in the Baltic States and the other Western countries in the BSR. Many of these activities continue to be highlighted in yearly reports published by the security services of Germany, Latvia and Lithuania, for instance.[106]

In the Western BSR countries, there are also a number of organizations and societies for the Russian diaspora or for friendship with Russia and the like. How many of these organizations actually exist is difficult to establish, but judging from the Swedish experience, some of them have sprung up since the spring of 2014 to promote Russian views. Nevertheless, their impact on public opinion tends to be marginal at best.

A more immediate source of concern is Russia's increased military activity in the BSR, which includes relatively frequent airspace and territorial water violations and incidents. For example, in June 2017, a Russian Su-27 Flanker flew dangerously close to a Swedish Air Force S102B Korpen on an intelligence gathering mission over the Baltic Sea.[107] As the general security situation has *deteriorated* and tensions have risen, there is a risk that such provocative behavior could lead to a miscalculation, mid-air accident, loss of human life and/or uncontrolled escalation.

Kaliningrad Oblast

Kaliningrad oblast, formerly the northern part of the German province of East Prussia, is an exclave sandwiched between Poland to the south and Lithuania to the north and east. As of February 2016, the oblast numbered 975,600 inhabitants and has an area of 12,430 square kilometers (4,799 square miles), roughly the size of Connecticut. The port of Kaliningrad is the only ice-free Russian port on the Baltic Sea. It is one of the largest regional port complexes both in terms of volumes of processed goods and in terms of technical support and services provided to cargo owners.[108]

East Prussia was partitioned and its northern portion was annexed by the Soviet Union in the aftermath of the Second World War (the southern section was appended to post-war Poland). Particularly starting in 1944, the region saw bitter fighting and suffered extensive destruction. As a result of the fighting and annexation, the German population either fled or was expelled. During the Soviet era, the renamed Kaliningrad oblast was a closed military zone; but that ended in 1991, when possibilities opened up for cooperation with foreign countries.[109] This raised hopes locally and abroad that the exclave would become a Russian gateway to Europe and a Baltic Hong Kong, hopes that have not materialized. In spite of its ice-free port and proximity to the EU, Kaliningrad oblast has relatively high unemployment and lower salaries than the Russian average. Additionally, customs and transport costs raise local consumption prices, which, combined with low salaries, lower Kaliningrad's living standards.[110]

A 1997 PONARS study suggested five possible future scenarios for Kaliningrad oblast:[111]

1. The continuation of a heavily militarized exclave under Russia's direct jurisdiction.
2. Far-reaching autonomy for the oblast with a continued military presence, though perhaps at reduced levels.
3. Far-reaching autonomy for the oblast and demilitarization.
4. A transfer of the oblast to Lithuania, Poland, or Germany.
5. An attempt by the oblast to secede or to negotiate independence.

Twenty years later, the first scenario has come to pass: Kaliningrad oblast is clearly a militarized exclave directly controlled by the central government in Moscow. As a result of the withdrawal of Soviet/Russian forces from Eastern Europe, the oblast become a reception area for those units and, consequently, became heavily militarized. In 1994, the Kaliningrad defensive district was formed and later, in 1998, renamed the Kaliningrad special district, unifying the ground, naval, air and air-defense units under a common command, i.e. the Baltic Fleet.[112] The 1990s saw a substantial (albeit temporary) downsizing of the military presence in oblast, with personnel reduced from 25,000 to 11,600; additionally, hundreds of tanks, combat vehicles and artillery were transferred to Russia proper or put in storage, and the number of ships in the Baltic Fleet was reduced from 200 to 40.[113] This changed in 2009, when the then–chief of the Russian General Staff, General Nikolay Makarov, declared that Kaliningrad oblast would be completely rearmed by 2012.[114] Later, in January 2015, the region was singled out as an area, together with the Arctic and occupied Crimea, to be given priority in terms of rearmament and development of military capabilities.[115]

But until 2016, not much happened in the Kaliningrad oblast compared with the Arctic and Crimea. The reason for this might be linked to the dismissal of the former commander of the Baltic Fleet, Vice Admiral Viktor Kravchuk, and a number of other officers in June of that year.[116] Alternatively, Moscow may have decided that, by 2016, the time had come to more assertively counter NATO in the BSR. Or perhaps, there appeared to be growing likelihood at that point of Sweden and Finland joining NATO.

Whatever the reason, developments in Kaliningrad oblast since 2016 have included, *inter alia*:

- The formation of the 11th Army Corps in April 2016.
- News suggesting an upgrading of the 7th Mechanized Regiment to a full brigade.[117]
- Rearming the 152nd Missile Brigade with Iskander-M theater ballistic missiles in November 2017.[118]
- The transfer of two corvettes from the Black Sea Fleet to the Baltic Fleet in November 2016; another three of the same class will reportedly be added prior to 2020.[119]
- Providing the 25th Coastal Missile Regiment with Bal missiles and possibly upgrading the regiment to a brigade.[120]
- Completion of equipping the 336th Naval Infantry Brigade with BTR-82A combat vehicles during 2017.[121]
- Providing the Baltic Fleet with Su-30SM fighters—one aircraft in 2016 and five in 2017.[122]
- Plans to set up two new air regiments.[123]

- Refurbishing of infrastructure—notably, Chakalovsk airbase.[124]
- A Russian-Chinese naval exercise in the Baltic Sea in July 2017.[125]

The above should not be treated as isolated events. They must be seen within the broader context of what has taken place in the Western Military District, which has a substantial impact on the BSR. According to the Chief of the Russian General Staff the following units have been set up in the Western Military District during 2012–2017:[126]

- One tank army, i.e. the 1st Guards Tank Army.[127]
- One army corps, i.e. the 11th Army Corps.[128]
- Three mechanized divisions, among them the 3rd and the 144th Mechanized Division,[129] and probably also the 2nd Guards Mechanized Division.[130]
- One tank division, probably the 4th Guards Tank Division.[131]
- Two artillery brigades.

This is not the complete picture, as a number of other units have also been organized. It cannot be excluded that additional military formations will be organized in the Western Military District over time, including potentially in Kaliningrad oblast, even though its size limits how many new units would be able to be housed locally. It remains open to debate whether the recently organized units are fully manned and equipped or what their operational capabilities actually look like in practice. Indeed, information gleaned from Russian open sources suggests that at least some of these units are not yet fully manned nor equipped and lack full operational capability. However, their weaknesses may still be rectified in the long run. It is worth noting that Russian military expert Aleksandr Golts assesses that the new divisions are cadre units, only to be manned with reservists during a full-scale mobilization in wartime—i.e., a return to Soviet practice.[132]

All that said, Russia has deployed substantial forces in and around the Baltic—ground, airborne/air assault, naval, and air defense units—giving Moscow the possibility to carry out either offensive or defensive operations in the BSR and to create a robust A2/AD bubble over the area. Moreover, the forces present in the Western Military District can easily be reinforced from elsewhere in Russia—something Moscow has annually practiced on a large scale. Indeed, this is a recurring feature in connection with the larger exercises carried out on a yearly basis, including Vostok, Zapad, etc. The Russian Armed Forces, including those of the Western Military District, are significantly better trained and operate under higher readiness levels today than they did than in 2008, during the war with Georgia. Moreover, the ongoing Syrian operation and intervention in eastern Ukraine have provided the Russian military with valuable combat experience.

Conclusion

Does Russia have a Baltic Sea strategy? The combination of documents laying out Russian doctrine and national security concepts coupled with Russian activities targeting the countries in the BSR certainly seems to point to one. The major doctrine and concept documents are written in general terms; therefore, the guidelines found therein can be applied to any region or activity, including the BSR. However, a deeper analysis of Russian activities in, or targeting, the BSR's other countries shows a remarkable degree of consistency, albeit adapted to the country in question—thus, indicating an underlying strategy founded on general principles but modified to suit the distinctive characteristics of the Baltic region. For obvious reason such a strategy is not in the public domain. But by linking the content of the government's planning documents with the observed reality of Russian activities, it is possible to formulate the apparent shape and set of objectives in Moscow's strategy toward the BSR:

- *Establish a position as an important actor, the key actor, in the BSR that cannot be ignored.*

From a Russian point of view, this is a logical objective due to its history of having long been a key player within the Baltic Sea area. However, it also linked to Russia's goal of substituting unipolarity—i.e., the unmatched US role and actions in international politics—with a multipolar world. Raising Moscow's status in the BSR, thus, locally contributes to counteracting US initiatives in this part of Europe.

- *Reestablish, maintain and advance bilateral relations— political, trade, cultural, etc.—with other countries in the BSR, with emphasis on Finland, while largely excluding the Baltic States.*

Russia's relations with the other states in the BSR are today more or less frozen. Reestablishing and developing these relations would be advantageous for Moscow, not least in order to gain influence and promote a positive image of Russia. Additionally, improved relations would contribute to reinforcing Russia's status as a major actor in the BSR. Finland has a special, longstanding and durable relationship with Russia; and this bilateral association has endured despite Moscow's annexation of Crimea. During a tense political situation, such as today, close ties to Finland may also enable Russia to convey its viewpoints to the West and vice versa, thus according the Helsinki-Moscow link additional value.

- *Destabilize the Baltic States to encourage the emergence of a political regime neutral or friendly toward Russia.*

An outright invasion of the Baltic States would be a risky enterprise for Russia. Undoubtedly, Russia has the military means to accomplish an invasion; but the move would almost certainly lead to a major war in Europe, and occupying Russian forces would face popular resistance, likely more intense and effective than the former Forest Brothers (Baltic partisans who opposed Soviet encroachment after World War II). Today, such resistance could not be as easily countered by the same means as in the 1940s and 1950s—i.e. terror, repression and collectivization. For one thing, modern-day Russia must contend much more with international reaction to its activities than the Soviet Union did. Moreover, it is questionable whether Russia could even allocate adequate forces to ensure an outright occupation. Therefore, "encouraging" neutral or friendly political regimes represents a better option than military force.

- *Establish and maintain a credible military force in or adjacent to the BSR in order to keep neighboring countries confused regarding Russian military intentions, offensive or defensive.*

To a certain extent this has already been accomplished, but further increased military presence in or adjacent to the BSR cannot be ruled out. That the BSR countries do not fully comprehend Russia's military intentions is obvious judging from the commentaries and speculation regarding Zapad 2017 prior, during and after that Russian military exercise. In this aspect, Moscow can be judged to have been successful.

- *Exercise military shows of force on the ground, on the sea and in the air.*

This is almost routine and obvious when looking at Russian military activities in the BSR, such as in connection with Zapad 2013 and a more recent naval exercise, on April 4–6, 2018, in the southwestern part of the Baltic Sea, close to

Sweden. Notably, that area of the sea had seldom or never been used for Russian naval exercises in the past.

- *Develop a non-military capability to incapacitate vital functions in countries in the BSR, but also to exert influence.*

Moscow is looking to be able to exert pressure on as well as influence political and other decisions favorable for Russia in the BSR countries without resorting to military means. These same non-military tools would presumably also allow Russia to gain concessions from or destabilize and incapacitate a potential or actual adversary.

- *Establish a robust and aggressive intelligence collection effort to support Russia's Baltic Sea strategy.*

Timely intelligence is of outmost importance for Russia due to the present situation in the BSR, marked by increased NATO presence and activity, the possibility of Sweden and Finland joining the Alliance, and Western countries contemplating or implementing various political actions directed against Russia or Russian interests.

- *Prevent Swedish or Finnish membership in NATO.*

Were Sweden and Finland to become NATO members, Russia would be completely surrounded by the North Atlantic Alliance in the BSR. Such a situation would dramatically change the security situation in the area, which Moscow would view as utterly disadvantageous—needing to be avoided using all possible means.

- *Undermine NATO's presence and exercise activities in the BSR, mainly in the Baltic States, preventing the further growth and, in the best case, actually diminishing the Alliance's regional presence.*

Moscow views NATO's presence close to the Russian border as a threat. It alleges that this represents a broken a promise by the West, at the end of the Cold War, not to enlarge NATO beyond the borders of a reunited Germany. As Russian President Putin said, in a speech on April 14, 2014, "… they have lied to us many times, made decisions behind our backs, presented us with a *fait accompli*. This happened with NATO's expansion [sic] to the East as well as with the deployment of military infrastructure at our borders."[133] A NATO withdrawal from the Baltic States—brought about by, for example, regime change or simply by influencing public opinion in the West—would be an important victory for Russia.

- *Influence the political establishment, media and public opinion though "active measures" in order to encourage local acceptance of Russian viewpoints and a more positive attitude toward Russia.*

Active measures represent a "soft" alternative to military pressure as a tool to incapacitate the vital functions of BSR countries and to further extend Russia's preexisting sources of influence.

- *Support political parties and organizations with positive views of Russia or more widely promote traditional values regarding the nation, family and religion.*

Such support, open or covert, is already ongoing and represents an important instrument with which Moscow seeks to gain influence and/or impact public opinion in the other countries of the BSR. Depending on the type of organization being supported, Moscow's goal may additionally be to inspire violent acts or to incite internal unrest. Unlike the Soviet Union, today's Russia is not ideologically constrained when choosing which foreign parties and organizations to support.

- *Protect and support the Russian diaspora and use it to promote Russian interests.*

Russian diaspora groups vary widely in size and activities across the BSR. But in each case, these communities can be exploited by the Kremlin as an instrument to promote Russian interests. The Russian protests against the transfer of the Soviet soldier statue in Estonia, in 2007, was an important case in point. More recently, supposed mistreatment of Russians and/or Russian speakers in eastern Ukraine served as a pretext for Moscow's intervention there in 2014. It is debatable whether Moscow might one day attempt to put forward the same kind of argument to justify a military invasion of the Baltic States; but regardless, any occurrences of discrimination or mistreatment of local Russian diasporas fuel Russian propaganda, disinformation and political activities.

Estonian journalist and European Council on Foreign Relations senior policy fellow Kadri Liik, in her Riga Conference Papers 2017 article, "The Baltic States and Russia—On Diplomatic Dimensions of Security," claims that Russia has essentially given up on being a dominant power in the Baltic States. Moscow perceives these three countries, she writes, as already having been lost to the US's sphere of influence.[134] Yet, that argument is difficult to fully accept when considering the continued scope of Russian activities in the BSR, a region important to Russia not least in light of increased NATO presence there as well as the continued possibility of Sweden and Finland joining the North Atlantic Alliance.

In this context, the question arises whether Moscow is giving the BSR priority over other strategic directions. In 2014, the chief of the Russian General Staff, Valery Gerasimov, singled out Kaliningrad oblast, Crimea and the Arctic as areas of precedence for the military.[135] And indeed, these three territories show a remarkable similarity from a military point of view: among other factors, all of them have seen deployments of S-400 surface-to-air missile (SAM) systems, the introduction of Bal and Bastion coastal defense missiles, as well as the organization of two new regiments, a new naval squadron and an army corps. Despite these similarities, it is still possible to argue that the Western strategic direction—i.e., the BSR—is currently being given priority by Moscow because of the fact that traditional West–East invasion routes traverse this region, due to the presence of NATO forces deployed close to the Russian border there, as well as the possibility of Swedish and Finnish NATO membership.

NATO's forces in the Baltic States act as a trip wire and a deterrent; but alone, they are not enough to counter a full-scale Russian attack. This fact poses a dual challenge for the Alliance. First, increasing the present forces in the Baltic States is hampered by the fact that additional available forces are difficult to come by. Furthermore, even if a reinforcement were successful, the forces are, in principle, stuck in the Baltics, making it problematic to redeploy them in case of a crisis or an armed conflict. Second, NATO would struggle to bring in reinforcements quickly enough before the forces already engaged on the ground become overwhelmed. In the latter context, the use of Swedish and Finnish territory and facilities would be of crucial importance; but they may not be wholly available, particularly if Russian pressure or outright threats push Stockholm and/or Helsinki to withhold their assistance.

Events during the last few years show continued Russian interest and increased activity in the BSR, which Moscow considers to be of strategic importance. Its regional Baltic strategy is likely to remain in force for the foreseeable future, thus continuing to pose a challenge to the other countries in the BSR. It is a challenge they have all begun to meet, although a little belatedly.

Notes

[1] "A meeting of the Collegium of the Ministry of Defense of Russia was held in Moscow," Russian MoD, October 27 2017, https://function.mil.ru/news_page/country/more.htm?id=12148569@egNews.

[2] Softschools.com, http://www.softschools.com/facts/seas/baltic_sea_facts/3312/.

[3] "The Military Doctrine of the Russian Federation," The Security Council of the Russian Federation, December 25 2014, http://www.scrf.gov.ru/security/military/document129/.

[4] JustFunFacts, "Interesting facts about the Baltic Sea," 2017, http://justfunfacts.com/interesting-facts-about-the-baltic-sea/.

[5] Ibid.

[6] The Baltic Ports Organization, "The Baltic Sea as a model region for green ports and maritime transport," http://www.bpoports.com/BPC/Helsinki/BPO_report_internet-final.pdf; ITE Transport & Logistics, "Russia & the Baltics: transport trials ready to be overcome," October 10 2017, http://www.transport-exhibitions.com/Market-Insights/Russia/Russia-the-Baltics-transport-logistics.

[7] Ibid.

[8] Nick Butler, "Nord Stream 2: a test of German power," *Financial Times*, July 3, 2017, https://www.ft.com/content/4875c9ff-0868-3798-8f66-4efa667eb5ba.

[9] The Swedish Government, Ett användbart Försvar, Regeringens proposition 2008/09:140,

http://www.regeringen.se/49bb67/contentassets/1236f9bd880b495f8a9dd94ce1cb71 de/ett-anvandbart-forsvar-prop-200809140.

[10] Ibid and Atlantic Council, "With a Little Help from My Friends: How Sweden is Balancing its Security in the Baltics," September 21, 2017, "http://www.atlanticcouncil.org/blogs/new-atlanticist/with-a-little-help-from-my-friends-how-sweden-is-balancing-its-security-in-the-baltics.

[11] "EU Strategy for the Baltic Sea Region," https://www.balticsea-region-strategy.eu/about.

[12] Council of the Baltic Sea States, *http://www.cbss.org/*.

[13] HELCOM (Baltic Marine Environment Protection Commission - Helsinki Commission), http://www.helcom.fi/about-us.

[14] Euroregion Baltic, http://www.eurobalt.org/.

[15] Daniel Workman, "Russia's Top Trading Partners," *World´s Top Exports,* March 27, 2018, http://www.worldstopexports.com/russias-top-import-partners/.

[16] Michail Nikolaevitj Tichomirov, "The struggle of the Russian people for exits to the sea in the 13th-17th centuries: Introduction," http://flot.com/history/io02.htm, "The Russian Quest for Warm Water Ports," Global Security, https://www.globalsecurity.org/military/world/russia/warm-water-port.htm and René Nyberg, The Baltic Sea – Sea of Peace?, September 7, 2017, http://www.anselm.fi/baltic-sea-sea-peace/.

[17] Eric Solsten and Sandra W. Meditz, editors. *Finland: A Country Study.* Washington: GPO for the Library of Congress, 1988, The Continuation War, .http://countrystudies.us/finland/20.htm.

[18] "Guerrilla war in the Baltic states" Wikipedia, https://en.wikipedia.org/wiki/Guerrilla_war_in_the_Baltic_states.

[19] "Finland - Soviet/Russia Relations," Global Security, https://www.globalsecurity.org/military/world/europe/fi-forrel-ru.htm.

[20] Eric Solsten and Sandra W. Meditz, editors. *Finland: A Country Study*. Washington: GPO for the Library of Congress, 1988, The Cold War and the Treaty of 1948, http://countrystudies.us/finland/24.htm.

[21] Ibid.

[22] "Baltic theatre of the Crimean War," The Gutenberg Project, http://www.self.gutenberg.org/articles/Baltic_theatre_of_the_Crimean_War#Baltic_theatre.

[23] "The National Security Strategy of the Russian Federation," The Security Council of the Russian Federation, December 31, 2015, http://www.scrf.gov.ru/security/docs/document133/.

[24] "Foreign Policy Concept of the Russian Federation," The Ministry of Foreign Affairs of the Russian Federation, November 30, 2016, http://www.mid.ru/en/foreign_policy/official_documents/-/asset_publisher/CptICkB6BZ29/content/id/2542248.

[25] "The Military Doctrine of the Russian Federation," The Security Council of the Russian Federation, December 25 2014, http://www.scrf.gov.ru/security/military/document129/.

[26] NATO Exercises, https://korrespondent.net/tag/175286/.

[27] Isabelle Facon, *Russia's national security strategy and military doctrine and their implications for the EU*, European Union 2017.

[28] Ibid, page 9.

[29] Ibid.

[30] The Maritime Doctrine of the Russian Federation," The Security Council of the Russian Federation,,http://www.scrf.gov.ru/security/military/document34/.

[31] "The Fundamentals of Russia's State Naval Policy Through 2030," July 20, 2017, Official Internet-portal for judicial information, http://publication.pravo.gov.ru/Document/View/0001201707200015?index=0&rangeSize=1&mc_cid=8dbd8574d4&mc_eid=3baefa44e9.

[32] Agnia Grigas, "Russia-Baltic Relations After Crimea's Annexation," Cicero Foundation Great Debate Paper, June, 2014, http://www.cicerofoundation.org/lectures/Agnia_Grigas_Russia-Baltic_Relations.pdf.

[33] "The Lithuanian president declares that she does not renounce cooperation with Russia," *Voenno-Promysjlennyj Kure*, December 27, 2017, https://vpk-news.ru/news/40563.

[34] About the portal, Rubaltic.ru, https://www.rubaltic.ru/about/.

[35] Statistics Estonia, June 9, 2017, https://www.stat.ee/34278, Latvia. Statistics in Brief 2017, http://www.csb.gov.lv/sites/default/files/nr_04_latvia_statistics_in_brief_2017_17_00_en.pdf; Jolanta Pivoriene, Ethnic Minorities In Lithuania, *Sociológa a S položnost' 1 / 1* (2016), http://www.sociology-society.ff.ukf.sk/archiv-cisel/c1/c1-jolanta-pivoriene.pdf.

[36] Dario Cavegn, "Monument of contention: How the Bronze Soldier was removed," *ERR.ee*, April 25, 2017, http://news.err.ee/592070/monument-of-contention-how-the-bronze-soldier-was-removed.

[37] Agnia Grigas, *Beyond Crimea: The New Russian Empire*, Yale University Press, Danbury, Connecticut, 2016, pp. 140–145.

[38] Swedish Embassy Tallinn, About Estonia, http://www.swedenabroad.com/sv-SE/Ambassader/Tallinn/Landfakta/Om-Estland/ and the Estonian government, Prime Minister Jüri Ratas, ,https://www.valitsus.ee/en/prime-minister-juri-ratas.

[39] Dario Cavegn, "Overview: Center Party's cooperation protocol with Putin's United Russia," *ERR.ee*, November 8, 2016, http://news.err.ee/119629/overview-center-party-s-cooperation-protocol-with-putin-s-united-russia.

[40] The Estonian government, Minister of Public Administration Mihhail Korb files his resignation, May 24, 2017, https://www.valitsus.ee/en/news/minister-public-administration-mihhail-korb-files-his-resignation.

[41] "The Mayor of Riga named Putin the best Russian president for Latvia," *Lenta.ru*, September 4, 2014, https://lenta.ru/news/2014/09/05/riga/.

[42] Dario Cavegn, "Latvia's Saskaņa party ditches agreement with Putin's United Russia," *ERR.ee*, October 10, 2017, http://news.err.ee/635146/latvia-s-saskana-party-ditches-agreement-with-putin-s-united-russia.

[43] "Lithuanian farmers party sweeps to victory in second round vote," *BNE IntelliNews*, October 24, 2016, http://www.intellinews.com/lithuanian-farmers-party-sweeps-to-victory-in-second-round-vote-108717/.

[44] Sanita Jemberga, Mikk Salu, Šarūnas Černiauskas, "The Kremlin's Millions, and its support of pro-Russian activists in the Baltics," *The Baltic Times*, September 7, 2015, https://www.baltictimes.com/kremlin_s_millions/.

[45] Nina Novikova, "Russia's influence in the Baltic States tends to reach zero," *Pravda.ru*, March 15, 2016, https://www.pravda.ru/world/formerussr/latvia/15-03-2016/1295133-korotchenko-0/.

[46] European Parliament, Briefing April 2016 The Russian ban on agriculture products, http://www.europarl.europa.eu/RegData/etudes/BRIE/2016/581971/EPRS_BRI%282016%29581971_EN.pdf.

[47] Information Note on the Russian Ban on Agri-Food Products From the EU, https://ec.europa.eu/agriculture/sites/agriculture/files/russian-import-ban/pdf/info-note-03-09_en.pdf.

[48] "Russia is Reducing Transit through Baltic States," The Analytical Center for the Government of the Russian Federation, May 29, 2017, http://ac.gov.ru/en/events/013079.html.

[49] "Meeting with the managing director of the company 'Transneft,' Nikolaj Tokarev," The Homepage of the Russian President, September 12, 2016,http://www.kremlin.ru/events/president/news/52879.

[50] "Baltic States Seek Security, Reduced Dependence on Russia," *BIZNESALERT*, June 13, 2017, http://biznesalert.com/baltic-states-seek-security-reduced-dependence-on-russia/.

[51] "EU to work with Baltic States on decoupling from Russian power grid," *Reuters,* June 1, 2017, https://www.reuters.com/article/baltics-energy-eu-russia/eu-to-work-with-baltic-states-on-decoupling-from-russian-power-grid-idUSL8N1IY455;" Integration of the Baltic States into the EU electricity system," *EU Publications,* June 2, 2017, https://publications.europa.eu/en/publication-detail/-/publication/8d3b7da2-562e-11e7-a5ca-01aa75ed71a1/language-en/format-PDF/source-31392329.

[52] https://www.fpri.org/article/2017/06/baltic-energy-sources-diversifying-away-russia/.

[53]Simon Hoellerbauer, "Baltic Energy Sources: Diversifying Away from Russia," *FPRI Baltic Bulletin,* June 14, 2017, https://www.ft.com/content/9d016276-43c3-11e4-baa7-00144feabdc0; Thomas Frear, Łukasz Kulesa, "Dangerous Brinkmanship: Close Military Encounters Between Russia and the West in 2014," *European Leadership Network,* November, 2014, https://www.europeanleadershipnetwork.org/wp-content/uploads/2017/10/Dangerous-Brinkmanship.pdf.

[54] "Drunkenness, rape and other "coforts" in the life of the NATO-soldiers in the Baltic States," *NewInforma,* February 22, 2017, https://newinform.com/45884-pyanstvo-iznasilovaniya-i-drugie-prelesti-zhizni-soldat-nato-v-pribaltike?utm_source=warfiles.ru; Anatolij Wasserman, Memo for Latvians: before you refuse a NATO soldier, think twice, *Sputnik,* June 20, 2017,https://ru.sputniknewslv.com/columnists/20170620/5093872/anatolij-vasserman-pamjatka-latyshkam-pribytie-soldat-nato.html.

[55] "NATO: Russia targeted German army with fake news campaign," *Deutsche Welle,* February 16, 2017, http://www.dw.com/en/nato-russia-targeted-german-army-with-fake-news-campaign/a-37591978.

[56] "Meeting of the Valdai International Discussion Club," September 19, 2013, The Homepage of the Russian President, http://en.kremlin.ru/events/president/news/19243.

[57] Hold Vinduet Åbent, En antologi om tilstandene i relationerne mellem Rusland og Vesten, *Rådet for International Konfliktløsning,* September 2016. http://riko.nu/wp-content/uploads/sites/11925/2017/02/samlet-1.pdf.

[58]"Danish MP Challenges Russian Stereotypes, Calls for 'Sober Analysis,' " *Sputnik*, September 9, 2016, https://sputniknews.com/politics/201609201045507209-denmark-russia-stereotypes-sober-analysis/.

[59] Udredning: Dansk diplomati og forsvar i en brydningstid, The Danish Foreign Ministry, May 1, 2016, http://um.dk/da/udenrigspolitik/aktuelle-emner/dansk-diplomati-og-forsvar-i-en-brydningstid/.

[60] Lars Kabel, "Danske mediers dækning af Rusland," *Danmarks Medie- og journalisthøjskole, December, 2016,*http://njc.dk/wp-content/uploads/2017/01/Danske-mediers-d%C3%A6kning-af-Rusland.pdf; Jens-Kristian Lütken, "Putins Rusland er en trussel mod Danmark og andre civiliserede lande," *Jyllands-Posten,* August 23, 2017, https://jyllands-posten.dk/debat/blogs/jenslutken/ECE9810567/putins-rusland-er-en-trussel-mod-danmark-og-andre-civiliserede-lande/.

[61] Martin Borre, Thomas Larsen, Rystet Claus Hjort: "Rusland har hacket det danske forsvar over to år," *Berlingske,* April 23, 2017, https://www.b.dk/politiko/rystet-claus-hjort-afsloerer-rusland-har-hacket-det-danske-forsvar-over-to-aar; "Denmark Says Russia Hacked Defense Ministry E-Mails," *Radio Free Europe Radio Liberty,* April 24, 2017, https://www.rferl.org/a/russia-denmark-defense-ministry-hacking/28448928.html.

[62] "Ruslands ambassadør: Danske skibe kan blive mål for russisk atomangreb," *Jyllands-Posten,* March 20, 2015, https://jyllands-posten.dk/indland/ECE7573125/Ruslands-ambassad%C3%B8r-Danske-skibe-kan-blive-m%C3%A5l-for-russisk-atomangreb/.

[63] Hans Redder, "Voldsom debat i Folketinget: - Dikkende lammehaler og Putins skødehunde," *TV2,* March 24, 2017, http://nyheder.tv2.dk/politik/2017-03-24-voldsom-debat-i-folketinget-dikkende-lammehaler-og-putins-skoedehunde.

[64] Caroline Damsgaard Christensen, "Russisk statspropaganda elsker Dansk Folkeparti, *mandagmorgen,* September 11, 2016, https://www.mm.dk/artikel/russisk-statspropaganda-elsker-dansk-folkeparti.

[65] "Germany's Steinmeier Tells Putin Improving Relations 'Essential'," *Radio Free Europe Radio Liberty*, October 25, 2017, https://www.rferl.org/a/putin-steinmeier-russia-germany-gorbachev-memorial-cathedral/28814600.html.

[66] Ulrich Schmid, "Die Beziehungen zwischen Russland und Deutschland sind auf einem historischen Tiefstand. Ulrich Schmid über die unterschiedlichen Perspektiven der Parteien auf Moskau," September 5, 2017, Universität St.Gallen, https://www.unisg.ch/de/wissen/newsroom/aktuell/rssnews/meinung/2017/septemb er/bundestagswahlen-beziehungen-russland-deutschland-5september2017.

[67] Olga Lebedeva, "Russian-German relations on the eve of 2018," *Mezjdunaraodnaja Zjizn*, September, 22, 2017, https://interaffairs.ru/news/show/18371.

[68] "Umfrage: Soll Deutschland bessere Beziehungen zu Russland haben?" *Contra Magazin*, https://www.contra-magazin.com/2017/10/umfrage-soll-deutschland-bessere-beziehungen-zu-russland-haben/.

[69] "Commentes in connection with the working visit of the Russian foreign minister to federal republic of Germany," The Foreign Ministry of the Russian federation, July 11, 2017, http://www.mid.ru/ru/maps/de/-/asset_publisher/Ho2VLi5PHLYX/content/id/2811896.

[70] Paul Carrel, Andreas Rinke, "Ties between Germany and Russia enter new chill," *Reuters*, April 4, 2016, https://www.reuters.com/article/us-germany-russia-relations-insight/ties-between-germany-and-russia-enter-new-chill-idUSKCN0X10NV; Stefan Meister, "The "Lisa case": Germany as a target of Russian disinformation," *NATO review*, July 27, 2016, https://www.nato.int/docu/review/2016/also-in-2016/lisa-case-germany-target-russian-disinformation/EN/index.htm.

[71] Katja Bauer, "Der "Fall Lisa" und sein bitteres Nachspiel," *Stuttgarter Nachrichten*, June 20, 2017, https://www.stuttgarter-nachrichten.de/inhalt.erfundene-vergewaltigung-der-fall-lisa-und-sein-bitteres-nachspiel.ece0548c-340c-4ae3-8d2c-e751c139e183.html; "Fake: Fall Lisa – Russisches Mädchen in Deutschland von "Flüchtlingen" entführt und vergewaltigt," *StopFake.org, January 17, 2016*, https://www.stopfake.org/de/fake-fall-lisa-russisches-madchen-in-deutschland-von-fluchtlingen-entfuhrt-und-vergewaltigt/.

[72] Bundestagswahl 2017, Der Bundestagswahlleiter, https://www.bundeswahlleiter.de/bundestagswahlen/2017/ergebnisse/bund-99.html;

"Gauland bestreitet Finanzierung der AfD aus Russland," *Zeit Online*, September 8, 2017, http://www.zeit.de/news/2017-09/08/deutschland-gauland-bestreitet-finanzierung-der-afd-aus-russland-08084604; "Umstrittene Osteuropa-Reisen: AfD-Männer sollen Beziehungen zu Russland-Spion haben," *Focus*, August 17, 2017, https://www.focus.de/politik/deutschland/umstrittene-osteuropa-reisen-lobby-arbeit-fuer-putin-afd-maenner-sollen-verbindungen-zu-russischem-spion-haben_id_7480861.html; "Gold-AfD lässt sich jetzt von Pleite-Putin beraten," *Focus*, December 7, 2014, https://www.focus.de/politik/deutschland/gold-shop-spielt-angeblich-keine-rolle-austausch-mit-diplomaten-macht-die-afd-jetzt-gemeinsame-sache-mit-putin_id_4328505.html.

[73] "Russlanddeutsche in der Bundesrepublik," Deutscher Bundestag, February 10, 2016, https://www.bundestag.de/blob/424502/e534deaef41f3f1f1efcf098f64cb013/wd-3-036-16-pdf-data.pdf; Manuela Roppert , "Russlanddeutsche - die verführbaren Wähler?," *BR24*, September 13, 2017, http://www.br.de/bundestagswahl/bundestagswahl-russlanddeutsche-manipulation-100.html.

[74] Ibid.

[75] Fabian Reinbold, "Was plant Moskau?" *Spiegel Online*, September 1, 2017, http://www.spiegel.de/netzwelt/web/bundestagswahl-2017-debatte-um-moegliche-manipulationen-durch-russland-a-1165520.html; Michael Schwirtz, "German Election Mystery: Why No Russian Meddling?" *New York Times*, September 21, 2017, https://www.nytimes.com/2017/09/21/world/europe/german-election-russia.html.

[76] "President of Poland: if we forgive Russia for Ukraine and Georgia, we are in for a tragedy," *UAWIRE*, November 13, 2017, https://uawire.org/polish-president-if-we-forgive-russia-for-ukraine-and-georgia-a-tragedy-awaits-us.

[77] "Polish FM says Russia uninterested in dialogue," *Radio Poland*, http://thenews.pl/1/10/Artykul/333941,Polish-FM-says-Russia-uninterested-in-dialogue.

[78] The Concept of Defence of the Republic of Poland, The Polish Ministry of Defense, May, 2017, http://www.mon.gov.pl/d/pliki/rozne/2017/05/KORP_DRUK_v03_mn2.pdf.
[79] Poland, Gazpormexport, http://www.gazpromexport.ru/en/partners/poland/.

[80] "Poland aims to stop buying Russian gas after 2022," *Radio Poland,* September 22, 2017, http://www.thenews.pl/1/9/Artykul/326978,Poland-aims-to-stop-buying-Russian-gas-after-2022-FM.

[81] Łukasz Wenerski, Michal Kacewicz, *Russian soft power in Poland,* Political Capital, Budapest 2017, http://www.politicalcapital.hu/pc-admin/source/documents/PC_NED_country_study_PL_20170428.pdf.

[82] Paulina Pacula, "New pro-Russia party emerges in Poland," *Euobserver,* March 23, 2015, https://euobserver.com/beyond-brussels/128075.

[83] "Poland detains pro-Kremlin party leader for 'spying,' " *The Guardian,* May 19, 2016, https://www.theguardian.com/world/2016/may/19/poland-detains-pro-kremlin-party-leader-mateusz-piskorski-spying.

[84] European Center for Geopolitical Analysis (ECAG), https://www.occrp.org/en/laundromat/profiles/european-center-for-geopolitical-analysis.

[85] "Rysslands president på arbetsbesök till Finland," The President of Finland, July 19, 2017, http://www.presidentti.fi/public/default.aspx?contentid=364575&nodeid=44809&contentlan=3&culture=sv-FI; Thelia Johnson, "Lavrov på besök i Finland – säkerheten kring Östersjön på agendan," *Sveriges Radio,* May 4, 2017, http://sverigesradio.se/sida/artikel.aspx?programid=83&artikel=6689526.

[86] "A century on, Finland has learnt to tame the Russian bear," *Financial Times,* December 5, 2017, https://www.ft.com/content/927b91be-d9c5-11e7-a039-c64b1c09b482.

[87] "Maria Sacharova: Russia and Finland maintains nonconfrontational relations," *RIA Novosti,* June 4, 2016, https://ria.ru/interview/20160604/1442590887.html.
[88] Statistics Finland, Trade, http://www.stat.fi/tup/suoluk/suoluk_kotimaankauppa_en.html#foreigntrade,2016.

[89] Lukas Lindström, Ann-Lis Fredriksson, "En klar majoritet av finländarna motsätter sig ett medlemskap i försvarsalliansen Nato," *Yle,* November 11, 2017, https://svenska.yle.fi/artikel/2017/11/05/hs-rungande-nej-till-nato-i-finland.
[90] https://www.reuters.com/article/us-finland-nato/finnish-president-says-joining-nato-would-require-referendum-idUSKBN1CZ2K6.

[91] Tuomas Forsell, Jussi Rosendahl, "Finnish president says joining NATO would require referendum," *Reuters*, October 30, 2017, https://www.defensenews.com/global/europe/2017/10/13/russia-promises-countermeasures-if-finland-joins-nato/.

[92] Mark Rivett-Carnac, "Finland and Russia Temporarily Close Border to Migrants," *Time*, March 23, 2016, http://time.com/4268754/finland-russia-border-restrict-migrants/.

[93] Katri Pynnöniemi, "Hybrid influence – lessons from Finland," *NATO Review*, June 28, 2017, https://www.nato.int/docu/review/2017/Also-in-2017/lessons-from-finland-influence-russia-policty-security/EN/index.htm.

[94] Tom Batchelor, "Finland stops Russians buying land near military sites amid invasion fears," *Independent*, February 13, 2017, http://www.independent.co.uk/news/world/europe/russia-finland-invasion-fears-military-sites-land-sales-blocked-a7578601.html; "Skypo misstänker att främmande makt kan ha köpt fastigheter till soldater," *Yle*, November 1, 2016, https://svenska.yle.fi/artikel/2016/11/01/skypo-misstanker-att-frammande-makt-kan-ha-kopt-fastigheter-till-soldater.

[95] Global Indicators Database, Pew Research Center, http://www.pewglobal.org/database/indicator/27/.

[96] Ryssland, The Swedish Governement, http://www.regeringen.se/sveriges-regering/utrikesdepartementet/sveriges-diplomatiska-forbindelser/europa-och-centralasien/ryssland/.

[97] Johan Pisoni, "Bara var tredje vill att Sverige går med i Nato," *Sveriges radio,* July 3, 2017, https://www.svt.se/nyheter/inrikes/bara-var-tredje-vill-att-sverige-gar-med-i-nato-fragan-politiskt-dod.

[98] "Putin emphasizes that Sweden's entry to NATO would jeopardize ties with Moscow," *TASS*, June 1, 2017, http://tass.com/politics/949067.

[99] Michael Winiarski, "Om Sverige går med i Nato kommer vi att vidta nödvändiga åtgärder," *Focus,* April 24, 2016, https://fokus.dn.se/lavrov/; "Ekot direktrapporterar från lördagsintervjun med ryske ambassadören," *Sveriges Radio,* October 1, 2016, http://sverigesradio.se/sida/artikel.aspx?programid=83&artikel=6531651; "Russia May Take 'Reciprocal Steps' if Sweden Joins NATO," *Sputnik,* September 10, 2015, https://sputniknews.com/politics/201509101026834982/.

[100] Memorandum of Understanding *(MOU)* between the Government of the Kingdom of *Sweden* and Headquarters, Supreme Allied Commander Transformation as well as Supreme Headquarters Allied Powers Europe regarding the Provision of Host Nation Support for the Execution of NATO Operations/Exeercises/Similar Military Activity, https://web.archive.org/web/20160214223359/http://natoutredningen.se/wp-content/uploads/140904-HNS-MoU-Sweden-NATO.pdf.

[101] "Russia spreading fake news and forged docs in Sweden: report," *The Local,* January 7, 2017, https://www.thelocal.se/20170107/swedish-think-tank-details-russian-disinformation-in-new-study.

[102] "Alexander, 34, är SD:s hemliga desinformatör," *Aftonbladet,* September 3, 2016, https://www.aftonbladet.se/nyheter/article23449197.ab.

[103] "Säpo: Rysk spion på svensk konferens, *Sveriges television,"* April 30, 2016, https://www.svt.se/nyheter/utrikes/sapo-rysk-spion-pa-svensk-konferens; Mikael Holmström, "Säpo: Ryska agenter motarbetar på svensk mark," *Dagens Nyheter,* April 30, 2016, https://www.dn.se/nyheter/sverige/sapo-ryska-agenter-motarbetar-pa-svensk-mark/?forceScript=1&variantType=large.

[104] David Cenciotti, "Russia Simulated A Large-Scale Aerial Night Attack On Sweden," *Business Insider,* April 23, 2013, http://www.businessinsider.com/david-cenciotti-russia-simulated-a-massive-aerial-attack-2013-4?r=US&IR=T&IR=T.

[105] "Rysslands ambassadör: Hög tid att Sverige och Ryssland sluter fred," *Dagens Industri,* October 12, 2017, https://www.di.se/debatt/rysslands-ambassador-hog-tid-att-sverige-och-ryssland-sluter-fred/?loggedin=true.

[106] Verfassungsschutzbericht 2016, Bundesministerium des Innern, https://www.verfassungsschutz.de/embed/vsbericht-2016.pdf, Annual Report for 2017, TheLatvian Security Police, http://www.dp.gov.lv/en/useful/annual-reports/;

"National Security Threat Assessment 2017," The State Security Department of the Republic of Lithuania and the Second Investigation Department under the Ministry of National Defence, https://www.vsd.lt/wp-content/uploads/2017/03/AKATSKT_DRAFT-3-31-EN-HQ.pdf.

[107] David Cenciotti, "Sweden Protests As Russian Fighter Buzzes Swedish Spyplane Over The Baltic Sea," *The Aviationist*, June 21, 2017, https://theaviationist.com/2017/06/21/sweden-protests-as-russian-fighter-buzzes-swedish-spyplane-over-the-baltic-sea/.

[108] "Lithuania – Russia Cross-Border Cooperation Programme 2014-2020," http://www.eni-cbc.eu/lr/data/public/uploads/2017/01/lt-ru-jop-_approved-2016-12-19.pdf; "Population," The Local Government Kaliningrad Oblast, https://gov39.ru/region/peoples.php; Natural resources, The Local Government Kaliningrad Oblast, https://gov39.ru/region/natural.php.

[109] "Kaliningrad profile – Overview," *BBC*, March 12, 2015, http://www.bbc.com/news/world-europe-18284828; "History," The Local Government Kaliningrad Oblast, https://gov39.ru/region/history.php.

[110] Beatrix Tolgyesi, "Kaliningrad – A bridge between two worlds or a military outpost?" *Baltic review,* April 28, 2016, http://baltic-review.com/kaliningrad-bridge-between-two-worlds/; Linas Kojala, Vytautas Keršanskas, (Un)convenient Kaliningrad and Kremlin's relationship, *Delfi,* December 7, 2016, https://en.delfi.lt/central-eastern-europe/unconvenient-kaliningrad-and-kremlins-relationship.d?id=73098334.

[111] Mark Kramer, "Kaliningrad Oblast, Russia, and Baltic Security," *PONARS Policy Memo 10*, October 1997, http://www.ponarseurasia.org/sites/default/files/policy-memos-pdf/pm_0010.pdf.

[112] "Kaliningrad Special region," The Ministry of Defence of the Russian federation, uhttp://encyclopedia.mil.ru/encyclopedia/dictionary/details_rvsn.htm?id=5867@morfDictionary; Svetlana Ivanova Adamovitj, "The cognitive project 'Kaliningrad Special Area,' " *Alye Parusa,* January 22, 2017, https://nsportal.ru/ap/library/drugoe/2017/01/22/poznavatelnyy-proekt-kaliningradskiy-osobyy-rayon.

[113] Dmitri Verchoturov, "Island Territories" of Russia, *KM.RU,* December 28. 2014, http://www.km.ru/v-rossii/2014/12/28/strategii-razvitiya-rossii/752972-ostrovnye-territorii-rossii; Olga Gontyarova, "How the Baltic Fleet Commander frightened

NATO," *Kpomsomolskaya Pravda,* May 18, 2017, https://www.kaliningrad.kp.ru/daily/26680.4/3702932/.

[114] Sergei Safronov, "The North Caucasian Military District and the Kaliningrad Special Area will be rearmed before 2012," *RIA Novosti,* June 17, 2009, https://ria.ru/defense_safety/20090617/174604357.html.

[115] Jevgenij Krutikov, "The strategic directions of defense will be significantly strengthened," *Vzgljyd,* January 30, 2015, https://vz.ru/politics/2015/1/30/727061.html.

[116] "The commander and the chief of staff of the Baltic Fleet were sacked for embellishing reality," *Lenta.ru,* June 29, 2016, https://lenta.ru/news/2016/06/29/za_upuschenia.

[117] Sergey Isityenko, "A US division has already Kaliningrad in its sights," *Svobodnaya Pressa,* October 12, 2017, http://svpressa.ru/war21/article/183432/.

[118] "The 152nd Guards Missile Brigade in Kaliningrad has received Iskander-M missile systems," *bmpd,* November 25, 2017, https://bmpd.livejournal.com/2970466.html.

[119] "Why the small missile boats 'Serpuchov' and 'Zeljonyi dol' arrived in the Baltic Sea," *Voennoe Obozrenie,* November 2, 2016, https://topwar.ru/103044-dlya-chego-mrk-serpuhov-i-zelenyy-dol-prishli-na-baltiku.html; Vladimir Tytjkov, "The Baltic Fleet asks for support," *Svobodnaya Pressa,* December 12, 2016, http://svpressa.ru/war21/article/162423/.

[120] "New missile systems have arrived in the Baltic Fleet," *Interfax,* April 15, 2017.

[121] Andrej Gavrilenko, "Both on the sea and on land," *Krasnaya Zvezda,* November 26, 2017, http://www.redstar.ru/index.php/2011-07-25-15-55-32/item/35208-i-na-more-i-na-sushe.

[122] "The airbase in the Kaliningrad oblast will be replenished with a Su-30SM fighter," *Vesti.ru,* December 8, 2016, https://www.vesti.ru/doc.html?id=2830689&cid=17; "The naval aviation of the Baltic Fleet received two more Su-30 SM fighters," *Novyi Kaliningrad,* May 29, 2017, https://www.newkaliningrad.ru/news/briefs/politics/13717780-morskaya-aviatsiya-baltiyskogo-flota-poluchila-eshche-dva-istrebitelya-su-30-sm.html; "Three new Su-30SM entered the naval aviation of the Baltic Fleet," *Voennoe Obozrenie,* August 29,

2017, https://topwar.ru/123702-tri-novyh-su-30sm-voshli-v-sostav-morskoy-aviacii-bf.html.

[123] "The Baltic Fleet will be strengthened by two air regiments," *Interfax*, October 10, 2017, http://www.interfax.ru/russia/582599.

[124] "Shojgu told which military airfields to be renovated in 2018," *Politika Segodnya*, December 22, 2017, https://polit.info/379581-shoigu-rasskazal-kakie-voennye-aerodromy-rekonstruiruyut-v-2018-godu.

[125] Magnus Nordenman, "China and Russia's Joint Sea 2017 Baltic Naval Exercise Highlight a New Normal in Europe," USNI News, July 5, 2017, https://news.usni.org/2017/07/05/china-russias-baltic-naval-exercise-highlight-new-normal-european-maritime.

[126] "Statement by Chief of the General Staff of the Armed Forces of the Russian Federation - First Deputy Minister of Defense of the Russian Federation, General of the Army Valery Gerasimov, at an open meeting of the Collegium of the Russian Defense Ministry on November 7, 2017," The Ministry of Defense of the Russian Federation, November 7, 2017, http://function.mil.ru/news_page/country/more.htm?id=12149743@egNews.

[127] "The formation of the 1st Guards Tank Army," *BMPD*, June 15, 2015, http://bmpd.livejournal.com/1324525.html.

[128] "The composition of the army corps created in the fleets," *Voennoe Obozrenie*, May 25, 2017, https://topwar.ru/116427-sostav-sozdannyh-na-flotah-armeyskih-korpusov.html.

[129] "Two new divisions of the Western Military District and the Southern Military District will be fully equipped in May 2017," *RIA Novosti*, November 11, 2016, https://ria.ru/defense_safety/20161111/1481182101.html; "A new mechanized division is beginning to be organized in the vicinity of Smolensk," *Vzglyad*, April 27, 2016, https://vz.ru/news/2016/4/27/807722.html.

[130] "In Russia, the Taman and Kantemirov tank divisions have been recreated," *Gazeta.ru*, May 4, 2013, https://www.gazeta.ru/social/news/2013/05/04/n_2890657.shtml.

[131] "4-ya gvardeyskaya Kantemirovskaya tankovaya diviziya (v/ch 19612)," *Voyskovyye Chasti Rossii*, June 22, 2015, https://voinskayachast.net/suhoputnie-voyska/tankovie/vch19612.

[132] Alexandr Golts, Military Reform and Militarism in Russia, *University of Uppsala*, 2017, http://www.diva-portal.org/smash/get/diva2:1138525/FULLTEXT01.pdf%20September%202017.

[133] Address by President of the Russian Federation, The President of Russia, March 18, 2014, http://en.kremlin.ru/events/president/news/20603.

[134] Security in the Baltic Sea Region: Realities and Prospects: The Rīga Conference Papers 2017, *The Latvian Institute of International Affairs*, 2017, pp. 148–158. http://www.liia.lv/en/publications/security-in-the-baltic-sea-region-realities-and-prospects-the-riga-conference-papers-2017-643.

[135] "Russia strengthens its geopolitical borders," *KM.RU*, January 15, 2015, http://www.km.ru/v-rossii/2015/01/15/vladimir-putin/753519-rossiya-ukreplyaet-geopoliticheskie-rubezhi.

Part II

Non-Conventional Elements of Strategy and Doctrine

5. Not 'Hybrid' but New Generation Warfare

Jānis Bērziņš

Introduction

Since the beginning of Moscow's 2014 annexation of Crimea, it has been difficult for many to find a term that adequately describes the way Russia conducted this operation. The most commonly accepted term, at least in the West, is "Hybrid Warfare." The North Atlantic Treaty Organization (NATO) itself has adopted this label. The seminal work on Hybrid Warfare is Francis G. Hoffman's "Hybrid Warfare and Challenges."[1] The author develops the idea of a hybrid strategy based on tactically employing a mix of instruments, resulting in the difficulty of fully understanding and establishing a proper counter-strategy for dealing with it. The main challenge results from state and non-state actors employing technologies and strategies that are more appropriate for their own field, in a multimodal confrontation. This may include exploiting modern capabilities to support insurgent, terrorist and criminal activities, as well as the use of high-tech military capabilities combined with terrorist actions and cyber warfare operations for use against economic and financial targets. Therefore, this strategy still largely presupposes the application of kinetic force or military power to defeat the enemy. Instead, as will be argued and explored in depth below, the more accurate term to apply here is "New Generation Warfare," which more fully captures the full range of tactics and strategies Russia employs against potential enemies or rivals.

The argument that Russia conducted Hybrid Warfare, whether in Crimea or elsewhere, presents two problems. First, this still presupposes the application of kinetic force, while Russian New Generation Warfare does not.[2] Second, it is a conceptual mistake to try to fit Russian New Generation Warfare, the result of a long military academic discussion, into Western concepts. Naturally, the word "hybrid" is catchy, since it can represent a mix of anything. However, its basic framework differs from the one developed by the Russians due to the former being a military concept and the result of American military thought. Moreover, the concept of New Generation Warfare actually includes conventional operations. In other words, Hybrid Warfare might be part of New Generation Warfare but cannot define it.

Therefore, it is a methodological mistake to try to frame a theory developed independently by the Russian military as a theory developed in another country. It reflects another culture's way of thinking and strategic understanding about the way warfare should be conducted. Specifically, what the Russians call New Generation Warfare is a combination of Asymmetric warfare with Low-Intensity Conflict, Network-Centric Warfare and Sixth-Generation Warfare, combined with components of Reflexive Control. Its main aim is to achieve political objectives; therefore, the use of military power may not even be necessary. To fully comprehend the way Russia sees warfare, it is necessary to understand Russia's security ambitions— and therefore its tactical objectives—as well as its military doctrine.

Russia vs. NATO and the United States: Geopolitical Enemies

The rhetoric that the transatlantic community, especially the United States, is Russia's main enemy, has been developing in Russia for some years. Albeit relatively marginal until about 2005, the idea that Russia is a victim of the US's vested interests, which are allegedly being implemented and executed by multilateral agencies and NATO, has been gaining legitimacy in Russian security circles. This idea has been gradually incorporated into Russian policymaking over the past ten years. It has also had significant influence on the military.

A very comprehensive analysis of NATO and the transatlantic community in relation to Russia was undertaken by Major General (ret.) Aleksandr Vladimirov, the president of Russia's Board of Military Experts. He is the author of more than 150 publications on defense and security issues. Vladimirov is also one of the protagonists of the idea that a war between the United Stated and Russia is inevitable within a decade. This notion was fully developed for the first time in his article "The Great American War" in 2008. The article begins with the statement *"Tsely Vashingtona—Polnomasshtabnyi kontroly nad prirodnymi resursami planet"* ("Washington's objective: total control of the planet's natural resources").[3] According to the retired general, this is the result of five factors.

First, economic: Although the United States has the most powerful economy in the world, it is also the most fragile, he argues. This is the result of American external debt—trillions of dollars that cannot be paid. The only way the United States can maintain its influence is to provide security to the world and demonstrate its superior power. Second, the military: The United States has extensive military and technological superiority over the rest of the world (including Russia and China). Third, information: The United States practically controls all major sources of information and is thus able to portray facts to its advantage, the president of the Russian Board of Military Experts asserts. Fourth, geopolitical: The United States can control the majority of the nations in the world, although this power is in decline. It includes controlling Europe and attempting to push European countries to the political periphery. Fifth, internal politics: In the United States, the basis for internal stability is a high level of consumption. Thus, any reduction in the level of individual consumption will certainly result in social unrest and a loss of political legitimacy. Since natural resources are limited, the US needs to guarantee control over these resources at any cost. The conclusion is that the United States never stopped conducting warfare against Russia on several levels and in various forms, with the objective being to submit Russia's national interests to the needs of the US.[4]

Vladmirov's two most relevant articles on understanding how the Russian military considers NATO and the United States strategically are: "*NATO v paradigme obshchey teorii voyny*" ("NATO in the Paradigm of the General Theory of War")[5] and "*SShA—Glavnyy Aktor Mirovoy Voyny*" ("The United States—The Main Actor in the World War").[6] In the first, the author develops the idea that there are many civilizations in the world, but only four are really relevant geopolitically. The first is the Christian/Western civilization (US, Europe and Australia), whose objective is to impose fundamentalist liberalism globally. The second is Orthodox civilization ("white" Russian), but its objectives are still developing. Third is Islamic civilization, whose objective is to expand radical religious Islamic fundamentalism. And the final is the Chinese civilization, whose project is to slowly expand Chinese chauvinism. By applying this division, all the significant conflicts in the world can be divided up as between the West and the Orthodox, the West against Islam, all of them against China, and vice-versa. The general rule is that each civilization is fighting alone and will lose alone. Thus, Russia has no other choice than to be independent and look for its own path of development and interests.[7]

Vladimirov contends that the Western civilizational project is, in reality, the United States' project. As such, there are four implications for NATO. First, the Alliance is intentionally and willfully failing to fulfil its obligations. In the preamble of the North Atlantic Treaty, it states that NATO members are "determined to safeguard the freedom, common heritage and civilization of their peoples, founded on the principles of democracy, individual liberty and the rule of law."[8] In other words, NATO's main objective is to guarantee the security of the Transatlantic community, and thus, of Western civilization and its cradle, Europe. Vladimirov claims that NATO is failing at this goal, however, because, in the face of the current war of civilizations between Western and Islamic civilizations, Muslim immigrants and their descendants are gradually physically displacing indigenous European ethnic groups on European soil. At the same time, while the West is losing the war of civilizations at home, it is doing nothing to ensure its own salvation. On the one hand, it engages in a pointless and costly war for freedom and democracy in places where these values are not important, or are even not wanted; on the other, the result is instead the radicalization of the Islamic people, not only in places where NATO soldiers have been fighting for freedom and democracy, but inside Europe and the United States.[9]

Second, in Vldimirov's view, NATO is not ready to contain the approaching "civilizational stress" that Europe is facing at this moment because of Muslim immigration. Europe, he insists, is doing nothing to save its own indigenous people; rather, it is instead hiding behind the ideology of political correctness. This he sees as extremely dangerous, since the result will, most probably, be a war between civilizations within Europe, as immigrant revolts in Paris and Stockholm have already signaled. Thus, he predicts Europe's implosion. Similar scenarios can be expected in the United States and Russia. Third, he says that NATO has lost its meaning and purpose and not yet found a new role. The North Atlantic Alliance's security guarantee to its members is still only to assure its members that first the Soviet Union and now Russia will not engage in a war against them. However, an annexation of Poland, Estonia, Latvia, Lithuania, or even non-NATO members Ukraine and Georgia is neither necessary nor strategically significant for Russia, Vladimirov writers. Therefore, in its present form, NATO is not needed for the defense of its European member states, although it remains a prime necessity for the United States, since the Alliance serves as an instrument to legitimize US actions. By utilizing NATO in missions abroad, the United States is, first of all, able to ignore the UN Security Council. Reliance on the Alliance also props up Washington's own bureaucracy. And third, Vlaidmirov argues, NATO is useful for splitting up foreign regimes, in the late Zbigniew Brzeziński's terms.[10]

Vladimirov writes that NATO never confirmed its friendliness toward Moscow. It continues to consider Russia an enemy and is constantly preparing for war against Russian military forces. Finally, NATO supports anti-Russian military-political trends in the regions within Russia's natural interests. Notwithstanding the difficult relationship between the North Atlantic Alliance and Moscow, they both need each other, he contends—first, as the basis for a certain continental bipolar stability; second, as a necessary strategic deterrent; third, as the "official" enemy; fourth, as an incentive for development; and fifth, as a potential strategic ally to win the civilizational war. In this sense, Russia's efforts to weaken NATO are counterproductive.[11]

The obstacle to Russia establishing a productive relationship with NATO countries, according to Vladimirov, is the United States. It has to maintain its global hegemony to guarantee the dollar as the global currency *par excellence*. This is necessary to guarantee financial stability, mostly because of the US's unpayable foreign debt. In addition, it gives the United States the power to buy unlimited amounts of whatever is necessary to maintain its global hegemony in the first place. The US pursuit of globalization results in a state of permanent war, causing poverty, injustice and lawlessness. Furthermore, in the United States, the formation of values and the development of financial, economic, ideological, technological, informational and organizational power, guaranteeing national survival were transferred from the state to private transnational corporations. The result, according to Vladimirov, is the establishment of global oligarchical fascism.[12]

More recently, the Kremlin backed the Izborsky Club's "Defense Reform as an Integral Part of a Security Conception for the Russian Federation: a Systemic and Dynamic Evaluation."[13] The first point made by the piece, attributed to military experts Aleksandr Nagorny and Vladislav Shurygin, is the understanding that the 1990s idea of Russia not having any direct external adversary has proved illusory. Moreover, the adoption of a strategy of unilateral diplomatic concessions—that is, showing Russia as a responsible and serious international player and, therefore, persuading the West to accept it in the international system as an equal partner—resulted in failure.[14]

The second point is that the main external threat to Russia consists of the interests of the United States and its Western allies. According to this idea, the West resists Russia restoring its status as a global power. Instead, it pursues policies, mostly economic, to force Russia to become a producer of raw materials, unable to develop its military strength. To achieve supremacy over Russia, the Euro-Atlantic community has been using so-called power instruments, including the imposition of unbalanced agreements on, for example, the reduction of strategic nuclear missiles and tactical nuclear weapons.

The authors of the Izborsky Club article conclude that Russia should prepare for three possible military conflict scenarios: First, a major war with NATO and Japan; second, a regional border-conflict scenario, i.e. disputed territories; and third, an internal military conflict as a result of terrorism. It is not believed that a direct military conflict with NATO in the short term can be expected. However, Russia has been facing severe pressure with the infringement of its strategic national interests. NATO has politically and militarily wiped out most of Russia's natural potential allies. This can be exemplified by NATO's "expansion" into the former Warsaw Pact space. The monetarist economic ideology imposed by the International Monetary Fund, the World Bank, and other multilateral organizations, not only had the objective of weakening Russian society overall, but resulted in the underfunding of the Armed Forces and, thus, an operational degradation.[15]

The authors argue for developing a strategy to neutralize the information-network war of controlled chaos the United States and NATO has been waging against Russia. The first step is to include in Russia's military doctrine the list of factors threatening the state: rebels, bandits and mercenaries, extremists, ethno-religious and nationalist organizations, as well as the conduct of warfare without any rules or outside classical canons. The most important threat to Russia, in the view of the authors, is a type of subversive weapon called "Westernization," that is, the imposition of a social system, economics, ideology, culture, and way of life similar to the West. The objective is to discredit Russia's political and social system, resulting in dividing the population into hostile groups, some of which are then supported by the United States and NATO.[16]

The core ideas discussed above have now been explicitly included in the latest versions of the Russian "Military Doctrine" (adopted in December 2014) as well as the "National Security Strategy" (December 2015). In both cases, the West, especially the United States, appears as Russia's main adversary, but not necessarily as the main enemy. Other problems affecting Russia's security are poor economic development, demographics and the environment, among others. Both documents stress the use of non-military instruments to achieve political goals, the most important one being social destabilization via color revolutions and terrorism.[17] Since it is a broader strategic document, the "National Security Strategy" also mentions radical public associations, the activities of criminal organizations, corruption, natural disasters, as well as the utilization of economic methods and instruments of financial, trade, investment and technological policy.[18]

Contrary to the idea of inevitable war among all civilization, the *National Security Strategy* explicitly mentions China as a key partner for maintaining regional and global stability, looking for an all-embracing partnership and strategic cooperation. This denies the idea of Russia feeling strategically encircled by a rising China. Other countries, regions, regional blocks, and international institutions of special interest to Russia are the BRICS (Brazil, Russia, India, China, South Africa), RIC (Russia, India, China), the Shanghai Cooperation Organization (SCO), Africa, Latin America, as well as the countries of the Asia-Pacific Economic Cooperation Forum. The Commonwealth of Independent States (CIS), the Republic of Abkhazia and the Republic of South Ossetia, the latter two being separatist regions of Georgia that have been occupied by Russian forces since August 2008, are also listed within the *National Security Strategy* as key strategic areas.[19]

As Putin and Medvedev stated many times, the idea is to form a multipolar world in which Western influence is limited. Since Russia considers itself a superpower, a multipolar world presupposes a territorial division into spheres of influence. This means it feels entitled to inherit the former Soviet space, and any attempt by those countries to become closer to the West is considered a violation of Russia's security interests. In other words, Russia's main strategic interest is to maintain its sphere of influence: annexing and occupying neighboring countries may not always be necessary in Moscow's view, but securing loyal governments along the Russian periphery certainly is. It is within this framework that Russia's military actions have to be evaluated. This also means that the occupation and annexation of Crimea is likely a unique case that, probably, will not be repeated.

The Russian Way of Warfare: New Generation Warfare

The Russian view of modern warfare is based on the idea that the main battlespace is the mind. As a result, new-generation wars are to be dominated by information and psychological warfare in order to achieve superiority in troops and weapons control, morally and psychologically depressing an enemy's armed forces personnel and civilian population. The main objective is to reduce the need to deploy hard military power to the minimum necessary, making the opponent's military and civilian population support the attacker to the detriment of their own government and country.[20] It is interesting to note the notion of permanent war in the *Military Doctrine*, since it denotes a permanent enemy. In the current geopolitical structure, this enemy is NATO, which—as Nagorny and Shurygin mentioned above—stands for Western civilization, its values, culture, political system, and ideology.

The main guidelines for developing Russian military capabilities by 2020 are to shift from:

1. direct destruction to direct influence;
2. direct annihilation of the opponent to bringing about its inner decay;
3. a war with weapons and technology to a culture war;
4. a war with conventional forces to specially prepared forces and commercial irregular groupings;
5. the traditional (physical, three-dimensional) battleground to information/psychological warfare and a war of perceptions;
6. a direct clash to contactless war;
7. a superficial and compartmentalized war to a total war, including targeting the enemy's interior and center of gravity;
8. war in the physical environment, to a war in the human consciousness and in cyber-space;
9. symmetric to asymmetric warfare via a combination of political, economic, information, technological, and ecological campaigns; and
10. war in a defined period of time to a state of permanent war as the natural condition in national life.

In other words, the Russians have placed the idea of influence at the very center of their operational planning and used all possible levers to achieve this: skillful internal communications, deception operations, psychological operations and well-constructed external communications. This is relevant for understanding its strategic significance, since it is the operationalization of a new form of warfare that cannot be characterized as a military campaign in the classic sense of the term. It is an opportunistic mix of different strategies. The key to understanding Russian strategy is realizing that Russians are eclectic, drawing on whatever works for a specific situation.

To fully grasp the foundational theory behind how Russia conducts warfare, it is necessary to review the Russian military literature. It is no surprise that chief of the General Staff General Valery Gerasimov's famous 2013 article discussing his view of modern warfare was called "The Value of Science in Prediction." It shows that, in Russia, military theory is expected to provide both a political and a military theoretical basis on which military art and military strategy are to be constructed—just like during the Soviet era. Presently, Russian military literature includes five main recurrent conceptual themes. The first and most important one is Asymmetric Warfare. It forms the main underpinning sustaining the next three. Second is the strategy of Low Intensity Conflict, as developed by the Pentagon's Joint Special Operations Command; third is Russia's own understanding and theoretical development of Network-Centric Warfare; and fourth is General Vladimir Slipchenko's idea of Sixth-Generation Warfare. It is their many possible combinations that define what, in a 2013 article for *Voennaia Mysl*, Sergei G. Chekinov and Sergei A. Bogadanov called New Generation Warfare.[21] However, there is also an additional, fifth factor: the strategic concept of Reflexive Control. Only when this fifth conceptual theme is applied to New Generation Warfare does the latter become fully operational. More recently, a new term has also appeared in the Russian literature—"New-type (Hybrid) Warfare"—but it has pointedly been used to refer to the allegedly Western strategy of Color Revolutions, i.e. what the Russians call "Hybrid Warfare."

Russian New Generation Warfare is not something new. Rather, it is the latest term for a particular understanding of Russian military thinkers about the evolution of military art, especially in the West. Although it is not correct to affirm that the Western way of conducting warfare determined how Russian military thinkers developed their own understanding on the subject, its influence is undeniable. Both the strategy of Low-Intensity Conflict and Network Centric Warfare were originally developed in the United States, while Sixth-Generation Warfare very much reflects Slipchenko's understanding about the strategic implications of Operation Desert Storm and the NATO bombing of Yugoslavia. Therefore, it is possible to affirm that the concept of Hybrid Warfare is strange to the Russian military, but New Generation Warfare results from the Russian military's own understanding and interpretation of Western military strategy. This explains why many people have been saying it is not new, while at the same time being unable to fully explain it. Similarly, the term "hybrid" became quite popular exactly because it can be understood as anything that is not monolithic.

As alluded to above, the fundamental operational applications of Russian New Generation Warfare were discussed in a 2013 paper by Chekinov and Bogadanov (2013) called "The Character and Content of New Generation Warfare" ("*O kharaktere i soderzhanii voi'ny novogo pokoleniia*").[22] Although their piece does not outline such a clear division, it is possible to draw from their analysis a set of eight phases that characterize New Generation Warfare. These phases are to be employed, preferably, in a sequential way; but at the same time, they are not rigid or mutually exclusive. Indeed, they can be engaged simultaneously, or individual phases can start at any point. Specifically, the eight phases are:

First Phase: non-military asymmetric warfare (encompassing information, moral, psychological, ideological, diplomatic, and economic measures as part of a plan to establish a favorable political, economic, and military situation).

Second Phase: special operations to mislead political and military leaders by coordinated measures carried out by diplomatic channels, media, and top government and military agencies by leaking false data, orders, directives, and instructions.

Third Phase: intimidation, deception, and bribing of government and military officers, with the objective of making them abandon their service duties.

Fourth Phase: destabilizing propaganda to increase discontent among the population, boosted by the arrival of Russian bands of militants, escalating subversion.

Fifth Phase: establishment of no-fly zones over the country to be attacked, imposition of blockades, and extensive use of private military companies in close cooperation with armed opposition units.

Sixth Phase: commencement of military action, immediately preceded by large-scale reconnaissance and subversive missions. All types, forms, methods and forces, including special operations forces, space, radio, radio engineering, electronic, diplomatic, and secret service intelligence, and industrial espionage.

Seventh Phase: combination of a targeted information operation, electronic warfare operation, aerospace operation, continuous air force harassment, combined with the use of high-precision weapons launched from various platforms (long-range artillery and weapons based on new physical principles, including microwaves, radiation and non-lethal biological weapons).

Eighth Phase: roll over the remaining points of resistance and destroy surviving enemy units by special operations conducted by reconnaissance units to spot which enemy units have survived and transmit their coordinates to the attacker's missile and artillery units; fire barrages to annihilate the defender resisting army units by effective advanced weapons; air-drop operations to surround points of resistance; and territory mopping-up operations by ground troops.

The first four phases are basically non-kinetic, using strategies of Low Intensity Conflict as understood by the Russians. The fifth phase is when military action really starts. It is important to mention the use of private military companies (PMC). The United States has extensively used them in Iraq and Afghanistan—from operating mess halls to providing security and, sometimes, performing military duties. For the Russians, PMCs must be understood as mercenaries. The objective is to have an active military force that cannot be linked to the Russian Armed Forces. These mercenaries can act as if they are locals, part of the enemy's Armed Forces, police, or whatever is necessary at that moment. They will often engage in sabotage, blackmail, subversive activities, terrorism, kidnapping, or any other activity that is not considered regular warfare. The Russian government, in turn, can and will deny any connection with its mercenaries, publicly accusing them of being part of the enemy's forces. The last three phases are a combination of Network Centric Warfare, Sixth-Generation Warfare and Reflexive Control.

Asymmetric Warfare

The main element defining the Russian way of war is Asymmetric Warfare. It provides the base on which Low-Intensity Conflict, Network-Centric Warfare and Sixth-Generation Warfare will be combined in different proportions to form the many faces of New Generation Warfare. This is one of the most ignored aspect of the Russian military art. Arguably, the biggest problem about using the term "Hybrid" is that it obfuscates the asymmetric and kinetic character of Russian tactics.

It is the basis for Russia's practice of creating an alternative reality as a military strategy. The idea is that, in a country at war, societal support for the state's strategic objectives—in other words, the legitimization of war—is fundamental for achieving victory. Thus, the success of military campaigns in the form of armed conflicts and local wars is very much dependent on the relationship between military and non-military factors—the political, psychological, ideological, and informational elements of the campaign. Whereas, military power is an isolated variable.

The objective of engaging in asymmetric warfare is to avoid direct military operations or overt interference in internal conflicts in other countries. Because Russia has been fighting exclusively weaker adversaries, the following strategy has been predominant for it: employment of small, specially trained troops; preventive actions against irregular forces; propaganda among local populations; military and material support given to certain groups in the country being attacked; as well as a scaling-back of combat operations and employing non-military methods to pressure the opponent. In general terms, the Russians consider the following points as the most important instruments of Asymmetric Warfare:

1. Measures to make the opponent apprehensive of the Russian Federation's intentions and responses;
2. Demonstrations of the readiness and capabilities of Russian troops (forces) located in a strategic area to repel an invasion with consequences unacceptable to the aggressor;
3. Actions by the troops (forces) to deter a potential enemy by guaranteed destruction of its most vulnerable military and other strategically important and potentially dangerous targets in order to persuade the enemy that attack on Russia would be hopeless;
4. The impact of state-of-the-art, highly effective weapons systems, including those based on new physical principles (remote versus contact);
5. Widespread employment of indirect force as well as non-contact forms of commitment of troops (forces) and methods;

6. Not always needing to seize and hold enemy territory; such actions are only undertaken if the benefits are greater than the "combat costs," or if the end goals of a war cannot be achieved in any other way;

7. Information warfare as an independent form of struggle along with economic, political, ideological, diplomatic and other forms;

8. Information and psychological operations to weaken the enemy's military potential by means other than armed force, by affecting the enemy's information flow processes, and by misleading and demoralizing its population and armed forces personnel;

9. Significant damage to the enemy's economic potential, with its effect showing up at a later time;

10. Pushing a clear understanding on a potential adversary that military operations could turn into an environmental and sociopolitical catastrophe.

It is interesting to note that much of what has been written by Russian military experts about Russia's strategic challenges reflects the way it has actually itself been conducting warfare. Notably, Nagorny and Shurygin, in analyzing Russia's most important strategic challenges, established ways and instruments the West could employ against it. Although their analysis mostly refers to so-called Color Revolutions—purported strategies of controlled-chaos deliberately being employed by the West—it reveals more about Russian strategy itself. In their paper, they formalize nine points that, although allegedly could be used by the West against Russia, in reality strongly reflects the Russian asymmetric strategy operationalized, for example, in Ukraine. The nine points Nagorny and Shurygin ascribe to the West are as follows[23]:

1. Stimulation and support of armed actions by separatist groups with the objective of promoting chaos and territorial disintegration;

2. Polarization between the elite and society, resulting in a crisis

of values followed by a process of reality orientation toward Western values;

3. Demoralization of armed forces and military elite;
4. Strategic controlled degradation of the socioeconomic situation;
5. Stimulation of a socio-political crisis;
6. Intensification of simultaneous forms and models of psychological warfare;
7. Incitement of mass panic and loss of confidence in key government institutions;
8. Defamation of political leaders who are not aligned with Russia's interests;
9. Undercutting possibilities to form coalitions with foreign allies.

The Russian view of Asymmetric Warfare is both systemic and comprehensive, simultaneously employing political, diplomatic, informational, economic, military and other indirect forms. It also can use strategic high-precision non-nuclear weapons systems, with the support of subversive and reconnaissance groups. Such asymmetric attacks can resulting in unacceptable damage to strategically significant targets like top government administration and military control facilities, fuel and energy plants, life-support facilities, chemical factories, or storehouses of poisonous agents, just to cite some examples.

Low-Intensity Conflict

Low-Intensity Conflict (LIC) was developed by the United States in the 1980s. It can be defined as:

...a political-military confrontation between contending states or groups below conventional war and above the routine, peaceful competition among states. It frequently involves protracted struggles of competing principles and ideologies. It ranges from subversion to the use of armed force. It is waged by a combination of means employing political, economic, informational, and military instruments. LIC's are often localized, generally in the Third World, but contain regional and global security implications.[24]

The main factors making LICs possible are change, discontent, poverty, violence, and instability. Change includes socio-economic and political factors that may result in raising tensions. If a government is not connected to or, in some cases, even concerned about the wishes of the people, the result might be discontentment leading to internal turmoil. Discontent can have many forms and is linked to feelings of injustice. Moreover, the level of social violence is directly related to the number of people sharing a common sense of such injustice, which in turn determines the level of discontent. Outside pressure can be a critical factor boosting such sentiment. Poverty, especially as a result of unstable economic conditions, is also an important factor influencing LICs. As a result, impoverished nations have a great potential for revolution and change. Very often, the spark can be a relatively simple need, but one that is ignored by the ruling government. It is, thus, possible for a domestic or outside actor to target what the population wants, stimulating revolutionary actions (violent or not) and creating instability. Therefore, instability can be considered an asset if it can be used to achieve one side's goals in an LIC mission.

Low-Intensity Conflict has five essential requirements. First is political dominance, meaning that the military of a country engaged in an LIC is subjugated to its civilian and political authorities. Second, there must be unity of effort or the integration of military actions with other government agencies' initiatives. Interagency coordination is critical, and commanders may answer to civilian chiefs or employ the resources of civilian agencies. Third, a country participating in an LIC must showcase adaptability to develop new approaches reflecting new situations. Fourth, the government needs to maintain legitimacy to rule. And fifth is perseverance, since an LIC involves protracted struggles. Additionally, Low-Intensity Conflict has four main operational categories: support for insurgency and counterinsurgency, combating terrorism, peacekeeping operations, and Peacetime Contingency Operations.

Returning to the Russian case, the main concept used by the Russians is "controlled chaos." It is mostly based on the US literature about Low-Intensity Conflict and Counterinsurgency operations, and is often referred to as a strategy of "Destruction and Attrition." Its objective is the geopolitical destruction of the victim state by a set of measures aiming to neutralize any geopolitical advantage the enemy might have, such as economic power, military might, international status, size of territory and population, etc. In Moscow's view, Color Revolutions and the Arab Spring are examples of how the West uses this concept.

"Controlled chaos" or "Destruction and Attrition" has three stages. First, there is crisis-inspired destabilization and internal conflicts. Second—degradation, impoverishment, and disintegration of the country making it a failed state. Third, the aggressor, posing as a benefactor and savior of the stricken country, steps in with troops to change the political regime. The closing is a stabilization operation. The main target is the self-awareness of the population, influencing the nation's mindset. The objective is to transfer aggression from the physical space to the information-network one. In other words—to attack the people's national and cultural identity.

The main instrument here is the "technique of information intervention"—already used during the Cold War—which predominantly utilizes extremist nationalist, religious, or separatist movements. All organizations and structures that might destabilize the internal political situation in the country can thus be put in play. This includes the direct and indirect support of subversive forces to take control of government organizations, the mass media, culture institutions, non-governmental foundations and social movements to promote the political and ideological values of the attacking country. The result is the destruction of the enemy's social and ideological system. Its mechanism of self-destruction and self-annihilation can be compared to a virus penetrating the internal structure and governance system. Also, it is conducted without any rules. There are no borderlines between the front and rear, close- and long-range combat, contact and non-contact actions, or offensive and defensive methods.

Sixth-Generation Warfare

The concept of Sixth Generation Warfare was developed by General Vladimir Slipchenko to reflect what he considered a new way of warfare. It is very much based on his views of Operation Desert Storm and NATO's aerial bombing campaign over Yugoslavia. It has three main components. First is the use of advanced conventional systems that approach nuclear effects, thus blurring the line on nuclear deterrence. Second is non-contact warfare. Third—the use of high-technology non-nuclear weapons. The main operational objective is to make obsolete the massing the large forces in a conventional war. However, since the aim of waging war is to achieve political objectives, the strategic goal is to use high-precision weapons to destroy the enemy's means of retaliation. This means employing high-precision non-nuclear weapons, together with the support of subversive and reconnaissance groups, to target strategic points that, if destroyed, result as unacceptable damage to the country being attacked.

Those key targets include top government administration and military-control systems, major manufacturing plants, fuel and energy facilities, transportation hubs and facilities (railroad hubs, bridges, ports, airports, tunnels, etc.), and potentially dangerous objects (hydroelectric power dams and complexes, processing units of chemical plants, nuclear power facilities, as well as storages of strong poisons, etc.). If the enemy's armed forces are mostly composed of ground units, it might not be necessary to destroy them. The idea is to make the enemy's political system collapse, with the local population turned into an instrument to achieve victory. In this case, the occupation of foreign territory might not be necessary. Russian bombings of hospitals and food storehouses in Syria in recent years are clear examples of Sixth-Generation Warfare.

Network-Centric Warfare

Although Network-Centric Warfare is a Western concept, for the Russians it has a double character. One of the best definitions is by Russian defense experts A. V. Raskin, V. S. Pelyak and S. A. Vyalov:

> Network-centric warfare is a war in which the combat strength of a troop (force) grouping is increased thanks to the creation of an information-communication network that would link information (intelligence) sources, control bodies and means of destruction (suppression). This can be done by giving the participants in operations reliable and complete information about the situation practically in real time. [25]

It presupposes (i) the organization of forces on the networking principle with higher autonomy; (ii) it is global; (iii) the notion of a "battlefield" includes emotions, figurative perceptions of reality and the adversary's state of mind (in other words, instruments of Reflexive Control); (iv) without global communication among forces, command and control (C2) is impossible; (v) that the proportion of non-military tools of coercion has dramatically increased, while at the same time there are no distinct state and national limits; and finally, (vi) the abandonment of the classical hierarchical command-and-control system for horizontal links between the parts involved.[26]

No longer based on divisions of between 15,000 and 20,000 troops, Network-Centric Warfare relies on smaller units of between 3,000 and 5,000 men. Each of these formations is essentially an autonomous module, able to independently conduct combat operations.

Depending on the conditions, smaller modules like a detached battalion, a reinforced company, or even a platoon or small special operations unit may be required to operate independently. It is of fundamental importance that each individual unit possess a degree of autonomy and capability to successfully perform its missions.

The autonomous information module assures proper cooperation between each autonomous combat module and the command and staff module. This is done by establishing a single information space based on an aggregate database of loops of information collected by the autonomous combat and command and staff modules. This collected information must include data on the adversary, own troops, intelligence, the navigation field and weather conditions, just to cite a few. The information database is to be used to provide continuous command and control, inform one's own troops, misinform the adversary (including by disrupting its information systems), protect one's own information systems, shape the desired image of reality to shape public opinion, and create psychological pressure on the adversary.

The autonomous information module has to be constituted of units and subunits of intelligence and psychological operations, Electronic Warfare, Information Warfare, one group of space-based support, automatic C2, and communications support. This structure changes the role of C2. First, command and control is redefined from a supervisory to a coordination role; second, the process of decision making and the conduct of combat operations is decentralized. Therefore, it is necessary to establish superiority in C2 by destructively taking control of the enemy's network-centric organization to create a situation of controlled chaos.

The first stratum must be understood as the procedures for reflexively controlling the adversary. It is done at the personal level, since it consists of selecting specific individuals from the adversary's military and political leadership to receive information to influence their decisions. The main aim is to adversely influence the opponent's process of decision making, creating favorable conditions for the controller's own forces. The second stratum consists of controlling the adversary in situations of uncertainty. The analysis of the information indicators of the situation is used to escalate the conflict rather than normalizing it. This is useful to decide the best courses of action in case of incomplete or divergent information about the opponent's behavioral profile. The third stratum focuses on the destructive control of the enemy's entire network with the objective of creating controlled chaos.[27]

Reflexive Control

Reflexive Control is the technique of providing the opponent (controlled) with especially enemy information to make her or him voluntarily take a predetermined action desired by the controller. It may occur by changing the enemy's information processing (cognitive) or by selecting the messages (informational). It can also be divided between "constructive" reflexive control, whereby the opponent is influenced to voluntarily make a decision favorable to the controller, and "destructive" reflexive control, when the objective is to destroy, paralyze, or neutralize the procedures and algorithms of the opponent's decision-making processes. Reflexive Control manipulates moral, psychological, and other factors, such as the personal characteristics of the opponent, using psychological deficiencies in deception operations.[28]

Conclusion

Since Russia annexed and occupied Crimea in early 2014, Western analysts have been trying to find a term to define the strategy Russia has been employing in Ukraine and across the post-Soviet space. "Fourth-Generation Warfare" was proposed initially, followed by suggestions of "Non-Linear Warfare," until NATO started using the term "Hybrid Warfare," probably when Major General Gordon "Skip"

Davis uttered it during a briefing to refer to the Russian tactics in Ukraine.[29] Yet, none of these terms adequately to describe what the Russians themselves call "New Generation Warfare." Although it is true that Western military thought has influenced Russian military thinkers, it is methodologically incorrect to try to frame Russian military thought within the Western rational framework. Therefore, to fully apprehend the theoretical developments that resulted in establishing the way Russia has been conducting warfare, it is necessary to review the Russian military literature with the objective of reversely deconstructing its theoretical fundaments.

Russian New Generation Warfare is not a new approach to warfighting. Rather, it codifies the particular understanding of Russian military thinkers about the evolution of military art. The concept, in fact, comes out of a combined use of Asymmetric Warfare, Low-Intensity Conflict, Network-Centric Warfare and Six-Generation Warfare, in various proportions or combinations, and based on Russia's own interpretation of these methods. However, it is only when combined with Reflexive Control that New Generation Warfare approaches become truly operationalized.

As seen in Russia's ongoing activities in Ukraine—but also against multiple countries in Europe, the United States and the West more generally—New Generation Warfare seeks to bring about political or military outcomes without necessarily resorting to overt conventional military means, although the latter is certainly not excluded. Crucially, New Generation Warfare is based on the idea that the main battlespace is the mind, which necessitates a predominant focus on information and psychological warfare so as to morally and psychologically depress an enemy's armed forces personnel and civilian population—preferably before overt hostilities can even break out. The main objective is to reduce the need to deploy hard military power to the minimum necessary, making the opponent's military and civilian population support the attacker to the detriment of their own government and country.

The West's answer to these threats must, therefore, be based on the concept of Asymmetric Warfare. In the Russian case, it has two meanings. First is the classic one, where the weaker fights the stronger. And Russia considers itself the weaker party. Second is the asymmetry resulting from the different views of what is, and what is not, acceptable in warfare. Russia is ready to go much further than what might be acceptable to the West. In this case, the weaker party inverts the asymmetric relationship, since it is able to exploit the stronger player's unwillingness to cross its own red lines. At this moment, NATO and Europe's greatest challenge is to establish a feasible strategy to cope with this, without jeopardizing their own values.

That is why NATO must develop a more pragmatic approach toward Russia and, at the same time, must be ready for the prospect of increasing instability on Europe's borders. Furthermore, that is why it is important to boost the presence of NATO in the frontline border states, such as the Baltics. At the same time, the Alliance will need to continue to engage in diplomatic talks with Russia to promote arms control and perhaps even the ban on the use of nuclear weapons.

Notes

[1] Francis G. Hoffman, "Hybrid Warfare and Challenges," *Joint Force Quarterly, Issue 52, 1, (2009): 34–40.*

[2] Janis Berzins, "Russia's New Generation Warfare in Ukraine: Implications for Latvian Defense Policy," National Defence Academy of Latvia Center for Security and Strategic Research, Policy Paper No. 2, 2014.

[3] Aleksandr I. Vladmirov, "Bol'shaya amerikanskaya voyna" ("The Great American War"), *Voyenno-promyshlennyy kur'yer*, September 24, 2008, http://vpk-news.ru/articles/1776.

[4] Voyenno-promyshlennyy kur'yer, "Bol'shaya amerikanskaya voyna" ("The Great American War").

5 Aleksandr I.Vladmirov, "NATO v paradigme obshchey teorii voyny" ("NATO in the Paradigm of the General Theory of War"), 2014, http://kadet.ru/lichno/vlad_v/NATO&Obschaya_teoriya_voiny.htm.

6 Aleksandr I. Vladmirov, "SShA - Glavnyy Aktor Mirovoy Voyny" ("The United States – The Main Actor in the World War"), 2012, http://kadet.ru/lichno/vlad_v/USA_gl_aktor.htm.

7 Vladmirov, "NATO v paradigme obshchey teorii voyny" ("NATO in the Paradigm of the General Theory of War").

8 North Atlantic Treaty Organization, "The North Atlantic Treaty," http://www.nato.int/cps/en/natolive/official_texts_17120.htm.

9 Vladmirov, "NATO v paradigme obshchey teorii voyny" ("NATO in the Paradigm of the General Theory of War").

10 Ibid.

11 Ibid.

12 "SShA - Glavnyy Aktor Mirovoy Voyny" ("The United States – The Main Actor in the World War").

13 Aleksandr A. Nagorny and Vladislav V. Shurygin, "Defense Reform as an Integral Part of a Security Conception for the Russian Federation: a Systemic and Dynamic Evaluation," Izborsky Club, http://www.dynacon.ru/content/articles/1085/. The Izborsky Club was formed by a group of Russian nationalists, some of them sympathetic to national-Bolshevik ideas. It has major influence on Vladimir Putin's thinking and policies, including in Eurasianism (as espoused by Aleksandr Dugin), geopolitics (Leonid Ivashov), socio-economic doctrine (Sergei Glaziev), and the concept of Russian civilization in a clash with the West (Andrei Platonov).

14 Nagorny and Shurygin, "Defense Reform as an Integral Part of a Security Conception for the Russian Federation: a Systemic and Dynamic Evaluation."

15 Ibid.

16 Ibid.

17 President of Russia, "Voyennaya doktrina Rossiyskoy Federatsii" ("The Military Doctrine of the Russian Federation"), December 26, 2014, http://www.kremlin.ru/acts/news/47334; "O Strategii natsional'noy bezopasnosti

Rossiyskoy Federatsii" ("On the National Strategy of the Russian Federation"), Ministry of Defense of the Russia Federation, July 26, 2017, http://stat.doc.mil.ru/documents/quick_search/more.htm?id=12074117.

[18] Ministry of Defense of the Russia Federation, "O Strategii natsional'noy bezopasnosti Rossiyskoy Federatsii" ("On the National Strategy of the Russian Federation").

[19] Ibid.

[20] Berzins, "Russia's New Generation Warfare in Ukraine: Implications for Latvian Defense
Policy."

[21] Sergei G. Chekinov, Sergei A. Bogadanov, "O kharaktere i soderzhanii voyny novogo pokoleniya" ("On the Nature and Content of a New-Generation War"), *Voennaia Mysl*, no. 10 (2013).

[22] Sergei G. Chekinov, Sergei A. Bogadanov, "O kharaktere i soderzhanii voyny novogo pokoleniya," pp. 13–24.

[23] Nagorny and Shurygin, "Defense Reform as an Integral Part of a Security Conception for the Russian Federation: a Systemic and Dynamic Evaluation."

[24] "Military Operations in Low Intensity Conflict," FM 100-20 / AFP 3-20, Departments of the Army and Air Force, Washington, DC, December 5, 1990, available at https://www.globalsecurity.org/military/library/policy/army/fm/100-20/.

[25] A. V. Raskin, V. S. Pelyak, S. A. Vyalov, "Kontseptsiya setetsentricheskoy voyny: za i protiv ("The Concept of Network-Centric Warfare: Pro and Contra")," *Voyennaya Mysl* (*Military Thought*), 2005, p. 7.

[26] Ibid.

[27] Ibid.

[28] Timothy L. Thomas, "Russia's Reflexive Control Theory and the Military," *Journal of Slavic Military Studies* 17 (2004), pp. 237–256, available at https://www.rit.edu/~w-cmmc/literature/Thomas_2004.pdf.

[29] The author heard this story from General Davis himself during a meeting at the NATO/SHAPE headquarters in Mons, Belgium.

6. Russian Nuclear Policy, Doctrine and Strategy

Stefan Forss

Introduction

As the Cold War was coming to an end, if not earlier, the leaders of the world's two superpowers largely came to believe that the enormous effort of building up and maintaining their vast nuclear weapons stockpiles had been a mistake. The nuclear arms race consumed extensive quantities of material and human resources in the United States, but particularly in the Soviet Union. It also remained unclear whether nuclear weapons could in fact be employed operationally in armed conflicts.[1]

In addition, the need to store tens of thousands of nuclear warheads was generating new problems of its own, as the aging nuclear stewardship facilities in both countries approached the end of their operational lives. Time was finally ripe for a radical change. Several ground-breaking bilateral and multilateral nuclear arms treaties were signed in just a few years' time: namely, the Intermediate-Range Nuclear Forces (INF) Treaty in 1987, the Strategic Arms Reduction Treaty (START) in 1991, the Lisbon Treaty between the United States, Russia, Ukraine, Belarus and Kazakhstan in 1992, as well as START II in 1993. Additionally, the US and the Soviet Union/Russia both signed unilateral legally non-binding commitments to reduce their non-strategic nuclear weapons, in 1991/1992. These have been referred to as Presidential Nuclear Initiatives (PNI).[2]

All five of the world's original recognized nuclear weapons states (the United States, Russia, the United Kingdom, France and China) are bound by their commitments made in the Non-Proliferation Treaty (NPT) to pursue a policy aiming for the abolition of nuclear weapons. The key commitment is found in Article VI: Each party

> undertakes to pursue negotiations in good faith on effective measures relating to cessation of the nuclear arms race at an early date and to nuclear disarmament, and on a Treaty on general and complete disarmament under strict and effective international control.[3]

In his State of the Union address in January 1984, then-President Ronald Reagan tackled the problem head on:

> People of the Soviet Union, there is only one sane policy, for your country and mine, to preserve our civilization in this modern age: A nuclear war cannot be won and must never be fought. The only value in our two nations possessing nuclear weapons is to make sure they will never be used. But then would it not be better to do away with them entirely?[4]

Reagan discussed this issue with his Soviet colleague, Mikhail Gorbachev, in Reykjavik in 1986. The Soviet president suggested, in January of that year, that nuclear weapons should be abolished altogether before the end of the century. That surprising move was generally not taken seriously. Both heads of state were, however, genuinely attracted to the idea of a world without nuclear weapons. In an interview in 2012, President Gorbachev reflected on that meeting:

We had said that a nuclear war cannot be won and must never be fought, we could not tolerate the situation that we had, we needed to deal with those mountains of weapons, to get rid of nuclear weapons. [...] It is strange that some people still think about nuclear weapons in terms of deterrence—that the positive role of nuclear weapons is that they deter. I have to say that this is not serious, if you look at the big picture. So, when we talk about nuclear weapons and what's to be done about them, the answer is to get rid of them.[5]

The idea of a world without nuclear weapons lived on, despite some unanticipated setbacks. For more than a decade, influential, bipartisan U.S. politicians and observers (notably, proponents of the so-called "Hoover Plan")[6] have strongly argued that such a world would certainly be in the interest of the United States. And in his speech in Prague, on April 5, 2009, President Barack Obama reiterated this same vision:

So today, I state clearly and with conviction America's commitment to seek the peace and security of a world without nuclear weapons. I'm not naive. This goal will not be reached quickly—perhaps not in my lifetime. It will take patience and persistence. But now we, too, must ignore the voices who tell us that the world cannot change.[7]

All US administrations from Reagan to Obama have undoubtedly acted in the spirit of the NPT and achieved impressive results. The same can essentially be said for Russia during President Yeltsin's administration and halfway into President Vladimir Putin's second term. The nuclear inventories in both countries have decreased to a small fraction of the inventories at the end of the Cold War.[8]

The elimination of a full category of land-based shorter- and medium-range ballistic missiles and cruise missiles, altogether 2,692 weapons systems during implementation of the INF Treaty in the early 1990s, was groundbreaking. [9] The symbolic value of that landmark treaty for the nuclear arms reduction process is difficult to overstate.

The reductions of strategic nuclear weapons proceeded well after the START treaty entered into force, in December 1994. Ratification was, however, delayed because of the sudden breakup of the Soviet Union and the necessity to handle the situation, with Ukraine, Belarus and Kazakhstan having a significant portion of the Soviet strategic nuclear weapon systems on their territory. All Soviet nuclear warheads in Soviet republics outside Russia had, however, been transferred to the Russian Federation, the successor state of the Soviet Union as custodian of nuclear weapons, already in 1992.

Yet, the simultaneous ratification process of START II, negotiated by the administration of George H. W. Bush, became stuck in the US Congress. That treaty carried a big prize, as it allowed only single-warhead, land-based intercontinental ballistic missiles (ICBM) and called for the complete elimination of the only heavy ICBM in the Russian inventory—the R-36UTTKh/M2 (SS-18 Mods 4/5 Satan)—the flagship of the Russian Strategic Rocket forces, which carried ten high-yield warheads. The United States had no comparable heavy ICBM at this time.

The bilateral US-Russian treaty-based regulation of strategic nuclear forces was intrinsically linked to restrictive measures in the field of missile defense. The Soviet/Russian political and military leadership was suspicious of President Reagan's utopian Strategic Defense Initiative and later more modest missile-defense aims.

President George W. Bush declared the US intention to withdraw from the 1972 Anti-Ballistic Missile (ABM) Treaty in December 2001, arguing that "the ABM treaty hinders our government's ways to protect our people from future terrorist or rogue state missile attacks." Russia's President Putin said the move, although not unexpected, was a mistake and that "the [ABM] treaty is a cornerstone of world security." Nonetheless, the Russian leader's assessment of the implications was sober:

As is well known, Russia and the U.S., unlike other nuclear powers, have for a long time possessed effective means to overcome missile defenses. [...] Therefore, I fully believe that the decision taken by the president of the United States does not pose a threat to the national security of the Russian Federation.[10]

Moscow's position has since then changed significantly.[11] The US missile-defense efforts may ultimately threaten Russia's strategic nuclear deterrence capability, the Russian side claims.

As the US withdrawal from the ABM Treaty came into force, on June 13, 2002, Russia declared the next day that it was no longer bound by START II.[12] This set the stage for developments that have become core issues one and a half decades later.

Russia's Changed Attitude Toward Nuclear Weapons and Nuclear Arms Control

The "Hoover Plan," the denuclearization agenda initiated in 2007 by senior US personalities, received wide international support, particularly in the West.[13] The official Russian response was less enthusiastic, and the country now largely rejects the Gorbachev-era idea of a world without nuclear weapons.

The changed attitude was felt, in 2008, in the United Nations Security Council Advisory Board on Disarmament Matters (ABDM), where the Russian delegate strongly resisted that US proposals on nuclear disarmament that were introduced on the ABDM agenda.[14] Two distinct motives help explain such a dramatic change in Moscow's approach to the total elimination of nuclear weapons: balance of power and Russia's global power status.

For Russia, a nuclear component is an irreplaceable counterweight to the perceived conventional superiority of its rivals. The political implications of possessing nuclear weapons, is as important as the military factor. Put another way, Russia without nuclear weapons would be reduced to a dwarf on the global scene.

Following the breakup of the Soviet Union—in President Putin's words one of the most catastrophic events of the 20th century—Russia's position as a major nuclear power was challenged in the mid-1990s.[15] The most important ICBM systems in service were manufactured in Ukraine; and the primary project of the strategic fleet, the development of the massive Typhoon-class strategic nuclear missile submarine (SSBN), had proved to be a major disappointment. Moreover, the industrial base and the economy of Russia could no longer support maintaining its strategic forces at even a fraction of their former levels. In this situation, the then–minister of defense, Army General Igor Rodionov, not only supported the START II treaty but also favored further reductions after meeting with Defense Secretary William Perry in Moscow, in October 1996.[16]

START II and the outline of START III never became legally binding. But even so, significant reductions on both sides continued during the first decade of the 21st century. Presidents George W. Bush and Vladimir Putin signed an unusually short (only a few pages long) framework document, the Strategic Offensive Reductions Treaty (SORT), without any meaningful negotiations in 2002. After the Yeltsin era, Russia had embarked on a major, and still ongoing, nuclear buildup, which consumes a significant portion of the defense budget. Although the START process began to show signs of tiring, it still was advantageous for Russia.

The Obama administration invested much political capital in bringing the START process back on track. It led to the signing of the New START Treaty in 2010, which is currently in force. The treaty ceilings had to be met in February 2018 and it expires three years later unless the parties agree to extend it for five years.

US efforts to start a new round of strategic talks and to expand these talks to also include non-strategic nuclear weapons met with firm resistance from Russia. The Global Zero Action Plan campaign, launched in Paris in February 2010, is a case in point. The day before the Paris Summit opened, Swedish and Polish Foreign Ministers Carl Bildt and Radek Sikorski co-authored an op-ed for the *New York Times*, advocating deep reductions in and eventual elimination of non-strategic (tactical) nuclear weapons stockpiles currently located in Europe. Accordingly, the authors called upon Russia to commit to a withdrawal of nuclear weapons from areas adjacent to European states and to the destruction of the relevant storage facilities. They also supported including non-strategic nuclear weapons in an arms control regime.[17]

When Russia refused to discuss non-strategic nuclear weapons, President Obama repeated his offer for a new round of START negotiations while in Berlin in June 2013.[18] His aim was to encourage Russia to agree to cut deployed strategic nuclear weapons by a third from the New START Treaty ceiling, to about 1,000 deployed strategic warheads. Russia's Foreign Minister Sergei Lavrov rejected the offer and declared that all subsequent nuclear reduction talks will have to be multilateral.[19] This position is a clear deviation from a several-decades-long tradition and a hard blow to the START process. It is included—albeit slightly less categorically—in Russia's foreign policy White Paper (The Foreign Policy Concept of the Russian Federation), adopted in late 2016.[20]

Non-Strategic Nuclear Weapons and INF Treaty Issues

Colonel General Leonid Ivashov, one of the most prominent Russian military officers of his time and chief of the international division of the Russian ministry of defense, gave a lecture about Russia's security and defense policy in Helsinki, Finland, in September 2000. He is well known as a nuclear hawk. In his address to the Finnish audience, he maintained that the world had never been as close to World War III as during the Kosovo War the year before.[21] This author asked him then to clarify the Russian implementation of the unilateral presidential PNI commitments given in 1991/1992. General Ivashov gave a lengthy answer with little information, but assured that Russia fully abided by the given commitments.

A summary of the Soviet/Russian Presidential Nuclear Initiatives is as follows:[22]

On October 5, 1991, Soviet President Mikhail Gorbachev responded to the US unilateral moves with reciprocal Soviet measures. Gorbachev committed to:

- eliminate all nuclear artillery munitions, nuclear warheads for tactical missiles, and nuclear mines;
- remove all tactical nuclear weapons from surface ships and multi-purpose submarines. These weapons would be stored in central storage sites along with all nuclear arms assigned to land-based naval aircraft; and
- separate nuclear warheads from air-defense missiles and put the warheads in central storage. A "portion" would be destroyed.

On January 29, 1992, Russian President Boris Yeltsin reaffirmed Gorbachev's commitments and expanded on them in response to a second round of unilateral US nuclear weapons cutbacks focused on strategic forces. (Following the Soviet Union's December 25, 1991, collapse, Russia assumed responsibility for the Soviet Union's nuclear complex and arms-control commitments.) Yeltsin said Russia would:[23]

- eliminate a third of its sea-based tactical nuclear weapons and half of its ground-to-air nuclear missile warheads; and
- halve its airborne tactical nuclear weapons stockpile. Pending reciprocal US action, the other half of this stockpile would be taken out of service and placed in central storage depots.

Ample evidence suggests, however, that Russia did not fully implement the above PNIs. This stands out particularly clearly for the ground forces. In 2002, Russia declared to a preparatory meeting for the Nuclear Non-Proliferation Treaty conference that it had "practically" implemented all of its PNI obligations, "with the exception of elimination of nuclear weapons in the army [i.e., the Ground Forces]."[24] But in 2007, Russia tried to clarify the meaning of the commitments to destroy the Army's nuclear warheads by implying that it was more a matter of removing them than actual elimination. A headline in *Pravda*, "Russia Determined to Keep Tactical Nuclear Weapons for Potential Aggressors," on October 31, 2007, is telling.[25] The current Russian position is clearly stated on the home page of the Missile Troops and Artillery of the Russian Ground Forces:[26]

> The Missile Troops and Artillery (MT & A) are an Arm of the Land Force, which is the primary means of fire and nuclear destruction of the enemy during conduct of combined-arms operations (combat actions).

Dr. Igor Sutyagin, a senior research fellow at the Royal United Services Institute in London, provided a thorough analysis of non-strategic nuclear weapons in Russia's armed forces in 2012.[27] In particular, he illuminated the dual-capable nature of many weapons systems in the ground and naval forces, including ballistic and cruise missiles, rocket launchers and artillery guns. The obvious conclusion is that Russia is no longer bound by the political commitments of the presidential initiatives.

The same Russian mindset is also at the core of the contentious INF Treaty issue. Deep mistrust of this treaty was voiced in the Russian nuclear weapons community more than two decades ago, in September 1996. "We may have to withdraw from the treaty on the elimination of medium- and shorter-range [INF] missiles and resume manufacture of theses arms, if the threat [from NATO expansion] becomes real," the influential Minister of Atomic Energy Viktor Mikhailov and two colleagues wrote at that time.[28]

Another prominent observer, Major General Vladimir Dvorkin, gave an equally clear signal that Russia may ultimately not respect the INF Treaty. In December 1999, he said that the Topol-M ICBM could easily be converted to a medium-range missile:[29]

> The missile would strike a target before its operator has time to smoke a cigarette. Besides, we also have the navy and the air force. They, too, can handle targets in Europe without ever leaving Russian territory.

Possibly the first high-level political indication of Moscow's new position on the INF was received in September 2004, when then–Minister of Defense Sergei Ivanov told reporters that Russia hoped to be able to pull out of the INF Treaty.[30]

Since then, Russian defense authorities have repeatedly raised the INF question in talks with the United States, despite objections from the Russian Ministry of Foreign Affairs. On his visit to Washington in January 2005, Defense Minister Ivanov asked his counterpart Donald Rumsfeld how the United States would react if Russia were to withdraw from the INF Treaty. This was repeated in August 2006, when the two top defense officials met each other in Fairbanks, Alaska.[31]

Ivanov returned to the question in February 2007.[32] His views garnered stronger political weight a few days later, when President Vladimir Putin stated that the INF Treaty no longer served Russia's interests and voiced serious concern regarding the US missile shield plans in Europe. At the Munich Security Conference, on February 10, 2007, Putin said,

Today many other countries have these missiles, including the Democratic People's Republic of Korea [North Korea], the Republic of Korea [South Korea], India, Iran, Pakistan and Israel. Many countries are working on these systems and plan to incorporate them as part of their weapons arsenals. And only the United States and Russia bear the responsibility to not create such weapons systems. It is obvious that in these conditions we must think about ensuring our own security. [...] Plans to expand certain elements of the anti–missile defense system to Europe cannot help but disturb us. Who needs the next step of what would be, in this case, an inevitable arms race? I deeply doubt that Europeans themselves do.[33]

On Moscow's initiative, the United States and Russia jointly proposed before the 2007 UN General Assembly and at the Disarmament Conference that the INF Treaty should be made universally binding.[34] This appeal was not successful, however.

In pursuing its new missile programs, Russia is following a long military-political tradition and has used US missile-defense efforts in general and the European missile shield issue in particular as legitimacy.[35] President Putin reaffirmed this position in in December 2017.[36]

Let's be clear: this is offensive infrastructure that is being created in Europe. This is about violations of provisions of the 1987 INF Treaty by the United States, unfortunately. [...]

For example, multi-purpose missile launchers have already been deployed in Romania, and are being deployed in Poland, as part of the missile defense system. Formally, they are deployed for interceptor missiles, but the point is, and experts are well aware of this, they are multi-purpose units. They can be used to launch existing sea-based cruise missiles with a range of 2,500 kilometers and, in that case, they cease to be sea-based missiles, and can easily be moved to land. That is, anti-missile launchers can, at any time, become units for medium-range cruise missiles.

Another example: target missiles used by the United State for testing anti-ballistic missile systems are identical to medium- and shorter-range ballistic missiles. They are already there and are operational. Their production in the United States may indicate the development of technologies outlawed by the INF Treaty.

Also, the Pentagon received funds for creating a mobile ground-based missile system with a range of up to 5,500 kilometers in 2018. Thus, the United States is, in fact, working towards violating the INF Treaty. They never stop looking for some kind of violation on our part, while consistently engaging in violations themselves, just like they consistently and persistently sought to pull out of the Anti-Ballistic Missile Treaty, which, eventually, as we know, they did in a unilateral manner. Of course, this significantly reduces the level of security in Europe and the world in general.

Shortly after Putin's 2007 Munich speech, the Chief of the General Staff of the Russian Armed Forces, Army General Yuri Baluyevsky, said that pulling out of the INF Treaty was possible, especially if the United States were to implement their missile-defense plans in Europe.[37]

Russia began to emphasize a policy of asymmetric response to address perceived threats in novel ways. The new dual-capable Iskander missile system became the tool of choice to nullify the alleged threat from missile-defense deployments in Europe.[38] A few months after Russia's war against Georgia in August 2008, where ballistic Iskander-M missiles were fired in anger for the first time, then-President Dmitry Medvedev declared Russia's intention to deploy Iskander missiles in Kaliningrad and to take other appropriate measures, should the US missile-defense plans be implemented.[39] From there on,

Russian missile plans for Kaliningrad became a political high-profile issue, which eventually caused concern particularly in the Baltic States and the Scandinavian countries.

The Russian 26th Missile Brigade in Luga, approximately 100 miles south of St. Petersburg in the Western Military District (MD), was among the very first units to receive Iskander missiles in late 2010. Pravda reported of a nervous reaction in NATO. [40] Viktor Litovkin, the editor of the prestigious military journal *Nezavisimoye Voyennoye Obozrenie* (NVO) explained why:

> The missile can be equipped not only with a conventional but also a nuclear warhead. The range of the tactical Iskander-M is 500 kilometers, and many military objects of the alliance will be threatened.

> If we place Iskander missiles in the Kola Peninsula, they would cover a significant part of the Scandinavian Peninsula, including a large area of Norway.

> If we place them in Leningrad and Kaliningrad regions, then all NATO facilities in the Baltic come under attack. Being stationed on the territory of Kaliningrad region, Iskander units also cover half of the territory of Poland.

The deployment of Iskander missiles to Luga did not become an issue in Finnish-Russian relations. Yet, it undoubtedly posed a new level of military-operational capability against Finland, too, as the missile's flying time to Finnish targets was only a few minutes. But there was not much Helsinki could do about that, so the Finnish government chose not to react. The concern in the West and particularly in the other Nordic countries rose as deployments to Kaliningrad gradually materialized.

After Iskander missiles were deployed with the 26th Missile Brigade, they were occasionally employed during exercises in the Kaliningrad region, such as the surprise readiness inspection in March 2015.[41] The 152nd Guards Missile Brigade in Chernyakhovsk, in Kaliningrad, still equipped with aging short-range OTR-21 Tochka-U (SS-21 Scarab) missiles, was the eleventh brigade to receive new Iskander missiles in late 2017.[42]

Defense Minister Sergei Shoigu declared in the upper house of Russia's parliament in May 2017,

> As for the general-purpose forces, self-sufficient groupings of troops and forces capable of adequately responding to any military security threats will be established in all the strategic directions, including the Arctic, by late 2020. The Army is expected to have been fully rearmed with modern Iskander-M missile systems by that time.[43]

The adopted Russian terminology for the operational-tactical Iskander missile system as well as restrictions imposed by the INF Treaty create confusion about the missile system itself and its key performance parameters, such as its range, which is limited to 500 kilometers by treaty.

The 9K720 Iskander missile system (SS-26 Stone) comes in two basic variants: the fast (Mach 6–7) ballistic missile 9M723-1 and the sub-sonic cruise missile 9M728 (a.k.a. R-500 or "Iskander-K"). Collectively, the two are known as "Iskander-M."[44] Iskander-M brigades consist of a mix of both ballistic and cruise missiles, providing significant operational advantages. [45] Footage from the Vostok-2014 exercise is quite illuminating, exhibiting launches of both missile types.[46] The Iskander-K was also fired in the Leningrad region during the Zapad-2017 exercise in September 2017.[47]

Although both Iskander missile types may reach targets well beyond 500 kilometers, the US has not formally accused Russia of INF treaty breach related to the Iskander missile system.[48] This is due to deficiencies in the treaty itself. Moreover, Russia's "treaty compliance" tends to blur the perception of the real capabilities of this missile system. Russian arms control expert Dr. Pavel Podvig quoted a colleague as implying that the range of the Iskander-K is dependent on how much fuel is pumped into the missile. Extended range comes with filling the fuel tank.[49] The nuclear arms control treaties have, in fact, become useful tools for deception.

Two recognized senior researchers, Roger McDermott and Dr. Tor Bukkvoll, described the military-political role of the Iskander missile system succinctly:

> Since its introduction in 2007, the Iskander features in Russia's operational-strategic exercises, and its presence appears to support President Putin's adherence to the "escalate to de-escalate" nuclear strike under certain circumstances. Putin also frequently refers to the Iskander during his speeches on defense issues. More recently its role in such exercises, as well as in separate brigade level exercises, has been to rehearse "pre-emptive" strikes on enemy targets.[50]

US concerns over possible Russian INF-related violations were voiced earlier, in the 2010s. But a formal accusation with no specific technical details was made in July 2014, in the State Department's annual Compliance Report:

> The United States has determined that the Russian Federation is in violation of its obligations under the INF Treaty not to possess, produce, or flight-test a ground-launched cruise missile (GLCM) with a range capability of 500 km to 5,500 km, or to possess or produce launchers of such missiles.[51]

The New York Times reported, in February 2017, that Russia had deployed two battalions of the new prohibited SSC-8 cruise missile.[52] American officials have voiced concerns since 2014 about the tests of this experimental missile, which they designated SSC-X-8. Dropping the "X" meant that the missile was considered operational, and it added substance to the accusation of INF Treaty breach. No details of the missile itself were disclosed, however.

International observers generally assumed that the Iskander missile system was at the core of the alleged treaty breach, but U. authorities denied that repeatedly. The missile in question was officially disclosed in November 2017 by National Security Council member Christopher Ford: the missile is Novator's cruise missile 9M729.[53]

Well-informed researcher Mikhail Barabanov, from the Center for Analysis of Strategies and Technologies (CAST), estimates that the missile is 1.3 meters longer than the same company's 9M728 (Iskander-K) missile, significantly increasing the volume of the missile's fuel tank. The missile obviously was too long to fit the Iskander 9P78-1 transporter erector launcher (TEL).[54] Because of the increased length of the missile, it was necessary to build a new launcher, presumable named 9P701, and also a new transport-loading machine, the 9T256. Both are built on the same Belarusian MZKT-7930 chassis, as are the Iskander launcher and loader vehicles. As such, they are not easily distinguished from each other, former NATO Supreme Commander General Philip Breedlove has observed.[55]

Barabanov describes the 9M729 missile itself as apparently being the same as the Kalibr land-attack cruise missiles deployed on ships and submarines.[56] The nominal range of the missile is 2,500 kilometers, with an operational range about a thousand kilometers less.[57]

Given, that the conventional deterrence value of the new Russian ground-based ballistic and cruise missile systems is limited, their dual-use nature has to be taken into account. The Swedish Defense

Research Establishment (*Totalförsvarets Forskningsinstitut*—FOI) continues to rely on Royal United Services Institutes' Senior Research Fellow Dr. Sutyagin as perhaps the best open source regarding the number of operationally assigned non-strategic nuclear warheads in the Russian arsenal.[58]

The number of offensive non-strategic nuclear weapons is growing. Sutyagin estimates that in mid-2016 there were 156–200 operationally assigned warheads for ship-launched cruise missiles, an increase of 50 percent since 2012. The number of operationally assigned warheads for the Tochka-U and Iskander-M short-range surface-to-surface missile systems has almost doubled to 248–372 warheads, according to Sutyagin, who also holds it possible that warheads still are operationally assigned to heavy artillery units. The marked increase in offensive nonstrategic nuclear weapons noted by Sutyagin is mainly due to the deployment of Kalibr and Iskander-M land-attack cruise missiles.

Regarding the distribution of warheads between Russia's Military Districts, Sutyagin's reports are the only available sources. Still, almost half of the operationally assigned warheads are located in the Western MD. However, the arsenal of the Southern MD has more than tripled since 2012, increasing from 87–103 to 287–369 operationally assigned warheads, surpassing the Eastern MD. The increase mainly consists of new offensive weapons, such as land-attack cruise missiles and warheads for Iskander-Ms and fighter-bombers. Noting that the increase in offensive non-strategic nuclear forces has been at least one and a half time faster in the western parts of Russia, Sutyagin concludes that Russia is rapidly improving its ability to wage offensive nuclear war in Europe."[59]

In order to understand to what lengths Russia is prepared to go to restore the capabilities that were lost at implementation of the INF Treaty, one also needs to reflect about the new ballistic missile RS-26 Rubezh, a.k.a. Yars-M, which, according to some sources, has already been accepted for active service.[60] From an operational, albeit not arms-control perspective, this missile should be compared with the flagship in the eliminated Soviet missile inventory, the RT-12M Pioner (SS-20 Saber), which was a two-stage, stripped version of the Temp-S ICBM, carrying three nuclear warheads.

In December 2013, the commander of the Strategic Rocket Forces, General Karakayev disclosed that the RS-26 is built on the basis of the RS-24 Yars ICBM.[61] In March 2015, it was finally acknowledged that the RS-26 Rubezh has fewer stages and shorter range than the RS-24 Yars.[62]

The first test of RS-26, in September 2011, failed; but the second test flight of the new missile, in May 2012, was successful.[63] The missile apparently flew with a light or empty payload from Plesetsk to the Kura missile range in Kamchatka, 5,800 kilometers, i.e. to intercontinental range. This automatically defined the missile as an ICBM, covered by the New START treaty. The following test, in October 2012, was performed from the Kapustin Yar proving ground to Sary Shagan, in Kazakhstan, over a distance of approximately 2,000 kilometers.[64]

This was the first public telltale signal of a possible diversion from a real intercontinental-range missile program toward the politically dubious INF ground. However, being START accountable, the RS-26 evidently is not formally violating any treaty. All subsequent tests have, however, been performed to the same medium-range distances, indicating that the real operational purpose of this missile is sub-strategic.

Although the RS-26 Yars-M is subject to New START's verification procedures, Russia has refused for several years to conduct the required treaty demonstration of the missile and its launcher. This treaty requirement involves viewing, measuring and photographing these items before deployment. But this exhibition had still not been conducted as of the autumn of 2017.[65]

The RS-26 case shows to what lengths Russia is going to mask its real intentions in the INF field. Letting the missile fly once beyond the 5,500-kilometer ICBM range definition was a clever way to disguise its real intent to reintroduce an improved version of the INF flagship SS-20.

Features Regarding the Development of Non-Strategic and Strategic Forces

Artillery as the "God of War" is an old maxim from Joseph Stalin's times, which the Russian Armed Forces still adhere to. Sweden's FOI covered Russia's materiel programs extensively in its major report "Russian Military Capability in a Ten-Year Perspective—2016."[66] And *TASS* gave a useful short summary about artillery and missile systems developments in November 2017.[67] Both reiterate that the Russian ground troops' missile forces and artillery are the primary means to inflict fire and nuclear damage on the enemy on the battlefield.

As the short-range ballistic Tochka-U missile systems will be completely phased out by 2020, they are being replaced with new and more capable Iskander-M systems. "The Iskander's large upgrade potential will allow it to operate on a par with foreign analogues up to 2030," *TASS* reports. "We continue further experimental design work on developing new missiles for the Iskander-M complex. It is constantly developed further. Several more missile types have been developed. Externally, they look alike but differ radically from inside. The complex currently has at least seven missile types or, perhaps, more," Valery Kashin Chief designer of the Machine-Building Design Bureau said.

Range is a key parameter that can be improved. Former commander of the Artillery and Rocket Forces Colonel General Zaritsky said in an interview for *Nezavisimaya Gazeta* already in November 2007 that the range can be increased if the political will to withdraw from the INF Treaty is there. The Iskander missile system will plug the gap in Russia's operational-tactical missile arsenal, created by the INF Treaty, the general emphasized.

According to Russian experts, the range could be increased to 1,000 kilometers without changes to the launcher.[68] Presumably, this would involve using a more effective propellant and advanced fly-by-wire steering techniques, facilitating the removal of unnecessary dead weight.

The military operational utility of ballistic Iskander-M missiles and Iskander-K cruise missiles in the same 1,000-kilometer operational-range ballpark is obvious. It would fill the gap in Russia's sub-strategic deterrence posture in Europe that was lost when the 1,000-kilometer-range 9K76 Temp-S missile (a.k.a. SS-22 Scaleboard) was eliminated.

An air-launched version of the Iskander-M ballistic missile was reported in March 2018. The launch of the Kh-47M2 missile, known as Kinzhal (Dagger), took place from a modified MiG-31BM Foxhound aircraft.[69] Not much is still known about this system, but given that it could also be carried by the Tu-22M3 bomber, the Kinzhal's range may be several thousand kilometers.[70]

In hindsight it is fair to say that the future of Russia's strategic nuclear forces looked increasingly bleak a few years after the breakup of the Soviet Union. All three legs of the strategic triad were affected. The bulk of the inventory of the Strategic Rocket Forces were built in Ukraine. Several missile fields were located outside Russia. The strategic fleet experienced severe problems, notably connected to the massive investment in the Project 941 Typhoon submarines. These colossal boats lay mostly in port, unable to perform their planned patrolling duties. The Typhoon division of the Northern Fleet was finally disbanded in 2004.[71]

Additionally, a significant portion of Russian strategic bombers were based in Ukraine. Production of the newest strategic bomber, the Tu-160 Blackjack had come to a virtual standstill, and the RuAF had to rely mostly on modernized versions of the vintage Tu-95MS Bear turbo-prop bomber.

This was the time for deep nuclear reductions and implementation not only of the START treaty but also START II, including its ban land-based ICBMs carrying multiple independently re-targetable re-entry vehicles (MIRV). However, a fouled-up ratification process resulted in START II being a lost opportunity. In the end, only the United States abided by that treaty, and the Minuteman III missile was converted to a single-warhead missile. Whereas, Russia ultimately expanded its MIRVed ICBM stockpiles.

The first domestically produced ICBM to be taken into active service in post-Soviet Russia was the silo-based and road-mobile RS-12M2 Topol-M (SS-27 Sickle-B/Stalin), deployed in December 1997 and 2006, respectively.[72] The design of this three-stage, solid-fueled missile was originally triggered by the United States' missile defense ambitions formulated in the Strategic Defense Initiative. In anticipation of entry into force of the ban on MIRVed ICBM warheads, mandated by the START II treaty signed in January 1993, the Topol-M was initially designed as a single-warhead missile.[73]

It is difficult to determine when exactly development work on a MIRVed version of the Topol-M began. But presumably it was several years before the first test-flight on May 29, 2007.[74]

With completion of the deployment of 78 Topol-M (SS-27 Mod 1) missiles in 2012, efforts have since shifted to deployment of a MIRVed version of the SS-27, known as SS-27 Mod 2, or RS-24 Yars in Russia. It is essentially the same missile as the Mod 1 version except the payload "bus" has been modified to carry multiple independently targetable warheads. Each missile is thought to be able to carry up to four such warheads.[75]

The START treaty prohibited increasing the number of warheads attributed to ICBMs. So Russia claimed the RS-24 was a completely new ICBM model to justify the designation "SS-29" instead of "SS-27 Mod 2," and thus to circumvent the treaty prohibition.

During the last five years, Russia produced 80 ICBMs, allowing for the rearmament of 12 strategic missile regiments with RS-24s.[76] The Strategic Rocket Forces will obtain 20 Yars launchers in 2018, and all single-warhead road-mobile Topol and Topol-M units will be rearmed with Yars ICBMs by 2026.[77] Dr. Pavel Podvig estimated, in mid-2017, that 84 Yars missiles were deployed with four warheads each.[78] One hundred-fourteen Topol and Topol-M missiles were eventually replaced.

The pride of the Russian nuclear weapons designers in their professional achievements is unmistakable: they invented both the world's largest (the 100-megaton-yield "Czar Bomb") and smallest (152-millimeter nuclear artillery round) nuclear weapons.[79] The same can be said about Russian designs of heavy ICBMs, a unique feature of the country's Strategic Rocket Forces.[80] The flagship, the liquid-fueled ten-warhead SS-18 Satan (lift-off weight of 210 tons and a throw-weight of 8 tons) was slated for complete elimination under START II. The last SS-18s—model R-36M2 (RS-20V) Voevoda—are to be retired as they are replaced by the new liquid-fueled heavy ICBM RS-28 Sarmat (SS-X-30), which is scheduled for initial combat duty in 2021. Serial production of missiles should begin in 2020. According to the commander of the Strategic Missile Forces, Colonel General Sergei Karakayev, the Voevoda will be in service at least until 2024, but their operation can be extended until 2027.[81]

The true specifications of the missile were withheld until March 2018. It was thought that the missile, designed and manufactured in Russia

(Makeev State Missile Center, Miass, Chelyabinsk region) would be significantly smaller than the SS-18 and only slightly heavier than the SS-19 Stiletto, which is just below the START treaty definition of heavy ICBMs.[82]

In his speech to the nation on March 1, 2018, President Putin disclosed that the weight of the Sarmat is over 200 metric tons, almost twice the lift-off (l-o) weight of the SS-19, equaling the l-o weight of the SS-18.[83] Ample photographic evidence supports the estimates of the Sarmat's huge size. According to Deputy Minister of Defense Yuri Borisov, the missile's payload may be ten tons. [84]

The Sarmat is likely to carry 8–10 warheads, but with yields lower than the 750-kiloton warheads carried by the SS-18. The modern missile's increased accuracy ensures that "effect on target"[85] will not be lost. It also employs advanced penetration aids to defeat enemy missile defenses. Finally, the missile has the option of carrying hypersonic glide vehicles (HGV) as maneuverable reentry vehicles.[86] *TASS* reported in July 2018 that the work on the Avangard HGV was completed and preparations made to accept the system for operational service in the Strategic Missile Forces.[87]

The RS-28 Sarmat development program has experienced multiple setbacks, and deployment by 2020 may be too optimistic. Three successful ejection tests were performed between December 2017 and late May 2018, paving way for real test flights yet to be performed.

Russia's Strategic Fleet Developments

The Russian nuclear submarine fleet experienced extreme difficulties during the first decades after the breakup of the Soviet Union. At dawn of the new millennium, the number of operational strategic missile submarines and nuclear powered and dual-use attack submarines had dwindled to a small fraction from the levels during the Cold War but have now stabilized.[88]

The biggest disappointment for Russian officials and the top brass was almost certainly the Typhoon-class (Project 941 Akula) submarine. Lack of funding and persistent maintenance problems kept most of the Typhoon boats moored in harbor, indeed as destabilizing sitting ducks as long as they carried their complements of SS-N-20 Sturgeon (R-39/D-19) submarine-launched ballistic missiles (SLBM). The final blow to this SSBN class was the failed effort to construct a reliable follower to the SS-N-20 missile.[89]

Russia's other operational SSBN classes experienced similar difficult problems; and routine patrolling went down from about 20 submarines at sea at any given time to about two.[90] Even the newest SSBN class from the Soviet era, the Delta IV (Project 667 BDRM Delfin), was affected. One of the seven boats, K-64 *Podmoskovye*, was eventually removed from the SSBN force and converted for underwater special operations in 2016. Production of the SS-N-23 Skiff (R-29RM/D-9RM) missiles had ceased in 1996 as development of an improved model began. The Russian government, however, made a decision to resume missile production in October 1999.[91] After a series of tests of the new version, the SS-N-23 (R-29RMU2 Sineva) SLBM was accepted for service in 2007.[92] It carries four 100-kiloton-yield warheads. Then followed a further upgraded version, the R-29RMU2.1 Liner, which may carry as many as 8–10 warheads. It was adopted into service in early 2014.[93]

Sineva and Liner missiles have improved navigation systems, upgraded warheads and penetration aids, and have flown in tests more than 11,500 kilometers, presumably with light payloads. The remaining six Delta IV–class boats have been thoroughly refurbished and serviced. Together with the new missiles, they will remain in service until 2030.[94]

Looking several decades ahead, the Borei-class SSBN (Project 955) is clearly the key project of the Russian strategic submarine fleet, as these boats will form the basis of Russia's maritime strategic deterrent and eventually carry the bulk of Russia's nuclear second-strike capability.

The development of the Borei-class boats—"Borei" is a reference to the North Wind—has also been a tedious and difficult process but is now basically on track. Development of the boat started in 1996 as a follow-on to the Delta-class boats, with their characteristic "hump backs" to allow for the length of the R-39UTTH "Bark" missile. The cancelation of this failed missile project led to a major redesign of the boat itself. It was to be equipped with the new R-30 Bulava (SS-NX-30), designed at the Moscow Institute of Thermal Technology (MIT, chief designer Yuri Solomonov). The institution is known for their Topol-M and Yars missiles, but has never before developed SLBMs. The Typhoon-class (Project 941) submarine *Dmitriy Donskoi* was refitted as a test bed for the Bulava missile system. The Bulava missile itself has had a mixed test history, but the major problems are solved.[95] After a successful salvo launch of four Bulava missiles on May 22, 2018, the Bulava missile was finally accepted for operational service.[96] The Bulava will carry six warheads.

Initial plans may have been to install 12 launch tubes. But after the larger Bark missile was discarded, the Borei-class boats will carry 16 Bulava launchers. According to some sources, the upgraded Project 955A *Borei II*-class boats may obtain 4 additional launch tubes, thereby increasing the missile load to 20, while others say that the number of launch tubes will remain at 16.[97]

The lead ship, *Yuri Dolgorukiy*, the first of the planned eight, joined the Northern Fleet in December 2013 and received its full complement of missiles in 2014. Subsequent Project 955 submarines are expected to join the Pacific Fleet. As of January 2016, three submarines had been accepted for service—the *Yuri Dolgorukiy, Alexander Nevskiy* and *Vladimir Monomakh*.[98]

The lead boat of the Project 955A Borei II series, *Knyaz Vladimir* (laid down in July 2012), set sail for the first time on November 17, 2017. Plans are that *Knyaz Vladimir* will be delivered to the Navy in 2018.[99] According to the Russian defense ministry, four other hauls are already being used to build the remaining four Borei II–class submarines: the *Knyaz Oleg, Generalissimus Suvorov, Imperator Alexander III* and *Knyaz Pozharsky*. Construction on these nuclear submarines is expected to be completed by 2025.[100]

The recovery of the Russian strategic fleet, literally from the brink at the end of the 1990s, is remarkable. One visible sign of this is that the operational tempo of the Russian submarine fleet has returned to former levels. Admiral Vladimir Korolev, the commander-in-chief of the Russian Navy, said in March 2017, "Last year, we returned to the level we had before the post-Soviet era in terms of the days at sea. Russia's submarine fleet has spent 3,000 days at sea."[101]

Defense Minister Shoigu's mention that 102 SLBMs had been produced during the last five years, is an indication that missile production corresponds to a little more than one yearly boat-load of missiles. SLBM and SSBN production seems to be in sync.

Nuclear missions are, however, not only the business of the Russian strategic fleet. Dual-use weaponry, such as SS-N-21 Sampson (S-10 Granat) and Kalibr cruise missiles, SS-N-19 Shipwreck (P-700 Granit) missiles as well as P-800 Oniks missiles, are found in the attack submarine fleet as well as in guided-missile submarines, diesel submarines and various surface vessels. The number of these are counted in several tens.

One additional Russian nuclear naval system in development is the alleged intercontinental-range nuclear underwater drone, Poseidon, a.k.a. "the multi-purpose Status-6 system" (codenamed Kanyon by NATO), disclosed in 2015.[102] If successfully developed and deployed, this weapon would be capable of transporting a megaton-yield nuclear charge and provide Russia with a "third strike" weapon, an ultimate doomsday weapon. It is said to be an asymmetric response to a US missile defense shield.[103] Citing Russian journalist Pavel Felgenhauer, Dr. Mark Schneider warned that this weapon "may further embolden the Kremlin to push for a new world order of its liking by intimidating the United States and its allies." Too little is, however, still known about Poseidon to provide definite answers regarding the qualities of the system. A video from July 2018 shows dimensions of the Poseidon drone to be far larger than ordinary torpedoes.[104]

Strategic Aviation

The third leg of the strategic nuclear triad, long-range aviation (*Dal'nyaya Aviatsiya*—DA), has always been inferior to the corresponding US force. In the 1980s the Soviet Union was able to produce a new heavy bomber aircraft, the Tu-160 Blackjack bomber, somewhat reminiscent of the US B-1B Lancer.[105] The Blackjack still remains the most potent of the Russian bombers, but the fleet of sixteen aircraft is worn out and the planes need both maintenance and modernization.

The plan is that the manufacturer of the Tu-160 bomber, Tupolev's Kazan Aircraft Plant (KAZ,) will both refurbish the present fleet and also produce 30–50 new modernized versions of Blackjack, called Tu-160M2. The plan is not only ambitious economically, it is also a military-industrial challenge: production at KAZ ceased in 1992, and the Soviet production chains no longer exist.[106] Deputy Defense Minister Yuri Borisov said, in April 2017, that Tu-160s will remain in service until the arrival of the new Tu-160M2s.[107] News that the first Tu-160M2 airframe had reached final assembly at KAZ is not entirely convincing.[108] The first upgraded Tu-160M2 bombers are expected to be built and delivered in the early 2020s.[109]

The old turbo-prop Tu-95MS Bear bomber, Russia's answer to the vintage US B-52 Stratofortress, is still operational. IISS's "Military Balance 2017" reports Moscow still wields 60 Tu-95 Bear aircraft in a few slightly different configurations.[110]

Russia lacks a strategic ground-attack aircraft that would be comparable to the United States' B-2 Spirit stealth bomber. Plans have been delayed for a new strategic bomber—for now, known as the PAK-DA. This aircraft will be built with significantly improved low-observability features and primarily replace the Tu-95 Bear. First flight can be expected in 2025–2026, with initial production starting a few years later.[111] Given that the plans for the B-21 Raider, a US successor to the B-2, are well advanced, it is likely that the United States will be able to maintain overwhelming superiority in penetrating strategic bombers.

Russia has used its strategic bombers for political signaling for more than a decade, testing the readiness of the air forces of potential adversaries around the world. This should not be interpreted as a typical operational pattern in areas where they cannot fly uncontested. This has largely been the case in Syria, where the Russian air force has been able to test new weapons systems, including smart bombs and cruise missiles.

Recognizing the operational limits of Russia's strategic bombers to penetrate strongly defended airspace, Russia increasingly sought to circumvent the problem by making a sustained effort to develop new air-launched long-range cruise missiles (ALCM), which could be safely launched from deep within Russian territory. In addition, Russia may reduce its aircraft's vulnerability to being wiped out on the ground by keeping them airborne in times of high tension.

This strategic choice evidently has borne fruit, as static objects in the whole of Europe and parts of the US can now be targeted from safe distances. The chief of the Russian General Staff, Army General

Valery Gerasimov, pointed out, in November 2017, that Russia is now able to strike targets with cruise missiles up to a distance of 4,000 kilometers.[112]

Increasing the range of the cruise missiles simply requires more fuel. This has been accomplished in various ways, such as making the missiles bigger or fitting them with external fuel tanks. In addition, more reliable navigation and homing systems are needed. The performance of Russian cruise missiles used in combat in Syria has been likened to that of the US Tomahawk cruise missiles used during Operation Desert Storm, in 1991.[113] The most powerful of Russia's new air-launched cruise missiles is the Kh-101, with a range of 4,500 kilometers, according to internationally respected Russian experts.[114] The nuclear variant is called the Kh-102.

In early July 2017, President Putin praised the performance of Kh-101 cruise missiles used in Syria, saying they "showed a high degree of reliability." At the same time, the Russian defense ministry reported that Russia's Tu-95MS long-range bombers had struck Daesh (the popular Arab name for the Islamic State) targets in Syria. The strikes were made from a range of about 1,000 kilometers and marked the sixth time that Russia has used the Kh-101 in combat, the ministry said.[115]

The Kh-101 was developed over a long period of time to replace the Kh-55 (AS-15 Kent), a Soviet/Russian ALCM. It has a low radar signature and is equipped with a terrain avoidance system. An opto-electronic flight correction system is used instead of a radio altimeter. Stealth features, better resistance against jamming, flying at low altitudes to avoid radars, and hiding behind terrain all contribute to the Kh-101's ability to defeat enemy defenses.

The Kh-101 uses the Russian GLONASS satellite navigation system for trajectory correction, which enables more complicated route planning, including flights over featureless terrain. The missile is reported to have an accuracy of five to six meters.

Kh-101 can be equipped with a high-explosive, penetrating, or cluster warhead. The conventional warhead contains 400 kilograms of explosives. The nuclear warhead of the Kh-102 is thought have a yield of 250 kilotons.

The Kh-101 is integrated with the Tu-160 (twelve missiles) and the Tu-95MS16 (eight missiles).[116] The weapon can be dropped at aircraft altitudes, between 3,000 meters and 12,000 meters. The medium-range Tu-22M3/5 bomber is likely to receive a smaller ALCM.[117]

Russian experts argue that the new Kh-101 ALCM is a more potent weapon than the Boeing AGM-86 ALCM carried by the B-52s. That may very well be true. Had the General Dynamics/Raytheon Advanced Cruise Missile AGM-129 not been retired in 2012, the situation may have been different.[118]

The Basics of Russia's Nuclear Doctrine

The massive nuclear buildup described above is not happening in a vacuum, but is based on first principles guiding Russia's military and security policy. This is where nuclear doctrine, part of military doctrine, enters. According to a long tradition, Russia's full nuclear doctrine remains secret. Nonetheless, it is known that the doctrine has gone through many twists and turns during the last few decades, as it has been revised and developed to suit present policies. And throughout this time, Russian military planners have not forgotten the Soviet legacy has not been forgotten.

Interviews by Pentagon consultants with former Soviet key officials in the early 1990s revealed key features regarding the Soviet nuclear doctrine in 1965–1985, also disclosing several potentially dangerous misunderstandings.[119] Although the US had repeatedly declared its nuclear strategy to be based on deterrence, the interviewed Russian professionals stressed that they did not believe that. From their point of view, the US strategy evidently was consistent with preparations for a first strike. Russia's own nuclear doctrine was built on this premise.

According to the Russian professionals, the development of the highly accurate MIRVed MX/Peacekeeper missile was one such sign of Washington's emphasis on a first strike.[120] The relative vulnerability of the US ICBM fields (silos and control centers) to ground bursts, was another. The Russians found out through realistic field tests performed in Semipalatinsk in 1964–1966 that ground bursts were extremely effective at destroying silo-based ICBM systems and their command centers. The charges used were evidently quite high but did not exceed the blast energy effect of a 500-kiloton nuclear warhead. Any ground burst closer than one kilometer away was highly likely to "kill" a silo-based missile system.[121] Having understood this, the Russians began planning road-mobile ICBM missile systems as well as hardening silos.

Other signs of US preparations for a nuclear first-strike were the large and varied arsenal of US tactical nuclear weapons in Europe, Washington's refusal to publicly adopt a no-first-use doctrine, and finally the deployment of Pershing II ballistic missiles. Ground- and sea-launched cruise missiles were thought to be capabilities sought to target the Soviet leadership itself in a surprise nuclear first strike. The US Presidential Directive PD-59 was seen in this context.[122] Similar thinking, unfortunately, seems to be resurfacing again in the current debate.

Soviet strategists considered the nuclear balance between the Soviet Union and the States to be unstable. The only truly stable nuclear situation was one in which one side had clear superiority over the other. The imbalance had to be in Soviet's favor. Therefore, throughout this period, the Soviets attempted to gain strategic superiority over the US, the primary goal not being to ensure victory in a nuclear war, but to ensure the general security of the Soviet leadership and the preservation of Soviet influence in Europe and around the globe.[123] The military leadership considered winning a nuclear war unattainable in any meaningful sense; thus, they believed nuclear war should be avoided at all cost.

The perception of the utility of nuclear weapons changed gradually, in parallel with the evolution of these weapons. A brief but useful summary of the changing Soviet nuclear doctrine was given, in 1991, by Colonel General Andrian Danilevich: The period of "Nuclear euphoria" between 1960 and 1965 was followed by "Descent to Earth" and ICBMs in 1965–1975, and finally "Strategic Balance" during 1975–1991.[124] Thus, in the early 1960s, it was thought that the importance of nuclear weapons almost made all other weapons superfluous. But with the ouster of Khrushchev, in late 1964, conservatism and realism returned, together with the realization that the main enemy of the Soviet Union possessed large numbers of nuclear weapons capable of inflicting "unrecoverable losses." A clearer appreciation of the devastating consequences of a full-scale nuclear exchange began to emerge. In a 1972 nuclear exercise 1972, Soviet leaders were presented with the results of a simulated US first strike using ground bursts against the Soviet Union. They were horrified.[125]

At first, Soviet policy was to respond with a full nuclear attack to even a single hit; but in the early 1970s, this policy was rejected. A more "controllable way of conduct of nuclear war" was called for. This led to doctrinal changes. Preemptive strikes were rejected as the only option, and retaliatory strikes gained in importance. The military situation was defining the preferred scenario of nuclear use, either global or regional. The course of war itself was expanded to four stages: a non-nuclear phase, a nuclear phase, follow-up actions and concluding actions. The most important ingredient was the gradual lengthening of the non-nuclear phase from hours to one week. With Marshal Ogarkov as chief of the General Staff from 1977 onwards, the conventional phase of war gained even more emphasis. The operational planning assumed that the first frontal operations would remain non-nuclear up through the advance to the Rhine.[126]

Rough parity in strategic systems characterized the period from 1975 to 1991. Until 1980, limited nuclear war was still officially rejected, but it was considered possible to conduct conventional war from beginning to end. A clear change of principle took place between 1980 and 1985. Limited nuclear war was now accepted in documents and in planning options offered to the political leadership. The options included nuclear use on the battlefield, against military targets, in limited strategic strikes, as well as proportional retaliation for enemy limited strikes.[127]

In the last five to six years before the collapse of the Soviet Union in 1991, a defensive nuclear doctrine was adopted. This, according to General Danilevich, was based on the realization that a nuclear war could not be won. Even a retaliatory strike with just 10 percent of the strategic nuclear inventory that had survived an enemy first strike would be enough to "put out of commission all elements of the viability of a state and put that state to death." Large-scale use of the enormous nuclear inventories available toward the end of the Cold War was inconceivable, as the aftermath of a first strike would have brought "irreversible changes in the world's ecology." As a result, a large-scale nuclear exchange "came to be perceived as the death of civilization and the death of the Soviet Union."[128]

General Danilevich's description of the thinking within the Soviet General Staff implies that the military was not opposed to negotiations of nuclear reductions in principle but had major misgivings about the INF and START treaties, which they found deeply unfair to Russia.

"Gorbachev talked about total reductions, but we in the GS [General Staff] did not think this would really happen. [...] We came from the premise that an acceptable level compatible with mutual deterrence should be found. We still maintain that nuclear weapons should be preserved as an element of deterrence, given the real possibility of the appearance of nuclear arsenals among third countries." Danilevich also called for "finding ways to use nuclear weapons so as to give them a role in deterrence, but also the role of a strategic military factor, a factor in armed conflict."

Escalate to Deescalate

In 2011, Russian defense expert Andrei Kokoshin formulated the basic challenge of nuclear doctrinal:[129]

> The nuclear deterrence concept has a deep internal contradiction. On the one hand, it is aimed to minimize the likelihood of a war by making it abysmally destructive. For this purpose, the state must have the nuclear forces that provide for annihilation of the adversary and infliction of irreparable damage to the enemy even if such a state is exposed to a first nuclear strike. On the other hand, in order to attain deterrence, it is necessary to make the threat of use of nuclear weapons credible and convincing.

Senior US nuclear experts published a thorough report, "A New Nuclear Review for a New Age," in April 2017. In that report, Russia's present nuclear doctrine was described as follows:

> Russian nuclear doctrine has undergone fundamental changes since the end of the 1990s, with an increasing salience for nuclear weapons. Open-source reports and testimony by US and NATO officials indicate that Russia has developed an "escalate-to-deescalate" or, more accurately, "escalate to win" nuclear strategy that includes the possibility of nuclear first use in regional and local conflicts in order to terminate a conflict on terms favorable to Russia.[130]

US Secretary of Defense James Mattis reiterated this assessment, in February 2018, in Congressional testimony, when he described the Russian nuclear doctrine as "escalate to victory and then deescalate."[131] This Russian doctrine is at the core of the debate of how the West should best respond. As the interviews with key Soviet military and defense officials in the early 1990s show, it should be kept in mind that the declared doctrine may differ substantially from the real doctrine. Referring to the respected Soviet bomb designer Yuri Trutnev, Dr. Kokoshin pointed out this fact:[132]

> As academician Yuri Trutnev rightfully observes, "a material basis means the weapon system defines the doctrine that exists in reality as opposed to the declared doctrine." One vital condition for conducting an effective national security policy is the absence of a gap between what Trutnev defines as the real doctrines and the declared doctrines.

Russia undoubtedly adheres to this policy. Its present nuclear weapons programs fit this picture, as the capability gaps in suitable hardware are obscured by empty declarations.[133]

The emphasis of the theoretical work on which the escalate to deescalate doctrine rests, is clearly at the lower end of the spectrum of nuclear use. Several important aims of this effort may be readily identified.[134] One is to find a formula for limited nuclear use in certain scenarios, deemed to be sufficiently decoupled from major nuclear use as to be worth employing without unduly high risk of escalation beyond control or with catastrophic consequences. The other aim is to erase the notion of a nuclear taboo, which only gains strength as time passes. In July 2045, a full century may have elapsed without nuclear weapons having been used in anger. A widely held perception that nuclear weapons lack credibility altogether as tools in military operations would evidently be unattractive for those who have invested heavily in these weapons.

De-escalation as a concept began to develop within the Russian military and nuclear communities in earnest in the 1990s. The role of nuclear weapons in Russia's future military policy was the subject of serious study. The aim and purpose of this effort was to find ways to expand the utility of nuclear weapons from a predominant deterrent role to possible employment in military conflicts without risking escalation to full-scale nuclear war. Several important publications appeared in 1999.

A basic reference is the article by Major General V. I. Levshin, Colonel A. V. Nedelin and Colonel (Professor) Mikhail E. Sosnovskiy, "On the Use of Nuclear Weapons for the De-Escalation of Combat Actions" in *Voennaia Mysl'* in May 1999.[135] Dr. Jacob W. Kipp identified this original paper as a critical new element in the Russian approach to war.[136] Accordingly, the following draws heavily on Levshin et al. Key quotes (bold face and italics inserted):

> In accordance with the Fundamentals of the Military Doctrine of the Russian Federation, a preemptive strike (any strike, not only a nuclear one) aimed at thwarting an aggression being prepared against Russia and its allies is absolutely inadmissible in any situation and nuclear weapons (NW) represent primarily a deterrent. Proceeding from this premise, nuclear weapons ought to be regarded not only as a means for bringing about a decisive rout of the adversary but also as *a means for de-escalating military operations if deterrence proves insufficiently effective and an aggression takes place after all.*

> Implementing the de-escalation function implies practical employment of NW both to demonstrate determination and directly deliver nuclear strikes against the adversary. It is expedient to deal with this objective by using non-strategic nuclear weapons, primarily operational-tactical nuclear weapons (OTNW), which may ward off a "landslide" escalation of nuclear warfare up to the point where an exchange of massive nuclear

strikes occurs, delivered by strategic assets. In this case, as we see it, the most acceptable thing for the adversary will be to stop military operations.

Levshin et.al. thus suggest singling out the following stages of OTNW employment buildup:

"demonstration"—delivery of single demonstrative nuclear strikes against desert territories (or water areas), against the adversary's minor, sparsely manned military facilities or such ones with no military personnel at all;

"intimidation-demonstration"—delivery of single nuclear strikes at transport hubs, engineer installations and other targets in order to localize an area of military operations in the territorial sense, and/or at separate elements of an opposing enemy force, against which strikes lead to a disruption (reduction of efficiency) of control over an invading force at the operational (operational-tactical) level and do not cause relatively high losses among the enemy forces;

"intimidation"—delivery of multiple strikes against the main enemy force in a single operational sector in order to change the balance of forces in this sector and/or eliminate an enemy breakthrough to the operational depth of defenses;

"intimidation-retaliation"—delivery of concentrated strikes at enemy theater operations (TO) force groupings within the limits of one or several adjacent operational sectors if a defense operation takes an unfavorable turn. The following objectives are due to be attained in the process: to remove the threat of a rout facing a friendly force; to resolutely change the balance of forces in an operational sector (sectors); to eliminate an enemy breakthrough of a defensive line held by an operational-strategic large unit, etc.;

"retaliation-intimidation"—delivery of a massed strike against an aggressor's armed forces grouping in theater operations (TO) in order to rout it and achieve a radical change in the military situation in one's own favor;

"retaliation"—delivery of a massed strike (strikes) at the adversary within the limits of an entire theater of war (if necessary, involving an engagement of separate military-economic targets of the aggressor), one characterized by the maximum use of all available forces and assets and coordination with strikes launched by the SNF [strategic nuclear forces], if these are going to be employed.

The choice of a scale, on which to use OTNW, will depend on how the situation shapes up at the moment of decision-making and after the delivery of nuclear strikes. *The initial employment is on the basis of a decision adopted by the Supreme Commander-in-Chief and only in accordance with a separate order (signal) issued by the Defense Minister (General Staff).*

If necessary, the decision to deliver subsequent nuclear strikes may come from persons authorized by the Supreme Commander-in-Chief, who operate within the framework of limitations as to the number and types of assets to be employed and targets to be engaged, which he has imposed. (Seemingly, the said persons should not be lower in position than commanders of operational-strategic large units; if operations are conducted in isolated sectors [in separate cases], they should not be lower in position than commanders of operational large units.) As the sixth stage in the employment of OTNW is reached after the first massed nuclear strike, the subsequent ones in individual cases may be delivered by decision of lower-level chain of command, this within the limits of their organic nuclear missile (NM) resources and upon authorization by a higher-level commander (as we see it, these persons should not be lower in position than commanders of operational large units, or commanders of operational-tactical large units).

The general rule is this: *the lower the stage of OTNW employment, the higher the command level adopting the decision to deliver each particular nuclear strike."*

Of particular interest for the present escalate to deescalate debate are the arguments presented by Levshin et al. concerning the use of a single nuclear weapon for demonstration purposes:

In definite conditions, the *delivery of single* or multiple nuclear strikes may be required at enemy targets located *outside of the zone of direct military operations* in order to cause a de-escalation of military operations. In this context, one ought to proceed from objectives pursued: *to effect containment at the regional level*, it is preferable to use OTNW, while at the global level (by intimidating the adversary with our readiness to go as far as mutual annihilation) it is possible to use operational-strategic and even strategic NW.

In the latter case, the degree of impact and effectiveness of engagement are things of lesser importance than the "test of nerves." The calculation is that the *fear of assured destruction will not permit the adversary to go over to employing strategic offensive forces* and will make him deescalate military operations. [...]

The most acceptable type of weapon for this kind of impact may be represented by sea-based *long-range cruise missiles*, which are launched from nuclear-powered attack submarines, this fact meaning that *the strike will not involve strategic nuclear weapons.* Moreover, their low flight altitude and small radar cross section, as well as the difficulty for the adversary to spot their possible launch areas make for greater undetectability of strikes by comparison with any other assets.

Reliance on other types of strategic nuclear weapons (SNW) for delivering single or multiple strikes in order to cause a de-escalation of military operations would lead to the detection of the Russian nuclear assets as early as at the launch stage and *increase the risk of the adversary launching full-scale nuclear retaliation*, particularly since a decision to that effect will be adopted in a situation where time is in dramatically short supply.

> Thus, employing SNW to deliver single (or multiple) nuclear strikes with a view to causing a de-escalation of military operations is warranted only if there are definite guarantees that the adversary will not regard these strikes as the beginning of a large-scale nuclear attack designed to destroy his military and/or military-economic potential.

Levshin et al.'s article was followed up by a few other equally detailed accounts.[137] But the window for open discussion closed by 1999 or so. These papers still form the basis for Western perceptions of Russian nuclear doctrine. While this useful early Russian debate gives insights about the Russian process of rethinking the role of nuclear weapons in theater, much remains opaque.[138]

Official doctrinal wordings are basically political statements. At the release of Russia's 2010 military doctrine, Secretary of the Security Council of the Russian Federation, Nikolay Patrushev summed up the nuclear doctrine:

> When do we reserve the right to use nuclear weapons? In response to the use of nuclear weapons or other weapons of mass

destruction against the Russian Federation and its allies, as well as in case of aggression against Russia using conventional weapons, if there is a threat to the existence of the state itself, its territorial integrity and inviolability.[139]

The Swedish Defence Research Establishment FOI observed, in December 2016, that there has been no public change in the Russian nuclear position at the doctrinal level.

The revised Military Doctrine 2014 has the same wording as was previously used to explain Russia's policy with respect to the use of nuclear weapons. Paragraph 27 states: "The Russian Federation reserves the right to utilize nuclear weapons in response to the utilization of nuclear and other types of weapons of mass destruction against it and (or) its allies, and also in the event of aggression against the Russian Federation involving the use of conventional weapons when the very existence of the state is under threat. The decision to utilize nuclear weapons is made by the president of the Russian Federation."[140]

Perhaps the first mention of the role of non-strategic nuclear weapons for deterrence in official doctrinal documents is found in a presidential decree on the "Fundamentals of the State Policy of the Russian Federation in the Field of Naval Operations for the period until 2030," in July 2017.[141] Section IV deals with "the Navy as an Effective Instrument of Strategic Deterrence." Whereas, Paragraph 37 addresses the role of non-strategic nuclear weapons:

37. During the escalation of military conflict, demonstration of readiness and determination to employ non-strategic nuclear weapons capabilities is an effective deterrent.

This is nearly an acknowledgement of the veracity of the escalate to win doctrine. It is interesting to note how the chief of the General

Staff, Army General Valery Gerasimov, described the role of nuclear deterrence in November 2017:

> Nowadays, the Strategic Nuclear Forces can deliver drastic damage against any aggressor, including one that possesses missile defense systems. At the same time, there are foundations laid for sustained growth of combat capabilities amid the limits imposed by international treaties on arms control.
>
> Non-nuclear deterrence forces have gained high momentum. Over the last five years, the Armed Forces have made a breakthrough in long-range high-precision weapons. Iskander-M missile systems, [as well as] underwater and surface warships with Kalibr missile systems are being supplied. Long-range aircraft are being upgraded to operate the new Kh-101 cruise missile.[142]

General Gerasimov's use of the term "non-nuclear" in this context is misleading. A more appropriate term to use would be "dual-use," as only the nuclear option has real deterrence value. Given, that Western perceptions of what constitutes acceptable loss in war, or particularly in nuclear war, has reduced markedly since the Cold War, a rather limited amount of land-based or sea-based operational-tactical nuclear weapons would make a difference.

In the opinion of one seasoned Russian observer, Major General (ret.) Vladimir Z. Dvorkin, "even the explosion of one powerful nuclear bomb in a metropolis is inadmissible. I do not know how this problem is looked at in China, but in the West damage at this level is now considered unacceptable. Even one explosion is unacceptable, as a result of which dozens or hundreds of thousands of people may die."[143]

Summary and Conclusions

Toward the end of the Cold War, US and Soviet leaders understood that the enormous nuclear buildup had been a mistake. Presidents Reagan and Gorbachev came to share a common view that "a nuclear war cannot be won and must never be fought." In addition, they believed in the pursuit of a nuclear-free world.

The two leading nuclear powers started a bilateral process of real, significant nuclear weapons reductions, which eventually brought profound results. The nuclear stockpiles were reduced to only a small fraction of the former inventories. The roles of nuclear weapons in the military doctrines of both countries were reduced accordingly. For nuclear arms control, the INF and START treaties were groundbreaking, and both countries genuinely committed themselves to the NPT, including its Article VI.

The turmoil after the breakup of the Soviet Union and the financial bankruptcy of Russia created opportunities for nuclear arms control. As successor to the Soviet Union, Russia assumed the responsibilities and rights as a recognized nuclear weapons state. The 1990s were a particularly difficult time. Russia's armed forces, including the nuclear forces and the nuclear community, were hit hard. Despite these difficulties, Russian nuclear weapons laboratories, major missile design bureaus and construction plants carried on their work and laid the groundwork for a second coming.

These circles of conservative hardliners, including the military and security sectors, received support when Vladimir Putin was elected president. After the US left the ABM Treaty in 2002, Russia's immediate response was to declare that it no longer was bound by the still unratified START II treaty, which forbid MIRVed ICBMs. The Strategic Rocket Forces, traditionally the backbone of the Soviet/Russian strategic nuclear deterrent, could again be developed in full. The strategic element of the Navy, which had sunk into such a sorry state that its whole existence was threatened, obtained a boost. Work to restore capabilities lost in the INF Treaty was also started.

The treaty-limited shorter- and medium-range land-based missiles had played a key part in the operational plans of the Soviet military in the 1980s—not in an offensive role, as perceived in the West, but as a deterrent against US/NATO first nuclear use in a large-scale conventional war in Europe. Sacrificing these weapons was a hard blow to the military, particularly because of the very asymmetric reductions, more than 2:1 in favor of the United States.[144]

President Putin's strongly worded landmark speech at the Munich Security Conference in 2007 was a clear indication of Russia's intention to abandon the post–Cold War European security order, built under the auspices of the OSCE and extending from "Vancouver to Vladivostok."

The United States and Russia still managed to conclude the New START treaty, in 2010; but Moscow categorically rejected bilateral negotiations with Washington on non-strategic nuclear weapons. The US may prefer a world free from nuclear weapons—as President Obama outlined in his speech in Prague in 2009—but for Russia, this is unacceptable. Russia repeatedly declined US invitations for a further round of strategic arms negotiations. After Obama's last effort in Berlin in 2013, Foreign Minister Lavrov responded that the time for bilateral negotiations is over. From now on, the talks would be multilateral, with all five NPT-recognized nuclear weapons states participating. That put nuclear talks in limbo.

The nuclear policies of Russia and the United States have been diametrically opposite for a decade. The US was committed to further large-scale nuclear reductions and a reduced nuclear role. Only one new nuclear weapon, the B61-12 nuclear bomb was in development.

Russia, on the other hand began to execute its ongoing massive strategic and non-strategic forces rearmament program. Russia saw a clear opportunity to use the US reluctance to invest more in nuclear weapons, despite the fact that the US strategic triad was ageing. From a Russian perspective, nuclear investments clearly were advantageous. The US would have to follow suit sooner or later, but the heavy costs of modernizing the US triad would diminish funds for development of new and more capable conventional precision strike weapons, an area where Russia could not compete seriously.

Russia's introduction of new missile systems in all three legs of its strategic triad is tilting the lifecycle comparison with the US triad in Russia's favor. The two are essentially out of step, and Russia may think that this advantage should be utilized. While history never repeats itself, some common features from the late 1970s can be found.

The magnitude of Russia's present strategic weapons programs clearly indicates the potential for growth well beyond the New START treaty limits.[145] Russia's economic possibilities to sustain all programs can, however, be questioned.

Formally Russia remained within agreed New START treaty limits, which took effect on February 5, 2018.[146] The treaty itself, however, facilitates creative accounting, which erodes the real substance of the declared numbers. Russian officials and experts, some of them close associates of the president, indicate that it is highly unlikely that New START will be extended in 2021.[147] One observer put it bluntly:

> Russia has declared time and again since 2010 that it will not accept new reductions in nuclear arms, including non-strategic types, in a changing strategic environment and that the New START treaty is more likely to be the last bilateral Russia-US "grand treaty" on the limitation and reduction of the nuclear arsenals.[148]

This Russian negative attitude toward extending New START is a new, if not particularly surprising feature. Arms control has not been a high priority on Russia's political agenda for more than a decade.

One of the major long-term priorities of the Russian Armed Forces has been to restore the capabilities lost following the implementation of the INF Treaty. Since the early 2000s, Russia has wanted to step away from the INF Treaty, at first through classic horse-trading with the US, but that failed to produce the desired results. Meanwhile, Russia's development of new land-based ballistic missiles and cruise missiles continued unabated. Some systems have already been deployed in significant numbers, such as a dozen Iskander-M brigades, consisting of both ballistic missiles and cruise missiles.

Interestingly enough, the US has never accused Russia of an INF Treaty breach related to the Iskander system. The reason is legal, not technical. The US has not been able to detect a smoking gun—that is, of Russia having tested either Iskander version to ranges in excess of the allowed 500 kilometers. Undoubtedly, however, the maximum range of both missiles is significantly higher; and the cruise missile could likely fly to at least twice the allowed range.

On the other hand, the slightly larger land-based SSC-8 cruise missile (9M729) is a clear treaty breach, although Russia denies this. On the contrary, Russia claims to abide by the INF Treaty and, in its turn, accuses the US of INF breaches.

The RS-26 Rubezh/Yars-M, essentially a strategic RS-24 Yars ICBM minus one stage, has yet to be deployed. It evidently will assume the same role as the famous SS-20, the Soviet flagship of the European-theater weapons of the Cold War. The new missile is classified as an ICBM, which may be one reason why Russia is uninterested in extending the New START treaty.

The current "escalate to deescalate" debate touches upon the core of these Russian developments. Yet, Russia vehemently denies that there is any such Russian doctrine. This became quite clear at the Munich Security Conference in February 2018. Former Russian ambassador to the US, Sergey Kislyak tried to blur Russia's real position and only reiterated a few sentences from the 2014 Military doctrine.[149]

Russia's position on negative security guarantees, of special interest for small countries in good standing committed to the Non-Proliferation Treaty, is troubling. Russia refuses to adopt the same policy as the US—i.e. to assure all such states that it will never use or threaten to use nuclear weapons against them. Denmark and Norway are examples of countries, which, in recent years, have received direct nuclear threats from Russian ambassadors, for miniscule reasons. Sweden, in turn, was the target of a simulated attack by Tu-22M3 Backfire bombers on Good Friday 2013.

Russia has pursued a very determined nuclear policy during President Putin's era. The general conditions for sustaining Russia's role as a leading nuclear power were extremely challenging after the breakup of the Soviet Union. A crucially important political decision was made in 2007–2008, when Russia finally discarded President Gorbachev's view and ambition to pursue a policy with a nuclear-weapon-free world as the final goal.

The Russian nuclear rearmament program has been surprisingly successful. For all practical purposes, Russia has now restored almost everything that was lost because of Gorbachev. It is prudent to assume that there are nuclear weapons available for the whole spectrum of distances, starting from the 152 mm nuclear artillery grenade to very long intercontinental ranges. The yields of the nuclear charges likewise encompass a full spectrum, starting from mini-nukes with a few tens of tons TNT equivalent yields to multi-megaton yields of some ICBM warheads. On the sub-strategic level, Russia has restored a whole triad.[150] All major services are able to operate non-strategic nuclear weapons. It is, however, fair to say that Russia's non-strategic nuclear warheads are still stored at central storage sites. [151]

Nuclear arms control has long served Russia well. Its main opponent, the United States, remained committed to President Reagan's policy toward a world without nuclear weapons for three decades and, more importantly, has continuously diminished its reliance on nuclear weapons in its defense policy.

Meeting with US President Donald Trump in Helsinki, in July 2018, President Putin suggested that the New START treaty should be extended to 2026 and reaffirmed Russia's commitment to uphold the INF treaty.[152] There are reasons to doubt both, as there were no firm commitments to resume START negotiations with a clear aim of new reduction goals. Russia's record regarding upholding the INF Treaty also lacks credibility. Russia evidently believes it has the upper hand and will be able to negotiate from a position of strength. Only time will tell.

Notes

[1] Forss, Stefan: "Yhdysvaltain ydinasepolitiikka" (US Nuclear Policy), Finnish National Defence University, Deparment of Strategic and Defence Studies, Publication Series 2, No. 34, 2006. As Vice Chairman of the Joint Chiefs of Staff, Admiral James A. Winnefield Jr. pointed out, "at the end of the Cold War, many felt that the international system had evolved to the point where a nuclear deterrent was obsolete." House of the Armed Services Committee Hearing on NUCLEAR DETERRENCE IN THE 21ST CENTURY, June 25, 2015, p.7, https://www.gpo.gov/fdsys/pkg/CHRG-114hhrg95318/pdf/CHRG-114hhrg95318.pdf.

[2] Eli Corin, "Presidential Nuclear Initiatives: An Alternative Paradigm for Arms Control," NTI, March 1, 2004, http://www.nti.org/analysis/articles/presidential-nuclear-initiatives/.

[3] UNODA, "Treaty on the Non-Proliferation of Nuclear Weapons (NPT), Text of the Treaty," https://www.un.org/disarmament/wmd/nuclear/npt/text.

[4] Ronald Reagan, "Address Before a Joint Session of the Congress on the State of the Union," January 25, 1984, http://www.presidency.ucsb.edu/ws/?pid=40205.

[5] CTBTO, "STORY: Gorbachev on Reykjavik and Nuclear Weapons Today," September 12, 2012, ftp://ftp.ctbto.org/Reykjavik_Press_Kit/VIDEO/Shotsheet_Gorbachev_soundbites_cutaways_final.pdf.

[6] George P. Shultz, William J. Perry, Henry A. Kissinger and Sam Nunn, "A World Free of Nuclear Weapons," *The Wall Street Journal*, January 4, 2007, (https://www.wsj.com/articles/SB116787515251566636). For a summary, see George P. Shultz, "The War That Must Never Be Fought," The Hoover Institution, March 12, 2015, https://www.hoover.org/research/war-must-never-be-fought-0.

[7] Barack Obama, "Remarks By President Barack Obama In Prague As Delivered", The White House, Office of the Press Secretary, April 05, 2009, https://obamawhitehouse.archives.gov/the-press-office/remarks-president-barack-obama-prague-delivered.

[8] Hans M. Kristensen, Robert S. Norris, "Estimated Global Nuclear Warhead Inventories 1945-2017," https://fas.org/wp-content/uploads/2014/05/history2017.jpg. See also Global Affairs Press, "Status of World Nuclear Forces 2017," February 28, 2017, https://globalaffairspressdotcom.wordpress.com/2017/02/28/status-of-world-nuclear-forces-2017/.

[9] U.S. Department of State, "Treaty Between The United States Of America And The Union Of Soviet Socialist Republics On The Elimination Of Their Intermediate-Range And Shorter-Range Missiles (INF Treaty)," Bureau of Arms Control, Verification and Compliance, (https://www.state.gov/t/avc/trty/102360.htm, accessed February 21, 2018). A total of 2,692 missiles were eliminated, 866 for the US and 1,826 for the USSR. SIPRI Yearbook 2007: Armaments, Disarmament, and International Security. New York, NY: Oxford University Press. p. 683.

[10] Terence Neilan, "Bush Pulls Out of ABM Treaty; Putin Calls Move a Mistake", The New York Times, December 13, 2001, http://www.nytimes.com/2001/12/13/international/bush-pulls-out-of-abm-treaty-putin-calls-move-a-mistake.html.

[11] Ministry of Foreign Affairs of the Russian Federation, "Foreign Policy Concept of the Russian Federation (approved by President of the Russian Federation Vladimir Putin on November 30, 2016)," December 1, 2016, § 27 g, http://www.mid.ru/en/foreign_policy/official_documents/-/asset_publisher/CptICkB6BZ29/content/id/2542248.

[12] Wade Boese, "U.S. Withdraws From ABM Treaty; Global Response Muted," *Arms Control Today*, July/August 2002, https://www.armscontrol.org/act/2002_07-08/abmjul_aug02.

[13] The Warsaw Reflection Group Report, "Arms Control Revisited: Non-proliferation and Denuclearization," The Polish Institute of International Affairs, Warsaw, November 20–21, 2008, https://www.pism.pl/files/?id_plik=2941.

[14] Private information from an advisor to the UN Secretary General, April 4, 2016.

[15] Stefan Forss, "Rysslands problematiska ställning som kärnvapenstormakt" (Russia's problematic position as nuclear superpower), *Proceedings of the Royal Swedish Academy of War Sciences*, No. 3, 1997, pp. 59–84.

[16] Ibid. See also, Glen M. Segell, "European Security and the Russian Duma," *Journal of Defense & Security Analysis*, Vol. 18, No. 1, 2002, pp. 75–84.

[17] Carl Bildt and Radek Sikorski, "Next, the Tactical Nukes," New York Times, February 1, 2010, http://www.nytimes.com/2010/02/02/opinion/02iht-edbildt.html. Mr Bildt spoke at the Paris Summit. In a private mail, the late French nuclear expert, Professor Thérèse Delpech soon reported: "What I can tell you, is that the Russians were furious."

[18] President Barack Obama, "Remarks by President Obama at the Brandenburg Gate -- Berlin, Germany," June 19, 2013, https://obamawhitehouse.archives.gov/the-press-office/2013/06/19/remarks-president-obama-brandenburg-gate-berlin-germany.

[19] Sputnik International, "Nuclear Arms Reduction Deals To Become Multilateral," June 22, 2013, https://sputniknews.com/world/20130622181811968-Nuclear-Arms-Reduction-Deals-to-Become-Multilateral--Lavrov/.

[20] The Ministry of Foreign Affairs of the Russian Federation, "Foreign Policy Concept of the Russian Federation (approved by President of the Russian Federation Vladimir Putin on November 30, 2016)," December 1, 2016, § 27 f,

http://www.mid.ru/en/foreign_policy/official_documents/-/asset_publisher/CptICkB6BZ29/content/id/2542248.

[21] The Finnish moderator at the event at the Finnish National Defence University, Colonel Heikki Hult challenged general Ivashov: "With all due respect, Sir, but what about the Korean War, the Berlin crisis, and particularly the Cuban missile crisis of 1962?" Ivashov did not answer.

[22] Arms Control Association, "The Presidential Nuclear Initiatives (PNIs) on Tactical Nuclear Weapons at a Glance," Fact Sheets & Briefs, July 2017, https://www.armscontrol.org/factsheets/pniglance.

[23] Arms Control Association, "The Presidential Nuclear Initiatives (PNIs) on Tactical Nuclear Weapons at a Glance," Fact Sheets & Briefs, July 2017, https://www.armscontrol.org/factsheets/pniglance.

[24] Igor Sutyagin, "Atomic Accounting – A New estimate of Russia's Non-Strategic Nuclear Forces" *RUSI Occasional Paper*, November 2012, p. 53, https://rusi.org/sites/default/files/201211_op_atomic_accounting.pdf.

[25] Ibid.

[26] Ministry of Defence of the Russian Federation, "Missile Troops and Artillery," http://eng.mil.ru/en/structure/forces/ground/structure/rvia.htm (accessed 3 December 2017).

[27] Igor Sutyagin, "Atomic Accounting – A New estimate of Russia's Non-Strategic Nuclear Forces."

[28] Vek, "NATO's Expansion and Russia's Security," Viktor Mikhailov, Igor Andryushin, Alexander Chernyshev; 20 September 1996. See also, C. Austin Reams, "Russia's Atomic Czar: Viktor N. Mikhailov," Center for International Security Affairs Los Alamos National Laboratory, LA-UR-97-234, December 1996, pp. 16-17, http://www.iaea.org/inis/collection/NCLCollectionStore/_Public/28/077/28077312.pdf.

[29] Oleg Odnokolenko, "Russian Hawks Are Heard in Europe," *Segodnya*, December 17, 1999, pp. 1, 3; *Defence and Security*, No. 150, 22 December 1999.

[30] Nikolai Zlobin, "A close look at Russia's leaders: Meeting Putin and Ivanov," *The Defense Monitor* 33, No. 5 (September–October 2004).

[31] George P. Shultz, Steven P. Andreasen, Sidney D. Drell, James Goodby, "Reykjavik Revisited: Steps Toward a World Free of Nuclear Weapons (complete report)," Hoover Institution, August 6, 2009, p. 147. See also: Hubert Wetzel, Demetri Sevastopulo, and Guy Dinmore, "Russia confronted Rumsfeld with threat to quit key nuclear treaty," https://www.ft.com/content/97c0ab8c-9013-11d9-9a51-00000e2511c8, March 8, 2005. See also: STRATFOR, "Geopolitical diary: A polite meeting about missiles," https://worldview.stratfor.com/article/geopolitical-diary-polite-meeting-about-missiles. Aug 29, 2006. See also: Nikolai Sokov, "Russia military debates withdrawal from the INF Treaty," October 2006. See also: Pavel Podvig, "Russia wants to pull out of the INF Treaty," August 25, 2006, http://russianforces.org/blog/2006/08/russia_wants_to_pull_out_of_th.shtml.

[32] Sputnik News, "Scrapping Medium-Range Ballistic Missiles a Mistake – Ivanov – 1," February 7, 2007, https://sputniknews.com/russia/2007020760350944/.

[33] Russian President Vladimir Putin, "Transcript: Putin's prepared remarks at 43rd Munich Conference on Security Policy," *Washington Post*, December 2, 2007 http://www.washingtonpost.com/wp-dyn/content/article/2007/02/12/AR2007021200555.html (accessed December 3, 2017).

[34] U.S. Department of State Archive, Office of the Spokesman, "Joint U.S.–Russian statement on the Treaty on the Elimination of Intermediate-Range and Shorter-Range Missiles at the 62nd Session of the UN General Assembly," Oct. 25, 2007, https://2001-2009.state.gov/r/pa/prs/ps/2007/oct/94141.htm and Vitaly I. Churkin, "Statement by Vitaly I. Churkin, the Russian Federation's Permanent Representative to the UN, in the UN General Assembly's first committee introducing the joint Russian – United States statement on the INF Treaty," Oct. 25, 2007, http://www.jstor.org/stable/pdf/10.7249/j.ctt3fh15z.16.pdf.

[35] The arguments presented follow two lines: suspicion of deployment of offensive arms in the BMD launchers, and fear of BMD eroding Russia's nuclear deterrent, strongly refuted by Russia's leading missile designers and professionals. President Putin: "if this missile [defense] system is put in place, it will work automatically with the entire nuclear capability of the United States. It will be an integral part of the U.S. nuclear capability." President of Russia, "Interview with newspaper journalists from G8 member countries, June 4, 2007," http://en.kremlin.ru/events/president/transcripts/24313. Yuri Solomonov, Chief missile designer: "It is becoming obvious now that all that ballyhoo over the US missile shield in Europe is just another bluff." "US ballistic missile shield for Europe: between propaganda and real threats," *Radio Voice of Russia*, June 6, 2013, n.l. Dr. Alexey Arbatov mentions several Russian top missile experts concurring. Alexei

Arbatov, "Strategic Dialogue: A Change of Priorities," Carnegie Moscow Center, December 10, 2013, http://carnegie.ru/2013/12/10/strategic-dialogue-change-of-priorities/h1ht#. See also, "US missile shield unable to repel massive Russian ICBM attack – chief of strategic missile forces," *RT*, December 16, 2015, https://www.rt.com/news/326121-us-missile-shield-russian-icbm/.

[36] President of Russia, "Expanded Meeting of the Defence Ministry Board", December 22, 2017, http://en.kremlin.ru/events/president/news/56472.

[37] "Russia to compensate for INF losses with Iskander system," *Sputnik International* (former *RIA Novosti*), November 14, 2007, https://sputniknews.com/russia/2007111488066432/.

[38] Roger McDermott and Tor Bukkvoll, "Russia in the Precision-Strike regime – military theory, procurement and operational impact," Nowegian Defence Research Establishment (FFI), August 1, 2017, p. 17 https://www.ffi.no/no/Rapporter/17-00979.pdf.

[39] President of Russia, "Address to the Federal Assembly of the Russian Federation," November 5, 2008, http://en.kremlin.ru/events/president/transcripts/1968.

[40] Sergei Balmasov, "Russia shows Iskander Missile systems to NATO," *Pravda*, December 17, 2010, http://www.pravdareport.com/russia/politics/17-12-2010/116249-iskander-0/.

[41] Johan Norberg and Fredrik Westerlund, "Russia's Armed Forces in 2016," in Russian Military Capability in a Ten-Year Perspective – 2016 (Gudrun Persson, ed.), The Swedish Defence Research Establishment (FOI), December 2016, pp.53-54, https://www.foi.se/rapportsammanfattning?reportNo=FOI-R--4326--SE.

[42] Alexander Bondar, "Oruzhie v Umelykh Rukakh," *Krasnaya Zvezda*, November 23, 2017, http://www.redstar.ru/index.php/component/k2/item/35173-oruzhie-v-umelykh-rukakh. See also Russian Defense Policy Blog, "Iskander-M in Kaliningrad," November 27, 2017, https://russiandefpolicy.blog/2017/11/27/iskander-m-in-kaliningrad/ and Live Journal, "152nd gvardeiskaya raketnaya brigda v Kaliningrade poluchilia raketnye kompleksy 'Iskander-M,'" Nov. 25, 2017, https://bmpd.livejournal.com/2970466.html.

[43] "Russian ground forces to be fully rearmed with ballistic Iskander-M missiles by late 2020," *TASS*, May 24, 2017, http://tass.com/defense/947360.

[44] For a good general technical description, see MilitaryRussia.ru, "Комплекс 9К720 Искандер - SS-26 STONE," http://militaryrussia.ru/blog/topic-816.html.

[45] Johan Norberg and Fredrik Westerlund, "Russia's Armed Forces in 2016." See also World Daily News, "Russia wants to increase the Iskander-M missile range," *World Daily News*, May 23, 2017, https://www.youtube.com/watch?v=uH9pcDbLKSM.

[46] "9K720 Iskander - SS-26 STONE," *Military Russia*, 2014, http://militaryrussia.ru/blog/topic-817.html.

[47] Ministry of Defence of the Russian Federation, "Zapad 2017: Iskander-K Tactical Ballistic Missile System launched a missile during active phase of drills (Leningrad Region)," http://eng.mil.ru/en/structure/forces/ground/media/photo/gallery.htm?id=45272@cmsPhotoGallery.

[48] The nominal range for the ballistic missile Iskander-M is estimated to be about 700 kilometers. The range of the cruise missile is 1,500–2,000 kilometers. A rule of thumb used by FOI is that operational ranges are about two thirds of nominal ranges. For a technical assessment of the ballistic missile Iskander-M, see Stefan Forss: "The Russian Operational-Tactical Iskander Missile System," The Finnish National Defence University, Department of Strategic and Defence Studies, Series 4: Working Papers No 42, 2012, https://www.doria.fi/bitstream/handle/10024/84362/StratL4_42w.pdf.

[49] Pavel Podvig, "The INF Treaty culprit identified. Now what?" *Russian Strategic Nuclear Forces Blog*, December 5, 2017, http://russianforces.org/blog/2017/12/the_inf_treaty_culprit_identif.shtml.

[50] Roger McDermott and Tor Bukkvoll 2017, p. 12, https://www.ffi.no/no/Rapporter/17-00979.pdf.

[51] The U.S. Department of State, "Adherence to and Compliance with Arms Control, Nonproliferation, and Disarmament Agreements and Commitments," July 2014, p. 8, https://www.state.gov/documents/organization/230108.pdf.

[52] Michael R. Gordon, "Russia Deploys Missile, Violating Treaty and Challenging Trump," February 14, 2017, https://www.nytimes.com/2017/02/14/world/europe/russia-cruise-missile-arms-control-treaty.html.

[53] Dave Majumdar, "Novator 9M729: The Russian Missile that Broke INF Treaty's Back?" *The National Interest*, December 7, 2017, http://nationalinterest.org/blog/the-buzz/novator-9m729-the-russian-missile-broke-inf-treatys-back-23547.

[54] Mikhail Barabanov, "Esho o razvertyvanii Rossei krylatyx raket 9M729," (More on the deployment of cruise missiles 9M729), CAST bmpd Blog, February 17, 2017 (https://bmpd.livejournal.com/2438303.html)

[55] Semen Kabakaev, "Russia Deploys Banned Missile and Brags about It," The Atlantic Council Blog, May 10, 2017, http://www.atlanticcouncil.org/blogs/ukrainealert/russia-deploys-banned-missile-and-brags-about-it. See also Military Update, "Kalibr NK: The Russian Cruise Missile - That Shocked the World," October 13, 2017, https://www.youtube.com/watch?v=dtMDmTcW00Y. The video is interesting as it also shows an animation of a land-based Kalibr system, possibly similar to the system the US claims is prohibited by the INF.

[56] See Barabanov "Esho o razvertyvanii Rossei krylatyx raket 9M729." See Dave Majumdar, "Novator 9M729: The Russian Missile that Broke INF Treaty's Back?" FAS researcher Hans Kristensen, however, tries to give the opposite impression from a simple small deletion in an intelligence report. See Hans M. Kristensen, "NASIC Removes Russian INF-Violating Missile From Report," Federation of the American Scientists, *Strategic Security Blog*, August 22, 2017 (https://fas.org/blogs/security/2017/08/nasic-2017-corrected/.

[57] See Norberg and Westerlund," Russia's Armed Forces in 2016."

[58] Ibid., p. 40.

[59] Ibid.

[60] Roman Azanov, "Russia's Strategic Missile Forces as its decisive defense," *TASS*, December 19, 2017, http://tass.com/defense/981811. See also Mark Schneider, "Additional Russian Violations of Arms Control Agreements," *RealClearDefense*, December 18, 2017, https://www.realcleardefense.com/articles/2017/12/18/additional_russian_violations_of_arms_control_agreements_112795.html.

[61] Pavel Podvig, "More news about the RS-26 missile," *The Russian Strategic Forces Blog*, December 18, 2013, http://russianforces.org/blog/2013/12/more_news_about_rs-26_missile.shtml.

[62] Pavel Podvig, "RS-26 missile is tested and ready for deployment," The Russian Strategic Forces Blog, March 26, 2015, http://russianforces.org/blog/2013/12/more_news_about_rs-26_missile.shtml. See also *Interfax*, "Razrabotka strategicheskoi raket' RS-26 – odin iz otvetnykhh shagov na rasvertyvanie PRO SshA – istotchnik v Minoborony' RF" (Developing strategic missile RS-26 - one of the reciprocal steps to the deployment of US missile defense - source in the Russian Defense Ministry), http://www.militarynews.ru/story.asp?rid=1&nid=370944.

[63] Pavel Podvig, "Russia tests new prototype of ICBM," *The Russian Strategic Forces Blog*, May 23, 2012, http://russianforces.org/blog/2012/05/russia_tests_prototype_of_a_ne.shtml.

[64] Pavel Podvig, "New ICBM tested in Kapustin Yar," The Russian Strategic Forces Blog, October 24, 2012, http://russianforces.org/blog/2012/10/new_icbm_tested_in_kapustin_ya.shtml.

[65] Aleksandr Golts, "Russia's Rubezh Ballistic Missile Disappears off the Radar," Eurasia Daily Monitor, September 27, 2017, https://jamestown.org/program/russias-rubezh-ballistic-missile-disappears-off-the-radar/.

[66] See Gudrun Persson, ed., "Russia's Armed Forces in 2016."

[67] "Russia's latest rocket and artillery systems," *TASS*, November 20, 2017, http://tass.com/defense/976431.

[68] See Stefan Forss, "The Russian Operational-Tactical Iskander Missile System." See also Viktor Myasnikov, "Full reverse," Defense & Security, No. 131, November 23, 2007, http://dlib.eastview.com/browse/doc/12998773.

[69] Tom Demerly, "Russia Test Fires New Kh-47M2 Kinzhal Hypersonic Missile," *The Aviationist*, March 12, 2018, https://theaviationist.com/2018/03/12/russia-test-fires-new-kh-47m2-kinzhal-hypersonic-missile/.

[70] Dave Majumdar, "Russia: New Kinzhal Aero-Ballistic Missile Has 3,000 km Range if Fired from Supersonic Bomber," *The National Interest*, July 18, 2018, https://nationalinterest.org/blog/buzz/russia-new-kinzhal-aero-ballistic-missile-has-3000-km-range-if-fired-supersonic-bomber.

[71] Pavel Podvig, "Typhoon submarines decommissioned," *The Russian Strategic Forces Blog*, April 29, 2004, http://russianforces.org/blog/2004/04/typhoon_submarines_decommissio.shtml.

[72] Military Russia, "RT-2PM2, RS-12M1 / RS-12M2 Topol-M - SS-27 SICKLE-B / STALIN," January 7, 2018, http://militaryrussia.ru/blog/topic-894.html.

[73] U.S. Department of State, "Treaty Between the United States of America and the Russian Federation on Further Reduction and Limitation of Strategic Offensive Arms (START II)," January 3, 1993, https://www.state.gov/t/avc/trty/102887.htm#treatytext. Reference: Article I, para 4(b) & 4 (c).

[74] Military Russia, "RS-24 Yars / Topol-MR - SS-X-29 / SS-29 / SS-27 mod.2 SICKLE-B," September 23, 2017, http://militaryrussia.ru/blog/topic-430.html.

[75] Hans M. Kristensen and Robert S. Norris, "Russian nuclear forces, 2017," The Bulletin of the Atomic Scientists, 73:2, 2017, pp. 115 – 126, http://dx.doi.org/10.1080/00963402.2017.1290375.

[76] Minister of Defense Sergei Shoigu, in President of Russia, "Expanded Meeting of the Defence Ministry Board," December 22, 2017, http://en.kremlin.ru/events/president/news/56472.

[77] Roman Azanov, "TASS highlights the Strategic Missile Force's modern combat potential and its prospects," TASS, December 19, 2017, http://tass.com/defense/981811. Past history indicates that annual production goals may not be achieved. An educated guess is that production in 2018 may be about half of that announced.

[78] Pavel Podvig, Strategic Rocket Forces," The Russian Strategic Forces Blog, June 22, 2017, http://russianforces.org/missiles/.

[79] Private information from Dr. Gunnar Arbman, Research Director, The Swedish Defence Research Agency (FOI), October 11, 2004. The Russian designers were particularly pleased that they were able to squeeze a nuclear charge into the 152 mm artillery round, thereby beating their American colleagues with 3 millimeters. Academician Yevgeny Avrorin confirmed this in an interview in 2013. See Российское атомное сообщество (Russian Atomic Energy Community), Академик Евгений Николаевич Аврорин: "Наука — это то, что можно сделать, а техническая наука — это то, что нужно сделать" (Academician Yevgeny Nikolaevich Avrorin: "Science is what can be done, and technical science is what needs to be done"), April 10, 2013, http://www.atomic-energy.ru/interviews/2013/04/10/41068.

[80] A heavy ICBM has a launch weight larger than 106 metric tons and a throw-weight larger than 4.35 tons. See U.S. Department of State, "START TREATY

DEFINITIONS ANNEX -TERMS AND THEIR DEFINITIONS,"
https://www.state.gov/documents/organization/27362.pdf.

[81] "Istochnik Pervyi Polk s Raketnoi 'Sarmat' Dolzhen Zastupit' Na Boeovoye
Dezhurstvo v 2021 Godu" ("Source: The First Regiment With a Rocket 'Sarmat'
Should Enter Combat Duty in 2021"), *TASS*, March 29, 2018, http://tass.ru/armiya-
i-opk/5076963.

[82] "PC-28 / OCD Sarmat rocket 15A28 - SS-X-30," *MilitaryRussia.ru*, March 31,
2018 http://militaryrussia.ru/blog/topic-435.html.

[83] President of Russia, "Presidential Address to the Federal Assembly", March 1,
2018, http://en.kremlin.ru/events/president/news/56957.

[84] Yuri Avdeev, "V oboime – 'Sarmat', 'Kinzhal', 'Avangard,' " *Krasnaia Zvezda*,
March 12, 2018, http://redstar.ru/index.php/newspaper/item/36438-v-obojme-
sarmat-kinzhal-avangard; "SS-30 ?? / RS-28 / 15A28 Sarmat New Heavy ICBM,"
GlobalSecurity.org, https://www.globalsecurity.org/wmd/world/russia/ss-30.htm.

[85] The accuracy of Soviet/Russian strategic missiles is generally believed to have been
lower than that of comparable US strategic missiles. Therefore, Moscow used
comparatively higher-yield warheads to ensure destruction of the designated target.
As missile accuracy has improved, the same effect on target can be achieved with
lower-yield warheads.

[86] Franz-Josef Gady, "Russia Completes Ejection Tests of RS-28 Sarmat ICBM," *The
Diplomat*, July 20, 2018, https://thediplomat.com/2018/07/russia-completes-
ejection-tests-of-rs-28-sarmat-icbm/; "PC-28 / OCD Sarmat rocket 15A28 - SS-X-30
(draft)," *Military Russia*, March, 31, 2018, http://militaryrussia.ru/blog/topic-
435.html. See also "Russia's RS-28 Sarmat ICBM: Hypersonic Disaster for US
Missile Defense Shield," *Sputnik News*, May 4, 2017,
https://sputniknews.com/politics/201705041053289933-russia-sarmat-us-missile-
defense/.

[87] "Russia completes work on Avangard hypersonic missile system," *TASS*, July 19,
2018, http://tass.com/defense/1014104.

[88] Stefan Forss, "Rysslands kärnvapenstyrkor," (Russia's nuclear forces), FOI
Strategiskt Forum, No. 7, January 2001. According to *Jane's Fighting Ships 1999–
2000*, Russia had only 17 SSBNs operational, a decline by almost ten in 1–2 years. In
addition, there were 27 SSGNs and SSNs capable of firing nuclear SS-N-21 Sampson
(S-10 Granat) cruise missiles and SS-N-19 Shipwreck (P-700 Granit) missiles. Harri

Tielinen, "Ryska marinen och dess framtidsperspektiv," (The Russian Navy and Its Future Prospects), FOA Strategiskt forum för säkerhetspolitik och omvärldsanalys, No.3. May 1998, The Swedish Defence Research Establishment (FOA), Stockholm. For 2017, the corresponding numbers are 13 SSBNs and 26 SSGNs and SSNs. IISS, "Chapter Five: Russia and Eurasia," The Military Balance 2017, p. 213, http://dx.doi.org/10.1080/04597222.2017.1271211.

[89] Ibid.

[90] Harri Tielinen, "Ryska marinen och dess framtidsperspektiv."

[91] Stefan Forss, "Rysslands kärnvapenstyrkor."

[92] John Pike, "R-29RMU / R-29RGU / RSM-54 Sineva / SS-N-23 SKIFF," *Global Security*, https://www.globalsecurity.org/wmd/world/russia/r29rmu.htm.

[93] Pavel Podvig, "Liner SLBM explained," Russian strategic nuclear forces, Blog, October 4, 2011 http://russianforces.org/blog/2011/10/liner_slbm_explained.shtml and "Liner version of the R-29RM SLBM accepted for service," April 2, 2014, http://russianforces.org/blog/2014/04/liner_version_of_the_r-29rm_sl.shtml.

[94] "VMF Rossii prinyal na vooruzhenie raketny kompleks s MBR "Lainer," *Voenno-Promyshlenniy Kourier*, April 2, 2014, https://vpk-news.ru/news/19774.

[95] Pavel Podvig, "Bulava missile test history," Russian strategic nuclear forces Blog, June 20, 2017, http://russianforces.org/navy/slbms/bulava.shtml.

[96] Pavel Podvig, "Bulava is finally accepted for service," *Russian Strategic Nuclear Forces Blog*, June 29, 2018, http://russianforces.org/blog/2018/06/bulava_is_finally_accepted_for.shtml

[97] Franz-Stefan Gady, "Russia to Launch Its Most Powerful Ballistic Missile Sub in November," *The Diplomat*, October 31, 2017, https://thediplomat.com/2017/10/russia-to-launch-its-most-powerful-ballistic-missile-sub-in-november/. See also, Lukas Andriukaitis, "#MeanwhileInTheArctic: Prince Vladimir Submarine Sets Sail," AtlanticCouncil's Digital Forensic Research Lab, November 27, 2017, https://medium.com/dfrlab/meanwhileinthearctic-prince-vladimir-submarine-sets-sail-71cebd22f77d.

[98] Pavel Podvig, "Strategic fleet."

[99] Minister of Defense Sergei Shoigu, "Expanded Meeting of the Defence Ministry Board," December 22, 2017, http://en.kremlin.ru/events/president/news/56472.

[100] Lukas Andriukaitis, "#MeanwhileInTheArctic: Prince Vladimir Submarine Sets Sail."

[101] Zachary Keck, "Russia's Nuclear Submarine Force Is Back (Maybe)," *The National Interest*, November 2017, http://nationalinterest.org/blog/the-buzz/russias-nuclear-submarine-force-back-maybe-23255?page=show.

[102] Dave Majumdar, "The Russian Defense Ministry Is Showing Off Some Truly Terrifying Weapons," *The National Interest*, July 22, 2018, https://nationalinterest.org/blog/buzz/russian-defense-ministry-showing-some-truly-terrifying-weapons-26496, Dave Majumdar, "Just How Much of a Threat Is Russia's Status-6 Nuclear Torpedo?" *The National Interest Blog*, January 16, 2018, http://nationalinterest.org/blog/the-buzz/just-how-much-threat-russias-status-6-nuclear-torpedo-24094?page=show. See also James Drew, "Russia's Doomsday Torpedo Is a 'Third Strike' Weapon," *Aerospace Daily*, January 24, 2018, http://aviationweek.com/defense/russia-s-doomsday-torpedo-third-strike-weapon.

[103] Mark B. Schneider, "Escalate to De-escalate," *US Naval Institute Proceedings*, February 2017 Vol. 143/2/1,368, https://www.usni.org/magazines/proceedings/2017-02.

[104]"Minoborony opublikovalo video podvodnogo bespilotnika 'Poseidon': polnaya neuyazvimost," MK.ru, July, 19, 2018, https://tv.mk.ru/video/2018/07/19/minoborony-opublikovalo-video-podvodnogo-bespilotnika-poseydon-polnaya-neuyazvimost.html; YouTube, "President Vladimir Putin predstavil Rossii novyie vidy vooruzhenii" (President Putin Introduced New Types of Weapons to Russia)," March 31, 2018, https://www.youtube.com/watch?v=cf_cjAutcY8.

[105] First flight was in 1981, series production begun in 1984, in service 1987. Pavel Podvig (ed.), "Ty-160 (Blackjack)," *Strategicheskoye yadernoye vooruzhenie Rossii*, Moscow, IzdAT, 1998, pp. 338–339.

[106] Thomas Malmlöf and Roger Roffey, "The Russian Defence Industry and Procurement," in Russian Military Capability in a Ten-Year Perspective – 2016 (Gudrun Persson, ed.), The Swedish Defence Research Establishment (FOI), December 2016, p. 158, https://www.foi.se/rapportsammanfattning?reportNo=FOI-R--4326--SE.

[107] Pavel Podvig, "Russia's ambitious plans for strategic bombers," *Russian Strategic Nuclear Forces Blog*, May 10, 2017, http://russianforces.org/blog/2017/05/russias_ambitious_plans_for_st.shtml.

[108] "Not Necessarily New," *Russian Defense Policy Blog*, July 17, 2017, https://russiandefpolicy.blog/2017/07/17/not-necessarily-new/.

[109] Pavel Podvig, "First Tu-160M2 takes flight, production contract for ten aircraft signed," *Russian Strategic Nuclear Forces Blog*, January 26, 2018, http://russianforces.org/blog/2018/01/first_tu-160m2_takes_flight_pr.shtml.

[110] IISS, "Chapter Five: Russia and Eurasia," *The Military Balance 2017*, p. 211, http://dx.doi.org/10.1080/04597222.2017.1271211.

[111] Pavel Podvig, "Russia's ambitious plans for strategic bombers," *Russian Strategic Nuclear Forces Blog*, May 10, 2017, http://russianforces.org/blog/2017/05/russias_ambitious_plans_for_st.shtml.

[112] Ministry of Defense RF, "Remarks by Chief of General Staff of the Russian Federation General of the Army Valery Gerasimov at the Russian Defence Ministry's board session (November 7, 2017)," Ministry of Defense RF, November 7, 2017, http://eng.mil.ru/en/news_page/country/more.htm?id=12149743@egNews.

[113] Giovanni de Briganti, "Kalibr SLCMs in Syrian Theater of Operations," *Defense-Aerospace*, http://www.defense-aerospace.com/articles-view/feature/5/178397/naval-cruise-missiles-and-russian-operations-in-syria.html. The three-part article builds on information from *TASS Defense*, October 26–28, 2016. Although Kalibr is a sea- and land-based cruise missile system, the navigation systems on air-launched cruise missiles are at least similar if not identical.

[114] "What Makes Russia's Advanced Kh-101 Cruise Missiles Such a Powerful Force," *Sputnik News*, July 8, 2017, https://sputniknews.com/military/201707081055365770-russia-kh101-cruise-missile/.

[115] Ibid.

[116] Ibid.

[117] "Х-50 / статья 715/9-А-5015" (Kh-50 / Product 715/9-A-5015), *Military Russia*, November 17, 2017, http://militaryrussia.ru/blog/topic-891.html.

[118] However important and representative the Kh-101 may be for Russia's ambitions regarding air warfare, it still is only one weapons system in the vast inventory of the Russian air force. The blog *MilitaryRussia.ru* offers a quality source to explore systems omitted here, including retired weapon systems, weapons in use and weapons in development, such as future hypervelocity weapons. See, "Raketny Kompleks Knizhal," *Military Russia*, 2018, http://militaryrussia.ru/blog/index-40.html.

[119] William Burr and Svetlana Savranskaya, "Previously Classified Interviews with Former Soviet Officials Reveal U.S. Strategic Intelligence Failure Over Decades," The Nuclear Vault, National Security Archive, Washington, DC, September 11, 2009, https://nsarchive2.gwu.edu/nukevault/ebb285/. The two-volume report by BDM Federal Inc. (John. G. Hines, Senior Author, Ellis M. Mishulovich and John F. Shull) on SOVIET INTENTIONS 1965 – 1985, written in September 1995, can be accessed using the links provided in Burr's and Safranskaya's summary.

[120] The period dealt with here was well before the MX program got under way in the 1970s, but that did not convince Dr. V.L. Kataev, Senior Advisor to the Chairman of the Defense Industrial Department of the Communist Party Central Committee. He claimed that Soviet intelligence had found references to the U.S. MX missile, a highly accurate counterforce weapon, were found possibly as early as 1963. BDM report, Vol. I, p. 2.

[121] Interview with Dr. Vitaly N. Tsygichko, December 21, 1991, in John. G. Hines, Senior Author, Ellis M. Mishulovich and John F. Shull, "SOVIET INTENTIONS 1965 – 1985, An Analytical Comparison of U.S. – Soviet Assessments During the Cold War," Volume II, BDM Federal Inc., September 22, 1995, pp. 150–151, https://nsarchive2.gwu.edu/nukevault/ebb285/vol%20II%20Tysgichko.PDF.

[122] Ibid.

[123] Ibid.

[124] Ibid.

[125] Interview with Colonel General (ret.) Andrian A. Danilevich, September 21, 1992, in John. G. Hines, Senior Author, Ellis M. Mishulovich and John F. Shull, "SOVIET INTENTIONS 1965–1985, An Analytical Comparison of U.S.-Soviet Assessments During the Cold War," Volume II, BDM Federal Inc., September 22, 1995, p. 27, https://nsarchive2.gwu.edu/nukevault/ebb285/vol%20iI%20Danilevich.pdf.

[126] General Danilevich was a key officer as Assistant for Doctrine and Strategy to Chiefs of the General Staff and having led the work on the top secret three-volume *Strategy of Deep Operations (Global and Theater)*, which was the basic reference document for Soviet strategic and operational nuclear planning for at least the last decade of the Soviet Union.

[127] This probably is one of the first times that thoughts of "escalation" or "de-escalation" in the sense it is discussed currently, was voiced.

[128] Hines et al., "SOVIET INTENTIONS 1965 – 1985, An Analytical Comparison of U.S. – Soviet Assessments During the Cold War."

[129] Andrei Kokoshin, "Ensuring Strategic Stability in the Past and Present: Theoretical and Applied Questions," Harvard Kennedy School, Belfer Center, June 2011, p. 34, https://www.belfercenter.org/sites/default/files/legacy/files/Ensuring%20Strategic%20Stability%20by%20A.%20Kokoshin.pdf.

[130] National Institute for Public Policy, "A New Nuclear Review for a New Age," National Institute Press 2017, April 2017, p. 25, http://www.nipp.org/wp-content/uploads/2017/06/A-New-Nuclear-Review-final.pdf.

[131] Jeff Daniels, "Pentagon chief sees new nuclear missile as bargaining chip against Russians" CNBC News, February 6, 2018, https://www.cnbc.com/2018/02/06/mattis-sees-new-nuclear-missile-as-bargaining-chip-against-russia.html.

[132] Andrei Kokoshin, "Ensuring Strategic Stability in the Past and Present: Theoretical and Applied Questions," Harvard Kennedy School, Belfer Center, June 2011, p. 4, https://www.belfercenter.org/sites/default/files/legacy/files/Ensuring%20Strategic%20Stability%20by%20A.%20Kokoshin.pdf.

[133] Ministry of Defence RF, "Remarks by Chief of General Staff of the Russian Federation General of the Army Valery Gerasimov at the Russian Defence Ministry's board session."

[134] Per Olov Nilsson, "Rysslands militärdoktrin i början av 2000-talet" (Russia's Military Doctrine in the Beginning of the 21st Century), *Proceedings of the Royal Swedish Academy of War Sciences*, No. 3, 2000, pp. 43-68; Jacob W. Kipp, "Russia's Nonstrategic Nuclear Weapons," *Military Review*, May-June 2001, pp. 27–38 http://cgsc.contentdm.oclc.org/cdm/singleitem/collection/p124201coll1/id/235/rec/

4; Stephen J. Blank, "Russian Nuclear Weapons: Past, Present, and Future," U.S. Army War College, Strategic Studies Institute, Carlisle, PA, 2011, https://ssi.armywarcollege.edu/pubs/display.cfm?pubID=1087; James T. Quinlivan and Olga Oliker, "Nuclear Deterrence in Europe – Russian Approaches to a New Environment and Implications for the United States," RAND Corporation, 2011, https://www.rand.org/content/dam/rand/pubs/monographs/2011/RAND_MG1075. pdf; Elbridge Colby, "Russia's Evolving Nuclear Doctrine and its Implications", Fondation pour la Recherche Stratégique, Note n°01/2016, January 12, 2016, https://www.frstrategie.org/web/documents/publications/notes/2016/201601.pdf.

[135] Major General V. N. Levshin, Colonel A. V. Nedelin, Colonel M. E. Sosnovskii, "O primenenii iadernogo oruzhiia dlia deeskalatsii voennykh deistvii," (On the Use of Nuclear Weapons for the De-escalation of Combat Actions), *Voennaia Mysl*, May 1999.

[136] Jacob W. Kipp, "Russia's Nonstrategic Nuclear Weapons."

[137] Stanislav N. Voronin and Sergey T. Brezkun, "Strategicheskii v'igodnaiia assimetria" (A strategically beneficial asymmetry), *Nezavisimoe Voennoe Obozreniie*, No 36, September 18, 1999, http://nvo.ng.ru/concepts/1999-09-18/assimetria.html; Vladimir F. Sivolob and Mikhail E. Sosnovskiy: "Realnost sderzhivaniia" (A Reality of Deterrence: Algorithms for Nuclear Weapon Use Should Become a Component Part of Military Doctrine), *Nezavisimoe Voennoe Obozreniie*, October 22, 1999, http://nvo.ng.ru/concepts/1999-10-22/reality.html.

[138] James T. Quinlivan and Olga Oliker, "Nuclear Deterrence in Europe – Russian Approaches to a New Environment and Implications for the United States."

[139] Matvei Kozhukin, "Iadernoe oruzhie – factor sderzhivaniia," (Nuclear weapons – a factor of deterrence), *Krasnaya Zvezda*, February 10, 2010, http://old.redstar.ru/2010/02/10_02/1_03.html.

[140] Jakob Hedenskog, Gudrun Persson and Carolina Vendil Pallin, "Russia's Armed Forces in 2016," in Russian Military Capability in a Ten-Year Perspective – 2016 (Gudrun Persson, ed.), The Swedish Defence Research Establishment (FOI), December 2016, p. 112, (https://www.foi.se/rapportsammanfattning?reportNo=FOI-R--4326--SE.

[141] Russia Maritime Studies Institute (Translation by Anna Davis), "Fundamentals of the State Policy of the Russian Federation in the Field of Naval Operations for the Period Until 2030," Russia Maritime Studies Institute, U.S. Naval War College, Newport, Rhode Island, 2017, http://dnnlgwick.blob.core.windows.net/portals/0/RMSI_RusNavyFundamentalsEN

G FINAL%20(1).pdf?sr=b&si=DNNFileManagerPolicy&sig=i110Z1rxZVzKbB%2B dHJ1CZuTxvwL3N7W34%2FLpksgT1Bs%3D, original in http://www.kremlin.ru/acts/bank/42117/page/2.

[142] Ministry of Defense RF, "Remarks by Chief of General Staff of the Russian Federation General of the Army Valery Gerasimov at the Russian Defence Ministry's board session (November 7, 2017)."

[143] Ilya Kramnik, "Nedopustim dazhe vzryv odnoi bomby" (Even the explosion of one bomb is inadmissible), *Izvestia*, October 16, 2017, https://iz.ru/658069/nedopustim-dazhe-vzryv-odnoi-bomby.

[144] U.S. Department of State, "Treaty Between The United States Of America And The Union Of Soviet Socialist Republics On The Elimination Of Their Intermediate-Range And Shorter-Range Missiles (INF Treaty)."

[145] Mark B. Schneider, "Will Russia Build 8,000 Nuclear Weapons by 2026?" *RealClear Defense*, January 26, 2018, https://www.realcleardefense.com/articles/2018/01/26/will_russia_build_8000_nucl ear_weapons_by_2026_112963.html.

[146] The Ministry of Foreign Affairs of the RF, "Foreign Ministry statement," February 5, 2018, http://www.mid.ru/en/web/guest/maps/us/- /asset_publisher/unVXBbj4Z6e8/content/id/3054864.

[147] Anton Troianovski, "Putin ally warns of arms race as Russia considers response to U.S. nuclear stance," *Washington Post*, February 10, 2018, https://www.washingtonpost.com/world/putin-ally-warns-of-arms-race-as-russia-considers-response-to-us-nuclear-stance/2018/02/10/23dd3cf2-0cf2-11e8-baf5-e629fc1cd21e_story.html.

[148] Dmitry Suslov, "Militarizing the Confrontation: Risks of the New US Nuclear Posture Review," Valdai Discussion Club, February 9, 2018, http://valdaiclub.com/a/highlights/militarizing-the-confrontation-risks/.

[149] Munich Security Conference 2018 Panel Discussion, "Nuclear Security: Out of (Arms) Control?" February 17, 2018, https://www.securityconference.de/en/media-library/munich-security-conference-2018/video/panel-discussion-nuclear-security-out-of-arms-control/filter/video/. Referring to the new "U.S. Nuclear Posture Review," ambassador Kislyak actually accused the US of adopting this posture. He also said that Russia is not going to change its position regarding negative security guarantees.

[150] Mark B. Schneider, "Russian Air-Delivered Non-Strategic Nuclear Weapons," *RealClear Defense*, June 15, 2018, https://www.realcleardefense.com/articles/2018/06/15/russian_air-delivered_non-strategic_nuclear_weapons_113537.html.

[151] Stefan Forss, "Extending the New START Treaty – Problems to consider," *The Royal Swedish Academy of War Sciences Blog*, August 14, 2018, http://kkrva.se/extending-the-new-start-treaty-problems-to-consider/.

[152] Bryan Bender, "Leaked document: Putin lobbied Trump on arms control," *Politico*, August 7, 2018, https://www.politico.com/story/2018/08/07/putin-trump-arms-control-russia-724718?cid=apn.

7. Putin's 'Asymmetric Strategy': Nuclear and New-Type Weapons in Russian Defense Policy

Stephen Blank

Introduction

Vladimir Putin has been at war with the United States and the West for over a decade.[1] Already, on January 18, 2005, Defense Minister Sergei Ivanov told the Academy of Military Sciences,

> Let us face it, there is a war against Russia under way, and it has been going on for quite a few years. No one declared war on us. There is not one country that would be in a state of war with Russia. But there are people and organizations in various countries who take part in hostilities against the Russian Federation.[2]

More recently, Dmitri Trenin, the director of the Moscow office of the Carnegie Endowment, observed that, for some time, "the Kremlin has been *de facto* operating in a war mode."[3]

Accordingly, this chapter focuses on a key aspect of that war, namely Russia's programs for nuclear weapons and hypersonics. These

251

weapons represent important parts of Putin's so-called asymmetric or indirect strategy. And their continuing procurement is unceasing. These sectors are critical not only because the Kremlin considers them procurement priorities but also because, until recently, Russia clearly envisaged the possibility of having to fight a limited nuclear war and may still think in terms of doing so. It is true that Russia's most recent military doctrines suggest a move toward greater reliance on what might be called non-nuclear or conventional deterrence.[4] But its procurement programs and exercises, like the recent Zapad 2017 war game, point to an entirely different conclusion: namely, anticipation of actual nuclear war-fighting. Therefore, the controversy over the role of nuclear weapons in Moscow's strategy and the question of whether or not Russia has a high or low threshold for nuclear use remains unresolved.[5]

Nevertheless, these deployments and plans clearly highlight the General Staff and government's strategy as still being one of (supposedly limited) nuclear war. Previously, key officials confirmed this interpretation, conceding limited nuclear war as Russia's officially acknowledged strategy against many different kinds of contingencies.[6] The correspondent Ilya Kedrov, in his 2010 discussion of armored vehicles, also ratified his understanding of the doctrine as affirming this strategy.[7] Likewise, Colonel General Nikolai Solovtsov, the commander-in-chief of the Strategic Rocket Forces (RVSN), stated in 2008 that new military uses for nuclear weapons are coming into being. Thus,

> The radical changes that have occurred since the end of the Cold War in international relations and the considerable reduction of the threat that a large-scale war, even more so a nuclear one, could be unleashed, have contributed to the fact that, in the system of views on the role of nuclear arms both in Russia and the US, a political rather than military function has begun to prevail. In relation to this, besides the traditional forms and methods in the

combat use of the RVSN, a new notion of "special actions" by the groupings of strategic offensive arms has emerged... Such actions mean the RVSN's containment actions, their aim to prevent the escalation of a high-intensity non-nuclear military conflict against the Russian Federation and its allies.[8]

At a September 2008 roundtable on nuclear deterrence, Solovtsov noted that Russia was giving explicit consideration to the concept of "special actions" or "deterring actions of the RVSN aimed at the prevention of escalation of a non-nuclear military conflict of high intensity against Russia." Solovtsov further stated that,

These actions may be taken with a view to convincingly demonstrating to the aggressor [the] high combat potential of Russian nuclear missile weapons, [the] determination of the military-political leadership of Russia to apply them in order to make the aggressor stop combat actions. In view of its unique properties, the striking power of the Strategic Missile Forces is most efficient and convincing in the de-escalation actions [9]

Whatever changes have occurred since then in actual operational planning, nuclear weapons remain Russia's priority procurement program item and new models are being developed with hypersonic capabilities even as Russia modernizes older systems. And the extent of these programs far outstrips current nuclear inventory modernization efforts by the United States.[10] Indeed, Russian officials—e.g. Viktor Bondarev, head of the Federation Council Defense and Security Committee—not only see no threat from recent US nuclear exercises, but Bondarev actually claims that "Russia's nuclear potential is significantly superior to America's."[11] According to a 2015 report by the Fairfax, Virginia–based National Institute for Public Policy,

Since the late 1990s, Russia has developed and deployed: two new types of intercontinental ballistic missiles (ICBMs), including a new road-mobile missile and a silo-based variant (Topol-M Variant 2 and Yars); a new type of sea-launched ballistic missile (SLBM), the Bulava-30, and two upgraded versions of an existing SLBM (Sineva and Liner); a new class of ballistic missile submarine (Borey); modernized heavy bombers, including the Tu-160 (Blackjack) and Tu-95 (Bear); and a new long-range strategic cruise missile (Raduga). Russia is also developing additional strategic nuclear weapons systems, including: a new road-mobile ICBM (Rubezh) and a new rail-mobile ICBM (Barguzin); a new heavy ICBM (Sarmat) with multiple independently targetable reentry vehicles (MIRVs); a new "fifth generation" missile submarine to carry ballistic and cruise missiles; and a new stealthy heavy bomber to carry cruise missiles and reportedly hypersonic missiles.[12]

In late 2017, the Barguzin project, which has been subjected to numerous cancelations in the past only to be resurrected, was once again terminated, presumably due to its cost—becoming unaffordable given Russia's difficult economic circumstances.[13] But considering the Barguzin's past history, it would not be surprising if the program is resurrected again at some later date.

Despite Moscow's professed interest in new arms-control treaties, this is clearly not the program of a state seeking disarmament. Furthermore, Moscow has long sought and is continuing to test weapons whose explicit purpose is to evade US missile defenses, which it continues to regard, in defiance of all science and innumerable American and Western briefings, as a major threat to its second-strike capability. In September 2017, Moscow tested both the road-mobile and silo-based versions of the RS-24 Yars solid-fuel ICBM in conjunction with the Zapad 2017 exercises, using "experimental warheads."[14] In addition, Russia announced impending plans to test a new generation of ICBMs that "can beat US defense systems" and hold the United States and Europe at risk. The new Sarmat (Satan-2) RS-28 ICBM can allegedly destroy an area the size of Texas or France, evade missile defenses and do so using hypersonic Multiple Independent Reentry Vehicles (MIRV) that are now permitted under the New START treaty. The hypersonic missiles that allegedly can be fitted to this system are currently in development under the title Project 4202, a label that evidently refers to the hypersonic glide vehicle (HGV), the Yu-71.[15] Russian sources claim an 11,000-kilometer range and up to 15 warheads for this weapon, a yield of up to 760 kilotons and the building of launch silos that could withstand seven nuclear strikes.[16]

Russian nuclear modernization programs also encompass all three legs of its triad of air, sea and land-based nuclear weapons, as well as short, intermediate and long-range nuclear weapons. In addition, in October 2017, Putin took the unusual step of publicly announcing his personal participation in a nuclear exercise using all three elements of Russia's nuclear triad and some of the newest models of Russian air, land and sea-launched nuclear weapons.[17] Putin also highlighted Russia's ongoing militarization by announcing that, as of October 27, over 2,500 military exercises had occurred in 2017.[18] Moreover, given current procurement plans and the counting rules under the New START Treaty, Russia could actually increase its nuclear weapons stockpile and still be in compliance with that treaty.[19]

Finally, all conventional plans and exercises have an accompanying nuclear component, so nuclear options are integrated into operational plans and rehearsed beforehand. Submarine-based nuclear strikes from the Arctic accompanied the recent Zapad 2017 exercises as did much less heralded nuclear exercises in Novosibirsk involving some of the newest nuclear weapons in Moscow's arsenal.[20] And this followed a pattern of coinciding nuclear and conventional exercises for Zapad 2009 and 2013.[21]

The Roots of Putin's Asymmetric Strategy

Putin's so-called asymmetric strategy has deep historical roots. In 2014, in his annual address to the Federal Assembly (upper chamber of the Russian parliament), Putin reiterated, "We have no intention to become involved in a costly arms race, but at the same time we will reliably and dependably guarantee our country's defense in the new conditions. There are absolutely no doubts about this. This will be done. Russia has both the capability and the innovative solutions for this."[22] Echoing such sentiments, Putin's advisor for military policy, General Alexander Burutin, wrote that, "A crucial element in our plans for the development of new armaments must be an orientation towards an asymmetric response to the development and entering into service of the expensive new systems of the developed foreign countries."[23] In this context, the Norwegian scholar Tor Bukkvoll remarked that, in Russian thinking, asymmetric technologies should have a disruptive effect on new Western technologies, be developed in areas where Russian defense industry has particular advantages, and be much cheaper to develop and produce than Western technologies. And these discussions also stress acquisition of anti-access and area-denial (A2/AD) systems and technologies.[24]

Therefore, this orientation toward an asymmetric strategy must emphasize nuclear weapons, including among them both long-range Tu-22M3 strategic bombers and the short-range Iskander dual-use ballistic missile, as well as ICBMs, nuclear-missile submarines, ground-based ballistic and cruise missiles, and a modernized conventional force to bypass the US's ballistic missile defense (BMD) network.[25] More recently, Putin has stated that Russia's acquisition of sea-launched and air-launched cruise missiles equalizes its status with the US. Moreover, he threatened that if Washington repudiates the Intermediate-Range Nuclear Forces (INF) Treaty, Russia will respond "immediately and symmetrically," i.e., start building its own intermediate-range (500–5,500 km) forces.[26]

Putin has repeatedly insisted that Russia focus on new and novel types of weapons.[27] Moreover, from Putin on down, Russian writers almost unanimously see the US threatening both Russia and, more broadly, the concept of strategic stability. Russia chides the US for simultaneously building BMD systems in Europe and Asia as well as for developing the capabilities to launch a Conventional Prompt Global Strike (CPGS) using high-precision conventional weapons, mainly delivered by air. Therefore, the aerospace attack is threat number one. These new Russian weapons under construction comprise nuclear, space, hypersonic weapons, and drones (unmanned aerial vehicles—UAV) many of which are intended to rebuff just such an attack, e.g. by using UAVs to counter UAVs.[28]

Putin's emphasis on creating new generations of weapons includes ones based on so-called new physical principles (beam, geophysical, genetic, psychophysical and other technology). He also singled out cyber, information and communications technology, noting that, as high-precision weapons proliferate and become common, they will become the main means for achieving a decisive victory over an opponent, including in global conflicts.[29] Evidently these are the categories of weapons that comprise the asymmetric strategy. Under the circumstances, the Armed Forces must follow a deterrence strategy and prepare for a quick and effective response to challenges, i.e. be ready for anything on the spectrum of conflict. Even so, nuclear weapons and thus deterrence, mainly of the US/NATO but also of China, in both the strategic and regional deterrence contingencies will remain the priority until and unless Russia can field high-tech competitive weapons. Subsequent directives regarding procurement have followed along these lines.

Moscow's deployment of nuclear and conventional weapons indicates that it believes the former deter not only nuclear but also conventional attacks. This mode of strategizing and thinking directly rebuts the complacent and groundless notion that nuclear weapons only deter other nuclear weapons. For Moscow, both sets of weapons are intended to deter the US and/or NATO aerospace attacks (as Russia calls it), thereby allowing Russia to operate offensively within the umbrella of its potent integrated air defense system (IADS).

In other words, Russian defense policy emphasizes medium- to large-scale conventional and even nuclear warfighting at the expense of insurgency, counter-insurgency, stability operations, and the like, even though those smaller-scale wars are the most likely threat its troops will face either in the North Caucasus, as is now the case, or potentially in Central Asia, once NATO leaves Afghanistan. Consequently, nuclear weapons are at the core of this so-called asymmetry in order to forestall the application of NATO's conventional superiority. In May 2016, complaining about US placement of missile defenses in Romania, Putin told the leadership of the Defense Ministry,

> As we have discussed already, we are not going to be drawn into this race. We will go our own way. We will work very carefully, without exceeding the planned spending on the rearmament of the army and navy, plans we have had for years, but we will adjust them in order to curb the threat to Russia's security.[30]

Thus, the impetus toward asymmetry vis-à-vis the West is a principled long-term Russian military strategy that is clearly oriented toward waging high-tech conventional war with substantial and potentially usable nuclear weapons on standby and always on display. Even in Moscow's wars of a new type, where information warfare (IW), cyber-strikes, media penetration, subversion, and so on play large roles, nuclear weapons, too, play a major role. They are integral to this "asymmetric" strategy and, in Russian thinking, this strategy could not succeed without those weapons.

For example, in both the Black and Baltic Sea theaters, NATO and US officials admit that Russia has created a combined-arms formation or network of land, sea, air and electronic weapons that can bar NATO entry to those "inland" seas.[31] Professionals call this an A2/AD strategy to bar NATO's access to those seas and to Russian territory— if not also the so-called near abroad. And in both cases, Russia's A2/AD posture is backed up by what appear to be credible threats of first-strike nuclear weapons use in defense of Russia.[32] In fact, Russia has openly deployed nuclear-capable weapons to both theaters and constantly talked of deploying the dual-use Iskander missile in Kaliningrad before deploying these nuclear-capable weapons there in 2016.[33]

Nuclear weapons must deter both nuclear and conventional scenarios, while also providing cover for what Moscow hopes will be limited conventional wars; moreover, the nuclear arsenal must be capable of intimidating all rivals and enemies. As a result, nuclear weapons are strategic procurement priorities for Moscow.[34] But when scholars look at published Russian literature discussing issues related to nuclear use it becomes clear that,

> The Russian General Staff officers working on nuclear deterrence theory attested that, despite their work, in 2010 there existed neither a mechanism nor an organ that connected all deterrence efforts in military and non-military fields. Lack of a main organ responsible for organization, planning, coordination, command, and control of deterrence policy is probably the best demonstration of the conceptual deficit around NSNW [non-strategic nuclear weapons]. Weapons procurement planners argued that deterrence based on TNW [tactical nuclear weapons] is a question not elaborate enough. There is no conceptual base

that enables Russia to establish the structure and quantity of this arsenal and thus procurement policy. Chaos is inevitable.[35]

Yet, large-scale procurement—despite the absence of a clear, coherent, and agreed-upon doctrine of nuclear use—is so robust in Russia that, under present conditions, it will surpass the presently agreed numerical thresholds of the New START treaty by mid-2018.[36] As nuclear weapons expert at the Carnegie Endowment Alexei Arbatov has observed,

> Firstly, developments in the sphere of offensive Strategic Nuclear Forces (SNF) are proceeding at full speed, [procurement plan] SAP-2020 stipulates the development by 2020 of 400 new intercontinental ballistic missiles, 8 nuclear-powered ballistic missile submarines, the creation of a new generation of heavy bombers (PAK-DA) with air launched long-range dual mission cruise missile X-101/102, and prior to that—relaunching the manufacture of the modernized Tu-160 bombers. These systems are intended to replace outdated equipment being withdrawn from operational use, i.e. they are aimed at renewing Russian strategic forces under the New START Treaty of 2010.[37]

Not unlike the US, we find a situation where Russian capabilities outpace doctrine; yet, the strategy is to use these weapons quite ostentatiously, as both political and warfighting weapons. Indeed, many Russian analysts now argue that the present-day defense sector, much like during the Soviet period, is virtually autonomous.[38] That means this sector is essentially producing, at least with regard to nuclear weapons, systems for which no real mission is indicated. Rather they are only producing what they can actually manufacture. Producers subsequently rationalize the mission, often couched in offensive and very threatening terms, to suit what is already produced instead of matching production to strategy.[39] If their analysis is correct, then in many respects the Russian defense industry, much like its Soviet predecessor, can supply many reasonably high-tech weapons, including nuclear ones, to the Ministry of Defense and the military. But also like its predecessor, Russia's present-day defense industry is regressing by imposing unfocused capabilities upon the state. And it is risking nuclear war because there actually may not be a truly coherent strategy for nuclear use in practice, rhetoric aside, at a time when Moscow is increasingly at odds with the entire West.[40]

Since Putin cannot and will not offer Russians "bread", i.e. economic reform, he must instead provide imperial circuses to solidify his domestic standing. And since the "war party" is ascendant in Russia, it too must orient policy toward repeated probes, if not confrontations, with the West.[41] Finally, as the chairman of the Center for Liberal Strategies, Ivan Krastev, has observed in fall 2017,

> In my recent discussions with Russian foreign policy experts, they have made clear that if Moscow wants to be a world power, on an equal footing with Washington, it should be able and willing to match the United States. Russian leaders believe that Washington interferes in their domestic politics and that the United States intends to orchestrate a regime change in Moscow. So if they take that as a given, the Kremlin should be able to similarly meddle and to show the world that it has the capabilities and will to do so. Reciprocal action is, after all, how you gain the respect of your enemies and the loyalty of your allies. The common sense in Moscow foreign policy circles today is that Russia can regain its great power status only by confronting the United States, not by cooperating with it.[42]

And beyond these factors, the geopolitical presence of China also drives Russia to confront the US. As Krastev also observes,

And contrary to conventional wisdom, Russia's craving for global power status is not simply about nostalgia or psychological trauma. It is a geopolitical imperative. Only by proving its capacity to be a 21st century great power can Russia hope to be a real, equal partner with countries like China, which it needs to take it seriously. Believe it or not, from the Russian perspective, interfering in the American presidential election was a performance organized mostly for the benefit of non-American publics.[43]

Therefore, we should expect more probes, including nuclear ones or conventional threats backed up by nuclear saber-rattling. For example, Russia may already be violating the New START treaty with its existing or impending capabilities. According to the state-run *Sputnik News*, under New START, Russia will have 2,100 actual deployed nuclear missiles. On the other hand, the Federation of American Scientists estimates that Russia will have 2,500 actual deployed strategic nuclear warheads by 2025. Those estimates preceded Russia's announcement of a program to build 50 new Tu-160 bombers. That program will push the number over 300 actually deployed nuclear warheads by 2030.[44] But it already appears that, by 2014, Russia had violated that treaty's numerical limits. According to Colonel General Sergei Karakayev, the commander of the Strategic Missile Forces, speaking in December 2014,

> Around 400 strategic missiles with warheads assigned for them are currently on combat duty. The problem is that under New START it is impossible to have more than around 300 deployed ICBMs consistent with the Russian declared number of deployed delivery vehicles.[45]

And the buildup continues. As Mark Schneider of the National Institute for Public Policy has observed, the announced Russian strategic nuclear modernization program includes:[46]

- A new road-mobile and silo-based Topol-M Variant 2 (SS-27 Mod 1) ICBM.
- A new SS-27 Mod 2 derivative with a Multiple Independently-targetable Re-entry Vehicle (MIRV) payload that the Russians call the RS-24/Yars.
- Improved versions of the Soviet legacy SS-N-23 submarine-launched ballistic missile (SLBM) called the Sineva and the Liner with many more warheads.
- A new MIRVed (six warheads) Bulava-30 SLBM being deployed on two types of new Borei-class submarines.
- A program to modernize the SS-19 with a hypersonic vehicle.
- A new stealthy long-range strategic nuclear cruise missile designated the KH-102.
- In December 2015, President Putin revealed that the long-range KH-101, which was supposed to be a conventional air-launched cruise missiles (ALCM), was nuclear capable.
- Modernization of Blackjack (Tu-160) and Bear (Tu-95) heavy bombers.
- In 2015, Russia announced that it would build at least 50 more of an improved version of the Tu-160.
- Development and deployment of the new Sarmat heavy ICBM with a mammoth ten tons of throw weight (which will reportedly carry 10 heavy or 15 medium nuclear warheads) in 2018–2020.
- Development and deployment of a new rail-mobile ICBM in 2018–2020. (This is the Barguzin project that was canceled in late 2017.)
- Development and deployment of a new "ICBM" called the RS-26 Rubezh, in reality, an intermediate-range missile, by 2016 or 2017. It is not yet clear if this weapon is operational, suggesting that the initial deadlines have not been met, and it is presumably still under development
- Development of a "fifth-generation" missile submarine carrying ballistic and cruise missiles.

- Development of a new stealthy heavy bomber that will carry cruise missiles and reportedly hypersonic missiles.
- Development of the "Maritime Multifunctional System Status-6," a nuclear-armed, nuclear-powered, 10,000 km range, very fast, drone submarine capable of operating at a depth of 1,000 meters, which the Russian press says, carries a 100-megaton bomb and possibly a cobalt bomb.[47]

Theater nuclear weapons are also undergoing comparable modernization and we have seen that they violate the INF Treaty. Late in 2017, a detailed revelation of recent Russian accomplishments in the fields of missile and aerospace attack and defense by the chief of Russia's General Staff, General Valery Gerasimov, openly admitted that Moscow has violated and is violating the INF Treaty and has developed multiple strike capabilities for ranges up to 4,000 km.[48] On November 29, 2017, Christopher Ford, of the National Security Council, publicly identified the weapon that violates the treaty as the Novator 9M729. And more than one Russian system may in fact be in violation of the INF. Specifically, Russia is developing a ground-launched cruise missile (GLCM) with a range capability of 500–5,000 km, thus able to target all of Europe. Nor do the violations end here. According to Schneider,

> Another possible violation or circumvention of the INF Treaty is the RS-26 "ICBM." At a minimum, the Russian RS-26 circumvents a basic prohibition in the INF Treaty and it may violate the INF Treaty or New START. Dr. Keith Payne and I have laid out the case in a *National Review Online* article that the RS-26 is a legal violation of the INF Treaty as it was interpreted to the Senate in 1988.[49]

Schneider has also written that,

The Russian R-500 cruise missile, now deployed, is also a likely violation of the INF Treaty. In 2013, Pavel Felgenhauer, a leading Russian defense columnist [and a] very well noted Russian journalist, said that there are two different versions of the R-500 cruise missile, one with a range of 1,000 km and the other with a range of 2,000–3,000 km. There are many similar Russian press reports concerning the range of the R-500.[50]

Beyond these troubling developments, the reported Iskander-M tactical missile (range: 600–1,000 km) is probably an INF Treaty circumvention, and the reported retention of the Soviet-era Skorost' IRBM is an apparent INF violation since in should have been declared and eliminated under the INF Treaty.[51] And the defense correspondent Felgenhauer even wrote back in 2010 that Moscow was planning to quit the INF Treaty covertly because its S-300, S-400 and forthcoming S-500 air-defense missiles, as well as the Moscow anti-ballistic missile (ABM) interceptors are nuclear armed and can function as "dual-use [...] conventional or nuclear medium or shorter range ballistic missiles."[52] If he is correct, in some cases these systems would then constitute violations of the INF Treaty.[53]

Meanwhile modernization and testing of low-yield weapons and the ongoing modernization of TNWs continue as well. Consequently, we see a comprehensive modernization of nuclear weapons across the board. According to President Putin, Russia is creating new-generation nuclear weapons that have hitherto not existed as well new kinds of delivery systems. For example, Russia is developing the drone intercontinental-range torpedo (Status-6), recently reported in the press, with a multi-megaton warhead for destroying naval bases and ports. It is also developing precision, low-yield, "clean" nuclear weapons. Russia has also stated that it could use EMP weapons without precipitating nuclear war—"discrete" EMP weapons may only cover an area of several dozen kilometers. Russia also has neutron weapons, which are significantly more effective than their US counterparts. Clearly, Russia is developing a spectrum of nuclear weapons with tailored effects and the means to deliver them in order to maintain escalation dominance all along the conflict spectrum. That spectrum runs the gamut—from "de-escalating" conflicts to conducting theater/strategic warfare for vital national objectives to major nuclear warfare up to the most destructive levels where the survival of the state is at risk.[54]

If we calculate all the programs for both new and incoming weapons as well as life extension of exiting platforms we could see, by 2022, a minimum of 2,976 warheads, and a maximum of 6,670 warheads, plus another 800+ bomber warheads. These capabilities could allow Russia a range of nuclear options from major nuclear war, where state survival is at risk, down to limited nuclear war being conducted to achieve vital national interests. For limited nuclear warfare scenarios, the forces needed for attacks on adversary military forces/bases, fleets and critical infrastructure to achieve conflict objectives could consist of:

- Accurate, low yield, "clean" weapons: Kill targets.
- Neutron Weapons: Kill military personnel/leadership.
- EMP Weapons (Discrete & wide area): Kill electrons.
- X-Ray Weapons: Kill satellites and reentry vehicles (RV). Nuclear weapons may play a major role in future space warfare scenarios.
- Gamma rays and other tailored effects: To be determined.[55]

Thus, Moscow appears to be reaching for a global strike capability comprising both nuclear and conventional weapons that could hold US, European and, if necessary, Chinese targets at risk. These developments portend serious threats. Russia is already violating the INF and Conventional Forces in Europe (CFE—which Moscow unilaterally "suspended" its implementation of in 2007) treaties. And before the end of 2019, it could be in violation of the New START or

Prague Treaty. Moreover, Moscow has broken a host of treaties with respect to Ukraine and Georgia. Second, it clearly has a first-strike capability that can hit targets throughout Europe while supposedly holding the US at bay. Lastly, it also is a state that refuses to accept any of the post–Cold War agreements of 1989–1991 concerning the territorial integrity or sovereignty of the states that either became independent then or regained their full actual sovereignty by leaving the Soviet bloc. Inasmuch as Moscow has repeatedly displayed its commitment to force and subversion and behaves like an outlaw state, it should be clear that the general threats both to international order and to regional security in Europe and the former USSR are enormous. Thus, the threat to vital US interests, apart from the threat to strike at the US with nuclear weapons, or as we are now seeing, through cyber strikes, and/or a potential combination of kinetic and non-kinetic means, is no less serious. However, new weapons developments do not end here.

Biological, Chemical and 'New Physical Principles' Weapons

Based on Russian combat activities in Chechnya and in Syria, there is reason to believe that Russia might not hesitate to use chemical weapons, including thermobaric weapons, against less well-armed opponents. In Syria there are reports of Russian use; and we know that in Chechnya Moscow employed thermobaric weapons.[56] Indeed, Igor Sutyagin of RUSI reports that flamethrower elements are being introduced into the structures of every Russian combined-arms formation as well as into chemical, biological, radiological and nuclear defense brigades.[57] The presence of such brigades itself testifies to Russia's expectation that nuclear, biological, chemical and/or radiological weapons may be used in future wars involving its forces. Earlier writings and statements by Russian commanders have explicitly referred to nuclear war-fighting's impact on tactical units and operations, so this is by no means a fanciful interpretation. In an otherwise unremarkable 2008 interview, General Vladimir Boldyrev, then commander-in-chief of Russia's Ground Troops, described the missions of Russia's tank troops as follows,

> Tank troops are employed primarily on main axes to deliver powerful splitting attacks against the enemy to a great depth. Having great resistance to damage-producing elements of weapons of mass destruction, high firepower, and high mobility and maneuverability, they are capable of exploiting the results of nuclear and fire strikes to the fullest and achieving assigned objectives of a battle or operation in a short time.[58]

Boldyrev's remarks, like those on armored vehicles, show that he, and presumably his colleagues, fully expected that Russia if not both sides will use nuclear weapons as strike weapons in combat operations.[59]

Such activities should additionally raise questions about Russia's adherence to the 1925 Chemical Weapons Convention, even though it is a signatory of that agreement. The use of chemical or possibly biological weapons (BW)—including new BW and chemical weapons, e.g., chemical warfare robots yet to be deployed or even invented— would not be a stretch. Indeed, the latter project is already underway.[60] Certainly we have seen repeated efforts by Moscow to defend Syria's use of chemical weapons in its civil war and block UN investigations into that use.[61]

First, we do not know whether or not Russia is continuing research and/or development of new biological techniques based on genetic manipulation that would create novel weaponized strains of bacteria and viruses developed after the 1992 closure of the Soviet BW program. Such weapons could interfere with immunological processes or genes that control behavior; in fact, this kind of research was at an advanced stage in 1991.[62] Second, as noted above, Putin has called for new-generations of weapons based on "new physical principles" that include, beam, geophysical, genetic, psychophysical and other technology.[63] Third, once Putin was reelected as president in 2012, the Ministry of Defense pledged to begin working on the creation of weapons based on these new physical principles; and certainly genetic weapons, as listed on the ministry's website, fall into those categories of weapons. Fourth, tripartite negotiations on BW among the UK, US and Russia, have long since broken down.[64] Consequently there is great concern that new labs and institutes or for-profit corporations might base their work on the Soviet research program and move forward with R&D on so-called "third generation" BW programs.[65] Given the range of our ignorance as to developments inside Russia—which is deliberately fostered by Russian opacity and refusal to be transparent or collaborative on these issues—it is not surprising that some experts "presume" that there is an ongoing BW R&D program currently operating in Russia.[66]

Another example of weapons development based on new physical principles is Russia's campaign to build and deploy hypersonic and directed-energy weapons. Persisting and recent reports in the Russian press contend that Russia is developing pulse weapons that could trigger an attack on the US electromagnetic sphere by being detonated in the atmosphere. This would make it an electromagnetic pulse (EMP) threat.[67] Similarly, there are reports of future land- and sea-based directed energy weapons that could destroy or disable sophisticated electronic guidance and navigation systems in both manned and unmanned aircraft and precision-guided missiles, as well as suppress foreign military satellites and their communications systems (SATCOM).[68] The development of such a weapon is not surprising given Moscow's proficiency in waging electronic warfare (EW) and its fears about an aerospace attack and corresponding efforts to build an integrated air defense system against it. And these are only some of the futuristic projects upon which Moscow is embarked.

Indeed, the list presented above of current Russian nuclear programs includes some hypersonic weapons systems, e.g. a new stealthy heavy bomber that will carry cruise missiles and reportedly hypersonic missiles. But in addition, as noted above, the Project 4202 vehicle that is to be delivered by the SS-19 Stiletto missile is also intended to be hypersonic.[69] And, as we have seen, the Sarmat or RS-28 is also going to carry hypersonic weapons.[70] These two programs suggest that both the SS-19 and RS-28 will be hypersonic nuclear weapons, aiming to evade US missile defenses and hold the United States and/or Europe at risk. Hypersonic vehicles, or alternatively boost-glide vehicles, travel at speeds between Mach 5 and Mach 10 (3,840–7,680 miles per hour). They use sophisticated technologies for maneuvering and boost in order to deliver warheads rapidly, evade defenses and target precisely. This allows for high rates of survivability against missile defense systems. Such qualities excite Russian designers and planners because Moscow fully believes that the US ballistic missile defense system now being built in Europe and Asia aims, despite all abundant evidence to the contrary, to neutralize Russia's nuclear strike capability against Europe and the US. Therefore the obsession—not too strong a word here—of Russian leaders is to build supposedly invulnerable nuclear weapons like hypersonic missiles that cannot be attacked by missile defenses.[71]

The development of such weapons strongly suggests that Moscow wants to hold the US itself at increased risk of nuclear strikes and sees military utility in nuclear weapons as warfighting instruments. The 2015 trials of the Project 4202 weapon comprised tests of what Russia calls the Yu-71 hypersonic attack aircraft, which can supposedly reach speeds of 7,000 miles per hour. In addition to being a warhead for the Sarmat, the Yu-71 can apparently also be adapted for Russia's advanced long-range strategic bomber.[72]

In 2016, Moscow reportedly tested another hypersonic attack aircraft, the Yu-74, evidently carried by the SS-19 Stiletto ballistic missile system. The new state-of-the-art Sarmat ICBM can apparently carry up to 24 nuclear-loaded Yu-74 gliders and can hit any target within a 6,200-mile radius in an hour.[73] Each Yu-74 glider can be equipped with a nuclear warhead and/or electronic warfare (EW) package or false target simulators to ensure penetration of any missile defense system and thus significantly raise the efficiency of Russia's Strategic Missile Forces.[74]

The search for missile penetration systems to break through any missile defense by means of the use of new kinds of weapons with hyper-modern technologies for maneuverability also helps explain the modernization of old systems like the SS-19 Stiletto to serve as launchers for these warheads. Although Russia's labels for the hypersonic vehicles are confusing, they suggest that these weapons are also being built along the lines of the modularity principle, with missiles that can be fitted onto one or more systems like the Sarmat and the Stiletto. Thus, the Yu-71 and Yu-74 hypersonic vehicles apparently conform to this modularity principle.

In deploying weapons with missile-defense-penetration capabilities, Russia is clearly not just relying on speed or MIRV-ing its systems; it is also building medium- or heavy-class weapons because the New START treaty does not impose any penalties or prohibitions for doing so, unlike START-1.[75] These plans for countering the US Ballistic Missile Defense program go back at least to 2004, when the latter was just being announced, and are clearly part of the asymmetric procurement strategy devised already at that time by Putin. As Alexander Savelyev, of the Russian Academy of Sciences, wrote in 2008,

> Russia declared that it would undertake effective "asymmetric" counter-measures in order to reduce this threat [of missile defenses] and to make the strategic situation more stable. One of these measures is to target the elements of the ABM system in

Europe with Russian strategic missiles. Alongside with this, some experts and even military officials, including the chief of the General Staff of the Russian Armed Forces, General Yuri Baluevsky, made rather straightforward statements about the possibility that Russia would withdraw from the INF treaty as a reaction and counter-measure to the deployment of an American ABM system in Europe.[76]

Meanwhile, the project to create hypersonic ALCMs that are quite similar to the Yu-74 is also allegedly entering its final phase.[77] Lastly, according to Savelyev,

> Ostkraft analysts emphasize that the Yu-74 gliders would not only evade NATO's missile defense systems but will also be capable of penetrating through the Terminal High Altitude Area Defense (THAAD) shield. The analysts argue that while the THAAD system is effective in intercepting outdated R-17 Elbrus tactical ballistic missiles, it is potentially vulnerable to the threat posed by advanced missile systems. [78]

Of course, if that is really the truth and Moscow can breach THAAD, then it remains a mystery why Moscow, if not Beijing, are so upset that South Korea, which clearly faces a serious missile and nuclear threat from North Korea, opted to join the US THAAD network.[79] Similarly, and in keeping with the idea that nuclear and futuristic weapons are valued as much for their power to intimidate as for their actual capabilities, it is not unusual to encounter statements of this kind in the Russian media even as Moscow endlessly fulminates that it is under threat from the US and its allies. Indeed, the following statement tangibly manifests the combination of overcompensation and groundless boasting to intimidate on the one hand, with ingrained paranoia of the Russian leadership on the other:

The Russian military are about to test the first prototypes of the S-500 Prometey air and missile defense system also known as 55R6M Triumfator M—capable of destroying ICBMs, hypersonic cruise missiles, and planes at over Mach 5 speeds; and capable of detecting and simultaneously attacking up to ten ballistic missile warheads at a range of 1,300 km. This means the S-500 can smash ballistic missiles before their warheads re-enter the atmosphere.

So [...] the S-500 would totally eliminate all NATO air power over the Baltic States—while the advanced Kornet missile would destroy all NATO armored vehicles. And that's not even considering conventional weapon hell [Russian thermobaric weapons].

If push came to nuclear shove, the S-400 and especially the S-500 anti-missile missiles would block all incoming US ICBMs, cruise missiles, and stealth aircraft. Offensive drones would be blocked by drone defenses. The S-500 practically consigns into the dustbin stealth warplanes such as the F-22, F-35, and the B-2.

The bottom line is that Russia—in terms of hypersonic missile development—is about four generations ahead of the US, if we measure it by the development of the S-300, S-400, and S-500 systems. As a working hypothesis, we could describe the next system—already on the drawing boards as the S-600. It would take the US military at least ten years to develop and roll out a new weapons system, which in military terms represents a generation. Every Pentagon planner worth his pension plan should know that.

Russian—and Chinese—missiles are already able to knock out the satellite guidance systems for US nuclear-tipped ICBMs and cruise missiles. They could also knock out the early alert warnings that the satellite constellations would give. A Russian hypersonic ICBM flight time, launched, for instance, from a Russian nuclear sub all the way to the US East Coast, counts for less than 20 minutes. So an early warning system is absolutely critical. Don't count on the worthless THAAD and Patriot to do their job. Once again Russian hypersonic technology has already rendered the entire missile defense system in both the US and Europe totally obsolete.

So why is Moscow so worried by the Pentagon placing the Aegis system so close to Russia's borders? A credible answer is that Moscow is always concerned that the US industrial-military complex might develop some really effective anti-missile missiles even though they are now about four generations behind.[80]

This long citation graphically combines the mendacity common to Russian propaganda with the paranoia that pervades the government and IW activity. Moreover, it epitomizes the use of false information about the Russian military that is disseminated precisely to intimidate or impress foreign audiences. Neither should we discount this paranoia as merely cynical window dressing for it pervades the entire defense sector and has been doing so for years. Felgenhauer long ago wrote that,

Russia has a Prussian-style all-powerful General Staff that controls all the different armed services and is more or less independent of outside political constraints. Russian military intelligence—the GRU, as big in size as the former KGB and spread over all continents—is an integral part of the General Staff. Through the GRU, the General Staff controls the supply of vital information to all other decision-makers in all matters concerning defense procurement, threat assessment, and so on. High-ranking former GRU officers have told me that in Soviet times the General Staff used the GRU to grossly, deliberately, and constantly mislead the Kremlin about the magnitude and gravity of the military threat posed by the West in order to help inflate military expenditure. There are serious indications that at present the same foul practice is continuing.[81]

More recently, a US Air Force medical wing tender for a medical research project asking for samples from Caucasians outside Ukraine led Putin to claim that the United States is collecting genetic material from all over Russia for the purposes of launching a biowar against his country.[82] Thus, little has been done to alter "Russia's virtual reality."[83] As long as this situation goes uncorrected—and considering the overall nature of Russia's political system, the role of defense and the military in that system, the pressures articulated above by Ivan Krastev, as well as the danger of ongoing probes—the threat of military and even nuclear confrontation remain too high for comfort, not to say complacency.

Meanwhile, Moscow's investment in hypersonics occurs not just because the US and China are also doing so but because the capabilities that the US and presumably China are now developing frighten Russia to no end. Specifically, Moscow knows it has no real defense against the US Conventional Prompt Global Strike (CPGS) program, which will rely on long-range hypersonics. It also fears that the US BMD network being built in Europe and Asia, including THAAD, can neutralize its first-strike nuclear capability. If both these programs are used together, Moscow believes Washington could decapitate its command, control, communications and intelligence (C3I) assets by conventional means, while its BMD system would neutralize any retaliatory Russian nuclear strike.[84] Therefore, nuclear weapons carried by hypersonic vehicles are needed to deter this conventional capability. As Sergei Karaganov, one of Russia's leading foreign policy and defense intellectuals recently observed, "Nuclear weapons, on the one hand, stimulate an arms race, but on the other hand, they contain it. [...] The nuclear factor does not allow any country to gain a decisive advantage in conventional forces."[85]

Statements by senior officials abundantly display Russia's fears and apprehensions. Special envoy Grigory Beredennikov, in February 2015, denounced the US missile defense program for upending deterrence. Supposedly the BMD network gives Washington the illusion it could strike Russian nuclear systems or their C3I with conventional weapons and use missile defenses to neutralize a second strike, thereby overcoming the bilateral deterrence relationship. But he also went further, reiterating that, for Moscow, strategic stability depends on a host of non-nuclear factors. Specifically he stated,

> We are prepared for a dialogue about further nuclear disarmament steps. At the same time, we are convinced that they are impossible without solving such problems as the unlimited growth of global U.S. missile defenses, the project of using strategic weapons with conventional warheads within the concept of "global strike"—the refusal of the United States to pledge not to deploy weapons in space, [and] the growth of qualitative and quantitative conventional imbalances.[86]

Therefore, Moscow constantly attacks BMD in Europe, the CPGS and US hypersonic programs, all of which, individually, or in tandem, would explode strategic stability as Moscow defines it.[87]

These Russian concerns are a major reason why, beyond development of both nuclear and conventional hypersonic weapons, Russia is also developing "next-generation" air defenses against the expected US and/or NATO or Chinese hypersonics.[88] But even though Moscow is developing such defenses, it is clear that its main thrust is to develop offensive strike capabilities that can threaten not just Europe but the continental US. Furthermore, Russian long-term acquisition plans manifest a desire to use nuclear weapons as warfighting weapons, not just as deterrents against conventional or nuclear attack. And this procurement policy is outrunning doctrinal efforts to regulate procurements in service of a coherent strategy. It has its own logic, as we have shown above, namely: controlling escalation processes and dynamics through all phases of any crisis.

Nuclear Strategy

The high-tech and nuclear elements of strategy and procurement as well as these "non-military" instruments of Russian power that represent critical components of Moscow's gravitation toward creative asymmetrical strategies, have their roots in Soviet thinking and practice. Furthermore, these procurements and concepts stem from at least 1991–2000, when the Soviet and Russian military establishments were fiscally, morally, and intellectually bankrupt and discredited due to their opposition to reform and inability to perform effectively, e.g. in the first Chechen war (1994–1996). As a result, the Russian "establishment" increasingly saw the US and NATO as manifesting an ever greater and conventionally unstoppable threat to Russian interests and self-identity as an imperial great power through NATO enlargement, the 1999 war in Kosovo, and subsequent democracy promotion.

Deliberately reckless rhetoric, nuclear overflights and submarine probes all comprise this aspect of contemporary wars; and none of these phenomena would be unfamiliar to the fathers of deterrence theory, Thomas Schelling, Bernard Brodie, Henry Kissinger, Albert Wohlstetter, Herman Kahn, *et al.* But such Russian tactics highlight the fact that the psychology and character of the regime are essentially those of an intimidation culture. As Andrei Soldatov and Irina Borogan observe, "The Putin system is all about intimidation, more often than actual coercion, as an instrument of control."[89] Accordingly the emphasis on nuclear weapons not only relates to this system or culture of intimidation, it also fully comports with the long-standing element of Russian political culture that relies on the external projection of fear in order to augment the regime's domestic support.[90]

Today, as Putin deliberately generates a war psychosis at home and abroad, the prominent display of Russian nuclear capability aims to frighten and reassure Russian audiences while intimidating Western ones.[91] Many writers have argued that Russia emphasizes its nuclear arsenal because it is one of the few things that enables it to claim parity with the United States and retain its overall great power status. However, we also cannot lose sight of the overall importance in Russian political culture of displaying the state's capacity to intimidate others. Just as Russia needs desperately to see itself as a great power, it equally needs to be feared abroad. But since intimidation expresses, above all, a psychological relationship between the parties involved, it makes perfect sense that the prominent display of nuclear weapons carries with it a powerful informational-psychological charge that also fully comports with Russian strategic thinking.

Russian writers from about 2005 onward, increasingly delineated IW and the manipulation of targeted adversaries' psychological states as the most crucial element in modern war.[92] The intimidation effect carried by the prominent display of nuclear weapons aims to convince gullible foreign observers that defying Russia means war and potentially a nuclear exchange. Since that is unthinkable, we must yield, at least in part, to Russian demands. Consequently, efforts at intimidation continue: regular probes, for example in the Baltic region, serve many objectives, including keeping those states and NATO psychologically off balance. And those probes regularly include nuclear threats, as do the probes we have seen against the UK, Sweden, Denmark, etc.

In a March 2015 meeting in Germany, Russian generals told Western delegates that any NATO effort to retake Crimea and return it to Ukraine would lead them to consider "a spectrum of responses from nuclear to non-military."[93] Apart from the obvious physical threat and its intimidation "quotient," the information conveyed here clearly partakes of IW—understood in Russian terms as manipulating opponents' psychological reactions and hence their ensuing policies. Putin, too, has made numerous remarks threatening nuclear strikes and the regular dispatch of bomber and submarine probes to all members of NATO, clearly intending to intimidate and deter as that is the mission par excellence of bombers and submarines in peacetime.[94] But it is equally indisputable that, for Russian leaders and commanders, nuclear weapons are also to be used for war-fighting missions and operations. Indeed, as Sir Richard Shirreff, who was NATO's Deputy SACEUR from 2011 to 2014, has stated, "Russia hardwires nuclear thinking and capability to every aspect of their defense capability."[95]

Thus, since NATO's Kosovo operation in 1999, Russia has gradually developed both a capability and a strategy involving nuclear weapons that Western elites either cannot or will not understand. And it is much broader than the catch phrase "escalate to deescalate" implies.[96] That formulation, unfortunately, exemplifies the increasing US tendency (as US understanding of foreign governments and their strategies decline) to mirror image countries like Russia and depict their strategies and goals as if they were Americans. In fact the nuclear strategy is much broader than the strategy that is imagined here.

Russia's nuclear strategy, as it has hitherto evolved, must be viewed within the context of its thinking about and conduct of contemporary war. Thus, in Moscow's view, we now face the challenge of an innovative kind of asymmetric warfare comprising of many simultaneous and constant conflicts that need not have any discernible starting point or phases as in US literature. To use the US military terminology, the world is always in phase zero, and there is no discernible gap between war and peace. Or, as Vladimir Lenin might have said, and certainly believed, politics is the continuation of war by other means. Ceasefires, actual conventional warfare and incessant information warfare—defined as attempts to alter mass political consciousness in targeted countries—occur together or separately as needed and are in constant flux. Regular forces can be used conventionally or as proxies, irregular or even covert forces allegedly for "peacekeeping" or other operations. The actual use of military force depends on the effectiveness of non-military instruments of power, including organized crime, ethnic or other irregular paramilitary groups, espionage, political subversion and penetration of institutions in the targeted country, economic warfare, IW, and special operations forces. Outright victory need not be the intended or victorious outcome. It may be enough to secure constant leverage and influence on the military-strategic, political and social situation in a state of no war and no peace. Therefore, both prosecution of such a war and resistance to it demands "quick decision-making processes, effective inter-agency coordination, and well trained and rapidly deployable special forces."[97] Unfortunately those are all areas where NATO, not to mention Ukraine in 2014, have been particularly deficient.

Russia's fundamental strategic posture involves the military primarily in conventional operations; and yet, it is actually a whole-of-state national security strategy, entailing the mobilization of much if not all of the state. As such, we must envision issues of Russian nuclear use in an innovative context.[98] Specifically, the issues of nuclear use must be seen in the context of this kind of war, where Russia may be seeking a slice of territory and permanent leverage rather than the destruction of its enemy or outright victory.

In other words, the most likely use (at least intended use before a war) of Russian nuclear weapons has until recently been for what would be considered a limited or local or regional war (the latter being the Russian terminology). Indeed, Russian writings on nuclear strategies distinguish between strategic deterrence contingencies and more localized or regional deterrence scenarios. The first could involve a "superpower" exchange of nuclear strikes with Washington, with ICBMs and SLBMs figuring prominently. Whereas, in the second, nuclear weapons may well be used in a warfighting context to control escalation throughout the entire crisis period and be used if necessary to force NATO to negotiate.[99]

This strategy goes far beyond the misconceived US idea that the strategy is "escalate to deescalate." That concept only applies in the context of Russia losing a regional war. In fact these weapons are to be brandished from the outset to deter and dissuade its rival from reacting at all in the first place. Russia's nuclear weapons would be deployed to prevent any kind of NATO reaction to war or to deter China from attacking in the East (though China's threat is rarely commented upon publicly in Moscow). Official or quasi-official statements make this point openly. For example, Deputy Foreign Minister Sergei Ryabkov has written that,

> The Russian side notes that nuclear-weapon states regard nuclear deterrence as a principal condition for preserving strategic stability. It is acknowledged, in particular, by the existing US national security policy documents as well as by the practical steps our US partners are taking with a view to improving their nuclear missile system.[100] In order to ensure strategic stability and equitable multilateral international cooperation, Russia is making the necessary efforts to maintain parity with the United States in strategic offensive weapons in the context of deployment of a global missile defense system and implementation of the concept of a prompt global strike with the possible use of strategic non-nuclear delivery vehicles.[101]

Nuclear weapons' psychological or intimidation effect is prominently displayed at all times, and especially from the onset of any crisis that could lead to war in order to control escalation from the outset and paralyze potential resistance from any quarter. Actual use to compel negotiations and a de-escalation is only a small part of this much broader strategy of employing nuclear war contingencies and weapons as an instrument of psychological or information war.

At least some Russian and Western scholars have observed this comprehensive deterrence and war-fighting strategy involving nuclear weapons as both a deterrent and potential war-fighting instrument. At a special June 2012 NATO workshop on the future of the Alliance's deterrence posture, one British participant observed that Moscow relies on nuclear weapons for "setting up a force field of inhibition operating at an even more fundamental level than generalized deterrence."[102] Thus, as Heather Williams of Kings College, London has written, that Russian strategy, "relies on nuclear coercion to avoid escalation."[103]

For obvious reasons, Russia's nuclear strategy and the conditions under which nuclear use might be entertained have been kept consistently opaque. But, as analyzed below, there is good reason to believe that it still is a first-strike strategy despite whatever has been written in its recent doctrines—and in spite of the considerable improvement in the last five years of Russia's non-nuclear deterrence capabilities.[104] Furthermore, there are reasons to believe it might even evolve into or contain tendencies toward preemptive use against NATO or China.

Certainly, the current construction projects of both new nuclear weapons and extensions of existing ones make no sense if at least some of these weapons are not intended for actual use. However, we argue here instead that, given the framework we have laid out, Russian nuclear strategy is much broader and more pervasive. The strategy's intention is for Russia to control the entire ladder of escalation, i.e. to gain and retain escalation dominance through every stage of the crisis.[105]

As described by Nikolai Sokov of the Middlebury Institute of International Studies, Russian nuclear forces are supposed to be used in a limited war scenario for limited purposes, namely to force a de-escalation of the war in response to a large-scale conventional attack beyond the capabilities of Russia's forces. These strikes would inflict what Russia calls tailored or pre-assigned damage (*zadannyi ushcherb*) upon the enemy that is subjectively unacceptable to it and would lead to de-escalation and presumably a return to negotiations. Thus, the actual strikes are a means of intra-war escalation control. Moreover, it is assumed that there is an asymmetry of interests wherein the US and NATO would be fighting for principles like democracy promotion, the self-determination of a particular group or the like, whereas for Russia the issue is the territorial integrity of the regime and even more importantly the survival of the governing system and the state. Lastly, the strategy only works when strategic stability—i.e., the ability to inflict a retaliatory strike even to a conventional strike that takes out Russian nuclear weapons or their C3I—is maintained. Therefore, from Russia's point of view, the US cannot be allowed to move forward on its prompt global strike or missile defense programs.[106]

This strategy makes considerable sense for Russia from its perspective. As Williams points out,

> Russia has a sufficiently strong conventional force to make a land grab on its periphery before NATO will be able to respond. The land grab will build on earlier stages of escalation in generating public support and utilizing regional military assets. However, this conventional force does not have the longevity to withstand a decisive and drawn out NATO response, largely due to the transportation and infrastructure problems. Therefore Russia must seize territory quickly. Then, in order to deter NATO intervention and maintain any geographic gains, Russia turns to nuclear coercion.[107]

Similarly, Gustav Gressel of the European Council of Foreign Relations agrees that the dominant fact we must consider is that Russia could start a war against its neighbors or even NATO but not be able to sustain it. And this fact will be the prevailing paradigm for at least another decade because Putin's system cannot survive without placing Russia in a state of constant cold war vis-à-vis the West.[108] As he and others have observed, that situation is fraught with the kind of misperceptions and cognitive failures of the opposing side that could lead to a much bigger war, particularly given Moscow's emphasis on overwhelming force to achieve a quick and decisive victory.[109]

Further adding to the risks on the Russian side is the fact that, throughout Russian history, protracted war, often arising from such a misperception of a quick and decisive victory, invariably put the Russian state's or political system's survival at risk. Those conditions are explicitly identified in Russia's national security and defense doctrines as justifying nuclear use.[110] This is especially true when the successful conduct of such supposedly quick and decisive wars and conflicts is a (if not *the*) precondition of the system's survival. Therefore, the nuclear threat does not come into play after having achieved strategic success but throughout all phases of the conflict, including pre-military ones. This makes that attainment of decisive strategic success in the initial or early phase/s of the war by conventional and so-called "hybrid" (New Generation Warfare) means all the more demanding a requirement—which is therefore more susceptible to deterrence if Russia encounters a determined conventional resistance.

Moscow might well launch short-range, tactical or low-yield nuclear weapons (once they are proven to be usable) against NATO or US targets in the initial period of the war—i.e., preemptively to short-circuit a NATO defense. However, it probably knows a prolonged war works against it since, historically, protracted wars put the Russian state under enormous and sometimes excessive strain. So if the continuation of the regime is in danger, this meets the doctrinal language in Russia's 2014 and 2015 defense and national security doctrines to justify nuclear use.[111] We are not just dealing here with hypotheticals.

Some Russian generals and leaders have already called for placing language in the defense doctrine or in the classified nuclear annex that would spell out the conditions under which Russia might launch a preemptive nuclear strike.[112] Similarly, in 2009, Russian National Security Council Secretary Sergei Patrushev revealed that Russian nuclear doctrine provided for the first and even preemptive use of nuclear weapons in local and regional wars, something not evident on its face.[113] It also appears that Russia has simulated such operations—for example, in a 2013 aerial exercise that practiced a nuclear attack on neutral Sweden.[114] And there are calls in the military literature for launching preventive or preemptive nuclear strikes against NATO in the event of a war in Europe. In a limited war, these strikes might aim to deescalate the war; but they also could be used in a bigger conflict, apparently and presumably to escalate the war.[115] Nevertheless, recent official statements expressly say that Russia regards the kinds of weapons that could be used in a preemptive attack—like TNW or low-yield high-precision nuclear weapons—as destabilizing because they inherently lower the threshold for nuclear strikes. Commenting on the recent announcement that the US is developing the B61-12 TNW, Deputy Foreign Minister Sergei Ryabkov said that,

> As soon as these plans emerged, we said that this is about creating a device that, according to publicly available information, will be relatively higher precision but lower yield compared to the existing types of such weapons in the US arsenal. This means that the threshold for use of such ammunition could theoretically be lowered, which of course destabilizes the situation to a certain extent.[116]

Therefore it should come as no surprise that many Chinese observers of Russian nuclear doctrine and strategy observe that since 1993 Russia has changed its posture from no first use to first use, and now to preemption. As they note, Russia abandoned the no first use pledge in 1993; declared in 1997 and 2000 that nuclear weapons would deter conventional conflicts and invasion; ordered the expansion of TNW production in 1999; and in statements in 2006 and 2010, cited nuclear deterrence as a national security pillar.[117]

Under these conditions, the attainment of decisive strategic success in the initial or early phase(s) of the war is, for Russia, all the more demanding a requirement. And it demonstrates that Russian nuclear strategy, contrary to far too much Western misunderstanding, is not merely escalating to deescalate if the tide of conflict goes against Russia. Instead, the purpose of the strategy is to obtain escalation dominance as quickly as possible and hold it throughout the crisis in all of its stages in order to intimidate adversaries against resisting conventionally as well as by nuclear means. Therefore, Moscow hopes not only to deter conventional responses to its aggression but also impose escalation control throughout all of the crisis' phases. Although Moscow might preemptively use nuclear weapons to forestall a NATO buildup during wartime, Russian strategy makes the necessity for a pre-positioned robust conventional deterrent all the more critical for the North Atlantic Alliance because NATO would then gain escalation control at a much lower level of conflict and trump Russia's strategy before a shot is fired. Therefore, for NATO, the primary strategic objective must go beyond merely deterring an attack. Rather it must be to retain conventional and nuclear escalation dominance from the start so that Moscow will be deterred both at the conventional and nuclear levels.

Conclusions

Much more could and has been said about Russian nuclear strategy. And based on the evidence of Zapad 2017, Moscow may be reconsidering the possibility of having to fight a major theater conventional war as a possible contingency that could quickly escalate to the nuclear level.[118] But in reality, a nuclear exchange would only occur if Moscow triggers actual combat hostilities (not IW as is now the case). Russia's most recent doctrinal statements all evince a preference for non-nuclear deterrence because it knows all too well what nuclear war means.[119] Nevertheless, as we have seen, Russia's nuclear procurements point toward first use rather early on, suggesting that Dmitry Adamsky is correct in postulating a serious disconnect between writings on nuclear war and Moscow's actual strategy, much as occurred under the Soviet Union.[120] This is disquieting and obliges us to take both doctrine and procurement, not to mention exercises, with utmost seriousness.

Tragically, it appears that here, too, in this aspect of war, Moscow is replicating Soviet precedents. And since Lenin introduced a state of siege, first into Social Democracy and then into international politics that spanned the entire Cold War, the reversion to past precedents carries great dangers, not least to Russia. Karl Marx memorably wrote that when history repeats itself, the first time is tragedy and the second time is a farce. But there is nothing farcical about nuclear weapons. And since Ivanov and Putin's behavior cited above reminds us that Russia sees itself in a state of war with the West, it is essential that we understand what is transpiring in Russia: as we have suggested, Putin and his team may not fully grasp the consequences of their restorationist policy. And if this new cold war persists, it is quite unlikely that they, like their Soviet predecessors, will go quietly into the night when they lose again.

Notes

[1] "Putin's Revenge," *Frontline*, PBS, October 25 and November 1, 2017, http://www.pbs.org/wgbh/frontline/film/putins-revenge/.

[2] M.A. Gareyev, *Srazheniya na Voenno-Istoricheskom Fronte*, Moscow: ISAN Press, 2010, p. 729 cited in MG I.N. Vorob'ev (RET) and Col. V.A. Kisel'ev (Ret), "Strategies of Destruction and Attrition," Moscow, *Military Thought*, in English, NO. 1, 2014, January 1-2014-March 31, 2014, accessed, June 2, 2014.

[3] Trenin quoted in Ivo H. Daalder, "Responding to Russia's Resurgence Not Quiet on the Eastern Front," *Foreign Affairs*, October 16, 2017, https://www.foreignaffairs.com/articles/russia-fsu/2017-10-16/responding-russias-resurgence.

[4] Text of Russian Defense Doctrine, www.carnegieendowment.org/files/2010russia_militarydoctrine.pdf; "Military Doctrine of the Russian Federation," February 5, 2010, www.kremlin.ru, *Open Source Center, Foreign Broadcast Information Service, Central Eurasia,* (Henceforth *FBIS SOV),* February 9, 2010; Voyennaia Doktrina Rossiiskoi Federatsii, December 26, 2014, www.kremlin.ru; *Natsional'naya Strategiya Bezopasnosti Rossii, do 2020 Goda,* Moscow, Security Council of the Russian Federation, May 12, 2009, www.scrf.gov.ru, in English it is available from *FBIS SOV,* May 15, 2009, in a translation from the Security Council website (Henceforth NSS); *Natsional'naya Strategiya Bezopasnosti Rossii,* www.kremlin.ru, December 31, 2015.

[5] Kristin Ven Bruusgaard, "The Myth of Russia's Lowered Nuclear Threshold," *War On the Rocks,* https://warontherocks.com/2017/09/the-myth-of-russias-lowered-nuclear-threshold/, September 22, 2017.

[6] Bildt Plays Down Russian Nuclear Threat," *The Local,* August 18, 2008," http://www.thelocal.se/13780/20080818; Mark Franchetti, "Russia's New Nuclear Challenge to Europe," *The Times Online,* August 17, 2008, https://www.thetimes.co.uk/article/russias-new-nuclear-challenge-to-europe-5kngpw8vj6q.

[7] Ilya Kedrov, "An Expert Evaluation: A universal Armored Vehicle; The Infantry Needs a Fundamentally New Combat Vehicle and Not a Taxi to the Forward Edge of the Battle Area," Moscow, *Voyenno-Promyshlennyi Kuryer Online,* in Russian, May 26, 2010, *FBIS SOV,* June 4, 2010.

[8] *FBIS SOV*, October 19, 2008.

[9] "Russia RVSN Military Academy Discussing Strategic Deterrence," *ITAR-TASS*, September 22, 2008, Johnson's Russia List, No. 173, September 22, 2008, ww.worldsecurityinstitute.org.

[10] National Institute For Public Policy, *Foreign Nuclear Developments: a Gathering Storm*, Fairfax, VA, National Institute For Public Policy, 2015, pp. 2-9; Dmitry Adamsky, "*If War Comes Tomorrow: Russian Thinking about "Regional Nuclear Deterrence,"* Mark B. Schneider, "Russian Nuclear Weapons Policy and Programs, the European Security Crisis, and the Threat to NATO," James R. Howe, "Future Russian Strategic Nuclear and Non-Nuclear Forces: 2022," All Forthcoming in Stephen J. Blank, Ed., *The Russian Military In Contemporary Perspective*, Carlisle Barracks, PA: Strategic Studies Institute, US Army War College, 2018.

[11] "Corridors of Power; Head of Federation Council Defense Committee sees no threat in U.S. nuclear exercise, *Interfax-America*, October 30, 2017, as made available to the author by Mark Schneider.

[12] National Institute for Public Policy, *Foreign Nuclear Developments: a Gathering Storm*, Fairfax, VA, 2015, pp. 2–9.

[13] "Barguzin Rail-Mobile Project Is Cancelled (Again)," *Russian Strategic Nuclear Forces Blog*, December 4, 2017, http://russianforces.org/blog/2017/12/barguzin_rail-mobile_icbm_is_c.shtml.

[14] Dave Majumdar, "Russia's Just Tested Its New ICBM Armed With "Experimental Warheads", www.nationalinterest.org, September 23, 2017.

[15] Franz-Stefan Gady, "Russia To Test Deadliest Nuke Twice Before Year's End," www.thediplomat.com, October 25, 2017.

[16] *Ibid;* Jon Sharman, "Russia to Test New Generation Of Intercontinental Missile That Can' Beat US Defense Systems," www.independent.co.uk, October 24, 2017.

[17] "Vladimir Putin Took Part In Strategic Nuclear Forces' Training, http://en.kremlin.ru/events/president/news/55929, October 27, 2017; Franz-Stefan Gady, "Russia Test Fires 4 Intercontinental-Range Ballistic Missiles,' www.thediplomat.com, October 27, 2017.

[18] "Presentation Of Officers Appointed To Senior Command Posts," http://en.kremlin.ru/events/president/news/55923, October 27, 2017.

[19] *Ibidem.*

[20] Michael Kofman, "Zapad 2017: Beyond the Hype, Important Lessons for the US and NATO," https://www.europeanleadershipnetwork.org/commentary/zapad-2017-beyond-the-hype-important-lessons-for-the-us-and-nato/, October 27, 2017; https://www.diplomaatia.ee/en/article/zapad-2017-what-did-these-military-exercises-reveal/; Roger McDermott, "Zapad 2017 and the Initial Period Of War," *Eurasia Daily Monitor*, Volume 14, Issue 115, The Jamestown Foundation, September 20, 2017, https://jamestown.org/program/zapad-2017-and-the-initial-period-of-war/; Pavel K. Baev, "Militarization and Nuclearization,": The Key Features Of the Russian Arctic," https://www.realcleardefense.com/articles/2017/11/01/militarization_and_nucleariz ation_the_key_features_of_the_russian_arctic_112562.html, November 1, 2017; https://forwardobserver.com/2017/10/recent-russian-nuclear-forces-exercises-larger-than-first-believed/; Lukas Andriukaitis, #Military Matters: Russia's Big Guns On the Move: Analyzing Russia's Strategic Missile Forces In Novosibirsk Oblast," www.medium.com, October 24, 2017.

[21] Stephen Blank, What Do the Zapad-2013 Exercises Reveal?" Liudas Zdanavicius and Matthew Czekaj Eds., *Russia's 2013 Zapad Military Exercise: Lessons For Baltic Regional Security*, Washington, D.C.: The Jamestown Foundation, 2015, pp. 8–13.

[22] "Presidential Address To the Federal Assembly," December 4, 2014, http://en.kremlin.ru/events/president/news/47173.

[23] Quoted in Tor Bukkvoll, "Iron Cannot Fight-The Role of Technology in Current Russian Military Theory," *Journal of Strategic Studies*, XXXIV, NO. 5,2011, p. 690.

[24] *Ibid.* pp. 690–691.

[25] Denis Telmanov, "Polite But Formidable,' Vladimir Putin Has Declared That the Country Will Not Get Bogged Down In Costly Rivalry With the West," Moscow, *Gazeta.ru*, in Russian, December 4, 2014, *FBIS SOV*, December 4, 2014.

[26] Zasedanie Mezhdunarodnogo Diskussionnogo Kluyba "Valdai," October 19, 2017, http://kremlin.ru/events/president/transcripts/55882.

[27] "Putin: Russia Not Going To Join New Arms Race But Will Develop Modern Nuclear Arms," *Interfax*, July 26, 2012, available at http://search.proquest.com/professional/login; "Meeting of the Military-Industrial Commission, " www.en.kremlin.ru, June 28, 2016; "Meeting of Russian Federation

Ambassadors and Permanent Envoys," www.en.kremlin.ru, June 30, 2016; "Putin Says, Russia Will Build New Weapons but Avoid Arms Race." *Yahoo! News*, www.yahoo.com, January 20, 2015.

[28] "Russian Military to Get "Drone-Killer UAV," *Izvestia*, October 23, 2017, Retrieved From BBC Monitoring, October 27, 2017.

[29] "Putin Says, Russia Will Build New Weapons but Avoid Arms Race." *Yahoo! News*, www.yahoo.com, January 20, 2015.

[30] "Meeting on Defense Industry Development," May 13, 2016, http://en.kremlin.ru/events/president/news/51911.

[31] Andrew Fink, "Russia, Iran, and Inland Seas," *The American Interest*, April 15, 2016, http://www.the-american-interest.com/2016/04/15/russia-iran-and-inland-seas/.

[32] Captain Steven Horrell (USN), speech at the event, "The Changing Military Balance in the Black Sea," Atlantic Council of the US, Washington, D.C., June 15, 2016, http://www.atlanticcouncil.org/events/past-events/black-sea-energy-and-security-conference.

[33] Jens Stoltenberg, "Adapting to a Changed Security Environment," Speech, Center for Strategic and International Studies, Washington, DC, May 27, 2015, available at http://www.nato.int/cps/en/natohq/opinions_120166.htm (accessed October 14, 2015); "Russia To Respond to NATO Black Sea Force By Deploying New Weapons – Report," https://www.rt.com/politics/329414-russia-to-respond-to-nato/, January 19, 2016; "Russia Deploys Nuclear-Capable Missiles In Kaliningrad," http://www.bbc.com/news/world-europe-37597075, October 9, 2016.

[34] Kristen Ven Bruusgard, "Russian Strategic Deterrence, Lecture at Lawrence Livermore Nuclear Laboratory, February 10, 2016, www.youtube.com.

[35] Dmitry Adamsky, "If War Comes Tomorrow: Russian Thinking about "Regional Nuclear Deterrence," Forthcoming in Stephen J. Blank, Ed., *The Russian Military In Contemporary Perspective*, Carlisle Barracks, PA: Strategic Studies Institute, US Army War College, 2018.

[36] Mark B. Schneider, "Russian Nuclear Weapons Policy and Programs, the European Security Crisis, and the Threat to NATO," James R. Howe, "Future Russian Strategic Nuclear and Non-Nuclear Forces: 2022," All Forthcoming in

Stephen J. Blank, Ed., *The Russian Military In Contemporary Perspective*, Carlisle Barracks, PA: Strategic Studies Institute, US Army War College, 2018.

[37] "Russian Defense Analyst" Russia's Being Drawn Into a New Arms Race With the U.S. and NATO Countries," www.memri.org, Special Dispatch No. 6449, May 26, 2016.

[38] As stated in the remarks of Pavel Podvig and Nikolai Sokov a the Program, "Russian Nuclear Strategy," Center for Strategic and International Studies, Washington, DC, June 27, 2016, https://www.csis.org/events/russian-nuclear-strategy.

[39] *Ibid.*; and for the Soviet period, Peter Almquist, *Red Forge: Soviet Military Industry Since 1965*, New York: Columbia University Press, 1992.

[40] Adamsky, "If War Comes Tomorrow: Russian Thinking about "Regional Nuclear Deterrence."

[41] Pavel Felgenhauer, "'Party Of War' Triumphs In Moscow," *Eurasia Daily Monitor*, Volume 14, Issue 137, October 26, 2017, The Jamestown Foundation, https://jamestown.org/program/party-war-triumphs-moscow/.

[42] Ivan Krastev, "Robert Mueller Will Never Get to the Bottom of Russia's Meddling," *The New York Times*, November 1, 2017, https://www.nytimes.com/2017/11/01/opinion/mueller-election-meddling-russia.html.

[43] *Ibid.*

[44] Hans M. Kristensen and Robert S. Norris, "Russian Nuclear Forces, 2015," *Bulletin of the Atomic Scientists*, April 24, 2015, p. 85, available at http://bos.sagepub.com/content/71/3/84.full.pdf+html (accessed October 14, 2015).

[45] Schneider, Russian Nuclear Weapons Policy and Programs, the European Security Crisis, and the Threat to NATO," Howe, "Future Russian Strategic Nuclear and Non-Nuclear Forces: 2022, Forthcoming in Stephen J. Blank, Ed., *The Russian Military In Contemporary Perspective*, Carlisle Barracks, PA: Strategic Studies Institute, US Army War College, 2018.

[46] U.S. Department of Energy and U.S. Department of Defense, *National Security and Nuclear Weapons in the 21st Century*, September 2008, p. 8, available at http://www.aps.org/policy/reports/popareports/upload/nuclear-weapons.pdf

(accessed October 14, 2015). "Military Dominance Over Russia Impossible, Nuclear Deterrent Top Priority – Defense Ministry," *RT*, January 30, 2015, available at http://rt.com/news/227811-russia-military-supremacy-modernization (accessed October 14, 2015); "New Heavy ICBM To Be Put Into Service in 2018—Karakayev," *Sputnik News*, May 5, 2011, available at http://sputniknews.com/voiceofrussia/2012_12_14/Russia-to-build-new-heavy-ICBM-by-2018-Karakayev/ (accessed October 14, 2015); and Steve Gutterman, "Russia Plans New ICBM to Replace Cold War 'Satan' Missile," *Reuters*, December 17, 2013, available at http://www.reuters.com/article/2013/12/17/us-russia-missiles-idUSBRE9BG0SH20131217 (accessed October 14, 2015); "Russia to Revive Nuclear Missile Trains—RVSN Commander," *Interfax*, December 16, 2014, available at http://search.proquest.com/Professional/login (accessed October 14, 2015); "Deployment of First Regiment With New Strategic Missile Complex Will Begin in 2014 -- General Staff," *Interfax-AVN*, June 7, 2013 (transcribed by World News Connection); Mark B. Schneider, "Russia's Noncompliance with Arms Control Obligations," Gatestone Institute, July 31, 2013, available at http://www.gatestoneinstitute.org/3906/russia-arms-control (accessed October 14, 2015); National Air and Space Intelligence Center, *Ballistic and Cruise Missile Threat*, 2013, available at http://www.afisr.af.mil/shared/media/ (accessed October 14, 2015); Vitaly Ankov, "Russian 5G Subs to Be Equipped with Ballistic, Cruise missiles—Source," *RIA Novosti*, March 19, 2011, available at http://en.ria.ru/militar_news/20110319/1630910 53.htm (accessed October 14, 2015); "Russia Goes Ahead with 5G Submarine Project," *RIA Novosti*, March 8, 2013, available at http://en.rian.ru/military_news/20130318/180092698/Russia-Goes-Ahead-with-5G-Submarine-Project.html (accessed October 14, 2015); "Russia Speeds Up Development of New Strategic Bomber," *RIA Novosti*, November 28, 2013, available at http://en.ria.ru/military_news/20131128/185110769/Russia-Speeds-Up-Development-of-New-Strategic-Bomber.html (accessed October 14, 2015).; "Russia's New Bomber to Carry Hypersonic Weapons – Source," *Sputnik News*, August 30, 2013, available at http://sputniknews.com/military/20130830/183062128/Russias-New-Bomber-to-Carry-Hypersonic-Weapons--Source.html (accessed October 14, 2015); "Meeting with Members of Political Parties Represented in the State Duma," The Kremlin, August 14, 2014, available at http://eng.kremlin.ru/transcripts/22820 (accessed October 14, 2015);"Russia to Produce Successor of Tu-160 Strategic Bomber After 2023," *Sputnik News*, June 4, 2015, available at http://sputniknews.com/military/20150604/1022954769.html; "The Kremlin, Meeting with Members of Political Parties Represented in the State Duma," August 14, 2014, available at http://eng.kremlin.ru/transcripts/22820 (accessed October 14, 2015); "Russia to Produce Successor of Tu-160 Strategic Bomber After 2023," *Sputnik News*, June 4, 2015, available at http://sputniknews.com/military/20150604/1022954769.html (accessed October 14,

2015); "Russia Developing Two Types of Advanced Liquid-Fuel ICBMs," *Interfax*, August 25, 2012, available at http://search.proquest.com/professional/login (accessed October 14, 2015); Lynn Berry and Vladimir Isachenkov, "Kremlin-Controlled TV Airs 'Secret' Plans For Nuclear Weapon," *Associated Press*, November 12, 2015, available at https://www.military.com/daily-news/2015/11/12/kremlin-controlled-tv-airs-ecret-plans-nuclear-weapon.html; "Text Of Russian TV Reports Featuring Classified Weapon System Status-6," *BBC Monitoring Former Soviet Union*, November 2015, available at http://search.proquest.com/Professional/login; Bill Gertz, "CIA: Leak of Nuclear-Armed Drone Sub Was Intentional," *The Washington Free Beacon*, November 19, 2015, available at http://freebeacon.com/national-security/cia-leak-of-nuclear-armed-drone-sub-was-intentional/.

[47] Schneider, "Russian Nuclear Weapons Policy and Programs, the European Security Crisis, and the Threat to NATO," Forthcoming in Stephen J. Blank, Ed., *The Russian Military In Contemporary Perspective*, Carlisle Barracks, PA: Strategic Studies Institute, US Army War College, 2018.

[48] Pavel Lisitcin, "Army; Russia sets Up Delivery Vehicles."

[49] *Ibid.*

[50] *Ibid.*

[51] *Ibid.*

[52] Pavel Felgenhauer, "Russia Seeks to Impose New ABM Treaty On the US by Developing BMD," *Eurasia Daily Monitor* Volume 7, Issue 136, July 16, 2010, The Jamestown Foundation, https://jamestown.org/program/russia-seeks-to-impose-new-abm-treaty-on-the-us-by-developing-bmd/.

[53] Schneider, "Russian Nuclear Weapons Policy and Programs, the European Security Crisis, and the Threat to NATO," Forthcoming in Stephen J. Blank, Ed., *The Russian Military In Contemporary Perspective*, Carlisle Barracks, PA: Strategic Studies Institute, US Army War College, 2018.

[54] Howe, "Future Russian Strategic Nuclear and Non-Nuclear Forces: 2022, Forthcoming in Stephen J. Blank, Ed., *The Russian Military In Contemporary Perspective*, Carlisle Barracks, PA: Strategic Studies Institute, US Army War College, 2018.

[55] *Ibid.*

[56] Lester Grau and Timothy Smith, "A 'Crushing' Victory: Fuel-Air Explosives and Grozny 2000, http://fmso.leavenworth.army.mil/documents/fuelair/fuelair.htm, 2001; Angela Dewan, "Reports of Chemical Gas Attacks in 2 Syrian cities," http://edition.cnn.com/2016/08/02/middleeast/syria-aleppo/index.html, August 2, 2016.

[57] Igor Sutyagin, "Russia Confronts NATO" Confidence-Destruction Measures," RUSI, Royal United Services Institute, Briefing Paper, 2016, p. 7.

[58] Artem Troitsky, "Interview With CINC Ground Troops General of the Army Vladimir Anatolyevich Boldyrev," Moscow, *Voyenno-Promyshlennyi Kuryer*, in Russian, October 1, 2008, *FBIS SOV*, October 19, 2008.

[59] Kedrov, *FBIS SOV*, June 4, 2010.

[60] "Russia Developing Chemical Warfare Robots," *The Moscow Times*, August 4, 2014, https://themoscowtimes.com/news/russia-developing-robots-for-military-use-54858.

[61] Karen De Young, "Russia, China veto At U.N. On Syria Chemical Weapons Is 'Outrageous,' U.S. Says," https://www.washingtonpost.com/world/national-security/russia-china-veto-at-un-on-syria-chemical-weapons-is-outrageous-us-says/2017/02/28/c69adcf4-fdeb-11e6-99b4-9e613afeb09f_story.html, February 28, 2017.

[62] Zilinskas, p. 44.

[63] Vladimir Putin, "Being Strong: We Should Not Tempt Anyone By Allowing Ourselves to Be Weak," Government of the Russian Federation, February 20, 2012, http://archive.premier.gov.ru/eng/events/news/18185/.

[64] Milton Leitenberg, "The Biological Weapons Program of the Soviet Union," Statement to the House Committee on Foreign Affairs, May 7, 2014; Zilinskas, p. 45.

[65] *Ibid.*, pp. 46-49; Leitenberg, "The Biological Weapons Program of the Soviet Union."

[66] "Expert Tells Congress He 'Presumes' Russia Has Biolo9igcal Arms Program," www.nti.org, May 9, 2014.

[67] Alexei Ivanov, "Electromagnetic Bombs Created In Russia," *Rossiyskaya Gazeta*, September 28, 2017, retrieved from *BBC Monitoring*, September 28, 2017.

[68] John Keller, "New Russian Directed Energy Weapon Could Complicate U.S. Military Strategic Planning, www.militaryaerospace.com, July 7, 2015.

[69] "Flight Test Of a New Project 4202 Vehicle," www.russianforces.org, March 3, 2015.

[70] Sharman, "Russia to Test New Generation Of Intercontinental Missile That Can' Beat US Defense Systems."

[71] "Russian Top Secret Hypersonic Glider Can Penetrate Any Missile Defense," *Sputnik News,* June 13, 2016, https://sputniknews.com/politics/201606111041185729-russia-hypersonic-glider/.

[72] Olga Bozhyeva, "Sources: Russia Successfully Tested New Missile Super weapon: Developers Called Launch of Sarmat ICBM Warhead a 'Fantastic Success,'" *Moskovsky Komsomolets,* April 20, 2016, *BBC Monitoring,* April 20, 2016.

[73] "Russian Top Secret Hypersonic Glider Can Penetrate Any Missile Defense," *Sputnik News.*

[74] *Ibid.*

[75] Olga Bozhyeva, "The 'Stiletto' Is In the Drawer – Russia is Testing Warheads On ancient Missiles From Penetrating American Missile Defenses," Moscow, *Moskovsky Komsomolets*, in Russian, October 22, 2011, *FBIS SOV*, October 22, 2011.

[76] Alexander G. Savelyev, "Russian Defense and Arms Control Policy and its Prospects After the Presidential Elections," *UNISCI Discussion Papers*, BNO. 17, May, 2008, p. 104 www.unisci.es.

[77] "Russian Top Secret Hypersonic Glider Can Penetrate Any Missile Defense," *Sputnik News.*

[78] *Ibid.* Ostkraft refers to the website www.ostkraft.ru.

[79] Stephen Blank," Missile Defense in Korea Further Roils US-Russian Relations," *Eurasia Daily Monitor*, Volume 13, Issue 133, The Jamestown Foundation, July 22, 2016, https://jamestown.org/program/missile-defense-in-korea-further-roils-us-russian-relations/.

[80] Pepe Escobar, "Beware What You Wish For: Russia is Ready For War," *RT*, May 22, 2016, https://www.rt.com/op-edge/344002-beware-russia-war-us/.

[81] Pavel Felgenhauer, "Russia's Imperial General Staff," *Perspective*, XVI, NO. 1, October-November, 2005, www.bu.ed./iscip/vol16/felgenhauer.

[82] Matt Bodner and Aaron Mehta "How a Pentagon Research Project Convinced Vladimir Putin Of a coming Biowar," *Air Force Times*, November 2, 2017, https://www.airforcetimes.com/news/pentagon-congress/2017/11/02/how-a-pentagon-research-project-convinced-vladimir-putin-of-a-coming-biowar/.

[83] Kirk Bennett, "Russia's Virtual Reality," *The American Interest*, November 1, 2017, https://www.the-american-interest.com/2017/11/01/russias-virtual-reality/.

[84] "The U.S. and Russia Plan For conflict," *Stratfor*, May 25, 2016, https://worldview.stratfor.com/article/us-and-russia-plan-conflict.

[85] Sergei Karaganov, "A Cold War: A Forecast For Tomorrow," *Rossiyskaya Gazeta*, October 22, 2017, retrieved from *Johnson's Russia List*, October 22, 2017.

[86] Quoted in Rumer, pp. 19–20.

[87] For descriptions of many of these programs see Amy F. Woolf, *Conventional Prompt Global Strike and Long-range Ballistic Missiles: Background and Issues,* Congressional Research Service, August 26, 2014.

[88] Ilyas Gilzatudinov, "Russian Work on Defense Against Hypersonic Weapons Systems In Full Swing," *Sputnik, Military and Intelligence,* July 3, 2016, http://sputniknews.com/military/20160703/1042360880/russian-anti-hypersonic-capabilities-development.html.

[89] Andrei Soldatov and Irina Bogoran, *The Red Web: the Struggle Between Russia's Digital Dictators and the New Online Revolutionaries*, New York: Public Affairs, 2015, p. 314.

[90] Robert Nalbandov, *Not By Bread Alone: Russian Foreign Policy Under Putin,* Washington, D.C.: Potomac Books, 2016, pp. 19–116; Jacek Durkalec, "Russia's Evolving Nuclear Strategy and What It Means For Europe," *European Council on Foreign Relations*, July 5, 2016, https://www.ecfr.eu/article/commentary_russias_evolving_nuclear_strategy_and_w hat_it_means_for_europe.

[91] Marcel H. Van Herpen, *Russia's Nuclear Threats and the Security Of the Baltic States*, Cicero Foundation Great Debate Paper, No. 16/05, 2016, pp. 3–6.

[92] Timothy L. Thomas, *Recasting the Red Star: Russia Forges Tradition and Technology through Toughness*, Ft. Leavenworth, KS: Foreign Military Studies office, US Army, 2011.

[93] Marvin Kalb, *Imperial Gamble: Putin, Ukraine, and the New Cold War*, Washington, D.C.: Brookings Institution Press, 2015, p. 233.

[94] Col. Thomas C. Kirkham, (USAF), "Modernizing the Nuclear Bomber Force: a National Security Imperative"; Lt. Col. Donald M. Neff (USAF); and Stephen J. Cimbala, "Nuclear Arms Reductions After *NEW START*: Obstacles and Options," all in Stephen J. Cimbala and Adam Lowther, Eds., *Defending the Arsenal: Why the Nuclear Triad Still Matters*, Forthcoming, Aldershot: Ashgate Publishing Company.

[95] Charlie Cooper, "NATO Risks Nuclear War With Russia 'Within a Year,' Warns Senior General," *The Independent*, May 18, 2016, https://www.independent.co.uk/news/world/europe/nato-risks-nuclear-war-with-russia-within-a-year-senior-general-warns-a7035141.html.

[96] Mark B. Schneider, "Escalate To Deescalate" *Proceedings of the US Naval Institute*, February 2017, https://www.usni.org/magazines/proceedings/2017-02/escalate-de-escalate.

[97] Margarete Klein, *Russia's Military; On the Rise?* Transatlantic Academy, 2015–2016 Paper Series, German Marshall Fund, 2016, pp. 8–9.

[98] Stephen Blank, "No Need to Threaten Us, We Are Frightened of Ourselves: Russia's Blueprint for a Police State," in *The Russian Military Today and Tomorrow: Essays in Memory of Mary Fitzgerald*, Stephen J. Blank and Richard Weitz eds., Carlisle Barracks, PA: Strategic Studies Institute U.S. Army War College, 2010, 19–150; Andrew Monaghan, "Defibrillating the Vertikal: Putin and Russian Grand Strategy," Chatham House, 2014; Andrew Monaghan, *Russian State Mobilization: Moving the Country on to a War Footing* – Chatham Hose, 2016, https://www.chathamhouse.org/expert/dr-andrew-monaghan#sthash.9Uf8wgVx.dpuf.

[99] Adamsky, "If War Comes Tomorrow: Russian Thinking about "Regional Nuclear Deterrence."

[100] Since little or no modernization of US nuclear weapons has taken place, this perfectly exemplifies the fictitious or mendacious, but certainly overwrought, nature of Russian threat perceptions.

[101] Sergey Ryabkov, "Changing Priorities in International Security," *Security Index*, XX, NO. 1, 2014, p. 23.

[102] David S. Yost, "NATO's Deterrence and Defense Posture After the Chicago Summit," U.S. Naval Postgraduate School Center on Contemporary Conflict, 2012, p. 21.

[103] Heather W. Williams, "Uncertainty in Escalation: Russian Strategy Interests and Avoiding Nuclear Coercion," unpublished paper, 2016.

[104] *Ibid.;* Schneider; Prezident Rossii, *Voyennaya Doktrina Rossiiskoi Federatsii*, The Kremlin, February 5, 2010; *Voyennaya Doktrina Rossiiskoi Federatsii,*" The Kremlin, December 26, 2014; *Natsional'naya Strategiya Bezopasnosti Rossii, do 2020 Goda*, Moscow, Security Council of the Russian Federation, May 12, 2009, in English it is available from *FBIS SOV*, May 15, 2009, in a translation from the Security Council website (Henceforth NSS); *Natsional'naya Strategiya Bezopasnosti Rossii*, The Kremlin, December 31, 2015.

[105] Heather W. Williams, "Uncertainty in Escalation: Russian Strategy Interests and Avoiding Nuclear Coercion," unpublished paper, 2016. Williams implies this but does not say so outright; this is also based on the author's conversations with high-ranking US officials in Washington, DC, during 2016.

[106] Nikolai Sokov, "Assessing Russian Attitudes Toward Phased, Deep Nuclear Reductions," *The Nonproliferation Review*, XX, NO. 2, 2013, pp. 251–252.

[107] Williams, "Uncertainty in Escalation: Russian Strategy Interests and Avoiding Nuclear Coercion."

[108] Gustav Gressel, "The Dangerous Decade: Russia-NATO Relations 2014 To 2024," European Council on Foreign Relations, July 5, 2016, https://www.ecfr.eu/article/commentary_the_dangerous_decade_russia_nato_relati ons_2014_to_2024.

[109] *Ibid.*

[110] *Voyennaya Doktrina Rossiiskoi Federatsii*, The Kremlin, February 5, 2010; *Voyennaya Doktrina Rossiiskoi Federatsii*, The Kremlin, December 26, 2014;

Natsional'naya Strategiya Bezopasnosti Rossii, do 2020 Goda, Moscow, Security Council of the Russian Federation, May 12, 2009, in English it is available from *FBIS SOV*, May 15, 2009, in a translation from the Security Council website (Henceforth NSS); *Natsional'naya Strategiya Bezopasnosti Rossii*, The Kremlin, December 31, 2015.

[111] *Ibid.*

[112] "Russian General Calls For Preemptive Nuclear Strike Doctrine Against NATO," *The Moscow Times*, September 3, 2014, https://themoscowtimes.com/articles/russian-general-calls-for-preemptive-nuclear-strike-doctrine-against-nato-39016.

[113] "Russia to Broaden Nuclear Strike Options," *RT*, October 14, 2009, http://rt.com/news/russia-broaden-nuclear-strike/; Schneider, *The Nuclear Doctrine and Forces of the Russian Federation*, op. cit., p. 21.

[114] Armin Rosen, "NATO Report: A 2013 Russian Aerial Exercise Was Actually a 'Simulated Nuclear Attack' On Sweden," *Business Insider*, February 3, 2016, https://www.businessinsider.com/nato-report-russia-sweden-nuclear-2016-2.

[115] Eugene Rumer, *Russia and the Security of Europe*, Carnegie Endowment for International Peace, Washington, DC, 2016, https://carnegieendowment.org/files/CP_276_Rumer_Russia_Final.pdf, p. 21.

[116] "Russia Says New US Nuclear bomb "Destabilizes Situation" *RIA Novosti*, August 3, 2016, retrieved from *BBC Monitoring*.

[117] Lora Saalman, Gu Guoliang, Zou Yunhua, Wu Riqiang, Jian Zhang, "China and Russia's Nuclear Relations," Carnegie-Tsinghua, July 7, 2013, https://carnegietsinghua.org/2013/07/07/china-s-and-russia-s-nuclear-relations-event-4167.

[118] "Presentation Of Officers Appointed To Senior Command Posts," October 27, 2017.

[119] *Voyennaya Doktrina Rossiiskoi Federatsii*, The Kremlin, December 26, 2014; *Natsional'naya Strategiya Bezopasnosti Rossii, do 2020 Goda*, Moscow, Security Council of the Russian Federation, May 12, 2009, in English it is available from *FBIS SOV*, May 15, 2009, in a translation from the Security Council website (Henceforth NSS); *Natsional'naya Strategiya Bezopasnosti Rossii*, The Kremlin, December 31, 2015; Kristin Ven Bruusgaard, "The Myth of Russia's Lowered Nuclear Threshold,"

War On the Rocks, https://warontherocks.com/2017/09/the-myth-of-russias-lowered-nuclear-threshold/, September 22, 2017.

[120] Adamsky, "If War Comes Tomorrow: Russian Thinking about "Regional Nuclear Deterrence.""

8. Russia's Offensive and Defensive Use of Information Security

Sergey Sukhankin

Introduction

Over the last decade and a half, Russian policies in the domain of information security have undergone a profound evolution in scope, complexity and sophistication. Moscow has traditionally viewed the information domain as a strategically crucial asset that allows it to effectively control the domestic population and project influence abroad. Yet, despite recent technological achievements, Russian information security policy continues to retain many classical Soviet traits that can be traced back to the writings of Vladimir Lenin and Joseph Stalin.[1] Russia's attitude toward information security in many ways dramatically differs from the Western approach. In the Russian reading, it is practice that plays a dominant role; whereas, theory (theoretical reflections) frequently appears post-factum, making Russian moves difficult to forecast and/or pre-empt.

Adopted on December 5, 2016, the new "Doctrine of Information Security of the Russian Federation"[2] ought to be seen as a complex phenomenon and an integral part of Russia's integrated strategy (that includes both military and non-military means) aimed at developing both offensive and defensive mechanisms in its confrontation with the West.

This chapter engages with both primary sources (with the text of the Doctrine forming the central pillar) as well as authoritative writings of prominent Russian thinkers and theoreticians in the information security domain. This approach enables an exploration of the issue from different angles and a discussion of Russia's information and cyber security doctrines from an interdisciplinary prospective.

Russian Stance on Information Security Between 2000 and 2010

Russia's current view of "information security" is in many ways still driven by the Soviet experience. This is reflected in two main ways:

- *Positive*: The Kremlin considers full and unconditional control over information (generation and dissemination) by the state as a useful means to secure greater mobilization potential for achieving specific/immediate goals and objectives. Post-1917 Russian/Soviet history witnessed numerous instances seemingly corroborating this precept.

- *Negative*: Russia's defeat in the Cold War is frequently linked in Russian writings with the state's forfeiture of control over information flows (particularly because of the so-called policy of *glasnost* introduced by Mikhail Gorbachev in the second half of 1980s) and Soviet inferiority in its information war with the United States.[3] Taken together, these two factors are seen as the main precursors to the collapse of the Soviet Union, which President Vladimir Putin has referred to as the "worst geopolitical catastrophe of the 20th century."[4]

After the dissolution of the Union of Soviet Socialist Republics (USSR), Russia's information security policy was left in a chaotic state, as demonstrated by the poor performance of the domestic mass media during the course of the first Chechen war (1994–1996)[5] and other instances. Toward the end of the 1990s (particularly after 1996), conservative circles inside Russia began to call for more consolidated state control over the domestic information space. Specifically, they suggested subjugating the country's major mass media outlets[6] and establishing the necessary legislative framework to regulate this transformation. The first step in this direction was made in 2000, with the adoption of Russia's Doctrine of Information Security. The document sparked alarm among the liberally minded segment of Russian society (The Union of Russian Journalists called it "the main danger to Russian information security itself"[7]), but the real extent of the peril was misunderstood. Both foreign and domestic observers paid excessive attention to details and formalities, eclipsing the doctrinal document's true purpose and potential, which not only paved the way for state control over the information sphere but also identified foreign countries as the main source of threat to Russia in the domain of information security. On the other hand, the document called for the inclusion of counter-propaganda among the government's primary tasks and urged the creation of "conditions for Russian representatives and organizations abroad to be able to neutralize disinformation regarding the foreign policy of the Russian Federation."[8]

Some measures—mainly those concerned with the consolidation of control over domestic information—were implemented throughout Putin's first term (2000–2004). Namely, on January 1, 2001, the state news agency *RIA Novosti* offered its "newsline" for free to all media outlets, thus essentially obtaining virtual control over the domestic information sphere.[9] Subsequently (2005), Moscow created *Russia Today* (later renamed simply *RT*).[10] This cable news channel, consciously styled to resemble *CNN* and *BBC International*, was designed to reach foreign audiences and convey Russia's take on both Russian domestic development and foreign events—in line with practical objectives laid out in the Doctrine. But in addition, *RT* specifically echoes Soviet-era practices of diversifying sources of propaganda to reach both "domestic" (performed by the Soviet Information Bureau) and "external" (*Comintern* and later *Cominform*) audiences.

Meanwhile, the early 2000s witnessed a surge in Russian theoretical thinking on issues related to information security. For instance, Russia's perception of "information" as a concept underwent a drastic transformation, notably owing to works by Igor Panarin, a chief-architect of the Russian theory of information confrontation/warfare. Panarin emphasized the term "social information" (*sotsialnaya informatsiya*), which, in his view, is one of the most essential criteria demonstrating effective functioning of a state and its national security apparatus. Specifically, he thought that the way information (transmitted by mass media) is processed by both individuals and groups of people has a direct effect on the ability of the state to maintain its internal stability and coordinate external actions. This is inseparable from the issue raised above, in reference to the collapse of the Soviet Union, of "who controls information flows, controls the destiny of the state." Panarin argued that ignorance of this factor would lead to "intellectual colonialism" (*intellektualnyi kolonializm*)[11] and ultimately the destruction of the state and nation, thus resembling the fate of the USSR. These ideas gained particular weight as the growing rift in relations between Moscow and the West started to acquire the shape of a veritable conflict toward the end of the 1990s.

Russia's stance on information security in the late 1990s and early 2000s became inseparable from external development, increasingly fixating on the United States and its actions and capabilities. For example, US activities in the domain of information security—from the implementation of concrete measures in the domain of cyber operations (October 1998), to the impressive performance of the US military during the Yugoslav conflict and initial stages of the Iraq war (especially use of the "psychological element"[12])—hugely contributed to shifting Russia's perspective from inward- to outward-looking.

This was underscored by two crucial transformations:

- The emergence and gradual popularization of the notion of an "information confrontation" (*informatsionnoe protivoborstvo*),[13] which drew on achieving information-psychological supremacy and the ability to provide an asymmetric response to external threats posed by technologically superior players;

- The notion of "information warfare" (*informatsionnaya voyna*) entering the Russian vocabulary and, having undergone critical changes compared to its original meaning in the West (as noted below), gaining immense popularity.

It is worth pointing out that, at first, both notions were rather incomplete and remained preoccupied with the US experience in local/regional conflicts.[14] The situation changed in light of the so-called "color revolutions," with Georgia (2003) and Ukraine (2004/2005) playing a decisive role. Events in Tbilisi and Kyiv demonstrated numerous weaknesses of Russian counter-propaganda (especially its information-psychological elements) and the lack of flexibility in the Kremlin's understanding of the notion of "information security." This gave rise to a renewed search for how to overcome these deficiencies. Consequently, by 2009, Russian theorists (Irina Vasilenko, in particular) came to see information warfare as a "systematic exertion of informational influence on the entire system of informational communication of an adversary, in order to set a beneficial global informational environment for conducting of various political and geopolitical operations."[15] This new perception exponentially broadened Russian understating of a "conflict" in the "information sphere/space" by specifically adding a "(geo)political" element, thus fully reflecting the course and trajectory of Russian foreign and security policy amidst the "cold peace" with the West (from Putin's Munich Security Conference speech in 2007 and onward). Nevertheless, at this point, both in terms of theory and practice, the Russian side was lagging behind not only leading players in the area of information security, but also much more modest actors, such as Sweden, Estonia, and Finland, which had adopted their own cyber security doctrines by 2008.

Crucial Changes: Evolution of Russian Information Policy, 2010–2016

The period from 2010 to 2016 had a decisive meaning for the development of Russian information security thinking, and owed to both internal and external developments. Rapid technological progress,[16] which transformed new media and the Internet into weapons of diplomacy and effective tools of foreign policymaking, pushed Moscow to re-consider a broad range of aspects related to information security.

Those transformations can be summarized in the following way:

1. The new role of information. For Russian policymakers, the Internet (as the cheapest and most effective means of transmitting information irrespective of state borders) came to be seen as a powerful medium for carrying out various "geopolitical tasks" (such as overthrowing "legitimate political authorities," in Russia's view), promoting ideology, and mobilizing/channeling public opinion. Furthermore, the continuing ideologization of foreign policy (with "inter-governmental" and "national-governmental" elements assuming a prominent role) made the proper dissemination of information absolutely essential;

2. The global "information space" as a zone of confrontation. From the early 2010s, Russia contested the assumption of the "global information/cyber space as a free area." Speaking in the Russian parliament (Duma) on April 20, 2011, Putin stated that "the main

Internet resources do not belong to us, they are located over the hill ['*za bugrom*'] or, to be more accurate, on the other side of the ocean. This allows some special services to use these resources for their own purposes."[17] As a result, many Russian theorists and practitioners stressed the need to make Russia's section of the Internet more autonomous from the rest of the global network;

3. *Information as a weapon of asymmetric response.* Events on the Bolotnaya Square (2011) and in the Middle East (from 2010 on) had a mixed effect on Russian perceptions of information security. They demonstrated that public protests could be "accelerated" with the help of new media and "channeled" against existing political regimes. At the same time, information came to be seen as a weapon of huge destructive power in an asymmetric conflict with militarily/economically/technologically superior adversaries. In this regard, aggravating relations with the West spurned Russian elites into intensifying their search for how to deal with opponents. These debates began to reflect on the reasons behind the Soviet defeat in the Cold War, summarized in the following citation: "having attained military parity with the US, the USSR was defeated on the information battlefield."[18]

By the 2010s, Russian experts came to view the concept of "information confrontation" as a combination of political, economic, diplomatic and military means—but comprised of two essential elements[19]:

1. *Information-technological confrontation* consisting of:

- Electronic Warfare (EW) and electronic intelligence;

- Electro-optical warfare ("*Elektronno-opticheskaya voyna*");

- Acoustic warfare;

- Computer warfare (so-called "hackers' warfare").

2. *Information-psychological confrontation*, which envisages targeting:

- Consciousness;

- Neurological systems (both individual and collective, including military formations);

- State ideology;

- National consciousness.

By the end of 2011, Russia's search resulted in a number of findings that contributed to the clarification of Russia's role and place in the global information space, the range of informational challenges faced by the country, as well as steps to be taken in order to boost its status, which included:

1. Recognition of the strategic importance of new media and social networks for Russian national defense and security[20];

2. A declaration of the state of "information war" and naming of the "foes." According to Vladimir Dobrenkov "our country [Russia] is in a state of information warfare that is waged on her territory and in regions that have traditionally been thought as a part of Russia's sphere of national interests (Ukraine, the Baltic States, the Caucasian Republics and others)";[21]

3. Identification of the main aims of information war "against Russia":

- Destruction of the will and intellectual capabilities of the political leadership of the Russian Federation;

- Demobilization of Russian society;

- Moral stagnation of Russian citizens;

4. An outline of the main outlets through which "information war" will be waged: television, radio, newspapers, books, magazines, songs, movies and popular culture. Strangely, some elements (such as the Internet and various social networks) were rarely mentioned by mainstream Russian theorists;

5. Identification of specific counter-measures and the mode of operation. It was argued that Russian policies in the domain of information security had to be coherent, multi-layered, goal-oriented and highly centralized. The list of counter-measures included:

- Correct detection of the adversary's weak spots (drawing on interdisciplinary analysis of an adversary and its/their capabilities);

- Employment of "active measures" (a clear reference to Soviet practices);

- Ability to use preventive and pre-emptive measures (developing offensive mechanisms);

- Rapid implementation of new analytical methods/technologies (modernization and innovation) via knowledge exchange and preparing of qualified specialists;

- Creation of a single organ/institution tasked with coordinating Russia's information policy (centralization).

In spite of the growing number of these and similar initiatives, the legislative framework in the domain of information security (still regulated by the Doctrine adopted in 2000), no longer corresponded to the challenges as well as the extent of technological progress attained by Russia and its competitors.

Aside from the already mentioned "Arab Spring," it was the "EuroMaidan" revolution in Kyiv (starting in late 2013) that once again intensified discussions (and this time, engaged military elites) on the new role of information within "new type" conflicts. Those ideas were extensively discussed in an article by the chief of the General Staff of the Armed Forces of Russia and first deputy defense minister, General Valery Gerasimov.[22] Perhaps for the first time in Russia's post-1991 history, non-military components of confrontation (including, among others, the "informational" element) started to not merely be viewed on par, but even prioritized in comparison with conventional means of warfare. Similarly, the role of Russian Defense Minister Sergei Shoigu is worth highlighting. Due to his personal advocacy, so-called "research units" (established in 2012/2013) were given a boost. These units (the 6th and 7th research units in particular), created under the umbrella of the Russian Armed Forces, should be viewed as a totally new element of information confrontation, which could develop both offensive and defensive mechanisms.[23]

Indeed, the Ukraine crisis was a turning point that allowed Russia to merge theoretical achievements with practice and to test the offensive side of its information security domain. The variety of measures introduced by Moscow between 2013 and 2016 highlights the "information/cyber revolution" that commenced in Russia within this period.

During the first stage of the Ukraine crisis (November 2013–February 2014), Russian actions were mainly concerned with offensive mechanisms of information-psychological confrontation that included the creation of (dis)information outlets and the launch of massive anti-Western/anti-Ukrainian propaganda. The second stage (from March 2014 onward) witnessed warfare entering a qualitatively new level. Using Ukraine as its "training ground," Russia tested the offensive side of its information and cyber capabilities by employing:

- an *"information-psychological"* element of information warfare through (counter)propaganda, disinformation and reflexive control techniques (leveled equally but with different purpose against Ukraine and its Western allies); and

- an *"information-technological"* element, with cyberwarfare and EW playing a decisive role (hacker attacks on various governmental institutions, major enterprises, EW operations against Ukrainian armed forces).

It is interesting to note that in the course of the Ukrainian events, Russia ended up combining both elements, using the "cyber" and "information" aspects of information warfare simultaneously.

Aside from the practical measures, the Russian government intensified its discourse pertaining to the creation of a new Information Doctrine (the first round of talks was initiated in 2013). On October 1, 2014, President Putin and members of the Russian Security Council discussed "problems related to counter-actions against threats to Russia's national security in the domain of information security."[24] Moreover, the Military Doctrine of the Russian Federation, adopted at the end of 2014, identified "information" as an integral ingredient for achieving "military-political objectives."[25]

The external factor must also not be downplayed. In late April 2015, the United States adopted a new Cyber Strategy, triggering an outcry of discontent from Russia, where the document was construed as an anti-Russian project.[26] Additionally, ongoing Russian disinformation enticed several prominent international media and investigative news agencies (including Google NewsLab, Bellingcat, DigDeeper, Eyewitness Media Hub, Emergent, Meedan, Reported.ly, Storyful and Verification Junkie) to unite under the roof of a joint project dubbed "First Draft News" (June 2015), which was subsequently supported by Amnesty International, the American Press Institute, *The New York Times*, *The Washington Post*, *The Telegraph*, *Le Monde*, *CNN* and *Al Jazeera*. The purpose of this alliance was primarily concerned with combating fake news and disinformation, which the Russian side recognized as an open challenge and a direct threat to Moscow's titanic efforts in the domain of (counter)propaganda aimed at the external audience.[27] At the same time, however, Russia felt threatened at the prospect of the European Union and the United State joining their efforts in confronting/containing Russian propaganda/disinformation, thus isolating Moscow and reducing its target audience to only the domestic segment. These concerns were reflected in the new "National Security Strategy" (December 2015), which stated that "independent conduct of foreign and domestic policy by the Russian Federation is causing counter-actions from the side of the United States and its allies, aspiring to preserve their dominant position in global affairs. Their policy of containment of Russia envisages exertion of political, economic and informational pressure."[28]

It is also imperative to mention the broader context in which work on the text of the new Information Doctrine was conducted. November 2016 witnessed renewed confrontation between Russia and the West triggered by alleged Russian cyberattacks against analytical centers and think tanks inside the United States, the broader US presidential election campaign, as well as governmental institutions in the EU and Ukraine. This caused a wave of alarm among European policymakers, urging the European Parliament to adopt a resolution (November 23) aiming to consolidate the European countries in countering "propaganda by third parties" and naming Russia as one of the main culprits.[29] Although non-binding, the European Parliament's resolution nonetheless sparked a great deal of discontent in Moscow. Commenting on this decision, Putin accused the EU of a "violation of the rights and freedoms of Russian journalists working abroad"[30] and a visible sign of the "degradation of European democracy."

Later, in his address to the Federation Council (the upper chamber of the Russian Parliament), on December 1, 2016, Putin specifically underscored the development of the domestic IT industry, the elaboration of defensive IT mechanisms, and the boosting of cybersecurity as Russia's strategic objectives in the domain of information security.[31] Incidentally, information security (its offensive element) became one of the main themes outlined in the Russian government's Foreign Policy Concept (adopted on December 1, 2016).[32] At the same time, in the beginning of December 2016, Russia's Federal Security Service (FSB) "uncovered" a plot allegedly staged by "foreign special services" that "were preparing massive cyberattacks against the Russian financial system" by hacking the webpages and official online portals of VTB Bank (element of cyberwarfare) and by "sending provocative messages" (element of information-psychological warfare), aiming to discredit the solvency of the Russian financial credit system.[33]

Assessing Russia's New Information Security Doctrine: Nuts and Bolts

The new "Doctrine of Information Security" reflects Russian national interests and official posture toward the goals and principles framing its information security policy. The Doctrine specifically identifies itself as a "document of strategic planning in the domain of Russia's national security,"[34] thus its scope and meaning are much broader than might appear on the surface. In comparison with previous iterations, the latest Russian information security doctrine contains numerous crucial distinctions.

New Concepts

First of all, it introduces a number of concepts (both brand new as well as previously mentioned but repackaged) that have in many ways reshaped Russian policies in the information security domain. For instance, the Doctrine finally includes a discussion of the Internet (absent previously), thus underscoring the growing number of Internet users in Russia, rising technological progress, as well as the increasingly critical role new media plays in terms of information delivery, transmission and dissemination.

Six other crucial new concepts in the December 2016 Doctrine include:

1. The information sphere ("informatsionnaya sfera"), which makes up a broad spectrum of elements, including "information, informatization objects, information systems and websites within the information and telecommunications network of the Internet, communications networks, information technologies."[35]

2. The national interests ("natsionalnye interesy") of the Russian Federation in the information sphere/space.[36] The notion encompasses a broad range of topics and issues that reflect shifts and transformations within Russian information security during 2010–2016, such as:[37]

- IT and external influence. The document points to the use of IT to preserve Russian cultural, historical and moral-spiritual values (*"dukhovno-nravstvennye tsennosti"*) and traditions.[38] As such, it links the "conservative turn" that promulgated in Russia since the 2010s with the information security domain;

- Import substitution, upgrades to the level of protection of Russian domestic IT infrastructure and common electric grid, as well as an emphasis on the development of R&D;[39]

- Promotion of Russian national interests, domestically and abroad. Referring to the necessity of developing counter-propaganda as well as counter-containment techniques, tools and measures, this segment stresses the vital importance of defending the "sovereignty of the Russian Federation in the information domain"[40] and preserving "national security in the domain of culture."[41]

Perhaps, the most crucial element is the necessity to maintain the "steady functioning of the Russian Federation's information infrastructure (primarily, critical information infrastructure) during both peace and war time."[42] Based on previous evidence (in particular, Russian activities during the Zapad 2013 strategic military exercises), the inclusion of this aspect suggests Moscow is likely to intensify drills and exercises aimed at preparing its information infrastructure for a potential military conflict. This could be carried out under the guise of various war games/military exercises. For instance, on September 10–12, 2017 (during Zapad 2017), Russian authorities practiced large-scale evacuations of civilian objects and institutions in major cities across the country[43]; such drills could certainly be linked with the above-mentioned aspect of the Doctrine.

3. The threat ("ugroza") to information security of the Russian Federation, understood as factors/activities that can pose a danger to Russia's national interests in the information space.[44]

4. Information security ("informatsionnaya bezopasnost") of the Russian Federation that emphasizes "sovereignty, territorial integrity, steady socio-economic growth [...], defense and security of the state."[45] In effect, this term was directly borrowed from the 2015 National Security Strategy document, which, in turn, undoubtedly was heavily shaped by the "Arab Spring," the EuroMaidan and subsequent events in southeastern Ukraine.

5. *The forces ("sily"), means ("sredstva") and system ("system") tasked with ensuring the maintenance of information security ("obezpechenie informatsionnoy bezopasnosti") of the Russian Federation.*[46] Taken together, these elements consist of:

- An inter-linked, coherent and mutually-supportive set of measures (including forecasting, detection, containment, forestalling and deflection, as well as dealing with the consequences of "anti-Russian" information and cyberattacks) aimed at coordinating and implementation Russia's information security policies;

- Forces (security forces, government bodies, local authorities) tasked with control and supervision of these policies;

- Means (legal, organizational, technical) to be employed by forces tasked with the supervision of the state's information security;

6. *Critical Information Infrastructure (CII) of the Russian Federation ("Kriticheskaya informatsionnaya ifrastruktura"),* which is defined as a "a compendium of informatization objects, information systems, Internet websites and communication networks located on the territory of the Russian Federation as well as on territories under the jurisdiction of the Russian Federation or used under international treaties signed by the Russian Federation."[47] This notion is crucial since it *de jure* renders certain specific foreign territories to be a part of Russia's domestic CII, which exponentially broadens the geographic scope (from East-Central Europe to Central Asia and the Middle East) to which this concept can theoretically be applied. It also means that Russia gives itself the right to activate both defensive and

offensive mechanisms in response to dangers to its CII (even regarding elements not physically present inside Russia's internationally recognized borders).

Information Security Domain Threats

Secondly, the Doctrine pays significant attention to threats faced by the Russian Federation in the information security domain. At this juncture, it is interesting to note that Russia views unrestricted trans-border information exchange (*"transgranichnyi oborot informatsyi"*)—that is, the free exchange of information across state lines—as primarily associated with risks and threats to the state in geopolitical, security and military-political domains. This is amplified when important IT components are acquired from abroad, since they could be used by opponents to undermine Russian information security.

Analysis of the Doctrine reveals at least four perils Russia deems crucial to defend against:

1. *Information-technology threats posed by foreign countries.* Those are reflected in "the accretion by some foreign countries of capabilities that can be used for the purpose of affecting the critical infrastructure of the Russian Federation for achieving military objectives... [as well as to carry out a] technical intelligence search against Russian state institutions, scientific organizations, [and Russia's] Military Industrial Complex."[48] This is seen by Moscow as part of a broader strategy pursued by "foreign countries" aspiring to employ information technologies for "military-political purposes," including steps aimed at undermining "Russian sovereignty, territorial integrity and political stability";[49]

2. *Information-psychological threats posed by special services of foreign countries.*[50] Here, three main elements are emphasized. First, the role

of "special services of foreign states" and "religious, ethnic, human rights and other NGOs [non-governmental organizations]" in applying "information-psychological pressure aimed at the destabilization of the political and social situation… [or to violate] the territorial integrity of countries." Second, activities performed by the above-mentioned actors for the purpose of using the Russian information space for their purposes. Third, exploitation of CII by terrorist and extremist organizations[51] "to influence individual, group and public consciousness; instigate inter-ethnic and social tensions; [spark] ethnic or religious hatred or hostility; [or to] spread extremist ideology." These aspects once again draw on Ukrainian events and the "Arab Spring" (which Moscow ascribes to destructive Western activities).

3. Technological inferiority of the Russian Federation in comparison with leading global IT players. This stems from the low competitiveness of most Russian IT products, insufficient levels of integration of domestically produced products in Russia's industry, as well as inadequately low levels of R&D in the IT domain.[52] Taken together, these factors hamper Russia's efforts to overcome its dependency on foreign IT (elements, components, software). This state of affairs enables "certain states" to, on the one hand, "use their technological dominance for the purpose of achieving their geopolitical objectives" (pointed out by Putin in 2011). And on the other hand, as noted in the Doctrine, these factors contribute to keeping "socio-economic development of the Russian Federation under dependence of geopolitical ambitions of foreign countries"; this is mainly as a result of economic sanctions imposed by the West in the aftermath of Russian activities in Ukraine and Russia's illegal annexation of Crimea.

4. Jeopardy of Russian counter-propaganda efforts associated with "open discrimination that Russian mass media and Russian journalists are facing abroad."[53] Undoubtedly, the inclusion of this aspect was motivated by measures taken by the EU and the US to combat Russian propaganda and disinformation efforts. As mentioned earlier, a combination of public diplomacy,[54] think tanks/non-governmental organizations, and "Russian societies" operating abroad with the support of multi-lingual information outlets constitute the main source of Russian "soft power" targeting external audiences—an element that was first emphasized in the first Doctrine (2000).

Areas of Strategic Importance

Thirdly, the document outlines areas of strategic importance that consist of:

- National defense;

- State and social security;

- Economic sphere;

- Science, technology and education;

- Strategic stability and equitable strategic partnership.

The Doctrine underscores that all the above-mentioned areas face numerous challenges stemming from both internal deficiencies and external threats, which nevertheless have a common denominator—a policy of containment pursued by the West. Therefore, current policies of the Russian Federation in these areas (given their strategic importance and technological-informational nature) are concerned with minimizing risks and threats. This primarily means that reliance on the Soviet experience (hedging from "external influence") will be increased. This is most visible in the national security and defense domain. For instance, the creation of the National Defense Control Center (NDCC), on December 1, 2014, claimed by Russian sources to be superior in comparison with foreign analogues (including the Pentagon), fully complies with this policy and should be seen as a *de facto* incarnation of Russia's most up-to-date "cyber" element of information confrontation. The Center's architecture is comprised of 73 federal and regional executive branch organs as well as 1,320 public and private firms from the military industrial complex (MIC).[55] Russian sources also claim the NDCC has a Supercomputer operating at a speed of 16 petaflops that is virtually immune to any type of cyberattack(s); reportedly, its hardware and software are capable of modeling crisis situations inside Russia and "everywhere in the world." Putin underscored that the NDCC will "work for all members of the CSTO [Collective Security Treaty Organization—a Moscow-led regional alliance],"[56] thus reiterating key provisions related to CII, engrained in the new Information Security Doctrine. Another notable example of the same trend pertains to work on a "military internet" and other types of communication designed for the Russian Armed Forces in order to "autonomate" internal information exchanges and minimize the threat of information being hacked/intercepted or damaged/corrupted.

Strengthening Capabilities in Five Key Strategic Dimensions

Fourthly, the document presents five strategic dimensions where Russia has to strengthen its capabilities:

1. In the field of national defense, strategic priority is "to protect the vital interests of the individual, society and the state from both internal and external threats related to the use of information technologies for military and political purposes," including "hostile actions and acts of aggression that undermine sovereignty and territorial integrity."[57]

This goal is to be achieved by pursuing the following measures:[58]

- Strategic deterrence/containment and prevention of military conflicts resulting from the use of information technologies (defensive element);

- Beefing up capabilities in the area of information security of the Russian Armed Forces (in particular, units/segments related to information confrontation). Presumably, this task will be primarily conferred to "research units," "cyber troops" and EW troops (including EW *spetsnaz*, created in Russia's Western Military District[59]). They will be charged with forecasting, detection and analysis of information threats faced by the Armed Forces (which adds an element of strategic planning and boosts the Russian military's defensive, offensive, as well as counter-offensive capabilities);

- Protecting the interests of allies of the Russian Federation in the domain of information security. The notion ("allies") was not explained. Yet, on the basis of other parts of the Doctrine, it appears that the geographic scope of the concept is extremely broad, including some members of the CSTO and the Shanghai Cooperation Organization (SCO) as well as certain state actors in the Middle East. Additionally, this point draws on Russia's readiness to use offensive and counter-offensive mechanisms of information confrontation on behalf of third parties;

- Neutralizing information-psychological pressure "leveled against historical and patriotic traditions concerned with the defense of the Motherland."[60] In this regard, the so-called "Youth Army" (*Yunarmia*)[61]—tasked with the "military-patriotic upbringing" of Russian youth—should be allocated particular attention. A lesser, but still important role is ascribed to various military-patriotic groups and organizations such as the AntiMaidan movement (emerged in 2015) and the Cossack movement, whose geographical area of activities has spread dramatically in the aftermath of the Ukraine crisis beginning in 2014.

2. *In the field of state and public security*, the key objectives are the need "to protect the sovereignty, maintain the political and social stability, and [defend the] territorial integrity of the Russian Federation" as well as "to protect the critical information infrastructure" of the state.[62]

Realization of these objectives rests on implementation of counter-measures in:[63]

- The information-psychological domain, where the effort should be leveled against "extremist ideology, xenophobia, and ideas of national exceptionalism for the purposes of undermining sovereignty and political and social stability, forcibly changing the constitutional order, and violating the territorial integrity of the Russian Federation."[64] This sub-section contains an implicit but important allusion to the United States ("*national exceptionalism*") and its European allies such as Ukraine, Poland and the three Baltic States, portrayed by Russian propaganda as Russophobic, far-right and ruled by illegitimate regimes. Emphasis is once again placed on the necessity to "neutralize the information impact that aims to erode Russia's traditional moral and spiritual values"; [65]

- The information-technology domain, where the most crucial elements are protection of CII against activities of "foreign states, special services and individuals," as well as the facilitation of a unified telecommunications network for the Russian Federation;[66]

- The military-industrial domain, which emphasizes "improving the methods and techniques of the manufacturing and safe functioning of types of arms and munitions and automatized systems of control."[67]

3. In the field of economics, the main objective outlined in the Doctrine boils down to the "minimization of negative factors stipulated by an inadequate level of development of the domestic IT and electronics industry,"[68] which may, among other things, be related to the adverse effect of economic sanctions imposed on Russia by the West in 2014.

This target is expected to be reached by implementing the following policies:

- Import-substitution and a drastic reduction of Russian industry's dependency on foreign IT products;

- Emphasis on innovative developments of IT and electronics, with the prospect of increasing the overall share of this sector in Russia's GDP, and subsequent higher penetration of the global market;

- Increase in the competitiveness of Russian companies by creating proper conditions and a more favorable material base.

The prioritization of this field was not only shaped by sanctions, but clearly stemmed from Russian experience gained during the Ukraine crisis. The success of Russian information-technology warfare in the Ukrainian theater (leveled both against military and civilian targets) was secured by Ukraine's dependence on Russian-produced IT products, Internet search tools (such as *Yandex*) and gadgets that rendered Ukrainian information/cyber security susceptible to Russian actions.

4. In the field of science, technology and education,[69] the Doctrine puts special emphasis on R&D in the information security sector, simultaneously underscoring perhaps the most acute problem Russia currently faces—the lack of qualified domestic IT experts and specialists. Given the unattractiveness of labor condition at Russian firms or for the government in comparison with leading international IT players, this issue might constitute one of the most serious challenges to meeting the goals outlined in the Doctrine. Most likely, the "research units" (employing an element of head-hunting) created under the umbrella of the Russian Armed Forces will be tasked with coping with this issue (thus partly replicating Soviet-era practices). The Doctrine also mentions the "formation of an individual culture of information security,"[70] but does not clarify what this means. However, on the basis of supplementary research, this objective may include (among other things) establishing a comprehensive grass-root system for recruiting those with a high aptitude for specialization in IT. Partly, this is reflected in Russian secondary school curriculums (currently, on an experimental basis) that stipulate integrating courses on the basics of cyber/information security.[71] Finally, a rather unusual phenomenon emerged in Russian in 2016—the so-called "Cossack cyber regiments," which were assembled and trained under the roof of the K. G. Razumovsky Moscow State University of Technologies and Management (the First Cossack University).[72] This may have represented a continuation of the same strategy.

5. In the field of strategic stability,[73] the document underscores that the primary objectives are ensuring the "sovereignty of the Russian Federation in the information space" and "[promoting] the position of the Russian Federation in international organizations"; to some extent, these goals intersect with the previously mentioned points. Most importantly, this section of the Doctrine points to the necessity of "developing a national system for managing the Russian segment of the Internet,"[74] thus addressing the so-called *Runet* (Russian-language segment of the Internet). Aside from confronting external factors, this initiative should be seen as a crucial element in Russia's regional integration efforts via the Eurasian Economic Union (EEU). Specifically, with Russia taking the major role in the EEU in terms of information/cyber security, the *Runet* becomes the main tool for increasing the international role of the Russian language within most of the post-Soviet space.

Division of Responsibilities Among Government Agencies

Fifth, the Doctrine establishes a multi-dimensional hierarchical framework that identifies the institutions and agencies responsible for maintaining Russian information security, which is acknowledged as an integral part of Russia's broader national security.[75] Notably, the document states that the Russian president has the power to "determine the entire structure of the information security system."[76]

Thus, the Doctrine presents:

1. The upper (institutional) level consisting of:[77]

- The Council of the Federation (upper chamber of parliament);

- The State Duma (lower chamber of parliament);

- The Government of the Russian Federation;

- The Security Council of the Russian Federation;

- Federal executive bodies;

- The Central Bank of the Russian Federation;

- The Military-Industrial Commission of the Russian Federation;

- Inter-agency bodies established by the President and Government of the Russian Federation;

- Executive bodies of the constituent entities of the Russian Federation (oblasts, krais, republics, etc.);

- Local governments and judicial bodies involved in information security activities.

2. *The lower (participatory/auxiliary) level* comprised of:

- Owners of critical information objects as well as organizations operating such objects;

- Mass media and mass communications;

- Monetary, foreign currency, banking and other financial institutions;

- Telecommunication operators;

- Information system operators;

- Organizations that create and operate information and communications systems;

- Organizations that develop, produce and operate information security tools;

- Organizations that provide information security services;

- Organizations that provide education services in this sphere;

- Public associations and other organizations and individuals involved in information security.

It is worth noticing that the document does not clarify the role/status of "cyber-squads" (*kiberdryzhiny*), an initiative launched in 2011 (which now involves 20,000 "volunteers" in 36 regions of the Russian Federation).[78] Nor does it address the Russian National Guard (*Rosgvardia*), which has been given additional powers in the realm of information security. For the rest, the Doctrine presents a sophisticated and all-encompassing framework comprised of bodies, institutions and agencies acting on a hierarchical principle. It also argues for "maintaining a balance between citizens' demands for the free exchange of information and restrictions related to national security."[79] In effect, this means that individual rights and freedoms can (and will) be limited/abridged for the purpose of maintaining information security.

The Doctrine also outlines the tasks and functions[80] that the above-mentioned institutions and agencies are expected to perform on a routine basis. These include a broad range of responsibilities: assessing the actual state of information security, forecasting/detecting information threats, overcoming their adverse effects, coordinating activities between various information security forces (including legal, organizational, operative investigative, intelligence, counter-intelligence, scientific and technical, informational and analytical tasks), as well as calculating state-sponsored support for non-state organizations operating in the domain of information security.

In addition to these measures, the document outlines steps for "developing and improving the information security system"[81] that the government bodies are to attain in the future.

In this regard, the following key areas are distinguished:

- The centralization and coordination of forces by establishing "vertical management" consisting of federal, inter-regional, regional and municipal levels (again, the Soviet tradition is apparent here);

- Regular practical drills as a means to boost the level of interaction between information security forces (an apparent parallel with NATO policies could be drawn);

- Inter-institutional interconnections between governmental (state institutions), local (local governance), collective (at the level of various organizations) and individual (between individuals) levels.

The document does not explicitly identify the time frame the above-mentioned steps are to be implemented. Although, it is stated that "in order to keep these documents updated, the Security Council of the Russian Federation shall compile a list of medium-term priority areas of information security."[82] However, given the pace of technological progress in the domain of information security as well as worsening political relations with Western counterparts, and the growing fear of internal destabilization (which can be precipitated with the help of new media), objectives set for a "mid-term" prospect might be implemented within a short-term period. In this regard, it would be worthwhile to study the quick progress attained by the EW segment of Russia's Armed Forces.

Impact of the Doctrine and Future of Russian Information Security

The adoption of the new Information Security Doctrine had surprisingly little impact on public or academic policy debates in

Russia. Moreover, many domestic specialists and experts (some of them quite prominent) construed the Doctrine as either "dated"[83] or "unlikely to become a guide for practical steps."[84] However, Russian military theorists seemed to evaluate the document's content as much more comprehensive and far-reaching. For instance, the editor-in-chief of the military magazine *Natsionalnaya Oborona*, Igor Korotchenko, claimed the document exemplifies Russia's ability to outpace its competitors. Reflecting on the new Doctrine and its meaning, the expert stated, "Today, we can see that a number of foreign states, primarily the United States and other members of NATO, are actively developing their cyber operations capabilities for achieving military objectives or to be able to destabilize the economic and socio-political situation, including by exerting pressure on the Russian Federation." Korotchenko particularly emphasized that, "under the auspices of NATO, specialized centers are created that are tasked with waging cyberwarfare. These are the NATO Cooperative Cyber Defense Center of Excellence, in Tallinn, and the Strategic Communications Center of Excellence, in Riga. At this juncture, the emergence of the Doctrine of Information Security represents a tangible step forward for Russia, Korotchenko argued, because it creates a powerful network that enables the Russian side to trace, prevent and deal with the consequences of cyberattacks, as well as helps to neutralize cyber threats."[85]

Indeed, since the end of 2013, this viewpoint (though subjective and containing questionable points) clearly reflects Russia's official posture on information security. The document contains a number of general trends that offer insight into how the Russian information domain will continue to develop over the next 3–5 years.

US/NATO-centric approach in Russian information policy. The Doctrine (as an integral supplement to other strategic documents) identifies the United States as the main source of threat to Russian "information sovereignty." Commenting on the Doctrine, member of the ruling United Russia political party Sergei Zheleznyak blatantly stated that this document is a response to "the US and its European partners, which have launched genuine information warfare against Russia, including [by attacking] its mass media and constantly accusing [Moscow] of non-existent aggression."[86] At the same time, it is difficult to overlook the presence of various elements (such as, for example, the role of information technology in command and control) that appear to have been influenced by the US experience. At this juncture, Russia's next move can be expected to officially distinguish the "cyber" layer as a separate pillar within the information security domain. Incidentally, the Russian Federation Council's original (beginning of 2014) resolution that formed the backbone of the new "Information Security Doctrine" was entitled "The Concept of a Cyber Security Strategy of the Russian Federation."[87] But it seems that the word "cyber" was ultimately dropped in favor of "information" because of Russian unfamiliarity with the concept (and the Western etymology of the word) as well as difficulties with formulating a "cyber doctrine's" key principles.

Protection of information security as a basis for geopolitical influence in its neighborhood. Having introduced the notion of CII, the Doctrine explicitly empowers Russia to use its offensive and counter-offensive potential in the information security domain while protecting the interests of its allies. This is a crucial aspect. Given the fact that the text of the document does not discuss the issue in-depth, retaining a share of ambiguity, this leaves the Russian side useful room for maneuver on the various ways that this point could be construed. Here, it is worth recalling Russian legislation on protecting "Russian compatriots abroad" as well as instances of Russian involvement in the affairs of sovereign countries under this pretext (most notably, Georgia and Ukraine). Given this element of the Doctrine, the next step made by Russia could include the recognition of cyber threats as tantamount to armed threats, thus creating a new foundation for Russia's potential involvement in the domestic affairs of other countries.

"Militarization" of information. A thesis presented by Chief of the General Staff Gerasimov that "information resources have become the most effective weapon" and "an essential element of hybrid warfare"[88] forms one of the most essential pillars of the Doctrine. The document presents a clear delineation between two main parts (technological and psychological) of a so-called "information confrontation." And each of them is deemed to be of crucial importance in terms of "new type warfare." Moreover, given Russian objectives during the so-called "initial period of conflict"—gaining control over the information space of an adversary via "information blockade/dominance"—the issue of information security becomes a critical factor for attaining complete and decisive success. Similarly, EW capabilities (also seen as a part of information security) are viewed as an integral part of Russia's Anti-Access/Area-Denial strategy, as tested in Kaliningrad Oblast.[89] On top of that, given current trends in Russian national security, there is every reason to believe that the EW branch will assume the leading role in terms of information security and its example is likely to be used by other branches of strategic importance.

The Doctrine as a foundation for further actions. Despite some assessments to the contrary, practical steps conducted by the Russian side suggest that the document is likely to be used as the basis for future legislation addressing the information security domain. Indeed, speaking in late 2016, Nikolay Nikiforov, the head of the Ministry of Telecom and Mass Communications of the Russian Federation, noted that it will take time to understand the way the Doctrine will be implemented and, if necessary, new laws will complement the document.[90] And already since then, Russia has adopted the "Strategy for the Development of an Information Society for 2017–2030,"[91] the Law on "Security of Critical Infrastructure"[92] (in July 2017) as well as a number of less significant pieces of legislation. Moreover, the Doctrine implies that some structural changes could take place. Namely, point 38 reads, "The findings from monitoring of the implementation of the Doctrine are to be reflected in the annual report on national security presented by the Secretary of the Security Council of the Russian Federation to the President of the Russian Federation." This shows that, despite the creation of an "information management vertical," the system will remain somewhat incomplete without a central organ/agency managing Russia's information security domain on a routine basis.

Emphasis on the defensive side of the "cyber" aspect. Given significant progress attained in the domain of information-psychological operations and EW (both tested in Ukraine), the next area likely to receive a boost may be the information-technological domain, with clear priority given to a defensive side of "cyber security" (in the Western reading of this notion). Following the example of the United States (once again highlighting Russia's fixation on the US experience), the Russian side is likely to concentrate its efforts on boosting the following elements:

- Protection Capabilities (including Computer Security and Information Security);

- Detection Capabilities;

- Reaction Capabilities.

Conclusions

Throughout the course of its post-1917 history, the Soviet Union (and contemporary Russia, although to a lesser extent) repeatedly demonstrated high proficiency in tactical operations thanks to its ability to effectively concentrate/divert and use the required resources for specific goals/objectives. Yet, despite this string of successes, the cumulative effect did not necessarily bring lasting victories.

By extensively relying on Soviet-era methods, the current Russian leadership is likely to commit similar mistakes as its historical predecessor. First, by prioritizing the military branch, the Russian side may undermine civilian informational security needs, thus creating a dichotomy in development, which was one of the most distinctive traits of the Soviet period. Similarly, a visible lack of competition could lead to a degradation in the commercial attractiveness of Russian IT products (since their most advanced innovations will routinely be restricted for military use). Incidentally, these were among the most crucial factors preventing the Soviet Union from achieving a breakthrough in the domain of information security and being able to catch up with the US.[93] At first glance, it might appear that the contemporary Russian strategy has undergone visible changes. However, those have been mainly cosmetic, largely preserving the Soviet-legacy substance. The current "Information Security Doctrine" explicitly argues for needed progress in upgrading the competitiveness of Russia's IT industry, via import-substitution and autonomation of the Russian information space. While, partly logical, this approach still looks flawed because of, as noted above, the authorities' Soviet-legacy inclination toward overemphasizing military requirements and limiting commercial competition.

Second, though presenting a clear framework of which agencies/institutions are responsible for aspects of Russian information security, the Doctrine failed to differentiate the separation of powers between these structures. Even more important, however, is the issue of responsibility-sharing between the "military" and "civilian" branches when it comes to ensuring Russian information security, not to mention the question of the supervision of their respective responsibilities. The current Doctrine ascribes responsibility for domestic information security to every agency/institution/organization/individual involved in this domain, which seems rather dubious and probably not feasible in terms of management and coordination.

Impressive as they may initially appear, Russian policies in the domain of information security will likely be very effective in the short to medium term, but perhaps less so over a longer period. Ambitious projects undertaken in the Soviet Union and the Russian Federation have one historically common feature: frequently effective in the beginning, those initiatives ultimately tended to be diluted due to a number of objective (lack of resources, red tape and excessive bureaucratization) as well as subjective (changing posture of political leadership on the issue and/or rivalries between institutions/agencies in charge) factors. This has generally led to decreasing effectiveness of the initiatives. On the basis of current trends visible in Russia—aging political elites, growing corruption and an excessive tilt toward militarization—the likelihood of implementing all the points of the Doctrine in practical terms looks improbable. The most likely scenario will be for Russia to choose the most essential aspects (primarily related to the development of offensive capabilities in the domain of information security) and prioritizing these over other, "less important" elements.

Notes

[1] For more information see: Igor Panarin, *Pervaya mirovaya informatsionnaya voyna. Razval SSSR*, (Saint Petersburg: Piter, 2010).

[2] The text is available here (in Russian): *Ukaz Prezidenta Rossiyskoy Federacii ot 05.12.2016 № 646 "Ob utverzhdenii Doktriny informatsionnoy bezopasnosti Rossiyskoy Federacii,"* December 6, 2016, Moscow, Kremlin, http://publication.pravo.gov.ru/Document/View/0001201612060002.

[3] Mariya Vasilyeva, "Informatsionnaya bezopasnost Rossii v usloviyah globalizatsii," *Vestnik MGLU* 25, 604 (2010): 31.

[4] "Munkhenskaya rech Putina," YouTube, accessed June 18, 2018, https://www.youtube.com/watch?v=bMnVVuoQiUo.

[5] Incidentally, the terrible performance of Russian media during this conflict made President Yeltsin publicly (and for the first time in Russia's post-1991 history) admit that nuclear deterrence along with measures in terms of information warfare were two prime tasks of Russian national security. For more information see: Igor Panarin, "Sistema vneshnepoliticheskoy propagandy Rossii," Panarin.com, accessed November 17, 2017, http://panarin.com/info_voina/88-sistema-vneshnepoliticheskoy-propagandy-rossii.html.

[6] Yuliy Nisnevich, "Gosudarstvennaya informatsionnaya politika Rossii segodnya I zavtra," *Informatsionnoe obshchestvo* 2 (1999): 4-9, http://emag.iis.ru/arc/infosoc/emag.nsf/BPA/8f09435324753a65c32568ba004420d3.

[7] Lev Roytman, "Informatsionnaya bezopasnost: ne v krasote, a v polnote," *Radio Svoboda*, September 19, 2000, https://www.svoboda.org/a/24202675.html.

[8] *Doktrina informacionnoy bezopasnosti Rossiyskoy Federacii (utverzhdennaya Prezidentom RF September 9, 2000, N Pr-1895)*, For more information see: http://base.garant.ru/182535/.

[9] Ekaterina Mikhaylovskaya, "Besplatnoe RIA byvaet tolko…" *Grani.ru*, December 17, 2000, https://graniru.org/Society/Media/Freepress/m.2820.html.

[10] "V Rossii sozdan propagandistskiy telekanal dlya inostrantsev," *Lenta.ru*, June 7, 2005, https://lenta.ru/news/2005/06/07/channel/.

[11] Igor Panarin, *Informatsionnaya voyna i Rossiya*, (Moscow: Mir bezopasnosti, 2000), 160.

[12] L. Polskikh, "O primenenii globalnoy kompyuternoy seti internet v interesakh informatsionnogo protivoborstva," *Zarubezhnoe voennoe obozrenie*, № 7 (2005).

[13] A. Manoylo, A. Petrenko, D. Frolov, *Gosudarstvennaya informatsionnaya politika v usloviyakh informatsionno-psikhologicheskoy voyny*, (Moscow: MIFI, 2003).

[14] Andrey Manoylo, *Gosudarstvennaya informatsionnaya politika v osobykh usloviyakh*, (Moscow: MIFI, 2003), 246.

[15] Irina Vasilenko, "Informatsionnaya voyna kak faktor mirovoy politiki," *Gosudarstvennaya sluzhba*, № 3, (2009): 81.

[16] For example, by 2014 the pool of Internet users in Russia reached 80 million people, whereas Russia occupied 6th global position (and 1st in Europe) in terms of number of active Internet users.

[17] "Doktrina informatsionnoy bezopasnosti RF. Dosie," *TASS*, December 6, 2016, http://tass.ru/info/3845810.

[18] Alexei Maruev, "Informatsionnaya bezopasnost Rossii i osnovy organizatsii informatsionnogo protivoborstva," *Problemny Analiz i Gosudarstvenno-Upravlencheskoe Proektirovanie*, №1, T.3 (2010): 49.

[19] Ibid.

[20] Evgeniy Kulikov, "Stikhiynye protsessy internet-kommunikatsy kak faktor ugrozy informatsionnoy bezopasnosti Rossii," *Usloviya i perspektivy natsionalnoy bezopasnosti sovremennoy Rossii*, (Moscow, 2011): 132.

[21] E. Andreev, V. Sergeev, "Problemy formirovaniya kulturnoy bezopasnosti v sovremennykh usloviyakh sotsialnykh izmeneniy," *Usloviya i perspektivy natsionalnoy bezopasnosti sovremennoy Rossii*, (Moscow, 2011): 132.

[22] Valeri Gerasimov, "Tsennost nauki v predvidenii," *Voenno-Promyshlennyi Kurier*, № 8 (476), February 27, 2013, https://www.vpk-news.ru/articles/14632.

[23] Sergey Sukhankin, "Russia Playing Catch-Up in Cyber Security," *Eurasia Daily Monitor*, Volume: 13, Issue: 172, October 26, 2016, https://jamestown.org/program/russia-playing-catch-cyber-security/.

[24] "Putin zastupilsya za Internet," *Tvzvezda.ru*, October 1, 2014, https://tvzvezda.ru/news/vstrane_i_mire/content/201410011040-fucn.htm.

[25] "Voennaya doktrina Rossiyskoy Federatsii," *Rossiyskaya gazeta*, Federalny vypusk №6570 (298), paragraph 12, December 30, 2014, https://rg.ru/2014/12/30/doktrina-dok.html.

[26] Elena Chernenko, "SSHA opredelilis s virtualnymi vragami," *Kommersant.ru*, April 30, 2015 https://www.kommersant.ru/doc/2720392.

[27] "Rossiya zanyala pervoe mesto v mire po gosudarstvennym zatratam na propaganda," *Pravda-tv.ru*, September 14, 2013, http://www.pravda-tv.ru/2013/09/14/26749/rossiya-zanyala-pervoe-mesto-v-mire-po-gosudarstvenny-m-zatratam-na-propagandu.

[28] "Ukaz Prezidenta Rossiyskoy Federatsii, December 31, 2015, № 683 "O strategii natsionalnoy bezopasnosti Rossiyskoy Federatsii," point 12, *Rossiyskaya gazeta*, December 31, 2015, https://rg.ru/2015/12/31/nac-bezopasnost-site-dok.html.

[29] "European Parliament resolution of 23 November 2016 on EU strategic communication to counteract propaganda against it by third parties (2016/2030(INI))," *EU strategic communication to counteract anti-EU propaganda by third parties*, (Brussels, November 23, 2016), accessed December 1, 2017, http://www.europarl.europa.eu/sides/getDoc.do?type=TA&reference=P8-TA-2016-0441&format=XML&language=EN.

[30] "Putin o rezolyutsii Evroparlamenta: khochu pozdravit zhurnalistov RT i Sputnik," *RIA novosti*, November 23, 2016, https://ria.ru/society/20161123/1482009865.html.

[31] *Poslanie Prezidenta Federalnomu Sobraniyu*, December 1, 2016, Moscow, Kremlin. Available at: http://kremlin.ru/events/president/news/53379.

[32] *Ukaz Prezidenta Rossiyskoy Federatsii ot 30.11.2016 № 640 "Ob utverzhdenii Kontsepcii vneshney politiki Rossiyskoy Federatsii,"* December 1, 2016, Moscow, Kremlin. Available at: http://publication.pravo.gov.ru/Document/View/0001201612010045.

[33] Federalnaya Sluzhba bezopasnosti Rossiyskoy Federatsii, *Inostrannye spetssluzhby gotovyat kiberataki, napravlennye na destabilizatsiyu finansovoy sistemy Rossii*, December 2, 2016, http://www.fsb.ru/fsb/press/message/single.htm%21id%3D10438041%40fsbMessage.html.

[34] "Doktrina informatsionnoy bezopasnosti RF. Dosie," *TASS*, December 6, 2016: http://tass.ru/info/3845810.

[35] *Doctrine of Information Security of the Russian Federation*, point 1, December 5, 2016, Moscow, Kremlin, http://www.mid.ru/en/foreign_policy/official_documents/-/asset_publisher/CptICkB6BZ29/content/id/2563163.

[36] *Doctrine of Information Security of the Russian Federation*, point 2, sub-point a.

[37] *Doctrine of Information Security of the Russian Federation*, point 8.

[38] *Doctrine of Information Security of the Russian Federation*, sub-point a.

[39] *Doctrine of Information Security of the Russian Federation,* sub-point c.

[40] *Doctrine of Information Security of the Russian Federation,* sub-point e.

[41] *Doctrine of Information Security of the Russian Federation,* sub-point d.

[42] *Doctrine of Information Security of the Russian Federation,* sub-point b.

[43] "Pochemu v rossiyskikh gorodakh sutki – massovye evakuatsii (eto ne ucheniya)," *Ura.ru,* September 12, 2017, https://ura.news/articles/1036272216?story_id=390.

[44] *Doctrine of Information Security of the Russian Federation,* point 2, sub-point b.

[45] *Doctrine of Information Security of the Russian Federation,* point 2, sub-point c.

[46] *Doctrine of Information Security of the Russian Federation,* point 2, sub-points d–g.

[47] *Doctrine of Information Security of the Russian Federation,* sub-point h.

[48] *Doctrine of Information Security of the Russian Federation,* point 11.

[49] *Doctrine of Information Security of the Russian Federation,* point 15.

[50] *Doctrine of Information Security of the Russian Federation,* points 12–13.

[51] In accordance with the "Yarovaya Package" (two pieces of legislation introduced on July 6, 2016) the dividing line between such notions as "terrorism" and "extremism," as well as the way these concepts are construed in Russia, has been blurred, leaving room for various readings and interpretations that could be used by the state in a manner deemed appropriate.

[52] *Doctrine of Information Security of the Russian Federation,* points 17, 18, 19.

[53] *Doctrine of Information Security of the Russian Federation,* point 12.

[54] Best-known examples are: The "Russian World" Foundation (2007), Rossotrudnichestvo (2008), The Alexander Gorchakov Public Diplomacy Fund (2010).

[55] Alexei Zakvasin, Anastasiya Shlyakhtina,"Pentagon odoleli pentabaytami: kak rabotaet noveyshaya rossiyskaya Sistema upravleniya oboronoy," *RT,* December 1, 2016, https://russian.rt.com/russia/article/337564-armiya-oborona-upravlenie-

tehnologii.; "W natsionalnom tsentre upravleniya oboronoii proshlo rasshirennoje zasedanije Kollegii Minoborony Rossii", Ministerstvo Oborony Rossijskoj Federatsii, December 22, 2016 https://function.mil.ru/news_page/country/more.htm?id=12106806@egNews.

[56] "Natsionalny tsentr upravleniya oboronoy RF budet rabotat dlya vsekh stran ODKB," *Tvzvezda.ru*, December 23, 2015, https://tvzvezda.ru/news/vstrane_i_mire/content/201412232053-sdcf.htm.

[57] *Doctrine of Information Security of the Russian Federation*, point 20.

[58] *Doctrine of Information Security of the Russian Federation*, point 21.

[59] Sergey Sukhankin, "Russia Introduces EW Spetsnaz to Western Military District," *Eurasia Daily Monitor*, Volume: 14, Issue: 143, November 7, 2017, https://jamestown.org/program/russia-introduces-ew-spetsnaz-western-military-district/.

[60] *Doctrine of Information Security of the Russian Federation*, sub-point e.

[61] Sergey Sukhankin, "Russia's 'Youth Army': Sovietization, Militarization or Radicalization?" *Eurasia Daily Monitor*, Volume: 13, Issue: 180, November 9, 2016, https://jamestown.org/program/russias-youth-army-sovietization-militarization-radicalization/.

[62] *Doctrine of Information Security of the Russian Federation*, point 22.

[63] *Doctrine of Information Security of the Russian Federation*, point 23.

[64] *Doctrine of Information Security of the Russian Federation*, sub-point a.

[65] *Doctrine of Information Security of the Russian Federation*, sub-point j.

[66] *Doctrine of Information Security of the Russian Federation*, sub-points b–d.

[67] *Doctrine of Information Security of the Russian Federation*, sub-point e.

[68] *Doctrine of Information Security of the Russian Federation*, point 24.

[69] *Doctrine of Information Security of the Russian Federation*, point 27.

[70] *Doctrine of Information Security of the Russian Federation*, sub-point e.

[71] "Master-klass po kiber-bezopasnosti proshel v shkole № 1770," *Nagatinsky zaton*, September 27, 2017, http://gazeta-nagatinsky-zaton.ru/2017/09/27/32936/.

[72] "RBK-TV potrollil Yandex, Kaspersky Lab I kiber-druzhyny kazakov," *Roem.ru*, November 25, 2016, https://roem.ru/25-11-2016/237089/rbc-kazachiy-yandex/.

[73] *Doctrine of Information Security of the Russian Federation*, points 28–29.

[74] *Doctrine of Information Security of the Russian Federation*, point 29, sub-point e.

[75] *Doctrine of Information Security of the Russian Federation*, point 30.

[76] *Doctrine of Information Security of the Russian Federation*, point 32.

[77] *Doctrine of Information Security of the Russian Federation*, point 33.

[78] For more information see: "Kiberdruzhyna" *Liga Bezopasngo Interneta*, accessed November 6, 2017, http://www.ligainternet.ru/liga/activity-cyber.php.

[79] *Doctrine of Information Security of the Russian Federation*, point 34, sub-point c.

[80] *Doctrine of Information Security of the Russian Federation*, point 35.

[81] *Doctrine of Information Security of the Russian Federation*, point 36.

[82] *Doctrine of Information Security of the Russian Federation*, point 37.

[83] "Novaya doktrina informatsionnoy bezopasnosti RF: borba s vcherashnimi ugrozami," *BBC*, December 7, 2016, http://www.bbc.com/russian/features-38225725.

[84] "Putin ogorazhyvaetsya ot mira `informatsionnoy bezopasnostyu`," *Vestnik CIVITAS*, December 7, 2016, http://vestnikcivitas.ru/news/4024.

[85] "Ekspert: Doktrina informbezopasnosti pomozhet uprezhdat kiberataki na Rossiyu," *RIA novosti*, December 6, 2016, https://ria.ru/defense_safety/20161206/1482968882.html.

[86] "V Gosdume rasskazali o preimushchestvah novoy doktriny," *RIA novosti*, December 6, 2016, https://ria.ru/defense_safety/20161206/1482931915.html.

[87] Sovet Federatsii, *Kontseptsiya strategii kiberbezopasnosti Rossiyskoy Federatsii (Proekt),* accessed November 20, 2017, http://council.gov.ru/media/files/41d4b3dfbdb25cea8a73.pdf.

[88] Valeri Gerasimov, "Po opytu Sirii", *Voenno-Promyshlennyi Kurier* № 9 (624), March 9, 2016, https://vpk-news.ru/articles/29579.

[89] See: Sergey Sukhankin, "From "Bridge of Cooperation" to A2/AD "Bubble": Dangerous Transformation of Kaliningrad Oblast," *The Journal of Slavic Military Studies,* Taylor & Francis. February 9, 2018, pp. 15–36, https://www.tandfonline.com/eprint/RBBXE9ajSWR9ZeEzdtTe/full.

[90] Nikiforov: Doktrina informbezopasnosti potrebuet vnesti popravki v zakony, *RIA Novosti,* December 6, 2016, https://ria.ru/politics/20161206/1482957170.html.

[91] *Ukaz Prezidenta Rossiyskoy Federatsii ot 09.05.2017 № 203 "O Strategii razvitiya informatsionnogo obshchestva v Rossiyskoy Federatsii na 2017 - 2030 gody,"* May 10, 2017, Moscow, Kremlin. Available at: http://publication.pravo.gov.ru/Document/View/0001201705100002?index=0&rangeSize=1.

[92] *Federalny zakon ot 26.07.2017 № 187-ФЗ "O bezopasnosti kriticheskoy informatsionnoy infrastruktury Rossiyskoy Federatsii,"* July 26, 2017, Moscow, Kremlin. Available at: http://publication.pravo.gov.ru/Document/View/0001201707260023.

[93] Henry R. Lieberman, "Soviet Devising a Computer Net for State Planning," *New York Times,* December 13, 1973, http://www.nytimes.com/1973/12/13/archives/soviet-devising-a-computer-net-for-state-planning-big-network-in-us.html.

Part III

Lessons Learned and Domestic Implications

9. Deciphering the Lessons Learned by the Russian Armed Forces in Ukraine, 2014–2017

Roger N. McDermott

Introduction

The senior leadership of Russia's Armed Forces has a long-established tradition of studying the military's involvement in conflicts and identifying appropriate lessons. This offers for the high command a deeper and more insightful understanding of the issues facing force development, modernization and the use of strategy and tactics.[1] Russia's intervention in Ukraine in early 2014, annexing Crimea in response to the Euro-Maidan revolution in Kyiv, and its subsequent fomenting of instability in southeastern Ukraine resulted in the most significant deterioration in US-Russia relations since the end of the Cold War. The Russian Armed Forces have been involved at varying levels of intensity in Donbas for almost four years. During this period, Russia's military high command has used the conflict in Ukraine to experiment with new systems, deploying forces on a rotational basis in the theater of operations, as well as training, equipping and supplying the various separatist groups. Undoubtedly, as in its previous experience of military conflict, the General Staff has identified and drawn lessons from this intervention. However, much of this is masked by the official Kremlin policy of denying Russia's involvement in Ukraine.

Indeed, reflecting on the Russian Armed Forces' involvement in conflicts since the disintegration of the Union of Soviet Socialist Republics (USSR) in 1991, the Russia-Georgia War in August 2008 yielded a vast deluge of information that made it possible to extrapolate the details of what the General Staff might learn. This helped to facilitate the reform of the Armed Forces that ensued shortly afterward.[2] The Ukraine conflict is entirely different. The fighting may have exposed the need for some tactical revision, and the experimentation could have offered deeper insights into existing and prototype systems trialed in combat. However, the lessons identified and learned officially remain shrouded in secrecy. That said, the lessons from Donbas appear to be part of a larger picture that explains Moscow's interest in high-technology assets for modern warfare, especially linked to force enablers and force multipliers.[3]

The following chapter seeks to unlock some of this by using extensive reporting on the conflict to decipher the type of lessons that the Russian General Staff may have drawn from the conflict to date. It argues that these need to be understood in the context of the condition and posture of Russia's conventional Armed Forces on the eve of the conflict in order to gauge the underlying reason for a subsequent shift in the organization of the Ground Forces and modifications to command and control (C2), especially over large forces.[4] It concludes that in terms of military basing closer to the Ukraine border, reorganizing land power to include a small number of divisions and reprioritizing the role of armor in combat operations, these were drawn from the conflict experience, as well as the periods of force build-up on the Ukraine border.[5]

Russia's Armed Forces on the Eve of the Conflict

While Russia's conventional Armed Forces remain a pale shadow of their Soviet predecessor, since the collapse of the USSR there were numerous failed attempts to reform the military. Often such reform efforts fell victim to institutional inertia, were consigned to limited experiments, or simply failed to achieve any substantive progress toward implementation. Yet, Russia's experience of small wars, from its first intervention in Chechnya (1994–1996) to the Five Day War with Georgia in August 2008, all presented operational challenges for the Soviet-legacy forces and impressed upon the political-military leadership that these structures had struggled to cope with the demands of such conflicts. On the eve of the Second Chechnya Conflict in 1999, Vladimir Putin was shocked to learn that Russia could only muster a maximum of 65,000 combat-ready forces.[6] Russia's military power was mitigated and hampered by preserving a system designed to wage a large-scale war in Europe that never happened. The decline in combat capability and combat readiness seemed to contradict the high aspirations of the Russian security elite and undermine claims to Russia's great power status.[7]

Strands of the Cold War–era tendency to exaggerate the strength of Russian military power remain apparent in contemporary analyses; a trend boosted by the Ukraine crisis that emerged in early 2014. For some states bordering Russia, any effort Moscow made to improve the country's military is treated with concern.[8] Equally, for those with an awareness of the past futile reform campaigns, there was skepticism as to whether this fresh attempt might avoid the same fate. Nevertheless, unlike previous bids to implement reform in Russia's Armed Forces, the plans first outlined by the political-military leadership in Moscow in September and October 2008 to fundamentally transform and modernize its conventional Armed Forces were, in fact, acted upon. In essence, this removed the very heart of the Soviet legacy forces by abandoning the mass-mobilization principle (still notionally in place at the time) and its skeleton or cadre units, moving instead to "permanent readiness" brigades fully staffed with well-trained officers and soldiers. Achieving the structural reorganization appeared relatively simple, particularly the transition from a division-based system to a new brigade-centric structure. But deeper long-term challenges in addressing issues of mentality and military culture, including corruption and abuse of office in relation to the officer corps, proved to be significantly more formidable for a defense ministry with no previous experience of planning or conducting such systemic reform.[9]

The 'New Look' Russian Army

Launching the reform so soon after the Five Day War in August 2008 certainly implied pre-planning, but does not testify to the quality of such planning. Initial official statements outlining the reform indicated broad designs and some specific aims, but it required a great deal of piecing together to assemble a larger picture of what the defense ministry intended. The then-president, Dmitry Medvedev, attempted such an outline during his visit to the Donguz training range, in Orenburg, on September 26, 2008. Medvedev had earlier approved *Perspektivny oblik Vooruzhennykh Sil RF i pervoocherednye mery po ego formirovaniu na 2009–2020 gody* (The Future Outlook of the Russian Federation Armed Forces and Priorities for its Creation in the period 2009–2020). However, the presidential summary of the impending reform, which he linked to the war with Georgia, arguing that future conflicts could erupt suddenly, was by no means a complete statement. Medvedev told military district commanders that the future capability of the Armed Forces would be determined by five factors: improving the organizational structure by transforming the divisions into brigades, abandoning the "mass mobilization" principle and adopting instead "permanent readiness" status; enhancing C2, including reducing the number of tiers to three (joint strategic command/military district, army, brigade), thus cutting the number of billets; reforming the system of personnel training as well as the military education system; equipping the Armed Forces with the latest high-technology weapons and equipment to promote air superiority, delivering precision strikes against ground and maritime targets and ensuring operational force deployment; and raising the social status of military personnel by vastly increasing salaries and offering a broader range of social support packages.[10]

More detail, though again only partial, was offered on October 14, 2008, by then–defense minister Anatoly Serdyukov. Following a briefing delivered by the defense minister to a closed session of the ministry's collegium, Serdyukov discussed the reform with a select group of journalists and spoke for a few minutes on *Zvezda TV*. He characterized this initiative as giving the military a "new look," which he stated involved speeding up the reduction of the overall strength of the Armed Forces to "one million," decreasing officer posts from 355,000 to 150,000, expanding the number of junior officers, carrying out major cuts in the defense ministry's central administrative staff, abolishing mass mobilization and divisions to form instead permanent readiness brigades, moving to a three-tiered command structure, drastically cutting the number of units, especially in the Ground Forces, as well as reforming military education. The Strategic Rocket Forces (*Raketnyye Voyska Strategicheskogo Naznacheniya—RVSN*) would be left largely unaffected, while some organizational change was envisaged for the Airborne Forces (*Vozdushno Desantnye Voiska—VDV*)—though they successfully preserved the division-based system in the VDV.[11]

Official statements concerning the aims of the unfolding reform were often at complete variance during the first three years of its implementation. Thus, Medvedev's explanation of the key features of the reform differed depending on the target audience and the timing of his speech. Medvedev's original "five key tasks" were notably different by March 11, 2011, suggesting these now included military procurement targets (achieving 70 percent new weapons and equipment by 2020), improved and joint C2, developing a unified ballistic missile defense system, enhancing border security, particularly in the Russian Far East (despite the ongoing border security challenges stemming from Afghanistan-related issues), and improving the officers corps.[12]

Army General Nikolai Makarov, then-chief of the General Staff, also demonstrated signs of vacillation, particularly on the issues of contract personnel and manpower. The then-commander-in-chief (CINC) of the Ground Forces, Colonel General Aleksandr Postnikov, suggested that downsizing the officer corps should not stop at 15 percent but continue to 9 percent, seemingly paying scant regard to 60,000 officers in the process. More remarkably, Serdyukov regularly departed from any sense of rationality when it came to explaining his reform aims. The defense minister at one point argued that no officers would be sacked, only posts would be reduced, while later declaring the downsizing complete and ahead of schedule. Serdyukov's grasp of whatever agenda may have existed was not only slippery, but he even suggested to brigade commanders in December 2010 that their input was required as it might prove to be necessary to "adjust the entire program on military reform."[13]

Some of these "adjustments" occurred after the defense leadership of Serdyukov and Makarov was replaced in November 2012 by Sergei Shoigu and Valery Gerasimov, respectively. The most notable changes involved the gradual limited reintroduction of divisions and the Soviet tradition of "snap inspections" of the Armed Forces.[14] The reform as such proved conceptually elusive, lacking coherence and reflecting at times chaotic and poor planning. Still, it is possible to discern some fundamental weaknesses related to manpower issues. Additionally, there has been a consistent theme of improving C2 and especially aiming to introduce a new unified automated C2 system as the state seeks to develop network-centric approaches to warfare, while more loosely trying to enhance combat capability (raising the quantity of modern equipment and weapons to 70 percent by 2020) and combat readiness (largely based on the readiness levels in the brigades).[15]

Command and Control

After much delay, the authorities announced the planned overhaul of the existing six military districts (MD) in April 2010. And during the operational-strategic exercise Vostok 2010, the replacement system was tested. However, the process was not completed until December 1, 2014, with the introduction of the Northern (or Arctic) Joint Strategic Command. The three-tiered simplified C2 structure was trialed in June 2010, with a declared target of forming four new military districts/joint strategic commands (*obyedinennyye strategicheskoye komandovanie*—OSK) by December 1, 2010. The new districts/commands were formed on four strategic axes: Western (headquarters in St. Petersburg), Eastern (headquarters in Khabarovsk), Central (Yekaterinburg) and Southern (Rostov-on-Don). Western MD/OSK was based on the Moscow and Leningrad MDs, and the Baltic and Northern Fleets. Eastern MD/OSK comprised of the former Far East MD, the eastern part of Siberian MD and the Pacific Fleet. Central MD/OSK included the western part of the Siberian MD and the Volga-Urals MD, while Southern MD/OSK merged the North Caucasus MD and the Black Sea Fleet and the Caspian Flotilla.[16]

In peacetime, these commands would function as MDs and transition to OSKs during military operations. Since their introduction, it appears that the operational control of forces is conducted by the OSKs and the day-to-day housekeeping activities is in the purview of the MDs; simultaneously. High-command elements of the Ground Forces, Air Force, Air Defense Forces as well as the Military-Maritime Fleet (*Voyenno-Morskoy Flot*—VMF) became structural subunits of the General Staff, and the command process was simplified by reducing the number of stages orders passed through from sixteen to four. General Makarov noted that the OSK commanders would have a much wider responsibility: "We shall be proposing to create, on the basis of the six MDs, four OSKs whose commanders will be in charge of all manpower and resources deployed in their areas, including the navy, air force and air defense forces. Moreover, these forces would be directly, not operationally, subordinate to the commanders." Part of the justification for this change was to place all military and security formations on these territories under a single command; in theory, during operations, such formations—extending to emergency and interior ministries or the Federal Security Service (FSB)—would be subordinate to the OSK. By September 2011 the operational-strategic exercise Tsentr 2011 rehearsed and refined such inter-agency coordination, though not without its peculiar problems, as these structures often used widely differing communications systems. Meanwhile, the VDV continued to be subordinate to the General Staff. This theme intensified under Shoigu and Gerasimov, as defense planners sought to improve C2.[17]

Overhauling and simplifying command structures formed part of the more challenging reform of C2, which had not only been exposed as a critical operational weakness in the Russia-Georgia War in August 2008, but time and again the political leadership and top brass had promised to revolutionize the C2 system. This meant digitizing all communications equipment and speeding up the work of introducing a "unified" automated C2 system throughout the Armed Forces. The strategy was also supported politically, and pressure was placed on the defense industry to cooperate with commanders in completing the design work and overcoming technical problems to facilitate the introduction of the long-awaited automated C2 system: the Unified System for Command and Control at the Tactical Level (*Yedinaya Sistema Upravleniya v Takticheskom Zvene*—YeSU TZ).[18]

Curiously, the automated system was publicized as "unified" and often presented by officials as a panacea that would guarantee immediate improvement in the speed of decision making and dramatically boost C2 while marking a significant milestone on the long path to developing network-centric warfare capabilities. Nonetheless, the VDV evidently had the makings of an alternative system, integrating their existing Polet-K with an advanced

Andromeda-D automated C2 system. In 2011, the Andromeda-D was introduced experimentally into the 76th Airborne Division, in Pskov, with plans to eventually outfit the entire VDV by 2015.

The mobile/fixed automated C2 system is under development for the VDV by the Communications and Command and Control Systems NII (Scientific Research Institute). Its production facilities consist of the Ryazan Radio Plant, Kaluga Telegraph Equipment Plant, Elektroavtomatika OAO (Open Joint Stock Company) (Stavropol) and Volgo NPO (Scientific Production Association) OAO. It is mounted on the chassis of BTR-D airborne armored personnel carriers, or BMD-2 and BMD-4 airborne fighting vehicles. Andromeda-D can support a wide range of communications packages to transmit information using traditional radio channels or high-speed networks, and its designers say it also has a state-of-the-art navigation system. Lieutenant General Nikolai Ignatov, the chief of staff and first deputy commander of the VDV, believed this would reduce the time involved in military decision making by up to 50 percent. Nevertheless, its designers reported that training programs held in the VDV to train personnel in using the system required around one year for ensuring sufficiently high standards; suggesting there would be profound problems in integrating the Andromeda-D and conscripts serving for only twelve months. The solution to this was to drastically increase the proportion of *kontraktniki* serving in the military.[19]

Defense ministry planners underestimated the extent to which introducing such technology will compel further revision of the manning structure. When the elite airborne forces are fully equipped with their own automated C2 system, how would this work with twelve-month serving conscripts? Would old and new C2 systems co-exist? Equally, how successfully would the VDV's system integrate with the YeSU TZ?

Once the design issues in the YeSU TZ were finally resolved, specialists estimate that the domestic defense industry had the capacity to equip five brigades annually; thus, after six consecutive years of introducing the automated C2 system, more than half the existing brigades would remain non-automated.[20] Many of these issues were obviously unresolved in the transition to the new defense leadership and were present in Russia's Armed Forces on the eve of conflict in Ukraine.

General Makarov, and other leading senior officers, consistently promoted the automated C2 and the adoption of network-centric warfare capabilities as central to the reform and modernization of Russia's Armed Forces. The future capability to conduct sixth-generation or non-contact warfare utilizing command, control, communications, computers, intelligence, surveillance and reconnaissance (C4ISR) became a guiding principle among the leading advocates of reform. The former CINC of the Ground Forces, General Postnikov, introduced conferences on network-centric warfare in the Combined-Arms Academy in Moscow and placed great emphasis on the capacity of the YeSU TZ to revolutionize the speed of the military decision-making process. Thus, this innovation would enhance the algorithm of battle management and allow a brigade commander to transmit his decisions in real time to his battalion commander displayed on his personal computer. Resolving the design flaws, largely linked to its lack of user-friendly graphics, has taken time, resulting in recrimination between the defense ministry and defense industry. By the fall of 2010, Dmitry Kandaurov, a Moscow-based expert on automated C2, examined some of the design problems related to the YeSU TZ in a series of articles in *Nezavisimoye Voyennoye Obozreniye*. These observations noted that the critical design challenge confronting the defense industry was the high-intensity graphics in the software, but the author placed these complexities in a broader context of improving the overall efficiency of C2. Yet, by August 2011, Kandaurov questioned whether the existing plans for introducing automated C2 would actually result in any real improvement.[21]

Military Manpower

The over-emphasis upon structural reorganization and technology at the expense of addressing issues concerning the future of military manpower exposed perhaps one of the single greatest weaknesses in the reform planning. These were key challenges facing the Shoigu-Gerasimov defense tandem, and it is primarily the result of an assessment of the Ukraine conflict that led to formulating answers. Prior to launching the reform, there was no serious consideration of whether the new brigade-based structures should be staffed by entirely contract-based personnel or mixed-manning retaining conscription, or indeed how to raise the standards of either personnel type, which according to the General Staff were woefully inadequate. This also permeated other central aspects of reform aims: was there a vision for a reformed officer corps? How would officers be separated from the notoriously high corruption levels? Would the defense ministry and General Staff agree on a model for the future development of non-commissioned officers (NCO)?

To begin with, given the inability of defense planners in Moscow to break the cycle of discussion on the merits of conscription opposed to a professional military manpower system, there was much evidence of constant switching of priority in this area. Commanders and senior officers openly admitted that the standards among conscripts were very low, beset by ill-discipline and institutionalized hazing or *dedovshchina*. This phenomenon seemed to perplex the defense ministry leadership, who were unable to understand why it had survived and grown even after reducing the length of conscript service to twelve months by 2008; the expected dividends simply never appeared. Equally, there was a consensus that standards among contract personnel (*kontraktniki*) were anything but desirable, reflecting the fact that many were bullied into signing contracts and simply wished to leave the Armed Forces.[22]

In the period 2008–2011, the "vision" for the precise form of "reformed" manpower in the new brigades went through constant zigzagging. Sometimes, the possibility of adopting an all-volunteer force and abandoning conscription was raised, then reversed or denied; *kontraktniki* were derided for simply being inadequate, but no plans were calibrated to redress this situation; advocates of the conscription system demanded continued high numbers of conscripts; consideration was given to increasing the maximum age to draft citizens from 27 to 30 only to realize this might fuel corruption and evasion. In an apparent policy vacuum, influential Russian military experts close to the reform even advocated learning from and adopting a variant of the Swiss militia system, without reference to how this might work.[23]

It became apparent that these larger manpower issues would not result in any clear policy direction on whether to pursue real professionalizing of the force structure or to persevere a mixed-manning system. However, the Shoigu-Gerasimov defense leadership consistently continued wider efforts to raise the numbers of *kontraktniki* serving in the Armed Forces without promising to ever eliminate conscription, which remains the key recruitment pool for the *kontraktniki*, despite efforts to recruit directly from the population by using mobile recruitment centers. In this context, on the eve of conflict in Ukraine, the General Staff had returned to relying on the forming of battalion tactical groups (BTG), and these remain the cornerstones of Russia's land power.

Ignoring the large body of evidence concerning the impact of Russia's demographic crisis on a dwindling conscription pool during the early stages of the reform, the authorities also exaggerated claims about the size of the Armed Forces and failed to resolve how the "permanent readiness brigades" could work in real terms with a mix of contract personnel and twelve-month serving conscripts. During this policy calamity, it was painfully obvious to officers that, with conscripts in very large numbers serving for twelve months and leaving the brigades twice annually (as the drafting process occurs in the spring and fall each year), combat capability and readiness levels were not particularly high. Moreover, the constant reference to "mobilization" in recent Russian security documents seems to exaggerate the state's capacity to generate genuinely trained reservists in a time of an escalating crisis.[24]

The Role of Russia's Armed Forces in Ukraine: Lessons Identified From Donbas

The Russian Armed Forces' involvement in Ukraine, especially in the latter country's southeastern regions, provides a unique and highly problematic experience for the military in terms of open discussion on its possible lessons. Arguably, this was never the "type" of conflict that would prove popular among the Russian officer corps. It has not yielded opportunities for career advancement and offered fewer challenges than the operations in Syria. Not coincidentally, of the five commanders in charge of the OSKs, four have combat experience gained in Syria. Of course, this is rooted in the policy of "plausible deniability," with the Russian government officially claiming non-involvement in the crisis, or not officially recognizing the presence of any Russian military personnel on the territory of Ukraine. While this deniability has been openly decimated by international media reporting and coverage by the analytical community, it does present serious issues concerning the effort to establish the possible lessons drawn from the conflict by Russia's top brass.[25] Unlike, for example, professional Russian military experts or even serving officers offering comment on the weaknesses exposed by the campaigns in Chechnya or in Georgia in August 2008, the deniability barrier on Ukraine means that the publicly available insights into how Russian officers perceived various aspects of the conflict, what the lessons were, or even to what extent the conflict is shaping Russian military thinking prove elusive.[26]

This elusive nature of the Russian military's lessons from Donbas is complicated still further due to a number of perception issues. That is to say, the entire conflict—possibly unlike Moscow's involvement in post-Soviet era conflicts—became highly politicized among governments and analysts. This is reflected also within Russian coverage, with reputable experts writing articles knowing full well that the Russian military was active in Donbas, but having to couch their analyses with great caution.[27] An innate tendency also existed in Western government and analytical circles to identify Russia's "New Generation Warfare" (dubbed by some as the "Gerasimov doctrine") or to seek to apply labels to better understand how Russian forces and their proxies were conducting operations.[28] At an early stage, many commentators rushed to dub the Russian actions in Ukraine as representing a breakthrough "Gerasimov doctrine," which avoided deeper analysis of what was actually taking place, misled governments, and misrepresented Russian military science. This "hybrid" theme, however, was never present within Russian specialist coverage and remains entirely alien in its coverage.[29]

Equally, many Russian analysts were sheltered from the full extent to which Moscow had interfered in Donbas. But the professional military journals are also largely silent in assessing the numerous challenges and experiments that emerged during the varied course of the conflict. Considerable cross-fertilization is apparent between the "lessons learned" approach based on the experience of Syria and Ukraine: both are important, and the Syria operations have clearly boosted both Russian combat readiness and, more importantly, operational experience.[30] Nonetheless, the experience drawn from Ukraine has served to influence Russia's force posture and the organizational structure of the Ground Forces.

In many ways, attempting to decipher the "lessons learned" from Russia's military involvement in Donbas is like looking at shadows on walls. Clearly, there is a much sharper and deeper picture of the operational environment and the tactics applied in Donbas known only to the Russian General Staff and within elite defense and security circles in Moscow.[31] Yet, despite these problems, some observations can be made concerning the most likely lessons drawn from the conflict, and the crossover into how operations were conducted in Syria.

These lessons loosely divide into the following categories: direct combat operations, combat support and service support, and command-and-control issues stemming from force build-ups on numerous occasions near Ukraine's border. At a more strategic level, the possible lessons divide into what worked, what has failed, and the C2 issues at the border. The argument presented here is that the conflict itself offers relatively little by way of failure to glean lessons for future conflict; the real lessons lie in the problems with forming temporary C2 during the periods of force build-up near the Ukrainian border.[32] This has resulted in some force reorganization, albeit on a small scale, and creating military infrastructure closer to the Ukrainian border, not only to resolve these issues but by way of messaging that Moscow is determined to protect its long-term strategic interests in Ukraine.

Since Russia's military operation to seize Crimea did not result in armed conflict, its study lies beyond the scope of this chapter, as the "lessons learned" would most likely revolve around an assessment of combat operations and the performance of the various support structures.[33] Therefore, the attempt to establish some of the lessons Russia's General Staff may have gleaned from the Ukraine conflict lies in its experience of Donbas during 2014–2017. As of early 2019, despite intense international diplomatic efforts to implement a lasting peace, the conflict shows no sign of ending. As the conflict unfolded, a number of different approaches to warfare were used, transitioning through these in different "phases" of the conflict.[34]

These types of warfare involved political, unconventional, a brief experimental use of hybrid (irregular and conventional) and limited use of conventional warfare. The early stage of the conflict was marked by political warfare, and by April 2014 armed rebellion in Donbas denoted the beginning of a period of unconventional warfare. In May to August 2014, Kyiv had renewed its Anti-Terrorist Operation (ATO), and in response, rebel groups and Russian forces used hybrid tactics that palpably failed as Russian conventional forces were required to mount a combined-arms operation in August 2014 to prevent Ukrainian forces from defeating the rebels; this operation ended with the routing of Ukrainian forces at the Battle of Ilovaysk, which precipitated the signing of the Minsk I agreement.[35] From that period to February 2015, Russia continued to fund, train and supply the rebellion (as it continues to do), and once again resorted to a combined-arms operation to achieve a fresh conventional success in Debaltseve, overlapping the signing of the Minsk II agreement. Since Minsk II, Moscow continues to arm, train and equip the rebel groups, maintaining low levels of violence and keeping its options open concerning conflict escalation in the future.

A number of factors also limit the value to Moscow of any potential "lessons learned" from the conflict in Donbas. These stem from the conflict's unique operational environment and the extent to which the Russian General Staff recognizes the uniqueness of each individual conflict and thus tends to eschew conflict "models" and a one-size-fits-all approach toward operational planning.[36] In other words, most of the lessons from the Donbas conflict will only really help to improve future Russian operations in Ukraine, rather than assist the further development of wider Russian military capabilities. A number of factors in Ukraine serve, therefore, to single out the Donbas conflict and Russia's handling of its involvement as unique and not readily exportable to other operational environments.[37] These are briefly outlined as:

- The presence within the political and economic system in Ukraine of large-scale and endemic corruption, with a few oligarchic individuals as its principal beneficiaries;

- The pre-existence of local networks Moscow could readily tap into in order to foment instability;

- Cultural, historical and linguistic affinity between the local population and Russia;

- Extensive and exploitable weaknesses within the Ukrainian state military and security structures, marked by Russian intelligence penetration, low combat readiness in the defense ministry units, and limited professional loyalty to the state on the part of local police (Kyiv's official estimates indicate that as many as 5,000 police officers in Donbas defected by August 2015 to join the separatists);

- Political and tactical errors by the interim government, which heightened separatist sentiment in Donbas. These included the move against the Russian language, actions against non-armed protesters that inadvertently paved the way for armed pro-Russian leaders to come to the fore, the disbanding of Berkut (implicated in Maidan casualties/violence) resulting in some of its members swelling separatist ranks, and action against the armed rebels prior to adequately preparing and training its defense ministry units for the task;

- The strategic context of the crisis: with a leadership coming to power promising to take the country in an entirely different economic direction, which Moscow judged to threaten its own strategic interests.[38]

Moscow's efforts to destabilize southeastern Ukraine met with only limited success, as these complex operations and use of proxies also exposed shortcomings. Russia's much-advertised and feared information warfare tools failed to inspire widespread support among the local population for the concept of "Novorossiya," which dropped out of the official lexicon in 2014. Indeed, it could be argued that the whole idea of Novorossiya taking root in Donbas and facilitating wider rebel aims was the single greatest failing of Moscow's Ukraine policy. Equally important, was the absence of achieving the strategic aim of federalizing Ukraine, which may explain the continued conflict stalemate.[39] However, these failings clearly lie more in the political than the military domain. Yet, despite obvious advances and an overall impressive performance in its Donbas involvement, the Russian military also encountered some problematic issues.

Notably, Moscow struggled to establish complete control over its proxy forces, which frequently caused problems as these groups would prefer to pursue their own aims and retain some level of autonomy. Even in the early stages of the Donbas instability, it was apparent that Moscow struggled to control the political warfare it had ignited. An additional failing stems from the brief "hybrid warfare" experiment, which gave way to traditional combined-arms operations in order to protect the separatists. At each point during the conflict when the separatist movement encountered stiff resistance from Ukrainian security forces, Moscow resorted to hard power, using its own units in order to revive and protect the separatist movement. In fact, despite fostering rebellion, investing in supplying the separatists with weapons and sustaining them throughout the period, devising a train-and-equip program and experimenting with lower levels of violence to leverage its longer-term interests, Moscow could only secure Minsk I and Minsk II ceasefire deals with Kyiv by using conventional combined-arms operations (Ilovaysk in August 2014, and Debaltseve in February 2015). Paradoxically, this may dissuade the Kremlin in the future from recourse to such tactics in favor of more direct action, such as is reflected in its operations in Syria.

After reviewing the available literature on the Ukraine conflict, it is possible to conclude that Russia's main military lessons may be as follows:

- Combat operations

  - Restore the traditional emphasis upon armor and its use in combat operations, reversing the trend in recent years to prioritize the development of the Aerospace Forces (*Vozdushno-Kosmicheskiye Sily*—VKS) for example;
  - Further improve targeting measures to facilitate the role of artillery and conventional fires;
  - Improve force protection by investing in strengthened armor;
  - Identify the strengths and weaknesses of C4ISR in order to achieve further C4ISR integration into future combat operations;
  - Assess the results of experiments with modern weapons and equipment and apply these lessons to future operational planning;
  - Assess and draw lessons from the use of proxy forces during operations and the role of Russian officers embedded in these units;
  - Improve C2 at all levels.

- Combat support and service support

  - Assess the level of progress in the use of force enablers and force multipliers such as electronic warfare (EW) specialists and assets to exploit the electromagnetic spectrum (EMS) as a warfare domain;
  - Assess the performance of EW, unmanned aerial vehicles (UAV) and fire control in an integrated network;

- o Improve the delivery of the train-and-equip program for proxies and examine how to improve C2 over these forces;
- o Draw lessons from the delivery of the train-and-equip program used in Syria to enhance the future effectiveness of training for Russian proxies;
- o Further integrate Russian commanders and proxy units to conduct independent operations and in conjunctions with Russian military units;
- o Enhance the effectiveness of information warfare (IW) as a tool to facilitate the achievement of strategic objectives;
- o Improve the use of psychological operations (PSYOPS);
- o Gain better control over serving military personnel using social media.

- Command-and-control issues encountered near Ukraine's border

  - o Temporary commanding organizations were required to establish working C2 over these forces during the force buildup near the Ukrainian border;
  - o The resolution of these C2 issues reinforced the General Staff perspective on the need to further vary the force structure to include divisions in the Ground Forces and not solely rely upon a brigade-based structure;
  - o Problems with moving and maintaining forces close to the Ukraine border convinced the General Staff to form divisions and move military infrastructure closer to the Ukraine border.[40]

Among the more significant lessons drawn from the Ukraine conflict, from Moscow's perspective, are the return to armor or promoting the interests of the Ground Forces in the ongoing military modernization and the issue of structural reorganization in the Ground Forces, with the formation of units closer to the Ukrainian border. Despite the political rhetoric used by the Russian political-military leadership, this on-the-ground shift appears driven not by reference to the North Atlantic Treaty Organization (NATO) but as a response to the C2 challenges identified during the numerous periods of force generation on the Ukraine border.

Reorganizing Russia's Ground Forces

In this wider context of defense reform and reorganization in recent years, coupled with lessons drawn from combat in Ukraine, further refinement of the order of battle (ORBAT) will take place in the Ground Forces. According to Colonel General Oleg Salyukov, the commander-in-chief of the Ground Forces, this process will continue to 2021 to ensure the "self-sufficiency" of the Army in all strategic directions. It corresponds to the effort to partly walk-back the Serdyukov-era reforms to modify the brigade-based structure to include some Ground Forces divisions. However, since the "walk-back" was introduced under Shoigu, as already noted, what has changed significantly in the ORBAT is that instead of BTGs being temporary formations they have become permanent structures.[41]

In February 2016 Salyukov noted that all brigades and divisions in the Ground Forces had formed BTGs. Chief of the General Staff Gerasimov later clarified that 66 BTGs in the Ground Forces were fully manned by *kontraktniki*, with a target set to achieve 125 BTGs by 2018.[42] These units are now also referred to as "strike" forces, in support of high-readiness formations such as the VDV; and more pointedly they constitute the backbone of unit training and evaluations.[43]

According to former VDV chief of reconnaissance Pavel Popovskikh, modern warfare lacks a clear and prolonged front line. Consequently, the importance of smaller units has increased in order to ensure the capacity to conduct independent tactical actions, not only to move over an extended front and depth but conducting combat operations on a fragmented battlefield. This autonomy to conduct independent action should be delegated from the "division-regiment" level down to the "battalion-company-platoon" level.[44]

During the early phase of the Ukraine crisis, in March 2014, Russia's Armed Forces deployed comparatively large forces near the Ukrainian border. This included ten brigades, four regiments, and several dozen BTGs. After the bulk of these forces withdrew from these positions in late April 2014, several BTGs from the MDs remained in place and were rotated every three or four months.[45] Interestingly, by way of illustrating the manning problems encountered at this point, in late 2014 a BTG was formed, subordinate to the 5th Tank Brigade in the 36th Combined-Arms Army and exclusively manned by *kontraktniki*. Yet, to achieve this, large parts of the manpower forming the BTG were reportedly forced to sign contracts. The 5th Tank Brigade was unable to secure enough professional troops from subordinate battalions for the BTG and was required to secure sufficient personnel and assets from the 37th Motorized Rifle Brigade, a sister unit also under the 36th Army.[46]

Moreover, media reports indicate that BTGs were earlier commanded by brigade-command-level officers (colonels); while more recently, BTGs are commanded by a battalion-level officer (lieutenant colonel or major).[47] Nevertheless, as noted in reference to the weaknesses exposed by the conflict in Donbas, the Russian Armed Forces' build-up on the Ukraine border served to expose issues with C2. In the course of building up this task force organization process, it was necessary to establish temporary commanding organizations to place these forces under C2. However, the 58th Army in the Southern MD was unable to undertake the task, because its subordinate units remained at their permanent bases. The Western MD's 20th Army experienced the same problem. To try to resolve this issue, the assembled forces were placed under the two operational groups' headquarters, consisting of the 58th Army and Southern MD staff as well as the 20th Army and Western MD staff. Despite this workaround, the planning and organization of headquarters tasks was actually carried out at a considerably higher level, though not without problems.[48] Essentially, this stemmed from a shortage of HQ personnel due to officer reductions under the former defense minister.

One MD officer attached as a staff member to a unit sent to the Ukraine border in 2014 explained that army corps or division HQ was used as a temporary command organization for C2 over large numbers of forces including brigades, regiments, and BTGs. This seemed to reinforce the idea that the divisional HQ, as an upper echelon C2, could prove useful as a coordinating and supporting organization in such circumstances.[49]

The Ukraine crisis inadvertently served to strengthen the case of those senior Russian officers advocating the benefits of the divisional structure and its utility in certain situations for C2. For example, General Salyukov noted that previously, as soon as senior officers had graduated from the Military Academy of the General Staff or completed their terms as brigade commanders, they were assigned as (deputy) commanders or chiefs of staff of armies, though lacking appropriate knowledge and experience. However, a restored divisional structure allows senior officers to broaden their experiences prior to their postings.[50] The brigade-based structure in the Ground Forces has been corrected to reintroduce a divisional element, which was ultimately driven by the Russian military's experience in the Ukraine conflict. The new Ground Forces divisions are located closer to the Ukraine border, and despite Moscow's political rhetoric this is not really calibrated as a "response" to NATO.

Russia's Ground Forces, moving away from the reform-inspired reliance on a brigade-based structure, reintroduced a small number of divisions in Western and Southern joint strategic commands, or OSKs, in order to address the aforementioned C2 issues and provide for controlling larger force groupings in the future as the need arises.

This involves establishing three divisions in western Russia, with two being constituted in the Western OSK/MD and one in the Southern OSK/MD. This was cast as a response to the United States' and NATO's posture toward Russia. However, its underlying driver seems to be a desire to back away from the reforms initiated by Serdyukov; the decision addresses the C2 issues that were identified during the force buildup periods near the Ukraine border.[51] On January 12, 2016, Defense Minister Shoigu addressed the top brass during a video conference at the National Defense Management Center (*Natsional'nyy Tsentr Upravleniya Oboronoy*—NTsUO), in Moscow. He outlined a series of plans to "counteract" NATO. This reflected measures already in place: forming the 1st Tank Army in the Western MD from units of the 20th Combined Arms Army (CAA) as well as conducting a limited reorganization from brigades to divisions.[52]

Russian General Staff sources suggest the 1st Tank Army and the 20th CAA in the Western MD upgraded to divisional status would contain four maneuver regiments like their earlier Soviet versions. The new divisions in the Western MD will be headquartered in Yelnya and Boguchar. Two Motorized Rifle Divisions (MRD) will form the basis of the 20th CAA by the end of 2016: these are located in Smolensk and Vorenezh, each MRD will have a personnel strength of 10,000. "Now, as it was in Soviet times, each tank division will have three tank regiments, a motorized rifle regiment, a self-propelled artillery regiment and an anti-aircraft missile regiment; and each motorized rifle division includes three motorized rifle regiments, a tank regiment, a self-propelled artillery regiment and an anti-aircraft missile regiment," noted a General Staff source. The division will include supporting units: intelligence, communications, logistics, electronic warfare, nuclear-biological-chemical (NBC) units, and others. These formations will be the first in the Ground Forces to procure T-14 Armata platforms and new Kurganets combat vehicles.[53]

Similar restructuring occurred in the Southern MD, to deploy a new MRD headquartered in Rostov. Also with 10,000 personnel and reflecting the structures formed in the Western MD, the defense ministry plans to build supporting infrastructure. Southern MD staff described the new MRD as "full-blooded" and estimated the initial costs for building its facilities at 5 billion rubles ($73 million).[54] In February 2018, the defense ministry initiated additional changes to the 58th Army in the Southern MD to strengthen the nucleus of general-purpose forces. This involves recreating two divisions based upon the 19th and 136th Motorized Rifle Brigades. These will be fully established by the end of 2018 by reinforcing these structures with additional battalions and regiments and arming them with BMP-3 infantry fighting vehicles and T-72B3 tanks. Viktor Murakhovskiy, the editor-in-chief of the journal *Arsenal Otechestva*, explained that these forces are aimed at deterring NATO on Russia's Western and Southern flanks: "The experience of combat operations and exercises has shown that the division is a more self-sufficient formation [*soyedineniye*] than the brigade. The latter usually requires reinforcement by combat and logistic support assets and weapons assets. The division is more adapted to the physical geographic features of the European part of Russia, where there are large expanses and a considerable length of lines of contact and of fronts."[55]

General Salyukov also explains these changes in reference to the result of assessments of the "snap inspections" and tests of combat readiness. Salyukov sees this reintroduction of some divisions as a correction to the Serdyukov reforms but does not stress the Ukraine element in its evolution. While noting the new divisions were formed on the basis of existing brigades, Salyukov adds that this aims to add to their firepower, strike force capabilities and the need to perform tasks along a "much wider battlefront." The General Staff wants to establish a variety of differing formations, from divisions to brigades and BTGs, to shape its responses to various potential theaters of conflict. Salyukov said the Ground Forces' command conducted a detailed study in 2014–2015 on the formation, support and use of tactical groups of forces in the Soviet Union, Russia and leading militaries to create an "optimal composition for the BTG formations of the

Ground Forces." These appear to have emerged as permanent structures, not originally planned in the reforms of 2008–2009, and they are manned exclusively by *kontraktniki*; the main effort is to prepare each BTG for action on any axis in "complex conditions" and in "unfamiliar terrain."[56]

Conclusion

The lessons identified and learned from Russia's military experience gained during its operations and support for separatist groups in Donbas is known for certain only to the select few in the General Staff. This study has sought to explain some of the possible lessons drawn by the General Staff by recourse to what the military is doing on-the-ground rather than placing too much emphasis upon political rhetoric.[57]

The main "lessons" from the conflict are the rediscovery of the importance of armor and the likely higher priority for re-equipping the Ground Forces in the continuing military modernization. The reorganization of some elements of the Ground Forces, including developing a divisional capability and creating supporting infrastructure near the Ukraine border, is less in response to NATO than it is rooted in aspects of the Ukraine conflict.[58] While the discussion concerning the need for divisions as well as brigades since the reform of 2008 was largely theoretical, the force build-up periods assembling tens of thousands of troops revealed in practical terms that the divisional C2 can prove to be quite useful. Moreover, the BTGs were a familiar feature of the Russian military in conducting its operations; and now many of these are permanent structures.[59]

The Ukraine conflict, above all, provided a real-time testing ground for Russia's approaches to modern warfare, training experience for its forces and the chance to experiment with new or existing systems, as well as supplying experience of conducting a train-and-equip program during a conflict. The success of this effort, combined with using an integrated approach to EW, UAVs, and targeting of fires, allowed Moscow to avoid deploying larger numbers of its military personnel in Donbas.[60] Russia's Armed Forces encountered a broader range of opportunities to train and experiment in Syria in more "open" conflict; and the lessons drawn from these campaigns will shape the organization and priorities of Russia's Armed Forces for many years ahead.

Notes

[1] See: Mikhail Barabanov, *Novaya Armiya Rossii*. Moscow, *Tsentr analiza strategiy i tekhnologiy*, 2010; B. Nygren, R. McDermott and C. Pallin (editors), *The Russian Armed Forces in Transition: economic, geopolitical and institutional uncertainties*, Routledge, 2012.

[2] D. R. Herspring, "Is Military Reform in Russia for 'Real'? Yes, But...," in S. Blank and R. Weitz (eds) *The Russian Military Today and Tomorrow: Essays in Memory of Mary Fitzgerald*, Carlisle, PA: US Army War College Strategic Studies Institute, 2010; V. Shlykov, "Tainy blitskriga Serdiukova," *Rossiya v globalnoy politike*, No 6, December 2009; V. Shamanov, Interview in *Bratishka* magazine for Russian special forces, Moscow, May 2009.

[3] "Shoygu anonsiroval stroitel'stvo 1740 voyennykh ob'yektov v 2018–2025 godakh," *Moskovskiy Komsomolets*, April 21, 2017.

[4] Mikhail Ivanov, Amaliya Zatari, "Mest v armii stanovitsya vse men'she," *Gazeta.ru*, April 21, 2017, http://www.mk.ru/politics/2017/04/21/shoygu-anonsiroval-stroitelstvo-1740-voennykh-obektov-v-20182025-godakh.html.

[5] Aleksey Ramm, "Proverka Ukrainoy," *Voyenno Promyshlennyy Kuryer*, April 29, 2015, http://www.vpk-news.ru/articles/25027.

[6] Carolina Vendil-Pallin, Fredrik Westerlund, "Russia's War in Georgia: Lessons and Consequences," *Small Wars & Insurgencies*, Volume 20, Issue 2, 2009, pp. 400–424.

[7] Oleg Vladykin, "1848 Hours and You are a Soldier," *Nezavisimoye Voyennoye Obozreniye*, July 1, 2011, http://nvo.ng.ru/realty/2011-07-01/1_soldier.html; Richard Weitz, "The State of the Russian Military," *RIA Novosti*, May 27, 2011.

[8] See: *Soviet Military Power*, US Department of Defense, Washington, 1983. The tendency to exaggerate Russian military power resurfaced in a report issued by Finland's National Defense University in September 2011, entitled: "Russian Politico-Military Development and Finland."

[9] For further detail see: Roger N. McDermott, *The Reform of Russia's Conventional Armed Forces: Problems, Challenges and Policy Implications,* Washington: The Jamestown Foundation, 2011; Dr. Lester W. Grau. Charles K. Bartles, *The* Russian *Way of War. Force Structure, Tactics, and Modernization of the Russian Ground Forces*, Foreign Military Studies Office, 2016, http://www.armyupress.army.mil/Portals/7/Hot%20Spots/Documents/Russia/2017-07-The-Russian-Way-of-War-Grau-Bartles.pdf.

[10] Viktor Baranets, "The Army Will Be Getting the Latest Weapons and Lodgings and Will Be Rid of Hazing: Dmitry Medvedev Has Formulated Five Principles of Development of the Armed Forces," *Komsomolskaya Pravda*, October 1, 2008; Nikolay Poroskov, "Military Arrangements," *Vremya Novostey*, October 8, 2008.

[11] "Russian Defense Minister Announces Overhaul of the Armed Forces Structure," *Zvezda Television,* 14 October, 2008.

[12] "Expanded Meeting of the Defense Ministry Board," Kremlin.ru, March 18, 2011.

[13] "Transcript of Meeting With Participants in the Assembly of Officers Commanding Force Groupings of the Armed Forces," Presidential website, November 25, 2010, http://kremlin.ru/transcripts/9609.

[14] "V VDV staklo na tri desantno-shturmovykh brigad bolshe," Ministry of Defense, October 21, 2013, http://function.mil.ru/news_page/country/more.htm?id=11859469@egNews.

[15] These dilemmas were also reflected in updated versions of Russia's security documents, see: Zatsepin, V. 'On a new version of the national security strategy of the Russian Federation', *Russian Economic Developments*, No. 2, 2016, pp. 82–85.

[16] Grigoriy Maslov, 'They Will Divide the Russian Armed Forces by the Compass,' www.infox.ru, April, 30, 2010.

[17] "Russian Army to Form Four Strategic Commands," *Interfax*, April 29, 2010; Viktor Litovkin, "Parade of Reforms Shows No Sign of Breaking: Russian Army Proceeds to New Stage of Modernization," *Nezavisimoye Voyennoye Obozreniye*, May 14, 2010, http://nvo.ng.ru/realty/2010-05-14/1_parad.html; "Organization of

Russia's New Operational-Strategic Commands will be Over in 2010," *Interfax,* June 11, 2010.

[18] Victor Litovkin, 'The Examination for the Seven Test Sites," *Nezavisimoye Voyennoye Obozreniye,* September 23, 2011, http://nvo.ng.ru/realty/2011-09-23/1_exam.html.

[19] Interview with Lieutenant-General Nikolai Ignatov, *Ekho Moskvy,* July 30, 2011.

[20] Roger N. McDermott, "Is Anybody There? Russian Military Command and Control," *Eurasia Daily Monitor,* Volume 8, Issue 182, October 4, 2011.

[21] Roger N. McDermott, 'Russian Military Command and Control: A Giant Leap of Faith?' *Eurasia Daily Monitor,* Volume 8, Issue 158, August 16, 2011; Dmitry Kandaurov, "Tanks Do Not Wash," Zavtra, August 3, 2011, http://www.zavtra.ru/cgi/veil/data/zavtra/11/924/print41.html; Dmitry Litovkin, "Defense Programme Failed the Internet War," August 1, 2011, http://www.izvestia.ru/news/496152Izvstia.

[22] "Medvedev Opens Discussion on Conscription Changes," July 23, 2010, http://kremlin.ru/news/8404; Valery Astanin, "New Look Soldiers," *Nezavisimoye Voyennoye Obozreniye,* January 21, 2011 http://nvo.ng.ru/realty/2011-01-21/3_new_face.html.

[23] Vitaliy Shlykov, "Conscript, Contractor or Citizen in the Form," *Voyenno Promyshlennyy Kuryer,* December 1, 2010, http://vpk-news.ru/articles/6964; Aleksandr Belkin, "And Still an Unsolved Problem. Who Could Protect the Country From Military Attack: Conscript or Contractor?" *Voyenno Promyshlennyy Kuryer,* November 10, 2010, http://vpk-news.ru/articles/6919.

[24] "Doktrina informatsionnoi bezopasnosti Rossiiskoi Federatsii [Information seurity doctrine of the Russian Federation]," http://www.scrf.gov.ru/documents/6/5.html; "Kontseptsiia obshchestvennoi bezopasnosti Rossiiskoi Federatsii [Concept for the security of the society of the Russian Federation]," http://www.scrf.gov.ru/documents/16/117.html; "Voennaia doktrina Rossiiskoi Federatsii [Military doctrine of the Russian Federation]," http://www.scrf.gov.ru/documents/18/-129.html.

[25] "NATO: Russian Troops Dying In 'Large Numbers' In Eastern Ukraine," *RFE/RL,* March 5, 2015, http://www.rferl.org/content/nato-russian-troops-dying-large-numbers-ukraine/26884296.html; James Kanter, Martin Fackler, "NATO Says Russia Pulled Some Troops From Ukraine," *New York Times,* September 24, 2014,

http://www.nytimes.com/2014/09/25/world/europe/ukraine-russia-nato-withdrawal.html?_r=0; Author interviews with SMEs and officials, Rome, September 8, 2014.

[26] "Lidery Ukrainskikh opolchentsev vychislili donskikh kazakov-predatelei, planirovavshikh sdat Lugansk natsgvardii," *Bloknot News Agency*, Rostov na-Donu, June 10, 2014, http://bloknot-rostov.ru/news/more/lidery-ukrainskih-opolchencev-zapodozrila-donskih-kazakov-pod-predvoditelstvom-atamana-kozicyna-v-predatelstve-20140610; "Control of Donbas," *The Economist*, October 1, 2014, http://www.economist.com/blogs/graphicdetail/2014/10/daily-chart; "Aleksej Zhuravlyov: Ukrainu nuzhno osvobodit ot fashizma i razgula rusofobii," Rodina Party Website, February 5, 2014, http://rodina.ru/novosti/aleksej-zhuravlyov-ukrainu-nuzhno-osvobodit-ot-fashizma-i-razgula-rusofobii; Vladimir Mukhin, "Rossia gotovitsa k mashtabnoi mirotvorcheskoi operatsii," *Nezavisimaya Gazeta*, August 25, 2014, http://www.ng.ru/armies/2014-08-25/1_peacemakers.html.

[27] Rimma Akhmirova, "Kto iz Rossii voyuyet protiv Kieva ha yugo-vostoke Ukrainy," Sobessednik.ru, July 16, 2014, http://sobesednik.ru/rassledovanie/20140716-kto-iz-rossii-i-pochemu-voyuet-protiv-kieva-na-yugo-vostoke; Ilya Barabanov, "Samovooruzhennaia respublika," *Kommersant Vlast*, June 2, 2014; Oleg Falichev, "Spetsnaz byl i ostaetsa elitoi," *Voyenno Promyshlennyy Kuryer*, February 26, 2014, http://vpk-news.ru/articles/19280.

[28] Valeriy Gerasimov, "Tsennost' nauki v predvidenii," *Voyenno Promyshlennyy Kuryer*, February 26, 2013, http://vpk-news.ru/articles/14632; For a detailed examination of some of the historical antecedents of the Gerasimov article see: Steven J. Main, "You Cannot Generate Ideas by Orders: The Continuing Importance of Studying Soviet Military History—G. S. Isserson and Russia's Current Geo-Political Stance," *The Journal of Slavic Military Studies*, Vol. 29, No. 1, 2016, pp. 48–72; Jacob Kipp, The Methodology of Foresight and Forecasting in Soviet Military Affairs (Fort Leavenworth, KS: Soviet Army Studies Office, 1988), http://www.dtic. mil/dtic/tr/fulltext/u2/a196677.pdf; and N. V. Ogarkov, Ed., *Military Encyclopedic Dictionary*, Moscow: Military Publishing House, 1983, p. 585.

[29] See: Aleksandr Golts, Heidi Reisinger, "Russia's Hybrid Warfare: Waging War Below the Radar of Traditional Collective Defense," Research Paper, NATO Defense College, Rome, November 2014; Marc Galeotti, "The 'Gerasimov Doctrine' and Russian Non-Linear War," *In Moscow's Shadows Blog*, July 6, 2014, http://inmoscowsshadows.wordpress.com/2014/07/06/the-gerasimov-doctrine-and-russian-non-linear-war/; US Government, State Department, White House, Department of Defense, CRS, Director of National Intelligence, Central Intelligence

Agency (CIA), *2014 Essential Guide to the Ukraine and the Crisis with Russia*. published by Progressive Management, 2014. Wilson, Andrew, Ukraine Crisis: What It Means for the West. Yale University Press, 2014; John Mearsheimer, "The Liberal Delusions that Provoked Putin," *Foreign Affairs*, September/October 2014; Michael McFaul, Stephen Sestanovick, John Mearsheimer, "Faulty Powers: Who Started the Ukraine Crisis?" *Foreign Affairs*, November/December 2014.

[30] Vladimir Mukhin, 'Rossiya gotovitsya k masshtabnoy mirotvorcheskoy operatsii,' *Nezavisimoye Voyennoye Obozreniye*, August 25, 2014, http://www.ng.ru/armies/2014-08-25/1_peacemakers.html; For an excellent Russian analysis of the course of the conflict in Ukraine see: Mikhail Barabanov, 'Prinuzhdeniye k miru-2: blizhayshaya perspektiva Rossii na Ukraine,' *Odnako*, December 2014–January 2015, http://periscope2.ru/2015/01/19/8298/.

[31] Aleksandr Tikhonov, "Where Threats to Peace Come From," *Kraznaya Zvezda*, May 27, 2014, http://www.redstar.ru/index.php/newspaper/item/16298-otkuda-iskhodyat-ugrozy-miru; Yury Gavrilov, "Games With Zero Outcome," *Rossiyskaya Gazeta*, May 26, 2014, www.rg.ru/2014/05/23/konferenciya-site.html; "Veroyatnoye budushcheye voyny za Novorossiyu," *Voyennoye Obozreniye*, August 29, 2014, http://topwar.ru/57093-veroyatnoe-buduschee-voyny-za-novorossiyu.html; Oleg Odnokolenko, "Vostochno-ukrainskiy front snova v ogne," *Nezavisimoye Voyennoye Obozreniye*, January 30, 2015, http://nvo.ng.ru/realty/2015-01-30/1_front.html.

[32] See section three below.

[33] Anton Lavrov, "Russian Again: The Military Operation for Crimea," Colby Howard and Ruslan Pukhov, eds. *Brothers Armed: Military Aspects of the Crisis in Ukraine*, (East View Press, 2014), pp. 157–186.

[34] Claire Bigg, "Vostok Battalion, A Powerful New Player in Eastern Ukraine," *RFE/RL*, May 30, 2014, http://www.rferl.org/content/vostok-battalion-a-powerful-new-player-in-eastern-ukraine/25404785.html; Konstantin Bogdanov, "Russia May Consider Establishing Private Military Companies," *RIA News Agency*, April 13, 2012, http://en.ria.ru/analysis/20120413/172789099.html; Enerud, Per (2013) "Can the Kremlin Control the Cossacks?" RUFS Briefing No. 18, Swedish Defence Research Agency, March 2013, http://www.foi.se/Global/V%c3%a5r%20kunskap/S%c3%a4kerhetspolitiska%20studier/Ryssland/%c3%96vriga%20filer/RUFS%20Briefing%20No.%2018%20.pdf.

[35] "V SNBO razyasnili pravovoj status rossiyan, prinimayuschich uchastie v konflikte ha Donbasse," *Inforesist*, September 8, 2014, http://inforesist.org/v-snbo-

razyasnili-pravovoj-status-rossiyan-prinimayushhix-uchastie-v-konflikte-na-donbasse/; Irek Murtazin, "Ustav. Otpravilis v otpusk," *Novaya Gazeta*, September 8, 2014, http://www.novayagazeta.ru/comments/65137.html.

[36] Kofman, Michael, and Matthew Rojansky, "A Closer Look at Russia's 'Hybrid War,'" *KennanCable*, No.7, Washington, DC: The Wilson Center, April 2015, http://www.wilsoncenter.org/sites/default/files/7-KENNAN%20CABLE-ROJANSKY%20KOFMAN.pdf, Korotchenko, Igor, "Nachalos Formirovaniye Otradov Armi Samoobrony Yugo-Vostochnoy Ukrainy," LiveJournal.com, March 23, 2014, http://i-korotchenko.livejournal.com/844693.html.

[37] Aleksei Ramm, "Pervyye pobedy rossiyskikh instruktorov — chast' I," *Voyenno Promyshlennyy Kuryer*, February 3, 2016, http://vpk-news.ru/articles/28995; Aleksei Ramm, "Pervyye pobedy rossiyskikh instruktorov — chast' II," *Voyenno Promyshlennyy Kuryer*, February 17, 2016, http://vpknews.ru/articles/29213.

[38] Based on a review of Russian and Western analyses of the conflict and discussions with defense specialists.

[39] See: T. Thomas, "Russia's military strategy and Ukraine. Indirect, asymmetric and Putin led," *The Journal of Slavic Military Affairs*, Vol. 28, No. 3, 2015; F. Westerlund and J. Norberg, "Military means for non-military measures: the Russian approach to the use of armed force as seen in Ukraine," *The Journal of Slavic Military Studies* Volume 29, Issue 4, 2016; A. Rácz, "Russia's hybrid war in Ukraine: breaking the enemy's ability to resist," *FIIA Report 43*, The Finnish Institute of International Affairs.

[40] Based on a review of Russian and Western analyses of the conflict and discussions with defense specialists.

[41] Oleg Salyukov, "Ratniki idut," *Voyenno Promyshlennyy Kuryer*, February 22, 2017, http://vpk-news.ru/articles/35285; Aleksandr Tikhonov, "S pritselom na budushcheye," *Krasnaya Zvezda*, , January 24, 2016, http://www.redstar.ru/index.php/component/k2/item/27444-s-pritselom-na-budushchee.

[42] Oleg Salyukov, Oleg Falichev, "Vozvrashcheniye diviziy," *Voyenno Promyshlennyy Kuryer*, http://vpk-news.ru/articles/29096, February 10, 2016; "Chislo batal'onnykh grupp, sostoyashchikh iz kontraktnikov, v rossiyskoy armii cherez dva goda dostignet 125 – nachal'nik Genshtaba VS RF," *Interfax-AVN*, http://www.militarynews.ru/story.asp?rid=1&nid=425709, September 14, 2016.

[43] "V Vozdushno-desantnykh voyskakh poyavilis' podrazdeleniya so statusom udarnyye," Ministry of Defense of the Russian Federation, May 19, 2017, http://function.mil.ru/news_page/country/more.htm?id=12124043@egNews.

[44] Olga Shilova, Pavel Popovskikh, "Razvedka VDV na smene epokh," *Natsional'naya Oborona*, December 1, 2010, http://old.nationaldefense.ru/284/112/index.shtml?id=3618.

[45] Aleksey Ramm, "Proverka Ukrainoy," *Voyenno Promyshlennyy Kuryer*, April 29, 2015, http://www.vpk-news.ru/articles/25027; Aleksey Chuykov, "Severnyye mechty Minoborony," *Argumenty Nedeli*, September 27, 2012, http://argumenti.ru/army/n358/204451.

[46] "My vse znali, na chto idem i chto mozhet byt," *Novaya Gazeta*, March 2, 2015, http://www.novayagazeta.ru/society/67490.html.

[47] "My vse znali, na chto idem i chto mozhet byt," *Op. Cit*; Yuriy Belousov, "Matritsa dlya lichnogo sostava," *Krasnaya Zvezda*, September 1, 2015, http://www.redstar.ru/index.php/component/k2/item/25548-matritsa-dlya-lichnogo-sostava.

[48] "Proverka Ukrainoy," *Op. Cit.*

[49] Igor Popov, "Divizii protiv brigad, brigady protiv diviziy," *Nezavisimoye Voyennoye Obozreniye*, July 12, 2013, http://dlib.eastview.com/browse/doc/34809412.

[50] "S pritselom na budushcheye," *Op. Cit*; "Vozvrashcheniye divizii," *Op. Cit.*

[51] Vladimir Gundarov, "Pyat milliardov dlya novoy divizii," *Nezavisimoye Voyennoye Obozreniye*, April 1, 2016, http://nvo.ng.ru/nvoevents/2016-04-01/2_mlrd.html.

[52] "Shoygu: Minoborony RF v 2016 godu sformiruyet tri novyye divizii na zapadnom napravlenii," *TASS*, January 12, 2016, http://tass.ru/armiya-i-opk/2579480.

[53] "Istochnik: divizii 1-y tankovoy i 20-y armiy na zapade Rossii budut imet' po shest' polkov," *TASS*, April 1, 2016, http://tass.ru/armiya-i-opk/3169104.

[54] Vladimir Gundarov, "Pyat milliardov dlya novoy divizii," *Nezavisimoye Voyennoye Obozreniye*, April 1, 2016, http://nvo.ng.ru/nvoevents/2016-04-01/2_mlrd.html.

[55] Nikolay Surkov, Aleksey Ramm, and Yevgeniy Andreyev, "Severnyy Kavkaz ukrepili diviziyami," *Izvestia*, February 16, 2018, https://iz.ru/705714/nikolai-surkov-aleksei-ramm-evgenii-andreev/severnyi-kavkaz-ukrepili-diviziiami.

[56] Oleg Salyukov, Oleg Falichev, "Vospreshcheniye diviziy," *Voyenno Promyshlennyy Kuryer*, February 8, 2016, https://vpk-news.ru/articles/29096.

[57] Aleksei Ramm, "Pervyye pobedy rossiyskikh instruktorov — chast' I," *Voyenno Promyshlennyy Kuryer*, February 3, 2016, http://vpk-news.ru/articles/28995; Aleksei Ramm, "Pervyye pobedy rossiyskikh instruktorov — chast' II," *Voyenno Promyshlennyy Kuryer*, February 17, 2016, http://vpknews.ru/articles/29213.

[58] "S pritselom na budushcheye," *Op. Cit;* "Vozvrashcheniye diviziy," *Op. Cit;* "Istochnik: divizii 1-y tankovoy i 20-y armiy," *Op. Cit.*

[59] Salyukov, "Vospreshcheniye diviziy," *Op. Cit.*

[60] Based on a review of Russian and Western analyses of the conflict and discussions with defense specialists.

10. Russian Lessons Learned From the Operation in Syria: A Preliminary Assessment

Dmitry (Dima) Adamsky

Introduction

This chapter deals with the lessons that the Russian strategic community and Russian experts have distilled from the operation in Syria and that can be traced to Russian sources. The main interest is in the lessons that will impact the three main components of prospective Russian military innovations: transforming the concept of operations, force buildup and organization structures.

This research contends with two major limitations to. First, it is still too early to talk about specific lessons, since the Russian experts themselves are in the process of exploring their own experience. Knowledge development, which started only recently, is an ongoing process, and will generate refined and deep insights only in the coming months and years. As of now, not even enough time has passed for the Russian strategic community to come out with anything beyond preliminary lessons. Moreover, while this chapter is based on open sources, the major portion of Russia's lesson-learning process is classified. The reliability of available sources is questionable, and their number is still too limited to offer any definite arguments. It will take time until the open commentaries, exercises, and actual military modernization programs in the realms of weapon procurement, doctrine and organizational transformations reflect the takeaways from the Syrian operation.

Consequently, this chapter offers a preliminary outline of the major themes and trends that Russian sources emphasize over others when debating the Syrian experience. It aims to highlight the main topics of interest and prioritization of the Russian military brass, theoreticians and experts, but does not seek to outline specific resolutions in each field. Nonetheless, it contributes by highlighting those themes that the Russian professional discourse has prioritized in terms of intellectual energy; and where possible, it speculates on linkages to force buildup and procurement tendencies. The chapter does not hypothesize about the lessons regarding strategy and operational art, which Russian practitioners are likely to deduce, but which, at this stage, are not reflected in the primary sources. These important insights are beyond the scope of this chapter and is worth exploring in a follow-up work.

The chapter consists of three sections. The first outlines the innovative conceptual climate, which fosters the lesson-learning process. The second section focuses on the reconnaissance-strike complex and its segments (intelligence, command and strike capabilities), which is the main leitmotif and frame of reference in the Russian process of learning. The third part covers other issues pertaining to operational art and strategy that already loom large in Russian knowledge development. Presumably, this way of addressing the subject matter reflects the Russian holistic mentality and complex approach to conceptualizing military innovations and the changing character of war.

Innovative Conceptual Climate

Without idealizing the contemporary Russian approach to military innovations, it seems that prior to, during and following the operation in Syria, the Russian strategic community has been functioning as a learning machine. Since 2008, from Georgia and then through the operations in Crimea, eastern Ukraine and Syria, one can identify a recurring pattern of innovation: first, the professional discourse explores a cloud of doctrinal ideas related to the changing character of war; exercises and snap inspections then refine the insights developed by theoretical discussions and introduce them into practice; these postulates then receive a reality check in actual military operations; finally, the energetic lesson-learning process during and following the operation again distills the conceptual takeaways from the experience and injects them into the theoretical debate, which further reactivates the above cycle of learning.

Some Western scholars have already admitted that in recent conflicts, Moscow demonstrated an aptitude for learning, transformation and scale of improvisation that are rather unorthodox for the post-Soviet Russian military. Indeed the learning process seems be tolerant of failure and has demonstrated conceptual flexibility and dynamism, new knowledge development by trial and error, constant experimentation, adjustments, and cycles of strategic-operational adaptation.[1] Russian Chief of the General Staff (CGS) Valery Gerasimov's statement in 2017 clearly illustrates this *modus operandi* of the Russian strategic community. According to him, "from the first day of the Syrian campaign, the GS [General Staff] thoroughly explored the combat experience," and among other things disseminated the lessons learned to the forces that were about to rotate to Syria. Moreover, the GS conducted several conferences on the subject of the lessons learned and issued several manuals summarizing the operational experience.[2] It was also a process of learning by friction, or what Western scholars would qualify as wartime adaptation,[3] when insights about the enemy's *modus operandi* generated adjustments (*korrektivy*) and transformation of the Russian concept of operations, organizational structures and force buildup trends.[4]

Moreover, from a relatively early stage, the GS turned the Syrian operation into an incubator of training and innovation. It sought to provide with combat experience (*"obkatat' v Sirii"*) the highest possible number of commanders from all the services and branches of the military. Eventually, in two years of the operation, 48,000 troops rotated through the Syrian theater in three-month deployments. All the commanders of the military districts, who one after another commanded the grouping of forces in Syria, and the commanders of the General Purpose (*obschevoiskvoye*), Air (*vozdushnye*) and Air Defense (*PVO*) armies went through Syria. They arrived with their chiefs of staff and with organic staffs from the military districts. Thus, all the staff apparatus, including staff officers from operations, intelligence, communications and rear departments, as well as the main branches of the Ground Forces—or in general, 90 percent of Russian commanders and more than 50 percent of regimental and brigade commanders—rotated through Syria.[5]

All these commanders acquired experience in combined arms warfare and inter-service cooperation, as well as "complex employment of intelligence, C2 [command and control] and fire destruction means" of their forces functioning in the form of a reconnaissance-strike complex.[6] Also, the crews of ships and submarines employing precision-guided weapons, along with almost the entire order of battle of the operational-tactical aviation, including the maritime aviation of the Northern Fleet, acquired combat experience.[7] Moreover, the Syrian baptism by fire was not confined only to the chain of command. The GS and Ministry of Defense (MoD) ensured the "uninterrupted military scientific-technological escort of the troops and weapons employment." Engineers, designers and scientists from the military design bureaus, scientific institutes and military industry were dispatched to Syria to accompany their products, to learn lessons, as well as to calibrate their products technologically and conceptually based on the hands-on experience on the ground. This applied, according to the CGS, to every type of weaponry.[8]

Reconnaissance-Strike Complex: The Leitmotif of the Innovation

A recurrent theme in the reflections of Russian experts and commentators on the operation in Syria is its definition as the first occasion on which a reformed Russian military eventually fought along the lines of the Information Technology Revolution in Military Affairs (IT-RMA) and materialized the principles of operational art associated with it. This notion, which was developed by Soviet military theoreticians during the 1980s under the titles MTR and RMA, and was known in the West as the Ogarkov Doctrine (after the then-Soviet CGS, Marshall Nikolai Ogarkov), has been popularized since the 1990s by Andrew Marshall and experts from the Office of Net Assessment in the Pentagon. The IT-RMA school of thought made a straightforward argument about the changing character of war: the overall tendency of military establishments in the information era would be to transform their armed forces into reconnaissance-strike complexes that link together intelligence capabilities, C2 systems and precision stand-off fire into an ecosystem of networked combined arms, uninterruptedly executing "sensor-shooter loops." The Soviet military lexicon defined this phenomenon at the strategic-operational level of war as a reconnaissance-strike (*razvedovatel'no-udarnyi*) and at the operational-tactical level as a reconnaissance-fire (*razvedovatl'no-ogenvoi*) complex. The very same notion in the Western military lexicon was given the title of network-centric warfare (NCW). The term also applies to the doctrine, organizational structures and weaponry that are associated with informational- (in contrast to industrial-) age warfare and was the driving force behind the US and NATO defense transformations in the late 20th– early 21st centuries.[9]

The Soviet Union, a pioneer in conceptualizing the changing character of war in the information era, never materialized this innovative notion. But following the post-Soviet collapse times of trouble, as Russia began rising from its geopolitical knees, defense modernization sought to head in this direction. It was only starting from 2008, however, that military reform with tangible changes began gathering momentum. The main flaws of the Russian military, which the war in Georgia highlighted, were in fact the pivots of the IT-RMA: the deficit of the PGMs and standoff weapons; an inability to wage NCW operations due to the low level of command, control, communications, computers, intelligence, surveillance and reconnaissance (C4ISR); and the low quality of ground forces, incapable of waging combined-arms warfare or functioning as reconnaissance-strike complexes. The main aim of the subsequent force modernization was to rebuild the conventional military after almost 20 years of decay, specifically focusing on the above three components, and thus to advance it as close as possible toward the ideal type of reconnaissance-strike complex. Modernizations implemented towards the operation in Crimea, then in Donbas but especially in Syria demonstrated a slow but steady improvement in this regard.

Russian experts argue that Syria represents the first instance that the Russian military has put into practice the ideas outlined by Marshall Ogarkov and fielded reconnaissance-strike complexes on the ground. The GS saw the operation in Syria as a testing ground for almost all types of modern Russian weaponry from each of the branches and services of the Armed Forces, and specifically the systemic use of ISR, C2 and fire systems integrated into unified reconnaissance-strike complexes.[10] Unsurprisingly, the Russian professional discourses and the lexicon of the senior officials with regard to the Syrian operation are saturated with the terms "reconnaissance-strike complex" (RSC) and "reconnaissance-fire complex" (RFC). Gerasimov's euphemism "Russia realized in Syria the principle of 'one target, one bomb' " is the most laconic expression of the IT-RMA warfare era—to be seen is to be shot, and to be shot is to be killed.[11] Accordingly, the following three sections focus on the lessons learned about the three main components of the complex—ISR, C2 and Strike—and what lies between them. This division is quite general and is mainly for the purpose of organizing the available material, as many topics easily fit into several categories.

ISR Segment of the Complex

A strong emphasis on precision-guided munitions (PGM), on which more below, demands a bank of targets prepared in advance as well as the ability to generate a bank of real-time intelligence. Russia's Special Operation Forces (KSO) Command, fleet of unmanned aerial vehicles (UAV) and the GLONASS satellite guidance system constellation, all of which contributed to these two missions, so far have received the most significant attention from Russian commentators discussing the ISR segment of the reconnaissance-strike complex. And all three elements of the ISR segment have been novel to Russian military practice.

For the KSO, a new branch in the Russian military, Syria became a period of professional and organizational establishment. The KSO forces in the theater of operations interchangeably took responsibility over the ISR, C2 and Strike elements of the RSC. When functioning as the ISR segment, the KSO played the most central role in the acquisition and designation of targets of strategic operational importance, such as leadership and C2 centers, for a strike by the artillery and air force (*navedenie I korrektsia udarov*).[12] Given the Syrian experience, it seems that the ISR responsibilities of the KSO as an organic part of the reconnaissance-strike (RS) and reconnaissance-fire (RF) complexes will continue to increase and become institutionalized.

Since 2012, the Russian Armed Forces have taken a huge leap forward in the quality and quantity of the UAV fleet. As part of the modernization in this field, the military established 38 new UAV units and detachments, which together operated more than 1,800 drones of various types. The aim was to improve the ability of the forces to conduct ISR missions to a tactical-operational depth of up to 500 kilometers, and to deploy them for the sake of so-called "Radio-Electronic Struggle (REB)[13], C2 and strike missions, in frames of the various RS and RF complexes; and to significantly increase the combat capabilities and effectiveness of the general-purpose forces, artillery and operational-tactical aviation.[14] The operation in Syria employed an unprecedented, in terms of types and numbers, fleet of UAVs. On average, at any given moment, 60–70 reconnaissance, strike and radio-electronic suppression UAVs have flown over the theater of operations. All branches have been using UAVs extensively in Syria in order to create reconnaissance-strike and reconnaissance-fire contours on the operational and tactical levels. As of this writing, in the midst of the lesson-learning process, the Russian high command does not envision future combat activities for any of the services that would not involve use of UAVs.[15]

All the ISR missions of the UAV fleet in Syria, as well as the subsequent feeding of the targets bank to precision weapons systems, sea and air cruise and ground ballistic missiles, as well as precision-guided bombs and the C2 architecture, were based on the GLONASS system. In 2011, the Russian MoD received for trial this satellite constellation, which provides navigation services, PGM satellite guidance and automated C2. In the subsequent years it entered service, both the space and ground segments of the system have been constantly improved. However, despite persistent upgrades and investments, it still falls short of satisfying "the most demanding applications, from mapping to high-precision weapons." In Syria, Russia field-tested all three abovementioned functions of the system. Despite losing several satellites in failed launches throughout the Syrian campaign, Russia had between 21 and 27 satellites in orbit. This was sufficient to provide 95 percent of the system's global availability to conduct its three main missions for most of the time.[16]

The main users of GLONASS included Su-24M, Su-25SM, Su-27SM3, Su-30, Su-34 and Su-35 jets, naval aviation aircraft, and Tu-22M3 long-range bombers equipped with targeting and navigation stations.

Moreover, satellite navigation technologies made it possible to radically improve the accuracy of the massive strikes with free-falling unguided bombs from the GLONASS-guided strategic bombers. According to a Russian expert, "the bombers can now automatically follow a preset course, and drop unguided munitions at a precise point in their flight."[17] The exact proportion of the PGMs used in the Russian operation in Syria is still unclear. According to expert on the Russian military Michael Kofman, less than 10 percent of the strikes conducted in Syria utilized PGMs. And in the case of precision strikes, Russian forces faced the greatest difficulty hitting small, maneuvering targets, which demanded the ability to rapidly close sensor-to-shooter loops and/or a fleet of strike-capable UAVs.[18] Russian sources mention around 200 air, sea and underwater missiles that were launched. All of these munitions, however, were GLONASS-capable and supported by C4ISR.[19]

According to Russian experts, GLONASS enabled the Russian Air Force to operate in the unfamiliar desert-mountain-urban terrain and to pinpoint well-disguised targets there. Seeking accuracy and caution in the densely populated areas was probably less of a demand for the Russian operators than for their Western or Israeli counterparts dealing with the same missions. Nonetheless, it was in fact much more important than the majority of Western commentators have tended to argue, frequently describing Russian aerial attacks as little more than indiscriminate carpet bombings.[20] The accuracy of the GLONASS-based PGM strikes in Syria, on which Russian sources report, suggests that Russia probably deployed ground correction stations in the theater of operations. The effectiveness of such strikes without this supporting system in the current state of affairs would probably drop significantly. The Russians are aware of this limitation and will probably, as one of the possible lessons from Syria, work intensively to improve in this regard in order to be able to further refine their ability to wage network-centric warfare and utilize the technologies supporting this ecosystem.[21]

C2 Segment of the Complex

The Syrian operation was a baptism by fire for the National Defense Management Center (NTsUO), which, in the words of the CGS and the MoD, fundamentally changed the Russian approach to the command, control and management of the armed forces and operations, and which is today the "key link in the system of state military management."[22] The establishment of the center in 2013 was probably one of the pivotal events in the realm of Russian C2 architecture and *modus operandi*. The NTsUO merges into one unified interagency system analogous centers at all the levels of management and in all the federal entities involved in national security—158 federal and regional state organs, and 1,320 state corporations and companies of the military-industrial complex. The intra-net, which supports the NTsUO, established a unified informational space for all the entities at all the levels. The daily combat duty shift of the NTsUO with representatives on the strategic, operational and tactical levels consists of 10,000 officers. It covers the entire range of subjects, from early warning on nuclear-missile attack, nuclear retaliation, air and missile defense, to managing actual combat activities in a given theater of operation.[23]

The center made it possible to establish during the operation in Syria a unique C2 architecture and procedures from the strategic level in Moscow to the tactical-operational level on the ground. It was tailor-made for the Syrian operation, but this novel architecture and the systems supporting it reflected the reforms aimed at improving the C2 in NCW operations since 2008.[24] Russian generals see the effective C2 segment as a pledge for the operation's overall success. Following the decision to intervene, a tri-level C2 architecture emerged. The highest-level operator was the Group of Combat Management within the NTsUO. The Command Post of the Grouping of Forces within the Khmeimim airbase was the second layer of C2, and Operational Groups of Advisors on all the tactical-operational directions was the lowest expression of this architecture.[25]

The Group of Combat Management consisted of around-the-clock shifts, which included representatives from all organs of military management. The tasks of the group included collection, analysis and assessment of the combat situation, of decisions made by the Command of the Grouping of Forces, and of the planned subsequent operational activities. The duty shifts provided regular situational updates on these issues to the MoD and the CGS. This constant situational awareness made it possible to rapidly adapt to the changing trends and situation on the ground. The Group coordinated with representatives of the United States, Turkey, the Special United Nations Envoys in Geneva and Damascus, the Cease Fire Monitoring center in Geneva, and also all Russian representatives interacting with the involved actors within international organizations. As such, it was responsible for the uninterrupted staff work on the military-political issues involving combat, diplomatic and humanitarian activities related to Syria.[26]

The Command Post of the Grouping of Forces, located in Khmeimim, ensured the coordination of activities of the Russian Forces in Syria with the Syrian Army, Republican Guard, and local and foreign militias. It consisted of representatives of all organs, services and military districts involved in the operation. The Post was also responsible for the coordination of combat activities and informational exchange in order to avoid accidents with the US operational centers in Jordan and Qatar, and with the Turkish and Israeli air force Command Centers. Operational Groups of Advisers— the lowest level of C2—coordinated on the tactical level through the C2 centers established within the Syrian Army Corps with the militias of all types supporting Syrian President Bashar al-Assad. The number of these groups varied according to the operational demands; during the most active phases of the operation, there were 15 groups of this kind.[27]

The NTsUO, which benefited from all the types of communication and data collection and analysis, became a hybrid of the traditional

Russian wartime supreme command (Stavka) and the GS. The CGS and MoD observed in real time all activities on the ground, including air, artillery, missile and long-range PGM strikes. The Command Post in Khmeimim waged the operation and did the staff work supporting it; however, it was fully and uninterruptedly accessible to the supreme military leadership in Moscow.[28] One may, thus, consider it the tactical-operational equivalents of the *Stavka* representatives during the war.

During the several years preceding the Syrian operation, special attention was paid to producing and deploying mobile automatic field C2 posts on the tactical-operational level, aimed at enabling effective and reliable combat management. When the Syrian operation started the development of an automatic C2 system of troops and weaponry on the tactical level was accomplished. It enables automatic collection and analysis of the information for the sake of the situation estimate, planning of combat activity, sending orders and combat missions, fire management, and logistical-rear support of the forces. The system was tested during the strategic exercises Kavkaz 2016 and Zapad 2017. From 2018, the equipment of this unified tactical-level C2 system, which the Syria war made possible to test and refine, will start arriving to the general-purpose forces.[29] GLONASS supported all tiers of these automated C2 systems, from the tactical to strategic levels. "The new Strelets reconnaissance, target designation and communication systems, which are part of the tactical automated C2 tier, are used to acquire target coordinates on the ground. The HQ of the Russian forces in Syria has been able to successfully coordinate the deployment of the different branches and services of the armed forces, as well as to coordinate strikes from the ground, sea and air. At the sub-strategic level, all the data on the coordinates of the battlefield assets and targets is fed to the National Defense Management Center."[30]

In support of the above C2 architecture, Russia deployed a communications system, which included cell, radio and video communication capabilities. Russian forces introduced full communication capacity into the non-equipped theater of operations and provided all segments of the tactical-operational level of C2 with a full spectrum of secured tele-, video and document connections. This facilitated rapid decision-making and execution as well as effective strikes. The equipment made possible a constant data flow for the UAV and other ISR sources on collective usage screens, which enabled better bomb damage assessment (BDA) and adjustments for the next rounds of fire and sorties. The system afforded interoperability of the communications system of the Grouping with the secured and closed telephony and intra-net and informational-telecommunication network of the MoD. The system was self-sufficient and deployed stationary and mobile complexes on the ground that maintained these secured tele-, video and radio communications. Data produced by the UAVs was transmitted to the collective usage displays in the Syrian theater of operations and in Moscow. All components of this triple architecture, including the operational C2 groups on the tactical level deployed within the C2 centers of the Syrian army, were interconnected. All the above enabled uninterrupted and effective command and control of the operation from Moscow.[31] In keeping with the canonical principles of Russian operational art, this C2 architecture linked all tactical activities in all directions with a unified operational plot (*edinyi operativnyi zamysel*) of the theater of operations, and orchestrated them all from the command post in Khmeimim.[32]

Probably due to the Syrian experience, new C2 structures were introduced and adjusted in one Ground Forces army and in the Northern Fleet.[33] According to Russian commentators, during 2017, the unified tactical-level C2 system, following training and adjustments, reduced the time needed for organizing combat activity by 20–30 percent, and accelerated the combat management tempo by 1.5–3 times.[34] Given the favorable assessment of its effectiveness and *modus operandi*, this C2 architecture is likely to be preserved in future practice.

Strike Segment of the Complex

In Russian military terminology, reconnaissance-strike complex, or RSC, refers to the strategic-operational combat activities and reconnaissance-fire complex, or RFC, to the operational-tactical ones, although there is not much consistency—commanders and commentators often use these terms interchangeably. In any case, the General Staff divided its strike capabilities according to concentric zones: for the far zone of destruction (a radius of 4,000 km), it used sea- (Kalibr) and air-based (Kh-101) cruise missiles and Tu-22M3 strategic bombers; in the medium zone of destruction (up to 500 km), it employed Su-24s and Su-33s, capable of conducting precision strikes thanks to a special targeting and guidance system; even in the near zone of destruction, it saw its activities as a "reconnaissance-strike contour," based on the C4ISR Strelets system and Su-24Ms. During the operation, the GS formatted and tested RS and RF complexes for the needs of the Missile Forces and Artillery (RViA), which enabled the destruction of the adversary in close to real time.[35]

Gerasimov's reflections on the Syrian operation clearly demonstrate an intent to wage modern warfare and a perception of the forces as RS and RF complexes. Also, the GS tested for the first time a massive sea-based and air-based precision-guided missile strike and their joint use in a coordinated salvo. It positively assessed the results of these three types of PGM usage.[36] In addition to the favorable estimate of air-based precision strikes launched from strategic aviation systems and from nonstrategic Su-34 bombers armed with KAB-500 bombs and laser-guided Kh-29L missiles, the GS was also satisfied with the use of unguided bombs by operational-tactical aviation. This was possible mainly thanks to the GLONASS-based SVP-24 Gefest aiming and navigation system, which enables nonstrategic platforms such as the Su-24M and Su-25SM to conduct strikes with unguided munitions, making their effectiveness comparable to that of the precision-guided strikes.[37]

The employment of main missile and artillery pieces, mortars and howitzers, as well as thermobaric weapons within the RviA arsenal—the non-precision weapons—also received a most favorable assessment. Some of these were modern systems and some several-decades-old pieces of weaponry. The overall estimate of these general-purpose forces is most positive.[38] Probably what ensures the high satisfaction with these systems are the conditions provided by the ISR and C2 segments, which enable maximum effectiveness of what may seem at first glance to be relatively dated systems. Similarly, the KSO, in addition to target acquisition and designation, was also involved in missions of leadership decapitation, and the destruction of critically important material, C2 and supply infrastructure objects in the operational and strategic rear.[39] As such, it functioned as an element in the Strike segment of the RSC.

Syria provided ample training and experience in combined-arms warfare and especially close air support (CAS). On the tactical level, forces on the ground closed sensor-shooter loops in real time using available ISR and striking jets. These ground units then conducted BDA by using the UAVs for another "observe, orient, decide, and act" (OODA) loop and self-synchronization.[40]

The ground forces' bid to enable their commanders to turn the forces under their command into RS and RF complexes is not novel. For example, in 2014, this was exactly the message of the RviA branch commander.[41] However, as the commander of the Russian Airborne Troop (VDV) forces put it in 2017, the Syrian experience enabled his and other branches of the general-purpose forces to train commanders to have under their authority and to employ the entire spectrum of ISR and fire capabilities. This sounds like the main takeaway from the Syrian operation and one of the main emphases that his branch and other services received from the CGS and MoD during a recent gathering of the Armed Forces high command. He did not envision this as a given skill, but as something that commanders should learn to employ.[42] Indeed, the annual gathering of the high command in July 2017 used the Syrian experience as the basis for further military modernization. That gathering, along with several military exercises that followed, emphasized, among other topics, the employment of RS and RF complexes.[43] The expectation of the Ground Forces from the State Armaments Program (GPV) is similar—to sustain highly mobile and self-sufficient brigades, capable of functioning as mini-RFCs thanks to their fire, ISR and C2 capabilities.[44]

Other Themes Pertaining to Operational Art

In addition to the lessons learned about the segments of the RSC, Russian sources have covered several other themes related to general questions of strategy, operational art and tactics. These insights relate directly to the lessons learned about RSCs but still form a separate category. Specifically, within the Russian professional discourse, the issues that have so far loomed large pertain to the state armaments program, strategic mobility, Radio-Electronic Struggle, exercises and the curriculum of military institutions, as well as qualities of modern commanders.

Self-Sufficient Groupings of Forces and State Armaments Program

The use of PGMs in Syria was a fruit of the incremental rearmament reform aimed at producing self-sufficient groupings of forces armed with precision-guided capabilities in strategically important theaters of operation. According to Gerasimov, by 2017, the accumulated arsenal of PGM capabilities, with an emphasis on Kalibr cruise missiles, Bastion shore-to-sea missiles and S-400 AD systems, made it possible to produce groupings of forces and deploy them in the Baltic, Barents, Black and Mediterranean Seas,[45] corresponding with the logic epitomized in the Western terminology of anti-access and area denial (A2/AD) bubbles.[46] Presumably, the Syrian experience will inject further conceptual and financial energy into promoting this trend. From now on, the high command envisions massive use of PGMs as part and parcel of all operations of the Russian Armed Forces.[47] With regard to the navy, according to the deputy chief of the General Staff, the effectiveness of the strike potentially enables long blue-water raids and patrols and affords the ability to conduct autonomous or joint strikes according to operational needs.[48]

Syria became the testing ground for new weapons and technologies in general as well as for cruise missiles, PGMs and UAVs in particular. Thus, just as the lessons from Georgia shaped the force buildup and modernization, Russian experts expect the lessons learned from Syria to leave an even more significant imprint on the State Armaments Program and force buildup.[49] Russian military experts Roger N. McDermott and Dmitry Gorenburg assumed that, in light of the Syrian lessons, the next GPV and military modernization plans will emphasize high-technology C4ISR assets and stand-off strike capabilities.[50] Indeed, one of the top priorities of the Russian force buildup is to produce a "new-generation military"; another is to create "self-sufficient, effective groupings of forces on the key directions for state security."[51] Providing guidance toward the new GPV, President Vladimir Putin urged that special emphasis be placed on equipping forces with sea-, air- and land-based PGMs, reconnaissance-strike UAVs, modern C4ISR and REB capabilities, as well as individual equipment for soldiers, such as Ratnik.[52] The next GPV, based on the lessons learned from Syria, pays special attention to the quality and quantity of the PGM arsenal and the C4ISR systems supporting it, including UAVs and space satellites as its main enablers in all the branches.[53] Russian officials and experts commenting on the next GPV see this as the strongest emphasis of the program, second only to the modernization of the nuclear triad.[54]

Further promotion of robotics is another takeaway from the Syrian experience; Moscow sees it as a force substitute and multiplier. It also resonates well with Putin's remark on the strategic competitive advantage that the control and skillful use of artificial intelligence (AI) provides, and corresponds with the initial emphasis on the subject that gave birth to the Fund of Prospective Research (the Russian equivalent of DARPA) in 2010. Presumably, at this stage at least, references made to "combat robots" relate less to developing a new generation of systems, and mainly to upgrading existing firepower through its informationalization and intellectualization. One of the main directions of procurement stemming directly from the Syrian experience will be an emphasis on automatic digital guidance and fire control of the artillery systems, which suggests that the introduction of robotics is about organically merging fire and C4ISR capabilities.[55]

Strategic Mobility

The Syrian campaign also offered rich experience in conducting a massive expeditionary operation. Never before had post-Soviet Russia deployed and sustained an expeditionary force so far from its borders, for such a long time and with such intensity. The reform in military logistics (*material'no-tekhnicheskoe obespechenie*— MTO), ongoing since 2010, made it possible to sustain stable lines of maritime and aerial supply, which enabled uninterrupted combat activities. Exercises and snap inspections in the years preceding the operation trained long-range forces in redeployment (*perebroska*) by using air, sea and railway transport. These laid the ground for the successful rapid and clandestine deployment of the forces.[56] Building the infrastructure to support strategic mobility, including improvements in the MTO system, started under Defense Minister Sergei Shoigu. But the Syrian operation made it possible to test and refine them. The prioritization of this segment is likely to remain intact.[57] Snap inspections, which have taken place since 2013, were, in fact, generally pre-announced; and they often turned into a *pokazukha* (an event staged for show), for personal and institutional reasons. That said, they still constituted a genuine effort to diagnose actual combat readiness problems and improve performance according to the findings. Operational effectiveness in Crimea and in the Syrian operation, which Russian commentators mention, attests to this.[58]

Russian experts reflecting on the Syrian experience concluded that victory depended in equal measure on combat activities, on maintaining a proper level of MTO, and on expeditionary capabilities (*vozmozhnosti operativnoi perebroski voisk*).[59] Gerasimov views an effective MTO system as one of the main factors of success in the Syrian operation that made it possible to project power and then sustain the forces on the ground with uninterrupted provision of armaments, spare parts and supplies. This resulted in uninterrupted combat activities—one of the main principles of Russian operational art.[60] Naturally, another of Putin's top-priority elements for the next GPV was an increase in force mobility and power projection capabilities. This relates to the "organization of logistics, transportation and supply of forces, their ability to rapidly deploy and act," in remote theaters of operation.[61] The strategic exercises Kavkaz 2016 and Zapad 2017 elaborated on the best and the worst practices from Syria and further refined operational and logistical procedures to ensure speed and effectiveness in transportation, supply, repair and technological maintenance.[62] The redeployment of forces in the framework of six snap inspections, which took place only during 2017, further refined strategic mobility skills. This experience of operational mobility is immediately relevant for Russia itself, in terms of deploying and redeploying forces in the hinterland.[63] Putin's guidance to the military for the strategic exercise Vostok 2018 urged it to test the ability to transport a large combined-arms expeditionary force to a distance of several thousand kilometers and deploy it in a faraway theater of operations as a self-sufficient grouping of forces.[64]

Experience related to strategic mobility acquired in Syria will be learned, refined and incorporated.[65] The implementation of some lessons is already evident. In 2017, probably influenced by the impact of the Syrian operation, the VKS established a new military-transportation air division (*voenno-transportnaia aviatsionnaia diviziia*) and a special-purpose air division (*aviatsionnaia diviziia osobogo naznacheniia*).[66] Also, the strengths and weaknesses of intensive maritime Syrian operations prompted Russian experts to recommend turning production of the landing ships into one of the main priorities of military-technical policy for the next decade. This refers to both the numbers and types, including a recommendation to produce bigger ships than those of Projects 775 and 1171. The lessons learned as regards the auxiliary fleet (*vspomogatel'nyi flot*), especially from the shortages of vessels which resulted in a crash program of hiring and purchasing old transport vessels even from Turkey, highlight the need to equip the VMF with its own, specialized naval transportation segment, which will have its own capacity to upload and offload various military cargo, including technique and armaments, in a self-sufficient manner.[67]

Radio-Electronic Struggle

A significant portion of the Russian discourse deals with the lessons related to Radio-Electronic Struggle (REB). As for other systems, Syria became a testing ground for REB assets of all types, both old and modern. Experts assume that the lessons from there are about to shape the next rounds of modernization in the field.[68] In the years preceding the Syrian operation, the MoD invested significantly in force buildup, concept of operations, and organization of the REB forces operating in the ground, aerial and naval domains. Since 2012, 19 new REB systems arrived to the forces, more than 2,000 pieces in total, which brought the overall share of modern types of REB equipment in the Russian military to 79 percent. The main trends were to expand the types of targets the REB systems can effectively engage, extend their ranges in terms of intelligence, defense and suppression missions, and enable their maximum compatibility with PGM systems and UAVs.[69] It seems that the constantly growing employment of REB systems for defensive, offensive and intelligence missions in recent conflicts, in Syria in particular, coupled with previous theoretical discussions, stimulated the REB senior commanders to claim broader organizational responsibilities. In 2017, they urged that the current status of REB be changed from being a supporting corps of the Ground Forces into a fifth branch, alongside Armor, Mechanized

Infantry, Missile Forces and Artillery, and Air Defense. Moreover, they claimed that this branch should be assigned the leading part in contemporary operations, which would imply a revision of the traditional roles of the branches, transforming REB into one of the main tools of victory in modern operations—a role, until recently, reserved for mechanized infantry and armor. Effectively, the REB branch would become the first among the four equals. Although discussions are still underway, the dominant role of the REB in ISR, C2 disorganization and anti-PGM defense in combined arms operations is already evident and is likely to continue growing. The same increasing role of the REB branch, according to the Russian sources, might be expected across the board in other services of the Russian Armed Forces in the coming years.[70]

Exercises and Curriculum of Military Institutions

In keeping with the innovation and transformation pattern described above, exercises, drills, maneuvers and adjustments in the curriculum of military institutions have already contributed to testing, training, refining and disseminating the Syrian experience. According to Gerasimov, the Armed Forces should constantly adjust and refine their field manuals and force training methods based on the Syrian combat experience, lessons from other military conflicts, and the analysis of the changing character of war.[71] In particular, his emphasis was on testing new forms of long-range and stand-off strike capabilities, and on the use of RS and RF complexes.[72] For example, the strategic annual exercise Zapad 2017 clearly underscored the main operational-tactical takeaway from the Syrian operation: training and disseminating across the brigades actual RSC and RFC skills saturated with precision-guided capabilities both in the theater of operations and at longer ranges.[73] Similarly, methods used in Syria were easily identifiable in the deployment of A2/AD bubbles during the Zapad exercise.[74] The Syrian experience featured in other training activities of the Western Military District (MD) during 2017. Armor, artillery, special forces, engineer and helicopter units train in combined-arms operations, adjusting to the reality of fighting against asymmetrical threats, training to use their own C4ISR and combined warfare.[75]

According to a district commander, who until recently headed the Grouping of Forces in Syria, the plan of operational and combat readiness activities for the Western MD in 2018, based on lessons both from Syria and from Zapad 2017, will further emphasize training forces to employ RS and RF complexes. Additional emphases of the training activities resonate with the dictum of the CGS and MoD about the qualities of commanders that Syria highlighted: competitiveness, self-education, learning, and a willingness to depart from the template and to express "reasonable initiative."[76] Similar activities, based on the lessons learned from Syria, took place in other military districts during 2017. For example, the artillery of the light combined-arms brigade of the Central MD tested fire support for new light brigades operating against "hybrid" actors in "mountain-desert terrain." The aim of the exercise was to destroy a maneuverable asymmetrical enemy (groupings of jihad-mobiles and shahid-mobiles) by combining air and artillery fire support with the fire capabilities of the light brigade's motorized infantry. The idea was to provide training in conducting nontraditional, not massive but surgical strikes to support maneuvering forces.[77]

In terms of operational-tactical themes, Russian sources have focused on waging combined-arms operations in urban, mountain and desert combat environments, as well as mining and demining operations, both standalone and as part of urban warfare.[78] Interestingly, next to relatively obvious tactical-op issues, they emphasize *maskirovka*, deception and military cunning, as well as the maintenance of a proper moral-psychological climate for the forces; they stress these as constant factors enabling operational success against this type of hybrid enemy.[79] As Russian military commanders continue to distill lessons from the Syrian experience, the annual strategic exercise Vostok 2018 will likely become the best opportunity to systematically test and refine all the experience that has been accumulated thus far.

In parallel, related activities have been evident within the sphere of professional military education. For example, the Moscow Highest School of All-Forces Commanders, the main educational institution of the Ground Forces, rotated almost half of its officers-professors from the Tactics Faculty on internship tours to Syria in order to adjust their theoretical insights and educational programs based on the insights from combat practice. In addition to participating in preparing the new Field Manual of the Ground Forces (especially the section on the employment of tactical battalion groups), based on the lessons learned, they incorporated their insights in the curriculum. In addition to insights about urban warfare and managing combined-arms warfare of small tactical groups using artillery, close air support and UAVs, special emphasis is laid upon cultivating among the future commanders creative tactical thinking and the ability to form a general picture of the dynamic and constantly changing combat situation and the organizing logic of the adversary, to foresee trends in its further development, as well as rapidly make decisions and formulate orders and missions for soldiers and units.[80]

Conclusion: Professional Qualities of Contemporary Commanders

According to Gerasimov, snap inspections and other training activities linked to commanders' skills and qualities have incorporated lessons learned from modern conflicts. They are aimed at cultivating commanders' abilities to rapidly assess the situation, foresee its development, make non-standard decisions, employ military cunning, act unexpectedly and surprise the adversary, opt for calculated risk, as well as capture and preserve the initiative.[81] Reform of the Armed Forces during the last decade has sought to cultivate these qualities, and Gerasimov further underscored them in reference to the training of commanders based on lessons learned from Syria. According to him, contemporary warfare demands uninterrupted deception and disinformation of the adversary; enemy forces should be surprised, disorganized and then destroyed; commanders should be creative, energetic, prone to initiative, not think by the book and employ military ingenuity (*voennaia smekalka*). "Template and blind sticking to the field manuals are not acceptable." Gerasimov sees the Syrian experience as invaluable for many reasons, *inter alia* because it highlighted talented commanders blessed with non-standard, ingenious and creative thinking. These qualities, more than anything else, will promise promotion according to Gerasimov.[82]

Importantly, such flexible and innovative qualities perfectly correspond with the skills needed for the effective creation and employment of RS and RF complexes.[83] Shoigu, during the meeting with the high command that looked at, among other things, the lessons from the Syrian campaign and commanders' ability to deploy and employ ROKs and RUKs, emphasized the need to think outside the box (*nestandartnoe myshlenie*)—that is, to develop the ability to find and realize new forms of waging operations.[84] This dictum corresponds with one of the main postulates of Soviet/Russian operational art—operational creativity (*operativenoe tvorchestvo*)—and resonates with Putin's references to a theory of victory based on qualitative and not quantitative superiority, on higher operational skills and strategic ingenuity.[85] During the last several years, the growing number of war games and sport-military competitions, in addition to patriotic *pokazukha*, indeed cultivated these skills.[86] In parallel, the Russian military brass has begun to intensively cultivate the principle of competitiveness among the troops (*printsip soztiazatel'nosti*) and incorporate it in all levels of command.[87] This principle makes it possible to further refine the qualities that the high command seeks to nurture and promote.

Notes

[1] For example, see: Dmitry (Dima) Adamsky, "From Moscow with Coercion: Russian Deterrence Theory and Strategic Culture," *Journal of Strategic Studies* 41, no. 1, 2018.

[2] Viktor Baranets, "Mi Slomali Khrebet Udarnym Silam Terrorizma," *KZ*, December 29, 2017.

[3] See: Dmitry (Dima) Adamsky and Kejell Inge Bjerga, *Contemporary Military Innovation: Between Anticipation and Adaptation* (London" Routledge, 2013).

[4] Viktor Baranets, "Mi Slomali Khrebet Udarnym Silam Terrorizma."

[5] Viktor Baranets and Iurii Avdeev, "Piatiletka Preobrazovanii," *KZ*, October 31, 2017; Editorial, "Itogi Spetsial'noi Operatsii v Sirii," *KZ*, December 24, 2017; "Vystuplenie Nachialnika GSh VS RF Valeriia Gerasimova na Otkrytom Zasedanii Kollegii MO Rossii," *MO RF*, Mil.ru, November 7, 2017.

[6] "Vystuplenie Nachialnika GSh VS RF Valeriia Gerasimova na Otkrytom Zasedanii Kollegii MO Rossi;" "Voennaia priemka. Aviatsiia v Sirii. Samolety. Chast' 2," *TV Zvezda*, August 14, 2017.

[7] Ibid.

[8] Viktor Baranets and Iurii Avdeev, "Piatiletka; Editorial, "Itogi Spetsial'noi Operatsii v Sirii"; "Vystuplenie Nachialnika GSh VS RF Valeriia Gerasimova na Otkrytom Zasedanii."

[9] See discussion: Dima Adamsky, *The Culture of Military Innovation: IT-RMA in Russia, the US and Israel* (Pale Alto: Stanford UP, 2010).

[10] "Vystuplenie Nachialnika GSh VS RF Valeriia Gerasimova na Otkrytom Zasedanii Kollegii MO Rossii."

[11] Editorial, "Genshtab: Rossiia v Sirii realizovala printsip odna tsel – odna bomba," *RIA Novosti*, November 7, 2017.

[12] Sergei Rudstkoi, "Osnovnye Etapy Operatsii VS RF v SAR i Osobennosti Organizatsii Sistemy Upravlenija," *Arsenal Otechestva*, no. 5(31), 2017, p. 25. Viktor Baranets Gavrilenko, Tikhonov, and Biriulin; Also see: Aleksandr Tikhonov, "Siriiskaia Proverka Boem," *KZ*, August 27, 2017.

[13] Generally known in the Western military professional lexicon as "Electronic Warfare" (EW).

[14] The work underway aims to provide the ability to conduct the entire range of missions to a depth of up to 3,000 km. "Vystuplenie Nachialnika GSh VS RF

Valeriia Gerasimova na Otkrytom Zasedanii Kollegii MO Rossii," *MO RF*, Mil.ru, November 7, 2017.

[15] Viktor Baranets, "Mi Slomali Khrebet Udarnym Silam Terrorizma."

[16] Anton Lavrov, "Russia's GLONASS Satellite Constellation," *Moscow Defense Brief*, no. 4, 2017.

[17] Ibid.

[18] Paul Iddon, "For the Russian Military in Syria, Old Habits Die Hard," *War Is Boring Blog*, December 9, 2017.

[19] Anton Lavrov, "Russia's GLONASS Satellite Constellation."

[20] Ibid.

[21] Also, the work is underway to develop satellite-guided shells for RViA; Ibid.

[22] Viktor Baranets, "Doklad pervogo zamestitelia MO RF Ruslana Tsalikova na Otrkrytom Zasedanii Kollegii MO Rossii," *MO RF*, mil.ru, November 7, 2017.

[23] Gavrilenko, Tikhonov, and Biriulin, "Vystuplenie Nachialnika GSh VS RF Valeriia Gerasimova na Otkrytom Zasedanii Kollegii MO Rossii," *MO RF*, Mil.ru, November 7, 2017. In that way, it further turned the GS and MoD into primus inter pares within the strategic community on matters of national security. See Golts, pp. 184–185.

[24] For the logic and essence of the reforms, see: Alexander Golts, *Military Reform and Militarism in Russia* (Uppsala: Uppsala University, 2017).

[25] Sergei Rudstkoi, "Osnovnye Etapy Operatsii VS RF v SAR i Osobennosti Organizatsii Sistemy Upravlenija."

[26] Ibid.

[27] Ibid.

[28] Viktor Baranets, "Doklad pervogo zamestitelia MO RF Ruslana Tsalikova na Otrkrytom Zasedanii Kollegii MO Rossii."

[29] "Vystuplenie Nachialnika GSh VS RF Valeriia Gerasimova na Otkrytom Zasedanii Kollegii MO Rossii," *MO RF*, Mil.ru, November 7, 2017.

[30] Anton Lavrov, "Russia's GLONASS Satellite Constellation."

[31] Also, for the first time ever Russian forces used a new method of secured and secret communication, utilizing the capacities of the local foreign operators' networks. Rudskoi, p. 26; Khalil Arsalanov, "Osobennosti Organizatsi Sviazi v Khode Boevykh Desitvii v SAR," *Arsenal Otechestva*, no. 5(31), 2017, pp. 27–30.

[32] Baranets.

[33] Gavrilenko, Tikhonov, and Biriulin; "Vystuplenie Nachialnika GSh VS RF Valeriia Gerasimova na Otkrytom Zasedanii Kollegii MO Rossii."

[34] Ibid.

[35] "Vystuplenie Nachialnika GSh VS RF Valeriia Gerasimova na Otkrytom Zasedanii Kollegii MO Rossii," *MO RF*, Mil.ru, November 7, 2017.

[36] Aleksandr Tikhonov, "Siriiskaia Proverka Boem," *KZ*, September 12, 2017. Also see: Gavrilenko, Tikhonov, and Biriulin.

[37] Ibid.

[38] Ibid. For additional discussion of the artillery systems, see: Iurii Liamin and Vitalii Moiseev, "Siriiskie Bogi Voiny," *Arsenal Otechestva* 31, no. 5, 2017; Leonid Kariakin, "Proverennye Boem," *Arsenal Otechestva* 30, no. 4, 2017.

[39] Rudstkoi, p. 25; Baranets; Gavrilenko, Tikhonov, and Biriulin, "Vystuplenie Nachialnika GSh VS RF Valeriia Gerasimova na Otkrytom Zasedanii Kollegii MO Rossii."

[40] Nikolai Surkov, "Siriiskaia shkola sovremennnoi voiny," *Izvestia*, December 29, 2017.

[41] Viktor Khudoleev, "Kursom k Razvedovatel'no-Ognevoi Sisteme," *KZ*, November 20, 2014.

[42] Editorial, "Udarnye i razvedpodrazdelenija VDV objedeniat pod odnim komandovaniem," *TASS*, July 31, 2017.

[43] Khairemdinov. The ability of the C2 organs to plan and conduct a joint combined arms ground operation was another major emphasis. "MO Sergei Shoigu v ramkakh sbora rukovodiashego sostava VS proveril gotovnost' organov voennogo upravleniia k boevomu primeneniju," *MO RF*, milru, July 19. 2017; "MO v ramkakh operativnogo sbora rukovodiashcego sostava VS pribyl vo Vladimirskuju oblast," *MO RF*, mil.ru, July 20, 2017.

[44] Gavrilenko, Tikhonov, and Biriulin; "Vystuplenie Nachialnika GSh VS RF Valeriia Gerasimova na Otkrytom Zasedanii Kollegii MO Rossii."

[45] "Vystuplenie Nachialnika GSh VS RF Valeriia Gerasimova na Otkrytom Zasedanii Kollegii MO Rossii," *MO RF*, Mil.ru, November 7, 2017.

[46] For example, see: Morgan Paglia, "The Role of Access-Denial in Coercive Diplomacy," *Asia Focus*, no. 55, IRIS, December 2017.

[47] "Vystuplenie Nachialnika GSh VS RF Valeriia Gerasimova na Otkrytom Zasedanii Kollegii MO Rossii."

[48] Aleksandr Tikhonov, "Siriiskaia Proverka Boem," *KZ*, September 12, 2017. Also see: Gavrilenko, Tikhonov, and Biriulin; "Vystuplenie Nachialnika GSh VS RF Valeriia Gerasimova na Otkrytom Zasedanii Kollegii MO Rossii." The jury is still out regarding the lessons related to the Russian air carrier *Kuznetsov*. Available comments by Russian experts suggest that the main directions for further modernization might be enhancement of the PGM and REB capabilities, and the ability to integrate itself into the RSC operating in the theater of operations by improvements of its own C4ISR capabilities. This would also further improve its ability to function as a self-sufficient RSC. Editorial, "Siriiskii opyt Kuznetsova," *TASS*, February 8, 2017. Also see: Roger McDermott, "Shoigu Promotes Russia's Effective Army Plans to 2025," *Eurasia Daily Monitor*, Volume 14, Issue 54, April 25, 2017.

[49] M. Iu. Shepovalenko, *Siriiskeii Rubezh* (Moscow: CAST, 2016), pp. 119–120.

[50] Roger McDermott, "High Technology Set to Dominate Russia's Rearmament Program," *Eurasia Daily Monitor*, Volume 14, Issue 154, November 29, 2017; Dmitry Gorenburg, "Russia's Military Modernization Plans: 2018–2027," *PONARIS*, no. 495, November 2017.

[51] Gavrilenko, Tikhonov, and Biriulin; "Vystuplenie Nachialnika GSh VS RF Valeriia Gerasimova na Otkrytom Zasedanii Kollegii MO Rossii."

[52] Given the very high estimate of the Ratnik individual equipment kit and frequent references to it by the Russian political and military leaders, it seems that massive acquisition is likely to turn into one of the main procurement trends. This is more than just a tactical issue; according to the Ground Forces commander, "the units equipped with this third-generation individual equipment will be autonomous and self-sufficient for the wide range of combat activities and capable of integrating themselves into RSCs." Gavrilenko, Tikhonov, and Biriulin. As the KSO experience suggests, the integration equally relates to the ISR, C2 and Strikes components of the complexes.

[53] Avdeev.

[54] Editorial, "Iadernye sily – glavnyi element sderzhivaniia," *NVO*, December 8, 2017.

[55] McDermott, "High Technology." Western scholars question, however, the move in this direction due to the potential obstacles from the military-industrial complex entities driven by parochial considerations. For example, see: John Grady, "Experts: Syrian War Prompting Russians to Expand Unmanned Systems," *The US Naval Institute*, October 9, 2017.

[56] Baranets. In the Gerasimov-Shoigu reforms, VDV troops have been developed as the basis of the rapid reaction forces, capable of swiftly regrouping, deploying and employing their battalion tactical groups in any strategic direction; "Vystuplenie Nachialnika GSh VS RF Valeriia Gerasimova na Otkrytom Zasedanii Kollegii MO Rossii."

[57] "Doklad pervogo zamestitelia MO RF Ruslana Tsalikova na Otrkrytom Zasedanii Kollegii MO Rossii," *MO RF*, mil.ru, 7 November 2017. For Serdiukov-Shoigu reforms see Golts, pp.185-194.

[58] See Golts, pp.185–194. "Vystuplenie Nachialnika GSh VS RF Valeriia Gerasimova na Otkrytom Zasedanii Kollegii MO Rossii," *MO RF*, Mil.ru, November 7, 2017; Surkov.

[59] Ibid.

[60] "Vystuplenie Nachialnika GSh VS RF Valeriia Gerasimova na Otkrytom Zasedanii Kollegii MO Rossii." Khmeimim was launching around 100 sorties daily.

[61] Gavrilenko, Tikhonov, and Biriulin; "Vystuplenie Nachialnika GSh VS RF Valeriia Gerasimova na Otkrytom Zasedanii Kollegii MO Rossii."

[62] For detailed discussion of the MTO and primary sources on the subject, see: Roger McDermott, "Zapad 2017: Myth and Reality," *Eurasia Daily Monitor* Volume 14, Issue 126, The Jamestown Foundation October 10, 2017.

[63] Gavrilenko, Tikhonov, and Biriulin; "Vystuplenie Nachialnika GSh VS RF Valeriia Gerasimova na Otkrytom Zasedanii Kollegii MO Rossii."

[64] Surkov.

[65] Baranets.

[66] Gavrilenko, Tikhonov, and Biriulin; "Vystuplenie Nachialnika GSh VS RF Valeriia Gerasimova na Otkrytom Zasedanii Kollegii MO Rossii."

[67] Shepovalenko, p. 129–131. Also see: M.L. Abramov, "Commentary," in Shepovalenko, p. 132.

[68] Sergey Sukhanin, "Syrian Lessons and Russia's Asymmetric Response to the US," *EDM* 14, no. 118, September 26, 2017.

[69] "Vystuplenie Nachialnika GSh VS RF Valeriia Gerasimova na Otkrytom Zasedanii Kollegii MO Rossii."

[70] Iu.I. Lastochkin Iu.L. Koziratskii, Iu.E. Donskov, A.L. Moraresku, "Boevoe primenenie voisk REB kak sostavnaia chast' operativnogo iskusstva ob'edeneniia SV," *Voennaia Mysl'*, no. 9, 2017, pp. 18–26; Editorial, "Russia's upgraded Mig-29 fighter jets to test new aircraft armament in Syria," *TASS*, December 7, 2017.

[71] "Vystuplenie Nachialnika GSh VS RF Valeriia Gerasimova na Otkrytom Zasedanii Kollegii MO Rossii."

[72] Ibid.

[73] Michael Kofman, "What Actually Happened During Zapad 2017," *Russian Military Analysis Blog*, December 22, 2017.

[74] Roger McDermott, "Zapad 2017 and the Initial Period of War," *Eurasia Daily Monitor*, Volume 14, Issue 115, September 20, 2017.

[75] Andrei Khokhlov, "V Voiska Vnedriaetsia pobednyi Siriiskii opyt," *Vecherniaia Moskva*, December 13, 2017.

[76] Andrei Kartapalov, "Okrug Udarnykh Zadach," *KZ*, December 6, 2017.

[77] Andrei Bondarenko, "Pod pritselom – dzhihad mobili," *KZ*, July 9, 2017.

[78] Surkov.

[79] Solomatin, page 32. Among the counterintuitive tactical insights that have emerged so far is the notion that tanks in this type of operations were not used in the canonical massive manner, maneuvering while supported by aviation and artillery deep into the operational depth to encircle, along the lines of 20th century tactics, but rather as standalone pieces of the offensive and defensive fire support and as multipliers of tactical effectiveness of the limited forces. It seems that in the course of a hundred years, the armor has come full circle and reacquired its early historical responsibility of providing support to the infantry. Iurii Liamin and Vitalii Moiseev, "Ural'skie tanki v Sirii," *Arsenal Otechestva* 27, no. 1, 2017.

[80] Nikolai Moiseenko, "Glavnaia Auditoriia – Poligon," *KZ*, December 14, 2017; Editorial, "MosVOKU vzialo na vooruzhenie Siriiskii opyt," *Voennoe Obozrenie*, December 15, 2017.

[81] "Vystuplenie Nachialnika GSh VS RF Valeriia Gerasimova na Otkrytom Zasedanii Kollegii MO Rossii."

[82] Editorial, "General Gerasimov: Siriiskii Opyt – Bestsennaia shkola dlia Rossiiskikh voisk," *POLITROSSIA*, 5 Febraury 2017; "V Voennoi akademii GSh VS RF proshlo ocherednoe zaniatie kursa Armiia I Obschestvo," *MO RF*, mil.ru, Febraury 3, 2017; "Vystuplenie Nachialnika GSh VS RF Valeriia Gerasimova na Otkrytom Zasedanii Kollegii MO Rossii."

[83] Despite the very important contribution of the VKS to the victory, eventually, according to Gerasimov, it was forged on the ground. This, in his view, further underscores the importance of the general-purpose ground commanders. Editorial, "General Gerasimov: Siriiskii Opyt – Bestsennaia shkola dlia Rossiiskikh voisk."

[84] Leonid Khairemdinov, "Siriiskii Opyt Kak Osnova," *KZ*, July 18, 2017.

[85] Gavrilenko, Tikhonov, and Biriulin; "Vystuplenie Nachialnika GSh VS RF Valeriia Gerasimova na Otkrytom Zasedanii Kollegii MO Rossii"; This strongly corresponds with his emphasis in previous years on the asymmetrical competitive strategies that Russia should adopt.
[86] Golts, pp. 180–182.

[87] Gavrilenko, Tikhonov, and Biriulin; "Vystuplenie Nachialnika GSh VS RF Valeriia Gerasimova na Otkrytom Zasedanii Kollegii MO Rossii"; "Vystuplenie

Nachialnika GSh VS RF Valeriia Gerasimova na Otkrytom Zasedanii Kollegii MO Rossii"; "Vystuplenie Nachialnika GSh VS RF Valeriia Gerasimova na Otkrytom Zasedanii Kollegii MO Rossii." The honorary title *"udarnyi,"* frequently used by Gerasimov and which is granted today to the units that have won in specific competitions, seems like a reincarnation of the old Soviet term with the similar meaning of a highly effective and productive "shock" or "strike" worker, who displays exemplary performance in labor (*udarnik*). By the end of 2017, the MoD granted the honorary term "udarnyi" to 265 military units.

11. The Concept of Mass Mobilization Returns[1]

Aleksandr Golts

Introduction

Attempts to modernize the Russian military machine during the post-Soviet period can be observed in the attitude of Russian authorities to the concept of mass mobilization, which has had a decisive influence on the domestic military culture and military planning over the last three hundred years. Since Peter the Great created the Russian regular army, the Armed Forces were formed on the basis of conscription, at the expense of volunteer recruitment. The Russian system of compulsory military service was, in fact, borrowed from Sweden, Russia's main opponent in the Great Northern War (1700–1721). But within the Russian Empire, conscription took on a fundamentally different quality. As historian William C. Fuller observes in his book, *Strategy and Power in Russia: 1600–1914,*

> Russian backwardness could be the font of tremendous military power. The very things that made Russia backward and underdeveloped by comparison with Western Europe—autocracy, serfdom, poverty—could paradoxically translate into armed might. The ruthless application of autocratic power could mobilize the Russian economy for war. The result may not have been a cornucopia of foodstuffs and goods, but it was just enough

to sustain protracted war. Similarly, because rural Russia was so unfree it could be tapped for money and, most important, for men. It did not matter that the recruits were raw, that rations were short, that equipment was missing. The peasant conscripts were already inured to hardship, and there were more where they came from.[2]

By the end of Peter I's reign, the Russian army was 210,000 strong;[3] yet, more than 50 drafts were conducted between 1705 and 1725, which together gave the Armed Forces a reserve of 400,000 men[4]—in effect, it was mass mobilization. A steady adherence to this concept provided Russian tsars and generals with the ultimate weapon—constant numerical superiority over the enemy in an era when, according to Napoleon Bonaparte, God was "on the side of the big battalions." During the 1870s, Russian War Minister Dmitry Milyutin completed his reforms, which radically changed the system of staffing—from one based on recruitment to a conscript service. As such, the government transformed Russia's high birth rate—which was typical for a peasant country—into a renewable resource of military power. Decades later, the ability to carry out a mass mobilization and to throw millions of poorly trained men into battle was key to the Union of Soviet Socialist Republics (USSR) winning the Second World War.

Mobilization as Foundation for Soviet Strategic Thinking

By the mid-20th century, the USSR wielded almost an "ideal system" of mass mobilization, allowing the Soviet leadership to rely on prodigious numerical superiority over the North Atlantic Treaty Organization (NATO), its main global opponent. In peacetime, the Soviet Union was able to keep a five-million-strong military force, which annually replenished a giant mobilization reserve. This permitted the Soviet General Staff to call up 6 million–8 million reservists[5] in the so-called "period of threat," when war seemed imminent. A significant portion of the Soviet Armed Forces consisted of skeleton divisions. These were made up of only 500 officers and 200 regular privates; the vast majority of remaining open positions were to be filled by incoming reservists. In war time, once a skeleton division accepted reservists, it was to be deployed to the battlefield, where the bulk of the troops were—according to the main military concept—likely to die in the opening exchange with the enemy. Soviet military planning was guided by the country's experience in the Second World War, in which a brigade would generally "fade" within three days. So these destroyed divisions had to be constantly replaced by fresh units made up of new reservists.

Not only people, but also military equipment—ships, tanks, planes, artillery systems, etc.—was deemed consumable in this way. Therefore, in the "period of threat," all industrial facilities had to immediately begin producing weapons and military equipment. To be ready to switch their production lines, all factories were obligated to, even in peacetime, maintain so-called mobilization capacities dedicated to military production. Arms production, rather than the manufacture of civilian and consumer goods, was the main goal of Soviet industry. Thus, the cost of the maintenance of these mobilization capacities was included in the value of civilian goods. This negatively affected both their price and quality. Such production could not be economically rational.

Almost every Soviet enterprise had a *mobzadenie* (mobilization task), that is, the preplanned production of components for weapons and military equipment. To support this planning, massive reserves of raw materials and huge idle production capacities were created. Final assembly took place at plants that formally belonged to the famous *devyatka* (nine defense-industry ministries: Aviation Industry, Defense Industry, General Machine Building, Radio Industry, Medium Machine Building, Shipbuilding Industry, Chemical Industry, Electronic Industry, and Electrical Industry). As a result of this mobilization set up, it was absolutely impossible to separate the "military" from the "civilian" sectors of the Soviet economy.

According to Vitaly Shlykov, perhaps the foremost researcher on the Soviet military-industrial complex, the USSR's commodities sector and basic industry were monstrously hypertrophied. They produced much more oil, metals and chemical products than were required for domestic industrial production. All these surplus stockpiles were intended to be released for weapons production, but only during wartime. "The whole economy was based on the fact that, in peacetime, such resources that were not required for war, were pumped into the civilian sector to maintain some of its balance,"[6] Shlykov insisted during seminars organized, in 2005, by the Liberalnaya Missiya foundation. Essentially, in this system, the civilian sector existed only to ensure military production could start on day one of a war; whereas, in peacetime, the goal was to consume the excessive, unnecessary economic resources. That arrangement was one of the main reasons for the overall inefficiency of the Soviet economy. For example, according to Shlykov, the Soviet General Staff planned that the Soviet industry should reach peak production of 30,000 aircraft per year within 3–6 months after the start of the war. To reach those aviation production goals, the USSR generated 4.5 million tons of aluminum per year, but the domestic economy could not use it all. Only 10–11 percent of this was consumed by military and civil aircraft production.[7] The rest—except for a portion used to make spoons and bowls (the Soviet Union was probably the only country in the world producing aluminum utensils)—had to be stockpiled without any practical use. The same types of arrangements dictated annual production of titanium, coal and rolled metal products.

As a consequence of this mass mobilization system of industrial production, the State Planning Committee (Gosplan), which artificially balanced prices on military and civilian goods, was vital to the overall Soviet economy. In preparing for global war, the Soviet Union created massive weapons stockpiles, producing and storing away, for example, more than 60,000 tanks between 1945 and 1991.[8] However, this system could only exist under conditions of severe isolation and autarky (that is, a regime of economic self-sufficiency, which minimizes external commodity turnover). Eighty years of steady growth of military production in conditions of economic crisis contributed greatly to the collapse of the Soviet Union: the system was doomed to collapse as soon as the goal of the state became something other than preparing the country for war.

A Concept That Broke the Army

Post-Soviet Russia inherited all elements of this mobilization system, which proved itself more enduring than Communist ideology. The military top brass, together with the military-industry leadership, firmly held on to the concept of mass mobilization: first, because it was a perfect "black hole," allowing for the extraction of additional income and sustaining a top-heavy officers corps, and second, because they just did not know a different system for preparation for war.[9] However, their attempts to save the Soviet mass mobilization military under the new political-economic conditions led to a substantial degradation of the Armed Forces in the 1990s.

The most important factors of social life and the economy on which the system of mass mobilization was based simply disappeared as the USSR fell apart. First of all, mass mobilization required a steady growth in the population: the population needed to be sufficient not only for the formation of a multi-million-strong military force, but also to provide the Armed Forces with weapons, equipment and all necessary resources. However, today's Russian Federation is heading into a demographic slump: in the year 2017, 570,000 young men were estimated to reach the age of 18, in 2018—600,000. And in 2019, 568,000 will reach conscription age.[10] As such, Russia will find it impossible to fully fill the ranks of a one-million-strong military, which will require a draft of around 700,000 people each year.

Despite the sharp deterioration of post-Soviet Russia's demographic situation during the 1990s, 80 percent of its military formations were retained as skeleton units. As a result, although it frequently boasted of having a 1.5-million-man army, Russia fielded almost no combat-ready units. All this became clear during the Second Chechen War, which broke out in August 1999. Years later, in a 2006 address to the Federal Assembly (upper chamber of the Russian parliament), President Vladimir Putin noted,

> When the need arose to counter a large-scale attack by international terrorists in the North Caucasus in 1999, the problems in the Armed Forces became painfully evident. I remember very clearly a conversation I had with the chief of the General Staff at that time. [...] In order to effectively repel the terrorists, we needed to put together a group of at least 65,000 men, but the combat-ready units in the entire army came to only 55,000 men, and they were scattered throughout the entire country. Our Armed Forces came to a total of 1,400,000 men, but there were not enough men to fight. This is how kids who had never seen combat before were sent in to fight.[11]

Besides these manning problems, a large part of the Soviet industry died during the 1990s. Those enterprises that managed to survive were redeveloped to produce different products. The current owners of these restructured companies no longer need to rely on defense orders. And any attempts to preserve their mobilization capacities will inevitably make their main products more expensive and, thus, less competitive. It is, therefore, no coincidence that, from time to time, the government floats suggestions of forcing private business to fulfill defense contracts under the threat of criminal prosecution.[12]

At the same time, those Russian commercial entities where industrial preparation for mass mobilization was preserved became a new opportunity for corruption. The Federal Tax Service and the Ministry of Finance regularly discovered massive levels of abuse in this sphere. The government was even forced to compensate factories for maintaining their mobilization capacities through tax incentives.

According to information leaked to the press in 2012, Russia annually lost about 1 billion–1.5 billion rubles (around $16 million–$24 million) of tax income from each of the 2,000 economic enterprises involved in the country's mobilization preparedness program.[13]

Rejection of Mobilization in the Name of Efficiency

The degradation of the Russian military during the nearly two decades following the collapse of the Soviet Union was further demonstrated during the war with Georgia, in August 2008. Military equipment that had been stockpiled for years in order to be used in war suffered from critically substandard quality. According to General Vladimir Shamanov, half of the tanks and armored vehicles of the 19th Motorized Rifle Division broke during the march on Georgia and did not reach Tskhinvali. The officer corps to lead Russia's various skeleton units was not ready either. "When those commanders were given troops and equipment, they were just confused, and some even refused to carry out their orders," the former chief of the General Staff, Nikolai Makarov, reflected in December 2008.[14]

Hence, it is no coincidence that the most radical Russian military reform in 140 years was started immediately after the war against Georgia. At the heart of the reforms was the rejection of the concept of mass mobilization. Russia's defense minister at the time (2007–2012), Anatoly Serdyukov, decisively eliminated all skeleton units. As a result, the number of divisions, brigades and regiments in the Russian Ground Forces decreased from 1,890 to 172.[15] He also abolished 115,000 officers' positions (in theory these commanders were needed to lead the regiments and battalions of reservists). While explaining the essence of the painful reforms, the aforementioned General Shamanov, who led the Main Combat Training Directorate of the defense ministry, noted that "regiments and divisions that had to accept mobilization resources and then deploy during a threat period have become a costly anachronism."[16] After a long period of hesitation, Russia's military reformers stated that the ultimate goal would be to fully staff the Armed Forces with volunteer contract soldiers (in Russian, so-called *kontraktniki*). As a result of the deep restructuring of the Armed Forces, the military command had at its disposal several dozen formations able to deploy within a few hours of receiving their orders.

Naturally, the "Serdyukov reforms," which dismissed tens of thousands of officers, were vehemently opposed by the "military community." Critics of the reforms concentrated in particular on the most important element of the changes being carried out—the rejection of mass mobilization. According to the detractors, Russia risked losing the main instrument of its defense—the ability to arm and send into combat millions of reservists. Then chairperson of the State Duma (lower chamber of parliament) defense committee, Admiral Vladimir Komoyedov, insisted that "contract" (volunteer) Armed Forces were a "bubble that [would] immediately burst."[17] The admiral firmly asserted that only a mass mobilization army could protect Russia.

Opponents of the reform had considerable administrative influence. In 2010, as skeleton units were being massively slashed based on Serdyukov's recommendations, the president signed a new Military Doctrine, which had been prepared by the Security Council. In that document, mass mobilization was notably mentioned more than a dozen times as a key element of the country's national defense. The 2010 Military Doctrine demanded that officials "ensure a rational correlation of formations and military units of permanent readiness and formations and military units designed for mobilization and deployment of the Armed Forces and other troops."[18]

The reformers tried to answer the criticism. They insisted that future military conflicts would be short-term wars, which is why a multi-million-man mobilization reserve was simply not needed. After a closed meeting of the then-chief of the General Staff, Nikolai Makarov, with members of the State Duma, it became known that in wartime, the Armed Forces would increase from 1 million troops to only 1.7 million.[19] This meant that even in war time, Russia would be mobilizing not millions but only 700,000 reservists.

Useless Experiments

Nevertheless, because of the strong resistance of conservative hardliners in the General Staff, a new reserve mobilization system was not officially established in Russia until 2013. Still, the new system looked revolutionary compared to traditional Russian military culture, which considers almost the entirety of the male population of the country to be a "mobilization resource." With adoption of the new approach to manning, after completion of conscript or active contract service, troops would now be able to voluntarily sign a contract to serve in the reserves. They would even receive a modest monthly compensation for their service—officers were to be paid approximately $120 and privates about $70 per month. To maintain this status, a reservist would have to be able to regularly pass training in special reserve units, which were to be created in each of the military districts. The new minister of defense, Sergei Shoigu, promised that four reserve armies would be formed. But the 2013 budget lacked the money for this project's implementation. It was not until July 2015 that President Putin signed a decree to carry out this "experiment." The number of reservists currently participating in this new system is unknown. But back in 2013, reports alleged that the number should be 9,000.[20]

Franz Klintsevich (at the time, a member of the Duma Committee on Defense) revealed in September 2015 that financial problems forced a postponement of the formation of the new reserve system until 2016.[21] Nonetheless, eventually reserve commands were established in each military district. These are charged with calling up reservists, forming units, and maintaining the weapons and military equipment intended for the reservists. Bases for storage and repair as well as military commissariats are subordinated to these commands. Nonetheless, this rational approach to the formation of a military reserve is still considered "experimental." Moreover, the insignificant number of reservists currently on call, as well as the minor sums of money spent on the organization of the reserve system, have allowed the opponents of this approach to easily manipulate the results of this "experiment."

Indeed, also in 2013, the Kremlin proposed an entirely different method to fill Russia's mobilization reserve. In his address to the Federal Assembly, President Putin announced his intention to carry out a true revolution in the organization of the military:

> We have to think [about] how to create highly trained reserve forces. There is another suggestion in this regard: keeping [conscription] deferrals for students and changing the very system of military training offered by institutions of higher education. This will enable all students to study [and simultaneously] receive military training for their next military assignment and a particular area of military specialization. This mechanism will allow us to train the right number of reservists for the most needed, primarily technical military specializations, while not drafting them into the Armed Forces.[22]

According to this proposed initiative, university students would devote one day a week to military education over the course of one and a half to two years. Upon completion of the course, they would need to pass a three-month summer boot camp. At that point, they would be signed up within the reserves as privates or sergeants and avoid having to spend a year in the active conscript service. The idea was strongly supported by the Russian defense minister. "We really want you to think of this as a good opportunity for easy learning without interrupting your educational process," Shoigu earnestly tried to convince students in 2013. He added,

> And for this purpose we will create worthy training centers. You will spend one day a week on theoretical education—it is not that

hard. After the theoretical course, you will have to pass a three-month-long training regimen. We have enough units, training grounds and equipment to do this. And believe me, we will try to do all this under humane conditions. But, of course, we will require complete output. We expect to recruit 80,000–100,000 people a year into the reserves.[23]

From the beginning, Shoigu was particularly interested in the success of this new reserve training program for university students. If this initiative became implemented as designed, he would have a chance to formally comply with Putin's order to raise the number of the Armed Forces personnel back up to one million servicemen. Under Russia's current demographic situation, this demand is only possible to meet through bureaucratic manipulation. Indeed, one such possibility would be for the defense ministry to record all of the country's male university students (approximately 2.3 million) as members of the Armed Forces. The size of the Armed Forces presently tops out at around 700,000–800,000 troops, so the rest of Putin's one-million-man army would have to be members of a paper "student army."

Predictably, the military top brass did not like this idea. Specifically, the enrollment of all students with military training into a mobilization reserve force would deprive supporters of a mass mobilization army of their main argument that only universal conscription is able to provide the Armed Forces with sufficient reserves. The Russian military annually calls up (with great difficulty) about 280,000–300,000 conscripts. And 10–15 percent of these draftees are university graduates; thus, the military did not want to lose them to a newly structured reserve force. As a result, the presidential initiative from 2013 was obstructed and delayed by the military leadership tasked with carrying it out. According to initial plans then announced by Shoigu, military training was supposed to be mandatory for all male students in the country by 2016. But that year, only 22,000 students were permitted to participate in the training program. The representative of the defense ministry's Main Directorate for Personnel, Colonel Ruslan Milyaev, offered a fundamentally different approach to military training for students than the one that Shoigu announced three years ago: "It all depends on the defense ministry's needs for specific specialists in particular regions; and of course it may not be for everyone. Besides, there is an issue of the cost for the state."[24] From this, one can conclude that all attempts to develop a new model for the formation of mobilization reserves have, to date, been sabotaged by conservative generals. As a result, mobilization planning today is an usual mixture of modern and old-fashioned approaches. This is evidenced by the results of strategic maneuvers held in 2016–2017, described below.

Mobilization Training

In 2016, Russia carried out mysterious snap military exercises from June 14 to 22. Although they were publicized in the media, the number of participants as well as the units involved were not mentioned. Russian Defense Minister Shoigu announced this snap inspection on the same day it began; the exercise was meant to "check the troops' combat and mobilization readiness." The minister further stressed that, "along with the troops' training for their missions in armed conflicts of varying intensity and in crisis situations, it is necessary to pay special attention to the mobilization component of the Armed Forces, the status of the troops' reserve components [as well as] weapons and military equipment stock."[25]

The scenario of various annual Russian strategic maneuvers regularly involves the mobilization of several hundred reservists from each military district. Such drills are designed to demonstrate readiness levels for the implementation of a partial mobilization in case of a local conflict. For example, about 1,000 reservists were mobilized in the Central Military District (MD) during Tsentr (Center) 2015 maneuvers. But exercises held in June 2016 looked totally different. For the first time since the collapse of the Soviet Union, mobilization stood as the main goal of the exercise. The snap exercise was held across all Russian military districts—that is, throughout the entire country. Within the framework of the exercise, mobile command centers were deployed in all districts. This, most likely, means that the inspection itself was rehearsing a so-called "threat period," during which time a war against a global adversary appears inevitable.

The fact that such specific exercises were held in the form of a snap inspection—and not as maneuvers announced in advance—was, of course, provocative. Russia announced a mobilization on the territory of the whole country and did not mention the number of participating reservists. It is appropriate to recall that the First World War started after opposing powers began mobilizing to scare and intimidate one another. Moreover, a "snap inspection" of troops announced by President Vladimir Putin on February 26, 2014, ended with the annexation of Crimea and the beginning of the "secret war" in the eastern Ukrainian region of Donbas. But as for the June 2016 snap inspection, the Russian Ministry of Defense considered it sufficient to only inform foreign military attachés present in Moscow—and only after it already started. The director of the Russian Ministry of Foreign Affairs' Department of European Cooperation, Andrey Kelin, tried to legitimize the snap exercise by noting: "[Such a] drill is not found in documents relating to confidence-building measures and arms control. Well, this is actually a new form [of exercise] and nothing more. There is absolutely no violation of existing agreements here."[26]

Though the June snap inspection was carried out in all four military districts and professed to cover the whole of Russian territory, it was in fact a bit more limited. According to defense ministry statements, only units located in Leningrad and Omsk oblasts as well as Primorsky and Krasnodar krais took part. A unit of the Western MD artillery brigade, manned with reserve servicemen, practiced firing Msta-B 152-milimeter howitzers at the Luga range, Leningrad oblast. In the Southern MD, a signal company formed from reservists received equipment at their base and then marched 200 kilometers to Molkino, in Krasnodar krai. Reservists making up part of a regular infantry fighting vehicle (IFV) unit participated in tactical and shooting exercises in Omsk oblast. And reportedly, the mobile command center of the Eastern MD was deployed under field conditions and practiced dealing with a simulated chemical attack.

Defense ministry statements suggested that the reservists called up to take part in the June 2016 snap exercises were incorporated into pre-existing brigades and battalions. This contradicts years of statements by military officials insisting that all Russian units are fully manned at all times. As such, this means that a functioning system of reserves in the Armed Forces did not exist.

The Russian General Staff clearly rehearsed a scenario of global conventional conflict during the summer of 2016. Following the June snap inspection mobilization drills, three military districts and the Northern Fleet were involved in additional snap exercises in late August. Then, on September 5–10, Russia held the strategic military exercise Kavkaz 2016, in the southwestern territory of the country. The chief of the Russian General Staff, Valery Gerasimov, said that during these exercises, the Armed Forces for the first time tested mobilizing reservists to fill territorial defense units. The Ministry of Defense, meanwhile, revealed that a division of territorial defense troops, manned by reservists, was created in Crimea, and a battalion of this unit took part in the Kavkaz 2016 drills. This formation is specifically designed to protect strategic facilities and infrastructure from saboteurs during wartime. However, the overall size of the mobilization during the exercises has been rather modest so far. Ahead of Kavkaz 2016, only one new battalion of 400 reservists was formed, on the basis of the Novosibirsk military school. In addition, they formed two companies and one platoon. Reportedly, however, around 4,000 reservists were called up in total. This means that most of the reservists were called up under the old rules—that is, not to establish new units, but to fill in existing ones.

Mobilization preparations in 2017 were developed in a particularly specific way. Zapad 2017 military exercises (September 14–20) were the main event of the Armed Forces training that year. The drills provoked a sharply negative reaction from nearby NATO member states, which have been particularly concerned by any Russian military activities since the annexation of Crimea and secret war in Donbas.

At first, Moscow repeatedly argued that the scale of Zapad 2017 was restricted to only 12,700 regular Russian troops, and no mention was ever officially made about practicing for a mass mobilization of reservists. However, two months later, in November 2017, President Putin suddenly revealed during a meeting with leaders of the Armed Forces and chiefs the defense industry that one of the main goals of that year's Zapad drills was to check "our mobilization readiness and ability to use local resources to meet troop requirements." He added, "Reservists were called up for this exercise, and we also tested the ability of civilian companies to transfer their vehicles and equipment to the armed forces and provide technical protection to transport communications."[27]

This aspect of the Zapad 2017 strategic exercise had only been featured occasionally, in fragmentary reports. Local press reported about mobilization being done in complete secrecy in the Kaliningrad region—reservists had to sign a non-disclosure agreement. Some hazy reporting on "mobilization actions" in Kursk region also appeared. The call-up of reservists was supposed to replace the need to transfer troops from elsewhere in the country. However, while addressing the defense ministry, Putin additionally noted that these mobilization activities during the 2017 Zapad exercise were unsuccessful and will need to be corrected.

New Units That Weaken Russia

All these contradictions in approaches to mobilization can be explained by the changes to the chief goals and priorities in Russian military planning. Based on the country's strengths, national interests, demographic situation and economy, Serdyukov and his team specifically created military forces capable of winning in a local conflict inside the post-Soviet space. But because of the Kremlin's current policies, Russia has locked itself into a conflict with the North Atlantic Treaty Organization (NATO), which is superior to the Russian Federation across all quantitative indicators—economic strength, all types of weapons and numbers of personnel. The only logical military response for Moscow in this situation, therefore, is to return to the ineffective and extremely cumbersome mass mobilization army. Indeed, this is happening now, as highlighted by the defense ministry's promise to create new military units.

Based on statements of representatives of the Ministry of Defense, the Russian Armed Forces created at least 50 new units between 2015 and 2017.[28] But the total number of Armed Forces personnel increased by only 10,000 troops in 2016. This can only mean that Russia has again begun creating Soviet-style "paper" skeleton divisions, to be staffed by heretofore non-existent reservists—in other words, the types of formations explicitly abandoned by Serdyukov. This would signify a return to the discredited Soviet concept of mass mobilization. As a result, the dispersed forces of existing brigades can be expected to lose their combat capabilities over time.

Another sign of the return of the concept of mass mobilization is a sudden shortage of officers. At a special session of top officials in charge of personnel matters, the chief of the Main Directorate for Personnel in the Russian Ministry of Defense, Colonel General Viktor Goremykin, stated that, in 2016, the Armed Forces found 11,000 officers for positions that otherwise would have gone empty.[29] In his words, the military used "non-standard" methods to fill these staffing gaps. In particular, reserve officers who left the Armed Forces were recruited again. It is worth noting that, on February 22, 2017, while speaking before the State Duma, Defense Minister Sergei Shoigu clarified that due to shortages of personnel in 2015, 15,000 troops previously dismissed had been returned to service.[30] Obviously this practice continued in 2016 and 2017.

Similarly, according to the Russian media, provincial newspapers increasingly feature advertisements publicizing the fact that one or another military unit is accepting previously retired Armed Forces personnel. Moreover, the commander of the Eastern Military District reportedly sent special recruiters to 22 Russian regions to persuade reserve officers to return to active service. In addition to such rapid replenishment strategies, Russia has also reduced the training period for officers at military academies from five years to four. Finally, the chiefs of personnel meeting in early February 2017 were particularly proud of the creation of special short-term courses for privates and sergeants that award the passing graduate an officer's star. Such a system directly recalls the Soviet experience in World War II.

The situation of Russia's military pilots is particularly critical. Defense Minister Shoigu revealed to the Duma lawmakers that the deficit had reached 1,300 pilots. To resolve this massive shortfall, the professional lifespan of pilots in the Armed Forces has been extended by five years. In addition, according to Colonel General Goremykin, "For the first time, a [shortened] 1.5-year pilot training course was organized for highly educated technical staff officers. Last year [2016], the first 49 such pilots graduated. Today, training was completed by another 50 troops."[31]

At first glance, blame for these chronic shortages in the officer corps might be attributed to former minister of defense Anatoly Serdyukov. As part of his important package of military reforms, Serdyukov had ordered a halt to any new cadets being accepted to military academies during 2009–2011. However, it should be recalled that his decision was triggered by the fact that, three years earlier, the Armed Forces were overwhelmed by a tremendous surplus of officers. At that time, open positions for lieutenants were virtually nonexistent, while graduates of military schools were appointed to positions usually occupied by sergeants. But suddenly, today, a monstrous deficit has appeared. Consequently, the number of uncommitted officers waiting for either dismissal or appointment has decreased by almost 20 times compared to those years. In 2012, Serdyukov's subordinates believed that an annual output of at 8,500 new lieutenants would thoroughly cover the military's staffing needs.[32] Now defense ministry leaders insist they need 16,000 new graduates each year. In contrast, the number of Russian troops has not doubled. Therefore, the only explanation for this sudden need to recruit twice as many officers is the excess number of lieutenants required to fill out the Russian military's new skeleton units. In fact, the staff of these divisions consists mostly of officers. These types of divisions are appropriate if one's goal is to report to the president about the increasing power of the Russian army. To establish such new "paper" divisions, one needs only several thousand officers, not hundreds of thousands of additional privates.

Staffing Problems

The controversial situation with the staffing of the Armed Forces in peace time also hints at the return of the mass mobilization concept. Periodically, Vladimir Putin makes populist statements promising to "move gradually away from the draft."[33] But at the same time, it is clear from official reports that the process of transition to an entirely contract-based service is frozen at the level from 2016. At the end of 2016, Defense Minister Shoigu said that there were already 384,000 *kontraktniki* in the military[34]; he repeated the same figure at the end of 2017.[35] Whereas, according to the Plan of Activities of the Defense Ministry for 2013–2020, there should be 425,000 contract soldiers under arms in 2017. Moreover, it is quite possible that the number of professional service members in positions of privates and sergeants has not been growing but is, in fact, shrinking. At an October 2017 meeting of the Public Council under the Ministry of Defense, Colonel General Michael Mizintsev mentioned a sensational figure: according to him, the number of Russian contract soldiers that year amounted to 354,000.[36] Mizintsev, as the chief of Russia's National Defense Management Center, is reportedly privy, in real time, to all possible data on the status of the Armed Forces, which adds credence to his cited lower number of contract soldiers.

With 250,000 conscripts, 354,000 *kontraktniki*, 220,000 officers, and 30,000 cadets at military academies, the total number of Russian military men at arms equals about 850,000. But the president's last decree set the number of troops in the Armed Forces at 1.013 million. Because of the demographic situation, it is physically impossible to achieve this goal. The gap of 160,000 troops between the nominal and real numbers will inevitably lead to decreased combat readiness. The only way to resolve this problem, thus, seems to be to boost reserve numbers with individuals who completed military service earlier. This is the reason to maintain the draft.

The Ministry of Defense intends to solve the military's manning problems via so-called short-term contracts. In 2016, the ministry received permission to conclude service contracts for a period of six months to a year. Contracts can be signed not only with individuals in the reserves, but also with conscripts a month away from completing their mandatory service. According to the draft law, these short-term contracts apply only during extraordinary circumstances, such as for dealing with a natural disaster or other emergency, when additional forces are needed to restore the constitutional order, or to maintain or restore peace and security abroad. Considering that Russian men are not rushing to sign long-term contracts, it is difficult to believe they would sign short-term contracts in "case of emergency." The only practical reason to offer such short-term contracts appears to be to essentially legalize the mercenaries that the government is rushing to send into Ukraine and Syria.

The Best Way to Destroy an Economy

The fact that the Kremlin is seriously considering a return to mass mobilization is underscored by official statements about the need to prepare the industry for a transfer to a war footing. Such statements appeared for the first time since the collapse of the Soviet Union during the military's summer 2016 exercises. The call-up of reservists was accompanied by a test of the readiness of industrial enterprises "to perform mobilization tasks." A year later, on November 22, 2017, speaking at a meeting of defense ministry leaders and the heads of defense-sector firms, President Putin focused on the theme of "mobilization preparations." "I want to say that the economic ability to increase the production of defense products and services quickly is a vital element of military security. All strategic and simply large companies, regardless of the type of ownership, must be able to do this,"[37] he declared.

If Putin is not bluffing, these statements show that he and his military advisers are ignoring reality. The domestic defense industry arguably cannot cope with the tasks set by the Kremlin due to evident difficulties with the mass production of weapons. In attempting to realize these tasks, the authorities risk further damaging the Russian economy. Nevertheless, to try to achieve the mobilization benchmarks, the government will likely first resort to "administrative" methods: using threats of criminal punishment to try to force businesses to produce military products. But participation in military production does not bring profits. And because of US sanctions, the participation in military production could destroy the civilian part of the business. Thus, if threats fail to increase military production, the Russian government might try to nationalize the industry—which could easily spiral into general autarky and systemic shortages, including of food. The idea of mobilizing industry contradicts Putin's remarks that the government would be moving away from a conscript army. After all, if the number of reservists is to be significantly reduced, such large-scale serial production of military equipment makes little sense.

Conclusion

The government's contradictory statements and policies pertaining to issues such as conscription and the civilian industry role in war time suggests a fierce, behind-the-scenes struggle in the top echelons of power over whether or not to adopt all key aspects of the mass-mobilization model of defense. Today, it is still unclear which side will prevail. Former defense minister Serdyukov's reforms were designed for a scenario in which Russia's conventional forces could win a local conflict within several days. But in the midst of today's new "cold war" against the West, the Russian General Staff is under pressure to explain exactly how the country intends to counter NATO, whose military surpasses Russia's by nearly every measure aside from nuclear weapons. In this case, a return to the idea of general mobilization is at least logical, which is why Moscow is evidently again embracing a defense organizational system that had already proved its inefficiency.

Everything related to Russia's mobilization programs is kept secret, and the public receives only fragmentary information. Moreover, turning the country into a besieged fortress helped create the necessary background for the re-election of President Putin. It is also clear that convincing everyone Russia is preparing for war is seen as an important element of military deterrence against the United States. Consequently, there is every reason to believe that the Kremlin is not going to back down from pushing the country on to a permanent war footing.

Notes

[1] This chapter draws heavily on some of the author's previously published articles (between 2016 and 2017) in The Jamestown Foundation's *Eurasia Daily Monitor*,

namely: "New Divisions May Reduce Russian Army's Combat Readiness" (Volume 13, Issue: 97), "Implementing Reserve System an Uphill Battle for Russia" (Volume 13, Issue 115), "Russia Returning to Concept of Mass Mobilization (Volume 13, Issue 157), "Short-Term Personnel Contracts Negate Goals of Russia's Military Reforms" (Volume 13, Issue 180), "The Russian Army Suffers Deficit in Officers" (Volume 14, Issue 25), "How Many Soldiers Does Russia Have?" (Volume 14, Issue 144), "Russian Military Mass Mobilization: Fact or Bluff?" (Volume 14, Issue 158). All are available on www.jamestown.org.

[2] William C. Fuller, *Strategy and Power in Russia: 1600–1914*, (Free Press: New York, 1992), p. 89.

[3] Gosudarstvennaia oborona Rossii, *Imperativy russkoi voennoi klassiki*, (Russkii put/Voennyi universitet), 2002, p. 490.

[4] *Istoriia Voyennoi strategii Rossii*, (Kuchkovo pole), 2000, p. 47.

[5] Ibid., p. 528.

[6] Aleksandr Golts, "Rossiskiyi militarism – prepyatstvie modernizatsyii starany" ("Militarism in Russia as obstacle to modernization"), *Liberalnaya missiya*, 2005 p.45.

[7] Ibid., p. 46.

[8] Viktor Litovkin, "Genshtab menyaet vzglyady na sovremennye i budushchie vojny" ("The General Staff Is Changing Views on Modern Warfare"), Nezavisimoe Voennoe Obozrenie, July 10, 2009.

[9] "General'skii demarsh" ("General's Demarche"), Nezavisimaia Gazeta. July 5, 2011.

[10] Problemyi i praktika perehoda voennoy organizatsii Rossii na novuyu sistemu komplektovaniya (Problems and practice of transition of military organization of Russia to new recruitment system) Nauchnyye trudy № 75. M.: Institut ekonomiki perekhodnogo perioda. 2004. S. 238.

[11] Vladimir Putin, "Annual Address to the Federal Assembly," May 10, 2006, http://en.kremlin.ru/events/president/transcripts/23577.

[12] "Administrativnaya otvetstvennost' za narushenie polozhenij Federal'nogo zakona ot 29.12.2012 N 275-FZ 'O gosudarstvennom oboronnom zakaze,' " "Administrative

responsibility for violation of provisions of the Federal law of 29.12.2012 N 275-FZ 'About the state defense order,' "
прогосзаказ.рф/uploads/2018/05/Административная%20ответственность%20по %20Закону%20%20№%20275-ФЗ-315.pdf.

[13] Ekaterina Karacheva, "FNS vyyavila khishcheniya milliardov pod predlogom podgotovki k voyne," *Izvestia*, July 30, 2012.

[14] *Interfax*, December 30, 2008.

[15] *Rossiiskaya Gazeta*, May 12, 2009.

[16] Vladimir Shamanov, "Neobkhodimost reform podtverdila voyna," *Krasnaya Zvezda*, February 11, 2009.

[17] Vladimir Voloshin. Ot Shoygu trebuyut uvelichit srok sluzhby v armii do polutora let. Izvestiya. November 22, 2012

[18] "Military Doctrine of the Russian Federation," *Kremlin.ru*, February 5, 2010, http://www.kremlin.ru/supplement/461.

[19] D. Telmanov, "V sleduyushchem godu zarplata leytenantov sostavit 50 tysyach rubley," Gazeta, November 14 2008, № 217.

[20] Yuri Gavrilov, "8 tysyach – 'partizanu' " ("8 thousands to 'partisan' "), Rossiyskaya Gazeta, March 22, 2013.

[21] "Sozdaniye mobilizatsionnogo lyudskogo rezerva Vooruzhonnykh sil RF nachnotsya na sistemnoy osnove v 2016 godu, soobshchayut v Gosdume," *Interfax-AVN*, September 11, 2015, http://www.militarynews.ru/Story.asp?rid=1&nid=388772.

[22] Presidential Address to the Federal Assembly, December 12, 2013, http://en.kremlin.ru/events/president/news/19825.

[23] Aleksandr Tikhonov, "Studencheskiy prizyv – v nogu so vremenem," *Krasnaya Zvezda*, December 19, 2013.

[24] "Khod uchebno-polevykh sborov so studentami vuzov po programmam voyennoy podgotovki serzhantov i soldat zapasa," *Ekho Moskvy*, July 16, 2016, https://echo.msk.ru/programs/voensovet/1802316-echo/.

[25] "Surprise combat readiness check begins in Russia," *TASS*, June 14, 2016, http://tass.com/defense/881746.

[26] Liza Dubrovskaya, "MID otvetil genseku NATO: obvinivshemu Rossiyu v nepredskazuyemosti," *Moskovsky Komsomolets*, June 15, 2016.

[27] "Meeting with Defence Ministry and defence industry senior officials and heads of ministries and regions," *Kremlin.ru*, November 22, 2017, http://en.kremlin.ru/events/president/news/56150.

[28] Nikolay Poroskov, "Nekolokolnyye interesy Rossii," *Nezavisimoye Voyennoye Obozreniye*, February 19, 2016, https://function.mil.ru/news_page/country/more.htm?id=12155960@egNews.

[29] Marina Eliseyeva, "S pritselom na perspektivu," *Krasnaya Zvezda*, February 5, 2017.

[30] "Shoygu: defitsit voyennykh letchikov v VKS v 2016 g. sostavlyal 1300 chelovek," *TASS*, February 22, 2017, http://tass.ru/armiya-i-opk/4045193.

[31] "V Moskve proshel spetsial'nyy sbor nachal'nikov kadrovykh organov Vooruzhennykh Sil Rossii," *Mil.ru*, February 2, 2017, https://function.mil.ru/news_page/country/more.htm?id=12110631@egNews.

[32] "V Minoborony rasskazali, skol'ko vypusknikov voyennykh vuzov nuzhno armii," *RIA Novosti*, March 23, 2012, https://ria.ru/defense_safety/20120523/655876063.html.

[33] "Rossiya postepenno ukhodit ot sluzhby po prizyvu. zayavil Putin," *RIA Novosti*, October 24, 2017, https://ria.ru/defense_safety/20171024/1507463335.html.

[34] "V ystupleniye Ministra oborony Rossi yskoy Federatsii generala armii Sergeya Shoygu na rasshirennom zasedanii Kollegii Minoborony Rossii," *Mil.ru*, December 22, 2016, https://function.mil.ru/files/morf/2016-12-22_MoD_board_extended_session_RUS.pdf.

[35] "Verkhovnyy Glavnokomanduyushchiy Vooruzhennymi Silami Rossii Vladimir Putin prinyal uchastiye v rabote rasshirennogo zasedaniya Kollegii Minoborony," *Mil.ru*, December 22, 2017, https://function.mil.ru/news_page/country/more.htm?id=12155960@egNews.

[36] "Sokrashcheniye kolichestva voyennosluzhashchikh po prizyvu pozvolyayet uluchshit' kachestvo ikh otbora," *Mil.ru*, October 20, 2017, https://function.mil.ru/news_page/country/more.htm?id=12147724@egNews.

[37] "Meeting with Defence Ministry and defence industry senior officials and heads of ministries and regions," *Kremlin.ru*, November 22, 2017, http://en.kremlin.ru/events/president/news/56150.

Contributors' Biographies

Dmitry Adamsky

Prof. Dmitry (Dima) Adamsky is a Head of the BA Honors Track in Strategy and Decision Making at the School of Government, Diplomacy and Strategy at the IDC Herzliya, Israel. His research interests include international security, cultural approach to IR, modern military thought, and American, Russian and Israeli national security policy. He has published on these topics in *Foreign Affairs, Security Studies, Journal of Strategic Studies, Intelligence and National Security, Studies in Conflict and Terrorism,* and *Journal of Cold War History.* His books *Operation Kavkaz* and *The Culture of Military Innovation* (Stanford UP) earned the annual (2006 and 2012) prizes for the best academic works on Israeli security. His recent book, *Russian Nuclear Orthodoxy* (Stanford UP, 2019) explores the nexus of religion and strategy in Russia.

Pavel K. Baev

Pavel Baev is a Research Professor at the Peace Research Institute Oslo (PRIO) and a Nonresident Senior Fellow in the Center on the United States and Europe at Brookings. He specializes in Russian military reform, Russia's conflict management in the Caucasus and Central Asia, and energy interests in Russia's foreign and security policies, as well as Russia's relations with Europe and NATO.

Baev graduated from the Moscow State University in 1979 with a master's degree in political geography, and worked in a research institute in the former USSR Ministry of Defense. After receiving a doctorate in international relations from the Institute for the U.S. and Canadian Studies, Moscow in 1988, he worked with the Institute of

Europe in Moscow until October 1992, when he joined PRIO. From 1995 to 2001 he was a co-editor of *Security Dialogue*, a quarterly policy-oriented journal produced at PRIO. From 2000 to 2004, Pavel was the head of the Foreign and Security Policies program. He held the NATO Democratic Institutions Fellowship from 1994 to 1996.

Baev's articles on the Russian military posture, Russian-European relations, and peacekeeping and conflict management in Europe have appeared in *Armed Forces & Society, Cambridge Review of International Affairs, Contemporary Security Policy, European Security, International Peacekeeping, Jane's Intelligence Review, The Journal of Peace Research, The Journal of Slavic Military Studies, Problems of Post-Communism, Security Dialogue, Studies in Conflict & Terrorism,* and *The World Today*. He also has a weekly column published in The Jamestown Foundation's *Eurasia Daily Monitor* and is the author of the blog, *Arctic Politics and Russia's Ambitions*.

Jānis Bērziņš

Dr. Jānis Bērziņš is the director of the Center for Security and Strategic Research at the National Defense Academy of Latvia. Previously Bērziņš was a senior fellow at the Potomac Foundation and has worked as Managing Director and Chief Economist at Lux Sit. He has held teaching positions at Riga Strandins University and the Universidade do Extremo Sul Catarinesese. He has authored more than 70 publications and has advised the United Kingdom House of Commons' Defence Select Committee as well as the governments of Sweden, Poland and Singopre. He has also provided expertise on strategic issues to the private sector. Dr. Bērziņš completed his PhD in Political Science at Latvijas Universitāte.

Stephen Blank

Dr. Stephen Blank is an internationally recognized expert on Russian foreign and defense policies and international relations across the former Soviet Union. He is also a leading expert on European and Asian security, including energy issues. Since 2013, he has been a Senior Fellow at the American Foreign Policy Council, in Washington. From 1989 until 2013, he was a Professor of Russian National Security Studies at the Strategic Studies Institute of the US Army War College in Pennsylvania. Dr. Blank has been Professor of National Security Affairs at the Strategic Studies Institute since 1989. In 1998–2001, he was Douglas MacArthur Professor of Research at the War College. Dr. Blank's MA and PhD are in Russian History from the University of Chicago. His BA is in History from the University of Pennsylvania.

Philip M. Breedlove

Gen. Philip M. Breedlove (Ret.) served as the Commander, US European Command, as well as the 17th Supreme Allied Commander Europe (SACEUR) of NATO Allied Command Operations, from May 2013 until May 4, 2016.

General Breedlove was raised in Forest Park, Ga., and was commissioned in 1977 as a distinguished graduate of Georgia Tech's ROTC program. He served in numerous operational, command and staff positions, and completed nine overseas tours, including two remote tours. He commanded a fighter squadron, an operations group, three fighter wings, and a Numbered Air Force. Additionally, he served as Vice Chief of Staff of the US Air Force, Washington, DC; Operations Officer in the Pacific Command Division on the Joint Staff; Executive Officer to the Commander of Headquarters Air Combat Command; the Senior Military Assistant to the Secretary of the Air Force; and Vice Director for Strategic Plans and Policy on the

Joint Staff.

Prior to becoming SACEUR, General Breedlove served as the Commander, US Air Forces in Europe; Commander, US Air Forces Africa; Commander, Air Component Command, Ramstein; and Director, Joint Air Power Competence Centre, Kalkar, Germany. He was responsible for Air Forces activities, conducted through 3rd Air Force, in an area of operations covering more than 19 million square miles. This area included 105 countries in Europe, Africa, Asia and the Middle East, and the Arctic and Atlantic oceans. As Vice Chief, he presided over the Air Staff and served as a member of the Joint Chiefs of Staff Requirements Oversight Council and Deputy Advisory Working Group. He assisted the Chief of Staff with organizing, training, and equipping of 680,000 active-duty, Guard, Reserve and civilian forces serving in the United States and overseas. General Breedlove flew combat missions in Operation Joint Forge/Joint Guardian. He was a command pilot with 3,500 flying hours, primarily in the F-16.

Breedlove currently serves on the Georgia Tech Advisory Board, as a Distinguished Professor in the Sam Nunn School of International Affairs at Georgia Tech, as a Senior Advisor to Culpeper National Security Solutions, and on the Board of Directors of the Atlantic Council.

Matthew Czekaj

Matthew Czekaj is the Senior Program Associate for Europe and Eurasia at The Jamestown Foundation and also serves as the Editor-in-Chief of Jamestown's *Eurasia Daily Monitor* publication, focused on the post-Soviet space. He has edited and prepared for publication numerous books and reports published by Jamestown, including *Russia's Zapad 2013 Military Exercise: Lessons for Baltic Regional Security*, and his writings have appeared in *EDM, Central Europe*

Digest as well as the *Atlanticist* blog. Prior to joining Jamestown, Mr. Czekaj was a Research Associate at the Atlantic Council, where he worked on issues of European Enlargement. Before that, he was a Research Assistant at the Center for European Policy Analysis (CEPA) Energy Security Program. Mr. Czekaj holds a Master's degree in Russian and East European Studies from Georgetown University's School of Foreign Service, and a Bachelor's degree in International Relations with a concentration in European Studies from The Johns Hopkins University. His research interests include Polish foreign and defense policy, Baltic Sea regional security, European enlargement, as well as pipeline politics and energy security.

Jörgen Elfving

Jörgen Elfving is a former Swedish army and general staff officer. During his military career, he mainly served in staff positions handling the Soviet Union/Russia. He has also previously been posted as a military attaché to the Baltic States. After retiring from the Swedish armed forces, Elfving has worked for a number of Swedish government agencies as a consultant and pursues a research project at the Swedish National Defense University regarding the development of Russia's military capabilities. In addition, he has been active as a translator and written a number of articles about the Russian military as well as a book about the reformation of the Russian armed forces.

Pavel Felgenhauer

Dr. Pavel E. Felgenhauer is a Moscow-based defense analyst and columnist for *Novaya Gazeta* as well as a Non-Resident Senior Fellow at The Jamestown Foundation. He served as senior research officer in the Soviet Academy of Sciences, from where he received his Ph.D. Dr. Felgenhauer has published widely on Russian foreign and defense policies, military doctrine, arms trade and the military-industrial complex. He comments regularly in local and international media on Russia's defense-related problems. Dr. Felgenhauer is also a weekly contributor to The Jamestown Foundation's *Eurasia Daily Monitor*.

Stefan Forss

Dr. Stefan Forss is a senior scientist and highly experienced defense researcher, at present working as an Adjunct Professor at the Finnish National Defence University. Professor Forss joined the Technical Research Centre of Finland (VTT), where he eventually became Chief Scientist. In 2005, he moved to the Finnish Ministry of Foreign Affairs' Policy and Research Unit, attached to the National Defence University, where he advised on arms control, particularly nuclear issues and the security policy implications of new weapons and weapon systems.

After retiring from government service in 2012, he has continued to publish on defense and security topics, including a series of high-profile reports on the implications for the Nordic States of a newly resurgent Russia. Professor Forss holds a Ph.D. in physics from Helsinki University.

Aleksandr Golts

Aleksandr Golts was born in 1955. In 1978, he received an MA in journalism from the Department of Journalism at the Moscow State Lomonosov University. From 1980 until 1996, he worked with the *Krasnaya Zvezda* (*Red Star*) editorial board, a Soviet and then Russian military daily based in Moscow. In 1996–2001, Mr. Golts served as military editor of *Itogi* (Moscow), a premier Russian news magazine. In 2001–2004, he worked for the Moscow-based magazine "Yezhenedelnyi Journal" ("Weekly") as deputy editor-in-chief. He currently works as a deputy editor for the website *EJ.ru* and is a regular contributor to The Jamestown Foundation's *Eurasia Daily Monitor*, where he writes on Russian military reform and defense issues.

Glen E. Howard

Glen Howard is the President of The Jamestown Foundation, a research and analysis institution based in Washington, DC. He is fluent in Russian and proficient in Azerbaijani and Arabic, and is a regional expert on the Caucasus and Central Asia. He was formerly an Analyst at the Science Applications International Corporation (SAIC) Strategic Assessment Center. His articles have appeared in *The Wall Street Journal*, the *Central Asia-Caucasus Analyst*, and *Jane's Defense Weekly*. Mr. Howard has served as a consultant to private sector and governmental agencies, including the US Department of Defense, the National Intelligence Council and major oil companies operating in Central Asia and the Middle East.

Ihor Kabanenko

Ihor Kabanenko is a retired admiral with the Ukrainian Navy. From 1983 to 1990, he served in the Soviet Navy in various positions up to Commander of the ship and Chief of Staff of Missile Ships Division. Since 1993, he served in the Ukrainian Armed Forces. He was appointed to the positions of Chief of Operations and Chief of Staff of the Ukrainian Navy, the Military Representative of Ukraine to NATO, Chief of Operations of the Ukrainian Armed Forces, and the First Deputy Chief of Defense. He retired in 2013, with the rank of Admiral. From May to August 2014, Admiral Kabanenko served as the Ukrainian Deputy Minister of Defense, and from August to October 2014—as Deputy Minister of Defense of Ukraine for European Integration. Currently, he is the president of UA.RPA (Ukrainian

Advanced Research Project Agency), which focuses on high-tech solutions and products for defense.

Roger N. McDermott

Roger N. McDermott is Senior Fellow in Eurasian Military Studies at The Jamestown Foundation, in Washington, DC. He is also a Visiting Senior Research Fellow at the Department of War Studies in King's College, London, as well as a Research Associate at the Institute of Middle East, Central Asia and Caucasus Studies (MECACS), at the University of St. Andrews, Scotland. McDermott is on the editorial boards of *Russian Law & Politics*, *Central Asia and the Caucasus* and the scientific board of the *Journal of Power Institutions in Post-Soviet Societies* and assistant editor of the *Journal of Slavic Military Studies*. He specializes in Eurasian defense and security issues. His interests in Russia's defense and security developments are mainly in the areas of defense reform, force structure, training, strategic exercises, military theory, perspectives on future warfare, planning and combat capability and readiness, as well as strategic and operational analysis.

Sergey Sukhankin

Dr. Sergey Sukhankin is a Fellow at The Jamestown Foundation and an Associate Expert at the International Center for Policy Studies (Kyiv). He received his PhD in Contemporary Political and Social History from the Autonomous University of Barcelona (UAB), with his thesis discussing the transformation of Kaliningrad Oblast after the collapse of the USSR. His areas of scientific interest primarily concern Kaliningrad and the Baltic Sea region, Russian information and cyber security, A2/AD and its interpretation in Russia, as well as the development of Russia Private Military Companies (PMC) after the outbreak of the Syrian civil war. Dr. Sukhankin's academic articles, expert opinions and commentaries, as well as policy-oriented analyses have appeared in leading international think tanks and research institutions, including The Jamestown Foundation, ECFR, CIDOB, *Diplomaatia*, RIAC, *New Eastern Europe*, *Kyiv Post*, *The New Republic*, *Business Insider*, *Rzeczpospolita*, *El Mundo*, *El Periodico* and *El Confidencial*. He was a Visiting Fellow (2016–2017) and subsequently taught a course entitled "Foreign and Security Policy of the Russian Federation" at The Institut Barcelona d'Estudis Internacionals (IBEI). He is based in Edmonton, Alberta, Canada.